CLASS ACTIONS AND OTHER MULTI-PARTY LITIGATION

IN A NUTSHELL®

SIXTH EDITION

ROBERT H. KLONOFF
Jordan D. Schnitzer Professor of Law
Dean of the Law School, 2007–2014
Lewis & Clark Law School

WEST ACADEMIC PUBLISHING

Nutshell Series, In a Nutshell and the Nutshell Logo are trademarks registered in the U.S. Patent and Trademark Office.

West, West Academic Publishing, and West Academic are trademarks of West Publishing Corporation, used under license.

Printed in the United States of America

ISBN: 978-1-64708-413-4

To my family

PREFACE

This text addresses class actions and other devices for litigating multi-party cases. It is intended for students taking courses in civil procedure, complex litigation, class actions, and mass torts. It is also designed for use by practicing lawyers who are involved in litigating multi-party cases. This edition follows the same approach and structure as the prior editions (1999, 2004, 2007, 2012, and 2017). A number of important judicial decisions have been rendered since 2017, and those decisions are discussed in this edition. Moreover, this edition discusses the 2018 amendments to Federal Rule of Civil Procedure 23.

This text provides citations for various propositions. It is not a reference book, however, and no attempt is made to provide case citations or other authority for every proposition. References to denials of *certiorari* (for U.S. Supreme Court cases) are provided only for cases in which the denial occurred in 2018 or later.

This text includes both scholarly analysis and a practitioner's perspective. In addition to teaching and writing about class actions, I served from 2011–2017 as the academic member of the Federal Advisory Committee on Civil Rules (having been appointed by Chief Justice John Roberts, Jr.) and previously served as an Associate Reporter for the American Law Institute's project, *Principles of the Law of Aggregate Litigation* (2010). I have prosecuted and defended more than 100 class actions as an attorney in private practice. I have also served as an expert witness in numerous class actions, both in federal and state court, including the *BP Deepwater Horizon*, *Equifax Data Breach*, *NFL Concussion*, *Volkswagen Clean Diesel*, and *Wells Fargo Unauthorized Accounts* cases.

In addition to those whom I acknowledged in the five previous editions, I would like to recognize the substantial contributions of my research assistants, Jacob Abbott, Sydney Lottes, and Cindy Lundt, who worked on this sixth edition. The statements and conclusions in this text are mine alone.

ROBERT H. KLONOFF

Portland, Oregon
September 2020

OUTLINE

TABLE OF CASES

References are to Pages

CLASS ACTIONS AND OTHER MULTI-PARTY LITIGATION

IN A NUTSHELL®

SIXTH EDITION

TEXT OF FEDERAL RULE OF CIVIL PROCEDURE 23. CLASS ACTIONS

(a) PREREQUISITES. One or more members of a class may sue or be sued as representative parties on behalf of all members only if:

(1) the class is so numerous that joinder of all members is impracticable;

(2) there are questions of law or fact common to the class;

(3) the claims or defenses of the representative parties are typical of the claims or defenses of the class; and

(4) the representative parties will fairly and adequately protect the interests of the class.

(b) TYPES OF CLASS ACTIONS. A class action may be maintained if Rule 23(a) is satisfied and if:

(1) prosecuting separate actions by or against individual class members would create a risk of:

(A) inconsistent or varying adjudications with respect to individual class members that would establish incompatible standards of conduct for the party opposing the class; or

(B) adjudications with respect to individual class members that, as a practical matter, would be dispositive of the interests of the other members not parties to the individual adjudications or would substantially impair or impede their ability to protect their interests;

(2) the party opposing the class has acted or refused to act on grounds that apply generally to the class, so that final injunctive relief or corresponding declaratory relief is appropriate respecting the class as a whole; or

(3) the court finds that the questions of law or fact common to class members predominate over any questions affecting only individual members, and that a class action is superior to other available methods for fairly and efficiently adjudicating the controversy. The matters pertinent to these findings include:

(A) the class members' interests in individually controlling the prosecution or defense of separate actions;

(B) the extent and nature of any litigation concerning the controversy already begun by or against class members;

(C) the desirability or undesirability of concentrating the litigation of the claims in the particular forum; and

(D) the likely difficulties in managing a class action.

(c) CERTIFICATION ORDER; NOTICE TO CLASS MEMBERS; JUDGMENT; ISSUES CLASSES; SUBCLASSES.

(1) *Certification Order.*

(A) *Time to Issue.* At an early practicable time after a person sues or is sued as a class representative, the court must determine by order whether to certify the action as a class action.

(B) *Defining the Class. Appointing Class Counsel.* An order that certifies a class action must define the class and the class claims, issues, or defenses, and must appoint class counsel under Rule 23(g).

(C) *Altering or Amending the Order.* An order that grants or denies class certification may be altered or amended before final judgment.

(2) *Notice.*

(A) *For (b)(1) or (b)(2) Classes.* For any class certified under Rule 23(b)(1) or (b)(2), the court may direct appropriate notice to the class.

(B) *For (b)(3) Classes.* For any class certified under Rule 23(b)(3)—or upon ordering notice under Rule 23(e)(1) to a class proposed to be certified for purposes of settlement under Rule 23(b)(3)—the court must direct to class members the best notice that is practicable under the circumstances, including individual notice to all members who can be identified through reasonable effort. The notice may be by one or more of the following: United States mail, electronic means, or other appropriate means. The notice must clearly and concisely state in plain, easily understood language:

(i) the nature of the action;

(ii) the definition of the class certified;

(iii) the class claims, issues, or defenses;

(iv) that a class member may enter an appearance through an attorney if the member so desires;

(v) that the court will exclude from the class any member who requests exclusion;

(vi) the time and manner for requesting exclusion; and

(vii) the binding effect of a class judgment on members under Rule 23(c)(3).

(3) *Judgment.* Whether or not favorable to the class, the judgment in a class action must:

(A) for any class certified under Rule 23(b)(1) or (b)(2), include and describe those whom the court finds to be class members; and

(B) for any class certified under Rule 23(b)(3), include and specify or describe those to whom the Rule 23(c)(2) notice was directed, who have not requested exclusion, and whom the court finds to be class members.

(4) *Particular Issues.* When appropriate, an action may be brought or maintained as a class action with respect to particular issues.

(5) *Subclasses.* When appropriate, a class may be divided into subclasses that are each treated as a class under this rule.

(d) CONDUCTING THE ACTION.

(1) *In General.* In conducting an action under this rule, the court may issue orders that:

(A) determine the course of proceedings or prescribe measures to prevent undue repetition or complication in presenting evidence or argument;

(B) require—to protect class members and fairly conduct the action—giving appropriate notice to some or all class members of:

(i) any step in the action;

(ii) the proposed extent of the judgment; or

(iii) the members' opportunity to signify whether they consider the representation fair and adequate, to intervene and present claims or defenses, or to otherwise come into the action;

(C) impose conditions on the representative parties or on intervenors;

(D) require that the pleadings be amended to eliminate allegations about representation of absent persons and that the action proceed accordingly; or

(E) deal with similar procedural matters.

(2) *Combining and Amending Orders.* An order under Rule 23(d)(1) may be altered or amended from time to time and may be combined with an order under Rule 16.

(e) SETTLEMENT, VOLUNTARY DISMISSAL OR COMPROMISE. The claims, issues, or defenses of a certified class—or a class proposed to be certified for purposes of settlement—may be settled, voluntarily dismissed, or compromised only with the court's approval. The following procedures apply to a proposed settlement, voluntary dismissal, or compromise:

(1) *Notice to the Class.*

(A) *Information That Parties Must Provide to the Court.* The parties must provide the court with information sufficient to enable it to determine whether to give notice of the proposal to the class.

(B) *Grounds for a Decision to Give Notice.* The court must direct notice in a reasonable manner to all class members who would be bound by the proposal if giving notice is justified by the parties' showing that the court will likely be able to:

(i) approve the proposal under Rule 23(e)(2); and

(ii) certify the class for purposes of judgment on the proposal.

(2) *Approval of the Proposal.* If the proposal would bind class members, the court may approve it only after a hearing and only on finding that it is fair, reasonable, and adequate after considering whether:

(A) the class representatives and class counsel have adequately represented the class;

(B) the proposal was negotiated at arm's length;

(C) the relief provided for the class is adequate, taking into account:

(i) the costs, risks, and delay of trial and appeal;

(ii) the effectiveness of any proposed method of distributing relief to the class, including the method of processing class-member claims;

(iii) the terms of any proposed award of attorney's fees, including timing of payment; and

(iv) any agreement required to be identified under Rule 23(e)(3); and

(D) the proposal treats class members equitably relative to each other.

(3) *Identifying Agreements.* The parties seeking approval must file a statement identifying any agreement made in connection with the proposal.

(4) *New Opportunity to Be Excluded.* If the class action was previously certified under Rule 23(b)(3), the court may refuse to approve a settlement unless it affords a new opportunity to request exclusion to individual class members who had an earlier opportunity to request exclusion but did not do so.

(5) *Class-Member Objections.*

(A) *In General.* Any class member may object to the proposal if it requires court approval under this subdivision (e). The objection must state whether it applies only to the objector, to a specific subset of the class, or to the entire class, and also state with specificity the grounds for the objection.

(B) *Court Approval Required for Payment in Connection with an Objection.* Unless approved by the court after a hearing, no payment or other consideration may be provided in connection with:

(i) forgoing or withdrawing an objection, or

(ii) forgoing, dismissing, or abandoning an appeal from a judgment approving the proposal.

(C) *Procedure for Approval After an Appeal.* If approval under Rule 23(e)(5)(B) has not been obtained before an appeal is docketed in the court of appeals, the procedure of Rule 62.1 applies while the appeal remains pending.

(f) APPEALS. A court of appeals may permit an appeal from an order granting or denying class action certification under this rule, but not from an order under Rule 23(e)(1). A party must file a petition for permission to appeal with the circuit clerk within 14 days after the order is entered, or within 45 days after the order is entered if any party is the United States, a United States agency, or a United States officer or employee sued for an act or omission occurring in connection with duties performed on the United States' behalf. An appeal does not stay proceedings in the district court unless the district judge or the court of appeals so orders.

(g) CLASS COUNSEL.

(1) *Appointing Class Counsel.* Unless a statute provides otherwise, a court that certifies a class must appoint class counsel. In appointing class counsel, the court:

> (A) must consider:

> (i) the work counsel has done in identifying or investigating potential claims in the action;

> (ii) counsel's experience in handling class actions, other complex litigation, and the types of claims asserted in the action;

> (iii) counsel's knowledge of the applicable law; and

> (iv) the resources that counsel will commit to representing the class;

> (B) may consider any other matter pertinent to counsel's ability to fairly and adequately represent the interests of the class;

> (C) may order potential class counsel to provide information on any subject pertinent to the appointment and to propose terms for attorney's fees and nontaxable costs;

(D) may include in the appointing order provisions about the award of attorney's fees or nontaxable costs under Rule 23(h); and

(E) may make further orders in connection with the appointment.

(2) *Standard for Appointing Class Counsel.* When one applicant seeks appointment as class counsel, the court may appoint that applicant only if the applicant is adequate under Rule 23(g)(1) and (4). If more than one adequate applicant seeks appointment, the court must appoint the applicant best able to represent the interests of the class.

(3) *Interim Counsel.* The court may designate interim counsel to act on behalf of a putative class before determining whether to certify the action as a class action.

(4) *Duty of Class Counsel.* Class counsel must fairly and adequately represent the interests of the class.

(h) ATTORNEY'S FEES AND NONTAXABLE COSTS. In a certified class action, the court may award reasonable attorney's fees and nontaxable costs that are authorized by law or by the parties' agreement. The following procedures apply:

(1) A claim for an award must be made by motion under Rule 54(d)(2), subject to the provisions of this subdivision (h), at a time the court sets. Notice of the motion must be served on all parties and, for motions by class counsel, directed to class members in a reasonable manner.

(2) A class member, or a party from whom payment is sought, may object to the motion.

(3) The court may hold a hearing and must find the facts and state its legal conclusions under Rule 52(a).

(4) The court may refer issues related to the amount of the award to a special master or a magistrate judge, as provided in Rule 54(d)(2)(D).

CHAPTER 1

INTRODUCTION

A class action is a suit in which a small number of representative parties proceed on behalf of a much larger, unnamed group of individuals who share common claims. The class action device is designed to avoid repeated litigation of the same issue, deter misconduct, and facilitate the prosecution of small claims that otherwise would not be brought.

The subject of class actions has received more attention from courts, legislators, scholars, and practitioners than any other area of civil procedure. Class actions—involving subjects such as school desegregation, airplane crashes, securities fraud, antitrust, consumer fraud, employment discrimination, civil rights, environmental disasters, tobacco, asbestos, human rights abuses, employee benefits, and many other high-profile issues—touch all of our lives.

The coronavirus pandemic forcefully illustrates the power of the class action device to seek group remedies. Almost immediately after the pandemic hit the United States, myriad class actions were filed. These include, among others:

- Class actions seeking refunds or reimbursements against airlines, cruise lines, universities, gyms, ticketing companies, music festivals, and many other businesses.

- Business interruption insurance class actions by restaurants, clubs, and other businesses against insurance companies for losses resulting from closures.

- Class actions under the Paycheck Protection Program forgivable loan program alleging that lenders violated state consumer protection laws or unfair competition statutes.

- Privacy class actions against video conferencing companies.

- Class actions by students against colleges and universities for tuition, fees, and housing costs because of campus closures resulting from the pandemic.

- Class actions by prisoners against prisons for failing to protect their health and safety, *e.g.,* not allowing prisoners to adhere to social distancing measures and not providing adequate protective equipment.

- False advertising class actions, such as suits by consumers against hand sanitizer companies for overstating the protection offered by their products.

- Class actions against cruise lines by passengers alleging that the companies failed to protect their health and safety.

- Consumer class actions claiming that companies selling products such as hand sanitizer, toilet paper, masks, and other products engaged in unlawful price gouging.

- Class actions by employees against employers alleging unlawful terminations, failure to provide sick leave, and other employment-related claims.

- Class actions against the Government of China by a wide variety of plaintiffs alleging that the Chinese government improperly covered up the seriousness and scope of the coronavirus.

- Securities fraud class actions by investors claiming that various companies misled them about the business risks arising from the coronavirus or that pharmaceutical companies overstated the prospects of a cure or vaccine, thus resulting in inflated stock prices.

Many of these suits involve overarching issues of liability and would be too costly to litigate as individual claims.

It is not surprising that few areas of civil procedure have been as controversial as class actions. On one side are those who claim that class actions should be used with greater frequency—to effect social change and to provide recourse for those who would otherwise find it economically infeasible to litigate their grievances. On the other side are those who claim that class actions have done little more than force corporations into bankruptcy, enrich attorneys, and clog the courts. Those in the latter camp have been working for years to convince Congress to overhaul the rules governing class actions. In 2005, they were partially successful: Congress enacted the Class Action Fairness Act (CAFA), which (1) permits defendants to remove most multistate class actions from state court to federal court, and (2) imposes restrictions on certain kinds of class action settlements.

Moreover, defendants have achieved many important victories in the courts. In the past decade, courts have imposed stringent new barriers to class certification—a trend described in depth by the author in an article published in 2013. *See* Robert H. Klonoff, *The Decline of Class Actions*, 90 Wash. U. L. Rev. 729 (2013). More recently, however, the Supreme Court has denied certiorari or issued narrow rulings in several high-profile class action cases, and the federal circuits have rejected many of defendants' efforts to impose additional restrictions on class certification. *See* Robert H. Klonoff, *Class Actions Part II: A Respite from the Decline*, 92 N.Y.U. L. Rev. 971 (2017).

The study of class actions can be challenging (hence the term "complex litigation"). The complexity of the subject is due in part to two distinct features of class actions: the impact of procedure on substance, and the impact of substance on procedure.

First, a class action is clearly a procedural device, one that is expressly authorized by the Federal Rules of Civil Procedure. As a theoretical matter, certification of a class action should not affect an individual class member's substantive rights. There is little doubt, however, that class actions can have powerful substantive effects. For instance, low-value individual claims that otherwise would not be litigated can be aggregated into a class action, thereby exposing the defendant to enormous potential liability.

Second, Federal Rule of Civil Procedure 23—like all of the Federal Rules of Civil Procedure—is trans-substantive, meaning that the Rule applies to a wide range of cases from different areas of law. Chapter 11 focuses on three such areas—mass torts, employment discrimination, and securities fraud—but class actions are common in numerous other areas. As will be discussed in Chapter 11 and elsewhere, substance does indeed impact procedure, and courts have described some categories of cases (such as securities fraud class actions) as more suitable for certification than other categories (such as mass torts). Thus, when considering a class action issue, one must consider not only Rule 23's requirements, but also how those requirements apply to the underlying substantive law implicated in the particular case.

The topic of class actions has received significant attention, generating a rich body of judicial and academic commentary. Courts have issued numerous groundbreaking class action decisions, and scholars have written literally hundreds of articles on various topics concerning class actions. In 2010, the American Law Institute (ALI) published a major work on the subject, *Principles of the Law of Aggregate Litigation*, a project on which the author served as an Associate Reporter. Rule 23 has also been amended in recent years, and those amendments have generated some important case law. Finally, in addition to the enactment of CAFA, various bills have been proposed in Congress that would significantly impact class action law and practice. *See* § 3.1.

The purpose of this text is to survey this important and controversial area of law. The field of class actions and other multi-party litigation covers a wide variety of topics and builds upon a host of basic civil procedure concepts. This text addresses the major topics of class action law and practice, including commencement of a class action, class action discovery, the class certification process, notice to class members, "opt-out" rights, communications with class members, constitutional issues, class settlements, jurisdictional issues, class trials, appellate review, and issue and claim preclusion. As noted above, it also focuses in detail on three important substantive areas of class action litigation: mass torts, employment discrimination, and securities fraud cases. In addition, it addresses three kinds of less traditional representative actions: defendant class actions, shareholder derivative suits, and suits involving unincorporated associations. Finally, this text surveys the relevant ethical issues.

Although most judicial and scholarly attention has centered on class actions, several other devices exist for resolving multi-party claims. These devices are important as well, and they are covered as topics in most courses on federal civil procedure and complex litigation. Accordingly, the final three chapters of this text address these various devices. Chapter 14 discusses transfers pursuant to the federal multidistrict litigation statute (MDL statute). MDL cases constitute roughly half of the federal civil court docket. Chapter 14 also discusses one device— informal coordination among federal and state courts—that is entirely voluntary and has no statutory foundation. Chapter 15 discusses various non-class devices—including joinder, impleader, interpleader, intervention, and consolidation—that are set forth in the Federal Rules of Civil Procedure. Finally, Chapter 16 covers additional aggregation devices, including transfers for the convenience of the parties and witnesses and in the interests of justice, and aggregation of parties pursuant to the Bankruptcy Code. Chapter 16 also addresses "mass actions" (sometimes called "quasi class actions") that are not brought as class actions but are frequently settled in the aggregate. These settlements are subject to an ethical restriction known as the "aggregate settlement rule."

All of these devices for litigating multiparty claims share a common goal: increasing the efficiency of judicial decision-making, thereby reducing time and expense to courts and parties. In addition, these devices all seek to reduce the likelihood of inconsistent adjudications. Some of these devices also enable nonparties to participate in litigation that might affect their interests. Others enable joint participation by individuals who would not find it cost-effective to litigate individually.

Nonetheless, while each device has its advantages, each can potentially yield unfair results. And, depending on the kind of case, each device has the potential to make matters *more*, rather than less, complicated. For these reasons, each device (with the exception of informal cooperation among courts) has specific, detailed requirements that must be satisfied. Furthermore, district courts are afforded substantial discretion in administering these devices.

While this text refers occasionally to procedures under state law (and in Chapter 7 includes a separate discussion of state court class actions), it focuses primarily on federal practice and procedure. In many of the areas addressed in this text, the approaches among states may differ from the federal approach. Even with respect to federal practice, the governing principles often differ from one federal circuit to another, and this text identifies important issues on which the federal circuits are divided (and on which there is no Supreme Court guidance). Thus, the student or litigator must carefully scrutinize the law applicable in the particular jurisdiction at issue.

In addition to numerous references to the ALI's *Principles of the Law of Aggregate Litigation* (mentioned above), this text refers in several places to two other important secondary sources: the Advisory Committee Notes and the *Manual for Complex Litigation (4th)* (the *Manual*).

The Advisory Committee Notes were written by the Advisory Committee on Civil Rules, whose members (from the bench, bar, and academy) are appointed by the Chief Justice of the United States and serve under the direction of the Standing Committee on Rules of Practice and Procedure. The

Advisory Committee is responsible for drafting proposed changes to the Federal Rules of Civil Procedure. (The author served as the academic member of the Advisory Committee from 2011–2017.) The Advisory Committee Notes are cited frequently by courts in construing the Federal Rules, although these notes must yield to the rules' plain language. (As discussed later in this text, the Supreme Court has cautioned against relying heavily on the Advisory Committee Notes.)

The *Manual*, published by the Federal Judicial Center (FJC), is used frequently by federal judges in managing complex cases and is an invaluable reference for attorneys. The fourth edition of the *Manual* was published in 2004, and is available on the FJC's website at http://www.fjc.gov/. (The website has other useful resources as well.) In addition to these sources, the student or litigator should also consult the local rules applicable in the particular judicial district at issue.

CHAPTER 2

EVOLUTION AND OVERVIEW OF FEDERAL COURT CLASS ACTIONS

Although this text focuses principally on class actions, as noted above many other devices exist for adjudicating the claims of multiple parties in one proceeding. For example, joinder under Federal Rule of Civil Procedure 20 allows multiple plaintiffs to sue (or multiple defendants to be sued) in one proceeding when common legal or factual questions exist and the claims arise out of the same transaction or occurrence or series of transactions or occurrences. Impleader under Rule 14 allows a defendant to bring in third parties who may be liable to the defendant for all or part of any claim that the plaintiff has against that defendant. Intervention under Rule 24 allows a nonparty, in certain circumstances, to join a lawsuit to protect its interests. Interpleader under Rule 22 allows multiple parties claiming entitlement to a particular fund or piece of real or personal property to have all issues of entitlement adjudicated in a single proceeding. Consolidation under Rule 42(a) allows a court to order a joint hearing or trial with respect to separate actions involving one or more common questions of law or fact. These and other devices (discussed in Chapter 15) share a common feature: all of the players are actually parties to the proceeding and present before the court.

Class actions are different. Unnamed members of a class action are not parties in the traditional sense and do not participate in—or usually even attend—

the classwide proceedings. Indeed, class actions exist precisely because, given the number of class members (and, in some instances, their geographic diversity), it is not practical to join all class members and try their claims individually. If the claims of class members share common issues, great efficiencies can be secured through aggregate pretrial and trial proceedings. In a class action proceeding, the named plaintiffs (also known as class representatives) and class counsel adjudicate the claims on behalf of the unnamed or "absent" class members. Assuming that the class representatives and counsel are adequate for the task, and that various other requirements for certification are met, the absent class members are bound by the adjudication of all common issues on behalf of the class. This is true whether the result of the classwide trial is favorable or unfavorable to the class. In some circumstances, class members can "opt out" (remove themselves from the case) before the judgment and pursue their claims individually. In other circumstances, however, the rules do not allow opt-outs.

Before a court will allow a class action to go forward, it must first conclude that various criteria are satisfied. Ultimately, these criteria (discussed in detail in later chapters) serve two purposes: (1) to ensure that the representative class members and class counsel will effectively represent the absent class members' interests, and (2) to ensure that a class action will be more efficient and effective than alternative methods for adjudicating the claims.

Although the basic model of a class action—a representative suit on behalf of a large number of people—has always been the same, the ground rules have changed substantially over time. In fact, at the federal level, multiple revisions of the rules governing class actions were necessary to establish that unnamed class members were in fact bound by a judgment in favor of or against the class.

The modern class action has its roots in English chancery practice. According to the Supreme Court, "class actions as we recognize them today developed as an exception to the formal rigidity of the necessary parties rule in equity, as well as from the bill of peace, an equitable device for combining multiple suits." *Ortiz v. Fibreboard Corp.*, 527 U.S. 815, 832 (1999). Although a detailed historical focus is beyond the scope of this text, this chapter provides a brief history of class action procedures in federal courts. Specifically, it summarizes the various federal class action rules enacted in 1842, 1912, 1938, and 1966, as well as amendments to Rule 23 subsequent to 1966. It also provides a brief summary of the Class Action Fairness Act of 2005 (CAFA).

§ 2.1 EQUITY RULE 48

The first codification of a federal class action rule in the United States occurred in 1842 and applied only in equitable proceedings. That rule, Equity Rule 48, provided that a case involving numerous parties could proceed on a representative basis without the need for each individual to appear personally. The rule made clear, however, that "in such cases, the decree shall be without prejudice to the rights and claims of all the absent parties." Thus, under the language of Equity Rule 48, and under the practice of most courts, a class action judgment had no binding effect upon those not actually before the court. These individuals could choose not to be bound if they did not like the result.

§ 2.2 EQUITY RULE 38

In 1912, Equity Rule 38 supplanted Equity Rule 48. Like its predecessor, Equity Rule 38 applied only in equitable proceedings. The main difference between Equity Rule 38 and the prior Equity Rule 48 was that the new rule specifically eliminated the reference to the non-binding effect of a judgment on absent class members. Under Equity Rule 38, which remained in effect until 1938, judgments in class actions could bind the absent parties in limited circumstances. Nonetheless, courts continued to display confusion as to when a judgment could bind an absent class member. The concern underlying this confusion—*i.e.*, whether a judgment that is binding on absent class members is consistent with each class member's due process right to a "day in court"—is still highly relevant today and will be explored in later chapters.

§ 2.3 THE 1938 VERSION OF RULE 23

The original version of Rule 23 was adopted in 1938. One of its major purposes was to make class actions available in both legal and equitable proceedings. (Indeed, a major purpose of the 1938

Federal Rules of Civil Procedure was to provide unified rules for both suits in equity and actions at law.) In addition, the rule sought to provide more guidance than the prior equity rules by attempting to fit class actions into one of three categories: (1) "true," (2) "hybrid," or (3) "spurious." These three categories, however, proved difficult to define, let alone to apply with precision.

The "true" category described the purest type of class action, where the "unity of interest" was "joint or common" to all members of the class. It included the situation in which a class member other than the owner of a primary right was entitled to enforce that right because the owner refused to do so. Examples of "true" classes included claims for breach of fiduciary duty resulting in the depletion of trust assets brought by trust beneficiaries against the trustee, and claims for conspiracy and interference with contract brought by labor union members against another labor union.

The "hybrid" category recognized interests that were "several" rather than "joint" but involved the same property or fund. Examples of "hybrid" classes included claimants to insurance policy proceeds, trust accounts, bank accounts, and other types of funds.

The last category created by original Rule 23, the "spurious" class action, again described the interests of the class members as "several," but recognized that aggregation was appropriate when "a common question of law or fact affected the several rights and common relief [was] sought." Actions brought by "spurious" classes included securities fraud claims by stockholders in which there was no common fund available for recovery.

Pursuant to the law that developed under the 1938 rule, the results of "true" and "hybrid" class actions were binding on unnamed class members; however, unnamed members of "spurious" classes were not bound until they actually appeared of record in the action. This problem—that not all class actions were binding on unnamed class members—was compounded by the fact that courts had difficulty distinguishing one category of class action from another. Further complicating matters was a practice known as "one-way intervention," whereby unnamed "spurious" class members—while not bound by an unfavorable judgment—could intervene before a favorable judgment became final and thus join the class only after success was assured. Needless to say, further revision was necessary to address a device that gave classwide effect to a plaintiff victory (through intervention) but gave the defendant no binding judgment when the class was unsuccessful. The revised rule did not emerge, however, until twenty-eight years later.

§ 2.4 THE 1966 VERSION OF RULE 23

The 1966 version of Rule 23 represented a substantial change from the original version. The Advisory Committee Notes discuss in detail the purposes behind the changes to Rule 23. As the Notes explain, the 1938 version of Rule 23 was abandoned because differentiating among true, hybrid, and spurious classes "proved obscure and uncertain." Moreover, the spurious class action proved to be of only limited utility because it did not "adjudicate the rights or liabilities of any person not a party." Finally, the Notes point out that the 1938 rule "did not squarely address itself to the question of the measures that might be taken during the course of the action to assure procedural fairness, particularly giving notice to members of the class, which may in turn be related in some instances to the extension of the judgment to the class."

To correct these concerns, the 1966 amendments to Rule 23 eliminated the true, hybrid, and spurious categories and adopted a practical and functional approach to representative litigation, with an emphasis on fair and adequate representation. Moreover, as the Notes indicate, the 1966 rule "provides that all class actions maintained to the end as such will result in judgments including those whom the court finds to be members of the class, whether or not the judgment is favorable to the class." The 1966 amendments thus closed the "one-way intervention" loophole described above and made clear that class action judgments were binding on all class members. In addition, the 1966 rule sets forth a variety of measures that trial court judges can use to assure the fairness of class actions. The following section contains a brief overview of the 1966 rule, as well as post-1966 amendments. Subsequent chapters describe the many issues that have arisen under the 1966 rule and the various amendments.

§ 2.5   OVERVIEW OF CURRENT RULE 23

The current version of Rule 23 is, in many respects, the same as the 1966 version, although some important changes were later made, as discussed below. Rule 23 contains numerous requirements that must be satisfied in order to maintain a class action. The burden is on the proponent of the class to show that each requirement is met.

Before analyzing the explicit requirements of Rule 23, the court must determine that certain threshold requirements are met. These requirements are arguably implicit in Rule 23 but are not set forth as freestanding, explicit requirements. Specifically, the court must find that: (1) a class exists that is capable of definition (including the requirement by some courts that identification of class members be administratively feasible); (2) the class representatives are members of the class; (3) the claim is live, not moot; and (4) Article III standing is satisfied. Next, four explicit requirements of Rule 23(a) must be met: (1) the class is so numerous that joinder of all members is impracticable; (2) at least one common question of law or fact exists; (3) the class representatives' claims are typical of those of the class; and (4) the class representatives and class counsel are adequate to represent the interests of the class. These four requirements are often referred to, respectively, as "numerosity," "commonality," "typicality," and "adequacy of representation." The failure to satisfy all of them will preclude class certification.

In addition to satisfying the threshold requirements and those specified by Rule 23(a), the proponent must also establish that a class is maintainable under at least *one* of the four categories established by Rule 23(b). The first category is 23(b)(1)(A), which applies when numerous individual actions would result in inconsistent standards of conduct for the party opposing the class. The second category, also part of Rule 23(b)(1), is 23(b)(1)(B). That subdivision applies in "limited fund" and other class actions in which numerous separate actions would substantially impair or impede the interests of individual class members.

The third category, 23(b)(2), is limited to suits seeking primarily declaratory or injunctive relief and does not extend to situations where money damages are the exclusive or predominant relief sought. Civil rights cases have historically been brought under (b)(2). In the past several years, however, Supreme Court and lower court precedent, discussed in § 4.3, has restricted the reach of (b)(2).

The fourth category, 23(b)(3), is appropriate when questions of law or fact common to the members of the class predominate over individual questions and a class action is superior to other methods of adjudication. As explained immediately below, unlike classes under Rule 23(b)(1) and (b)(2), which are mandatory classes (unless the court orders otherwise), members of Rule 23(b)(3) class actions have the right to receive notice of class certification and to "opt out" of the suit.

Rule 23(c), amended in 2003, provides courts with managerial authority over class actions. Subdivision (c)(1) addresses the timing of the certification decision, stating that the court must determine whether to certify the case as a class action at "an early practicable time." This language provides courts with more flexibility than the pre-2003 version of Rule 23(c), which mandated that the certification determination be made "as soon as practicable after commencement of an action." Subdivision (c)(2) addresses issues of notice to absent class members of class certification decisions. It requires notice and opt-out rights for absent class members in class actions maintained under (b)(3), and also provides that the court in its discretion "may direct appropriate notice to the class" in suits under (b)(1) and (b)(2). With respect to the judgment, in suits under (b)(1) and (b)(2), Rule 23(c)(3)(A) requires that the judgment describe the members of the class. In suits under (b)(3), Rule 23(c)(3)(B) requires that the judgment specify or describe the class members to whom notice was sent and who did not opt out. Rule 23(c)(4) permits the court to certify particular issues for class action treatment, and Rule 23(c)(5) permits the court to create subclasses.

Rule 23(d) enables the court to enter appropriate orders dealing with procedural matters, such as requiring notice to absent class members of important developments and imposing conditions on class representatives or intervenors.

Rule 23(e) requires the court's approval prior to any settlement, voluntary dismissal, or compromise of a certified class action. That provision also requires notice to class members of the settlement, dismissal, or compromise in such manner as the court directs. Any class member is entitled to object to any proposed settlement or voluntary dismissal that requires approval under Rule 23(e). As amended in 2003, Rule 23(e)(4) gives courts authority to permit class members in cases certified under Rule 23(b)(3) a second opportunity to opt out of the class if they do not wish to be bound by a proposed settlement. Rule 23(e)(3) requires that parties seeking approval of a settlement, voluntary dismissal, or compromise under Rule 23(e) "file a statement identifying any agreement made in connection with the proposal."

Rule 23(f), which became effective in 1998, permits immediate appeal (at the discretion of the court of appeals) of orders granting or denying class certification. In 2009, the period for seeking immediate appeal following such an order was increased from ten to fourteen days, consistent with the Federal Rules' overall efforts to simplify the calculation of filing deadlines.

Rule 23(g), added in 2003, provides that the court shall appoint class counsel upon certification of a class, and contains a list of criteria that the court must consider in making such an appointment. It addresses situations where multiple applicants seek to serve as class counsel, as well as situations where there is only one applicant. Rule 23(g) also reiterates Rule 23(a)(4)'s adequacy requirement in the context of class counsel.

Rule 23(h), also added in 2003, authorizes reasonable attorneys' fees and nontaxable costs upon the filing of a proper motion. It allows class members or the party from whom payment is sought to object to such a motion. The court must include findings of fact and conclusions of law with its decision on fees.

Several changes to Rule 23 became effective in 2018, including detailed provisions to address meritless objections to class settlements, changes to the notice rules (to emphasize the use of electronic mail and social media), and an amendment to Rule 23(f) clarifying that preliminary rulings are not subject to interlocutory review.

The foregoing requirements of Rule 23, including the various amendments discussed above, are examined in detail in the following chapters. Because many states have adopted class action rules that are patterned after Federal Rule 23, *see* § 7.2, federal authority interpreting Rule 23 may often be relevant even in state courts. The student or lawyer should not necessarily assume, however, that a similarly worded state court rule will be construed the same as Federal Rule 23. *See, e.g., Smith v. Bayer Corp.*, 564 U.S. 299 (2011) (noting that the class certification requirements of Federal Rule 23 are applied differently than the similarly worded West Virginia rule).

§ 2.6 CLASS ACTION FAIRNESS ACT OF 2005

On February 18, 2005, then-President George W. Bush signed into law the Class Action Fairness Act of 2005 (CAFA). CAFA affects two important areas: (1) the jurisdiction of federal courts over multistate class actions involving state-law claims, and (2) various types of class action settlements in federal court.

A. JURISDICTIONAL PROVISIONS

As described in detail below, *see* § 8.3, CAFA significantly expands the original jurisdiction of federal district courts over class actions involving state-law claims. Under CAFA, federal courts have jurisdiction over state law class actions if: (1) the case involves 100 or more class members, (2) there is "minimal diversity" between the parties, and (3) the aggregate amount in controversy for the class exceeds $5 million.

There are several exceptions to this expanded jurisdiction, discussed in detail in § 8.3. One group of exceptions is designed to keep truly local controversies in state court. Another exception pertains to class actions in which the primary defendants are government entities or officials. CAFA also does not apply to actions involving securities or internal corporate affairs. (As discussed in detail in § 11.3, other federal legislation specifically addresses securities claims.)

In addition to expanding original federal jurisdiction to cover many more state law class actions, CAFA also authorizes removal from state to federal court of cases covered by the statute. *See* § 8.3. As a result of CAFA, most major multistate class actions involving state-law claims are now adjudicated in federal court.

B.   SETTLEMENT PROVISIONS

CAFA also addresses class action settlements in federal court. In particular, it imposes significant restrictions on how class counsel can be compensated for "coupon settlements" (in which class members receive, for example, coupons good for discounts on future purchases of the defendant's product(s)). *See* § 9.2. CAFA also imposes restrictions on "net loss settlements" (*i.e.*, settlements resulting in a monetary loss to class members); prohibits settlements in which some class members receive more compensation merely because of their closer proximity to the courthouse; and requires that the parties to a federal class action settlement notify appropriate federal and state officials regarding the terms of a proposed settlement. The settlement provisions of CAFA do not apply to class actions in state court, even if those class actions could have been removed to federal court.

CHAPTER 3

CLASS CERTIFICATION REQUIREMENTS: THRESHOLD REQUIREMENTS AND RULE 23(a)

Before a case is "certified," or allowed to go forward as a class action, it is often referred to as a "putative" or "potential" class action. Likewise, the members of the proposed class are often referred to as "putative" or "potential" class members. To obtain certification of a putative class, the proposed class representatives (or named plaintiffs) must satisfy the explicit requirements of Rule 23(a)—numerosity, commonality, typicality, and adequacy of representation—as well as the requirements of one of the subdivisions of Rule 23(b)—(b)(1)(A), (b)(1)(B), (b)(2), or (b)(3). The burden of proof is on plaintiffs to meet those standards. Along with the Rule 23(a) and (b) requirements, courts generally require that the class representatives satisfy various threshold requirements.

§ 3.1 THRESHOLD REQUIREMENTS

Most courts and commentators agree that four threshold requirements must be satisfied before a class can be certified: (1) the existence of a definable class (and in some circuits, an administratively feasible method for identifying class members); (2) the presence of at least one representative who is a member of the class; (3) the existence of a claim that is live, not moot; and (4) the existence of standing under Article III of the U.S. Constitution. Because the text of Rule 23 provides little or no guidance on these requirements, courts have struggled to articulate clear and consistent criteria.

§ 3.2 A DEFINABLE CLASS

A. BASIC REQUIREMENTS

A clear, precise definition of the class is critical to the proper functioning of the class action device. The class definition determines who is entitled to favorable relief obtained in the suit and who is bound by an adverse ruling. It also determines who will receive notice in circumstances where notice is required. Surprisingly, despite the importance of the class definition, Rule 23 says nothing about how to define a class. To be sure, Rule 23(c)(1)(B), which was added in 2003, does state that "[a]n order that certifies a class action must define the class and the class claims, issues, or defenses." Beyond this general directive, however, the rule does not provide any meaningful guidance for defining a class.

Nonetheless, guidance can be found in the case law and in the *Manual for Complex Litigation (4th)*. As an initial matter, the class definition should be sufficiently precise such that a court can delineate the members of the class and thereby determine specifically who is bound by the ruling. For example, a class comprised of individuals "active in the peace movement" or "affected by the defendants' discharge of pollutants" may be viewed by a court as too vague because words like "active" and "affected" are ambiguous. Similarly, the class definition should not turn on each class member's subjective state of mind. For instance, a class should not be defined as all persons who "believe" that the defendant's emissions harmed their real property, because such a definition is too subjective. Likewise, a class definition should not depend upon resolution of the merits of the case (for instance, all persons who suffered illness "caused by" defendant's defective breast implants). In other words, the class definition should not create a situation where the court cannot identify a significant number of class members until the merits of the claims are fully resolved.

Generally, a class definition should focus on the defendant's alleged conduct and should include geographical, temporal, or other objective parameters that circumscribe the membership of the class. The class definition should capture the parties necessary for a fair and efficient resolution of common questions of law or fact in a single proceeding. If a class definition fails in this regard, the court may decline to certify the class or may elect to employ a number of alternatives at its disposal, such as designating subclasses with separate representatives and counsel. *See* § 5.2.

The level of judicial scrutiny that courts apply to class definitions depends in part on the type of class action involved. Thus, a damages "opt-out" class under Rule 23(b)(3) requires a very specific definition, because notice to class members is required under Rule 23(c)(2), and class members must be given the chance to exclude themselves from the class. *See* § 6.1. To provide such notice, courts must be able to identify with precision those who are, and are not, members of the class. By contrast, the class definition in Rule 23(b)(1) or (b)(2) cases need not be as precise. For instance, because notice is required under (b)(3) but generally not under (b)(1) and (b)(2), *see* § 6.1, a class definition that includes future members (*i.e.*, those who have not yet suffered injury but will suffer injury in the future) is more likely to be upheld under Rule 23(b)(1) or (b)(2) than under Rule 23(b)(3).

In recent years, the requirement of an adequate class definition has taken on greater significance in the certification decision. Between 1966 and 2000, relatively few putative class actions were rejected at the certification stage because of a flawed class definition. For the most part, courts were flexible in permitting class counsel to modify flawed definitions (and, in some instances, courts modified the definitions themselves to correct deficiencies). Since 2000, however, courts have denied certification in many cases because of flawed definitions. Two examples are *Romberio v. UnumProvident Corp.*, 385 F. App'x 423 (6th Cir. 2009), and *Oshana v. Coca-Cola Bottling Co.*, 225 F.R.D. 575, 578 (N.D. Ill. 2005), *aff'd*, 472 F.3d 506 (7th Cir. 2006). Some courts, however, have remained liberal in upholding class definitions or allowing counsel to amend flawed definitions. The Seventh Circuit, for example, has recognized that crafting an adequate class definition "is more of an art than a science," and has said that definitional flaws "can and often should be solved by refining the class definition rather than by flatly denying class certification on that basis." *Messner v.*

Northshore Univ. HealthSystem, 669 F.3d 802, 825 (7th Cir. 2012).

B. HEIGHTENED ASCERTAINABILITY

In recent years, some courts have imposed a heightened standard, requiring that plaintiffs establish an "administratively feasible" means of identifying class members. This is often referred to as the "heightened ascertainability" requirement, and some courts have adopted it as an independent threshold requirement for class certification.

The most prominent example is *Marcus v. BMW of North America, LLC*, 687 F.3d 583 (3d Cir. 2012), in which the Third Circuit overturned certification of a class alleging defective tires, concluding that plaintiffs had not presented an administratively feasible way to identify class members whose tires had gone flat. The court stated: "If class members are impossible to identify without extensive and individualized fact-finding or 'mini-trials,' then a class action is inappropriate." *Id.* at 593. The court explained that affidavits from class members were insufficient, stating that "[f]orcing [defendants] to accept as true absent persons' declarations that they are members of the class, without further indicia of reliability, would have serious due process implications." *Id.* at 594. Notably, in 2015, the Third Circuit appeared to retreat from its strict approach, characterizing heightened ascertainability as a "narrow" requirement. *Byrd v. Aaron's Inc.*, 784 F.3d 154, 165–67 (3d Cir. 2015).

Other courts have rejected heightened ascertainability as an independent requirement for certification. For example, in *Mullins v. Direct Digital, LLC*, 795 F.3d 654 (7th Cir. 2015), the Seventh Circuit rejected the Third Circuit's ascertainability jurisprudence, noting that a heightened ascertainability requirement is found nowhere in Rule 23 and "does not further any interest of Rule 23 that is not already adequately protected by the Rule's explicit requirements." *Id.* at 662. On the other hand, the court explained, "the costs of imposing the requirement are substantial." *Id.* Among other things, the *Mullins* court noted that heightened ascertainability would effectively preclude certification of many low-value consumer class actions, particularly where potential class members lack documentary proof that they purchased the defendant's product. And the court noted that, at least in Rule 23(b)(3) class actions, concerns about identification of class members are best addressed by that rule's manageability requirement (*see* § 4.4). Finally, the court disagreed with the Third Circuit's categorical rejection of affidavits from class members, noting that "[w]e are aware of only one type of case in American law where the testimony of one witness is legally insufficient to prove a fact." *Id.* at 669 (referring to U.S. Const. art. III, § 3, cl. 1 requiring two witnesses to convict for treason).

Legislation introduced in Congress—for example, The Fairness in Class Actions Litigation Act of 2017, H.R. 985, 115th Cong. (2017)—seeks to codify heightened ascertainability. Such legislation would arguably impose a more stringent standard than the Third Circuit, prohibiting class certification in cases involving monetary relief unless the plaintiff "affirmatively demonstrates that there is a reliable and administratively feasible mechanism (a) for the court to determine whether putative class members fall within the class definition and (b) for distributing directly to a substantial majority of class members any monetary relief secured for the class."

Heightened ascertainability has been discussed extensively by commentators. For an especially insightful discussion, *see* Geoffrey C. Shaw, *Class Ascertainability*, 124 Yale L.J. 2354 (2015).

§ 3.3 A REPRESENTATIVE WHO IS
A MEMBER OF THE CLASS

A second threshold requirement for class certification is that the class representative must be a member of the class that he or she seeks to represent. Although most courts recognize this requirement, they disagree as to its source. Some courts derive the requirement from the opening clause of Rule 23(a), which states that "[o]ne or more *members of* a class may sue or be sued as representative parties on behalf of all members only if" Rule 23(a)'s four requirements are met (emphasis added). Some courts derive the requirement by implication from Rule 23(a)(2), which requires "questions of law or fact common to the class." Others derive the requirement from Rule 23(a)(3), which provides that "the claims or defenses of the representative parties [must be] typical of the claims or defenses of the class." Others derive it from Rule 23(a)(4), which requires that "the representative parties will fairly and adequately protect the interests of the class." Finally, other courts derive the requirement from the constitutional mandate (U.S. Const. art. III, § 2, cl. 1)—fully applicable to class actions—that an individual must have standing to assert a claim. Whatever the source relied upon, the analysis employed by the courts is largely the same: Does the class representative have the same basic interests and the same type of alleged injury as the other class members?

A leading case applying the requirement of class membership is *East Texas Motor Freight System Inc. v. Rodriguez*, 431 U.S. 395 (1977), which held that, because the named plaintiffs in an employment discrimination suit lacked the qualifications for the job positions at issue, they "were not members of the class . . . they purported to represent," and thus could not serve as class representatives. *Id.* at 403. Similarly, a class of individuals complaining about the wording of a government notice (such as a notice describing the procedures for revocation of a driver's license) could not be represented by someone who did not receive the challenged notice; class members claiming antitrust injury from anticompetitive conduct could not be represented by someone who did not participate in the affected market; and a class of employees claiming discrimination on the basis of a certain disability could not be represented by an employee who did not suffer from that disability. The cases tend to be very fact-specific, however, and some courts are more rigorous than others in applying the membership requirement.

§ 3.4 A CLAIM THAT IS NOT MOOT

A. GENERAL PRINCIPLES

As a general matter, courts do not allow someone to serve as a class representative if his or her claim is moot. The mootness doctrine derives from Article III of the Constitution (U.S. Const. art. III, § 2, cl. 1) and requires that the litigant have a personal stake in the outcome in the form of a live controversy. As applied in various class action circumstances, however, the mootness doctrine is extremely complex.

For instance, the Supreme Court has held that if a class representative's claim becomes moot after the class is certified, the class action itself is not rendered moot. *Sosna v. Iowa*, 419 U.S. 393 (1975). *Cf. Nielsen v. Preap*, 139 S. Ct. 954, 963 (2019) (the "fact that the named plaintiffs obtained some relief before class certification [did] not moot their claims") (plurality op.). Likewise, if a class representative's claim becomes moot after class certification is *denied* (for instance, a prisoner challenging parole guidelines is released from incarceration after the denial of certification), the class representative can still appeal the denial of class certification. *U.S. Parole Comm'n v. Geraghty*, 445 U.S. 388 (1980). And under the exception to the mootness doctrine that allows review of claims that are "capable of repetition yet evading review," even if a class representative's claim becomes moot *prior* to a ruling on class certification, the class representative may be able to serve in that capacity if other class members' claims are likely to become moot in a short time frame as well. *Gerstein v. Pugh*, 420 U.S. 103 (1975). On the other hand, if the "capable of repetition" doctrine does not apply and the class representative's claim becomes moot before class certification, then the entire suit should be dismissed unless a new class representative with a live claim can be substituted.

The mootness doctrine is also sometimes applied in class actions when the defendant voluntarily ceases the conduct challenged by the plaintiff, and the plaintiff seeks no damages for prior wrongdoing. The case will not become moot, however, unless the defendant can demonstrate that the alleged wrongdoing is not likely to be repeated. Courts closely scrutinize the defendant's motivation to determine if the defendant *deliberately* mooted the controversy to evade judicial review of the conduct at issue. Courts have broad discretion in deciding whether to declare a case moot based upon the defendant's assurances that the alleged wrongdoing will not recur.

B.   PICK-OFFS OF CLASS REPRESENTATIVES

Another important mootness issue is defendants' use of offers of judgment under Federal Rule of Civil Procedure 68 to "pick off" class representatives prior to certification. Rule 68 provides, in pertinent part:

[A] party defending against a claim may serve on an opposing party an offer to allow judgment on specified terms, with the costs then accrued. . . . An unaccepted offer is considered withdrawn[.] . . . If the judgment that the offeree finally obtains is not more favorable than [an] unaccepted offer, the offeree must pay the costs incurred after the offer was made.

Defendants have increasingly attempted to create mootness by formally offering the full judgment sought by class representatives. Such a defendant will then move to dismiss the case, arguing that the offer of judgment mooted the class representative's individual claim by providing him or her with complete relief. The goal, of course, is to terminate the putative class action by "picking off" the class representatives with the hope that no other representatives will come forward.

The Supreme Court confronted this issue in *Campbell-Ewald Co. v. Gomez*, 136 S. Ct. 663 (2016), a putative class action involving the Telephone Consumer Protection Act (TCPA). There, the defendant filed a Rule 68 offer to pay the class representative, Gomez, his litigation costs and the maximum treble damages that he could claim for each violation of the TCPA. Gomez allowed the offer to expire without accepting it. The defendant subsequently moved to dismiss for lack of subject matter jurisdiction, arguing that "its offer mooted Gomez's individual claim by providing him with complete relief." *Id.* at 668. The Court rejected that argument, holding that the unaccepted offer of judgment did not moot Gomez's claim because he "remained emptyhanded" when the offer expired.

The Court noted, however, that "[w]e need not, and do not, now decide whether the result would be different if a defendant deposits the full amount of the plaintiff's individual claim in an account payable to the plaintiff, and the court then enters judgment for the plaintiff in that amount." *Id.* at 672.

Campbell-Ewald thus left open the question of whether *payment* of complete relief into an account payable to the plaintiff will suffice to moot a class representative's claims. Post-*Campbell-Ewald*, a number of defendants have followed that approach in an effort to preserve the "pick off" strategy after the Supreme Court's ruling. The Supreme Court has not yet addressed the question left open in *Campbell-Ewald*, and the lower courts have reached varying conclusions. Notably, the Third and Ninth Circuits have held that, even if payment of complete relief to the court were to moot a class representative's individual claim, the representative must be given "a fair opportunity to move for class certification" before entry of judgment. *Chen v. Allstate Ins. Co.*, 819 F.3d 1136, 1147 (9th Cir. 2016); *accord Richardson v. Bledsoe*, 829 F.3d 273, 283 (3d Cir. 2016). By contrast, other courts have held that a tender of complete relief can successfully moot a putative class action. *E.g.*, *Demmler v. ACH Food Companies, Inc.*, No. 15–13556–LTS, 2016 WL 4703875 (D. Mass. June 9, 2016) (sending plaintiff two checks prior to class certification that exceeded statutory damages, both of which plaintiff rejected, mooted individual and class claims). The Seventh Circuit has held that a defendant's settlement offer, accompanied by a deposit of the offered funds with the court, did not

moot the class representative's individual claims.
Fulton Dental, LLC v. Bisco, Inc., 860 F.3d 541 (7th
Cir. 2017). The court concluded that "an unaccepted
offer to settle a case, accompanied by a payment
intended to provide full compensation into the
registry of the court . . . is no different in principle
from an offer of settlement made under Rule 68." *Id.*
at 547.

§ 3.5 STANDING

Under Article III of the U.S. Constitution (which
limits judicial authority to "cases" and
"controversies"), a litigant must have "standing" to
sue. In *Lujan v. Defenders of Wildlife*, 504 U.S. 555
(1992), the Supreme Court identified a three-part
test that a litigant must satisfy to establish standing:
(1) the plaintiff must have suffered an "injury in
fact," (2) there must be a "causal connection between
the injury and the conduct of the defendant," and (3)
it must be "likely," not just "merely speculative," that
a favorable decision rendered by the court would
redress the injury presented. *Id.* at 560–61.

The Supreme Court has addressed standing issues
in the class action context. In *Spokeo, Inc. v. Robins*,
136 S. Ct. 1540 (2016), the plaintiff filed a putative
class action under the Fair Credit Reporting Act,
claiming that the website known as "Spokeo" posted
inaccurate information about plaintiff, thereby
harming his prospects for finding work. The
defendant argued that the plaintiff had suffered no
actual injury but was simply speculating about
possible harm. In a 6–2 opinion, the Court held that

for standing purposes, an injury must be both "concrete *and* particularized." *Id.* at 1545 (emphasis in original). The Ninth Circuit had focused on particularity but had failed to address concreteness, and thus its "standing analysis was incomplete." *Id.* at 1550. On remand, the Ninth Circuit held that plaintiff has properly alleged concreteness, *Robins v. Spokeo, Inc.*, 867 F.3d 1108, 1118 (9th Cir. 2017), and the Supreme Court denied certiorari, *Spokeo, Inc. v. Robins*, 138 S. Ct. 931 (2018).

In *Frank v. Gaos*, 139 S. Ct. 1041 (2019), three named plaintiffs brought a class action claim against Google, claiming that "Google's transmission of users' search terms in referrer headers violated the [Stored Communications Act]." *Id.* at 1044. Google moved to dismiss for lack of standing, an argument accepted by the district court but rejected by the Ninth Circuit on appeal. The Supreme Court granted review on a separate issue regarding the legitimacy of a *cy pres* settlement, but decided—based on *Spokeo*—to remand the case so the Ninth Circuit could reconsider standing based on *Spokeo*.

The federal circuits have grappled with various other standing issues in the class action context. For instance, defendants have argued that, even if the named plaintiffs have standing, Article III is violated if a substantial number of unnamed class members are unable to allege an "injury in fact." Some courts have rejected this argument, holding that a class action can go forward as long as at least one named plaintiff has standing. *See, e.g., Neale v. Volvo Cars of N. Am., LLC*, 794 F.3d 353, 364 (3rd Cir. 2015);

Kohen v. Pac. Inv. Mgmt. Co., 571 F.3d 672, 676 (7th Cir. 2009). Other courts, however, have held that all (or at least the vast majority) of the class members must have standing for the case to go forward. *See, e.g., Denney v. Deutsche Bank AG*, 443 F.3d 253, 264 (2d Cir. 2006).

Standing issues have arisen in a variety of contexts, including consumer and data breach class actions. For instance, in two separate consumer class actions, washing machine purchasers alleged that their machines were defective because the machines were susceptible to mold growth. *See In re Whirlpool Corp. Front-Loading Washer Prods. Liab. Litig.*, 722 F.3d 838 (6th Cir. 2013); *Butler v. Sears, Roebuck & Co.*, 702 F.3d 359 (7th Cir. 2012), *vacated*, 569 U.S. 1015 (2013), *judgment reinstated*, 727 F.3d 796 (7th Cir. 2013). In both cases, the defendants argued that because most class members had not experienced the mold problem, there was no Article III standing. Both Circuits rejected the argument. As the Sixth Circuit noted in *Whirlpool*, "not all class members must demonstrate manifestation of biofilm and mold growth in their [washing machines] before those individuals may be included in the certified class." 722 F.3d at 857.

In data breach class actions, important Article III issues have arisen. For example, in *Remijas v. Neiman Marcus Group, LLC*, 794 F.3d 688, 696–97 (7th Cir. 2015), the Seventh Circuit held that the plaintiffs—customers who had used payment cards at the defendant's stores prior to a large data breach—had Article III standing because they had suffered a substantial risk of future harm (potential fraudulent charges and identity theft). By contrast, in *Reilly v. Ceridian Corp.*, 664 F.3d 38, 46 (3d Cir. 2011), the Third Circuit held that the plaintiffs—employees who alleged negligence and breach of contract against the payroll processing firm as a result of a data breach—lacked standing because they could not show that the compromised data at issue was actually used to cause them financial injury.

§ 3.6 RULE 23(a)

Rule 23(a) sets forth four explicit requirements that must be satisfied in every federal class action. Again, these are generally known as numerosity, commonality, typicality, and adequacy of representation. Failure to satisfy any of these four requirements is fatal to class certification. Although some courts have applied these requirements liberally, in *Wal-Mart Stores, Inc. v. Dukes*, 564 U.S. 338 (2011), the Supreme Court reaffirmed an earlier statement made by the Court in *General Telephone Co. of Southwest v. Falcon*, 457 U.S. 147, 161 (1982): "[C]ertification is proper only if 'the trial court is satisfied, after a *rigorous analysis*, that the prerequisites of Rule 23(a) have been satisfied.'" *Dukes*, 564 U.S. at 350–51 (emphasis added) (quoting *Falcon*).

The Supreme Court and most of the federal circuits have recognized that a court may not avoid inquiring into the substantive merits of class claims at the certification stage if the merits overlap with an element of Rule 23. That is, the district court must "consider carefully all relevant evidence and make a definitive determination that the requirements of Rule 23 have been met before certifying a class." *In re Hydrogen Peroxide Antitrust Litig.*, 552 F.3d 305, 320 (3d Cir. 2008). And, as the Supreme Court made clear in *Dukes*, the district court's "rigorous analysis" will often "entail some overlap with the merits of the plaintiff's underlying claim." 564 U.S. at 351. Thus, although these decisions do not alter the substantive requirements of Rule 23(a), plaintiffs face a heightened evidentiary burden at the certification stage.

In 2013, however, the Supreme Court issued an important opinion, cautioning that the class certification stage is not the place to decide the merits. In *Amgen v. Connecticut Retirement Plans & Trust Funds*, 568 U.S. 455 (2013), the Court explained that "Rule 23 grants courts no license to engage in free-ranging merits inquiries at the certification stage. . . . Merits questions may be considered to the extent—but only to the extent— that they are relevant to determining whether the Rule 23 prerequisites for class certification are satisfied." *Id.* at 466. Following *Amgen*, numerous courts have likewise emphasized that class certification is not the place to adjudicate the merits. *Amgen* and subsequent cases are discussed in more depth in § 5.2.

Nonetheless, despite the Supreme Court's clear message in *Amgen* that courts addressing class certification should focus on the requirements of Rule

23 rather than the strength of the underlying claims, the class certification process remains heavily fact-intensive, with both sides developing and relying on evidence as opposed to mere allegations. The certification hearing may involve the resolution of conflicting expert or other testimony. Moreover, in many instances, the certification issues cannot even be addressed without extensive merits discovery. Consequently, Rule 23(a)'s threshold requirements are more important than ever.

§ 3.7 NUMEROSITY

A. OVERVIEW

Rule 23(a)(1) provides that "[o]ne or more members of a class may sue or be sued as representative parties on behalf of all members only if: (1) the class is so numerous that joinder of all members is impracticable." This requirement—commonly known as "numerosity"—lies at the heart of a class action. If joinder under Rule 19 or Rule 20 is practicable (*see* §§ 15.1–15.2), then there is no need for a representative action; each allegedly aggrieved individual can sue individually or as part of a collective, non-class case. The numerosity standard requires only that joinder be impracticable or difficult; joinder need not be impossible. In determining whether Rule 23(a)(1) has been satisfied, the trial judge has considerable discretion and will not be reversed on appeal absent abuse of that discretion.

B.   SIZE OF THE POTENTIAL CLASS

Rule 23 imposes no requirement of a minimum number of claimants necessary to bring a class action. Thus, absent a separate statutory requirement (such as the requirement of at least 100 class members to invoke federal jurisdiction under CAFA), numerosity must be evaluated on a case-by-case basis. Cases can be found certifying classes with fewer than twenty known members, whereas other cases can be found holding that numerosity is *not* satisfied with more than 300 members. Some courts have suggested that classes of twenty-five or more are generally sufficiently numerous to satisfy Rule 23(a)(1), while others have set the number at forty or more. Several courts have stated that focusing on numbers alone is improper, and that all relevant factual circumstances must be examined, such as the geographic dispersion of the class. Courts generally agree, however, that small numbers are more likely to be acceptable in cases seeking only injunctive relief, because the benefits of injunctive relief often run to individuals not formally included within the suit.

In many cases, particularly those that indisputably involve large numbers of class members, the defendant will not challenge numerosity. Attorneys in such cases reason that they would have no chance of succeeding under the governing law and would only undermine their credibility when they contend that other Rule 23 criteria have not been met.

C.   POSSIBLE FUTURE CLAIMANTS

In addition to evaluating the size of the potential class, courts sometimes take into consideration possible future claimants. For example, in a class suit claiming discrimination against women in intercollegiate athletics, a court might look not only at the existing students claiming injury, but also at the likelihood that future students will be subjected to the same discrimination. *See Pederson v. La. State Univ.*, 213 F.3d 858 (5th Cir. 2000). Thus, the existence of unknown, future claimants makes it easier for plaintiffs to satisfy the numerosity requirement. Such claimants necessarily increase the sheer numbers and also confirm the impracticability of joinder.

D.   OTHER FACTORS BEARING ON NUMEROSITY

In addition to size, other factors may in some cases be given significant weight. This is because the touchstone of the analysis is impracticability of joinder, not mere numbers.

One such factor is the geographical dispersion of the class. Obviously, if a class is spread out, joinder will be more difficult than if a class of the same size were limited to a small geographical area. For example, because of the difficulty in coordinating claims of plaintiffs dispersed throughout the country, a putative class of twenty-five such class members could easily satisfy the numerosity requirement. On the other hand, if all twenty-five putative class members lived in the same city, it would be far less difficult to join all of them.

Similarly, some courts reason that impracticability of joinder is more easily satisfied when each potential class member's claim is small, or when the potential class members lack the resources to pursue their claims individually. In these circumstances, class members are unlikely to litigate *at all* unless a class is certified, thus making joinder in the absence of a class all but impossible. Such cases—in which the claims likely would not be brought but for a class action—are commonly referred to as "negative-value" cases.

The facts of a specific case may indicate other reasons why joinder is impracticable. For example, impracticability of joinder may be found where employees fear reprisals from suing their employer individually. Likewise, impracticability was found in one case alleging police brutality where the events occurred in "a Chicago bar primarily frequented by homosexual and bisexual men," and the court found that "the potential social prejudice against homosexuals . . . may deter class members from suing in their own name[s]." *Patrykus v. Gomilla*, 121 F.R.D. 357, 360–61 (N.D. Ill. 1988). And joinder is often deemed impracticable, even with respect to relatively small classes, when the putative class members are poor, uneducated, or otherwise not inclined or able to bring individual actions. Furthermore, a court may deem joinder impracticable if several of the putative class members reside outside the court's jurisdiction.

These kinds of facts will frequently tip the scale in favor of finding numerosity satisfied in cases where sheer numbers alone would be insufficient.

E.   APPLICABILITY TO SUBCLASSES

When a court is considering whether to certify subclasses under Rule 23(c)(5), each subclass must independently satisfy Rule 23(a)(1) (along with the other elements of Rule 23(a) and (b)). Thus, when multiple subclasses are proposed, the court must consider separately the number of members and the impracticability of joinder within each subclass.

F.   RE-EVALUATION OF NUMEROSITY

Satisfaction of numerosity at the outset of a case does not necessarily mean that the issue is resolved conclusively for the entirety of the litigation. For instance, a large number of class members "opting out" might disqualify a class that at one time satisfied Rule 23(a)(1). On the other hand, even where a putative class initially did not satisfy numerosity, the entry of intervening parties may later render it sufficiently large to qualify under Rule 23(a)(1). Therefore, courts will sometimes revisit the numerosity issue, as well as other Rule 23 requirements, during the course of the litigation.

G.   RECENT TRENDS

Until recently, numerosity was rarely a barrier to certification. Because classes as small as twenty-five to forty often qualified under Rule 23(a)(1), defendants frequently stipulated to numerosity.

Recently, however, numerosity has become a more significant barrier, and many courts have denied certification on numerosity grounds. These rulings are frequently based on plaintiffs' failure to put forward sufficient evidence of class size, even in circumstances where common sense would suggest a class size of well over forty members.

For example, in *Vega v. T-Mobile USA, Inc.*, 564 F.3d 1256 (11th Cir. 2009), a class action involving only T-Mobile employees in Florida, the court held that the mere fact that T-Mobile was a large company with many employees nationwide did not excuse the plaintiffs' failure to produce evidence of the number of allegedly aggrieved T-Mobile employees *in Florida*. That is, speculation as to numerosity based on T-Mobile's size and large number of employees nationwide was insufficient.

Similarly, in *Marcus v. BMW of North America, LLC*, 687 F.3d 583 (3d Cir. 2012), the Third Circuit held that proof of defendant BMW's sale and lease of many cars with allegedly defective tires nationwide was insufficient to prove that the number of purchasers and lessees specifically in New Jersey satisfied Rule 23(a)(1). The court explained that, where a plaintiff attempts to certify a nationwide class and a state-specific subclass, "evidence that is sufficient to establish numerosity with respect to the nationwide class is not necessarily sufficient to establish numerosity with respect to the state-specific subclass." *Id.* at 595.

Other courts, however, have been willing to take a less stringent approach in finding numerosity. In

Johns v. Bayer Corp., 280 F.R.D. 551, 556 (S.D. Cal. 2012), for example, the court held that numerosity was satisfied where the defendant's nationwide sales figures made it "reasonable to assume" that a sufficient number of people in California had purchased the product at issue. *See also, e.g., Pederson v. La. State Univ.*, 213 F.3d 858, 868 (5th Cir. 2000) (involving alleged discrimination against female athletes at Louisiana State); *Verdow ex rel. Meyer v. Sutkowy*, 209 F.R.D. 309, 312 (N.D.N.Y. 2002) (involving allegedly improper denials of Medicaid benefits across the State of New York).

In 2016, the Third Circuit identified the criteria that courts should consider in assessing the impracticability of joinder:

> The non-exhaustive list [of factors for courts to consider] includes: judicial economy, the claimants' ability and motivation to litigate as joined plaintiffs, the financial resources of class members, the geographic dispersion of class members, the ability to identify future claimants, and whether the claims are for injunctive relief or for damages.

In re Modafinil Antitrust Litig., 837 F.3d 238, 252–53 (3d Cir. 2016) (overturning certification of 22-member class for failure to satisfy numerosity).

§ 3.8 COMMONALITY

A. OVERVIEW

Rule 23(a)(2) states that a class action may not be certified unless the case presents "questions of law or fact common to the class." This requirement, known as "commonality," focuses on the group of persons who would make up the class and requires that a court assess whether the group shares one or more issues relevant to the dispute that could be adjudicated on a collective basis. The "commonality" requirement seeks to ensure that group adjudication will achieve efficiencies without unfairness to the litigants. If a proposed class consists of individuals whose legal claims share either common legal theories or common factual circumstances, adjudication of their claims on a classwide basis may achieve efficiency without imposing substantial unfairness on either class members or their opponents. If, however, a proposed class is diverse with respect to critical facts, or if the legal theories presented by putative class members are dissimilar, trying the claims on an aggregate basis may be both inefficient and unfair.

The commonality requirement serves other purposes in addition to achieving efficiencies. By focusing the court's and litigants' attention on whether the proposed class presents common issues, Rule 23(a)(2) helps to refine the definition of the class itself. The commonality inquiry also influences the determination of "typicality" under Rule 23(a)(3), *see* § 3.9, since a potential class representative must present the allegedly "common" issues in a way that makes the claims or defenses being asserted "typical" of those of the class as a whole.

Like the numerosity requirement—but unlike the typicality and adequacy requirements, *see* § 3.9–3.10, both of which focus on the individual class representatives—the commonality requirement focuses on the *group* that seeks to proceed as a class. At the same time, commonality, typicality, and adequacy all focus on similarities and differences among representatives (and thus the class as a whole). Accordingly, the Supreme Court has observed that adequacy, commonality, and typicality "tend[ ] to merge." *Amchem Prods., Inc. v. Windsor*, 521 U.S. 591, 626 n.20 (1997) (citation and internal quotation marks omitted).

It is not difficult to identify issues that could be deemed common. For instance, in a securities fraud case, a common question might be whether defendant deliberately misstated its earnings. In a product defect case, a common question might be whether an appliance performs as promised in the owner's manual or in advertisements.

B. THE LANDMARK OPINION IN *DUKES*

Prior to the Supreme Court's decision in *Wal-Mart Stores, Inc. v. Dukes*, 564 U.S. 338 (2011), most actions brought as class actions easily satisfied the commonality requirement. Many courts found the standard satisfied where class members shared a legal question even with divergent underlying facts, or shared common underlying facts despite differing legal standards. To be sure, even prior to *Dukes*, courts occasionally cited commonality as a ground for denying class certification. But those cases tended to be outliers. Indeed, defendants often stipulated to commonality and, in (b)(3) cases, most defendants focused instead on the more demanding requirement of "predominance," under which common questions must not only exist but must *predominate* over individualized questions. *See* § 4.4.

In its 2011 opinion in *Dukes*, however, the Supreme Court provided its definitive interpretation of commonality under Rule 23(a)(2) and formulated a definition that, in the view of the dissent, is in reality a "predominance" test. A thorough understanding of *Dukes* is critical in applying Rule 23(a)(2).

In *Dukes*, a federal district court certified a class consisting of approximately 1.5 million current and former female Wal-Mart employees alleging systematic sex discrimination in pay and promotions in violation of Title VII of the Civil Rights Act of 1964. The women alleged that Wal-Mart maintained a "corporate culture" that "permitted bias against women to infect . . . the discretionary decisionmaking of each one of Wal-Mart's thousands of managers—thereby making every woman at the company the victim of one common discriminatory practice." 564 U.S. at 345. Although each side presented a wealth of statistical and anecdotal evidence, the Court ultimately held (in a five–four decision with respect to commonality) that the potentially disparate questions underlying each putative class member's claim prevented plaintiffs from satisfying the commonality requirement. The Court found no evidence that Wal-Mart "operated under a general policy of discrimination," and no evidence that all of the company's managers exercised their discretion in a common way such that each class member suffered a common injury. *Id.* at 354–56.

In its decision, authored by Justice Scalia, the Court articulated the test for commonality as follows:

> [The] common contention . . . must be of such a nature that it is capable of classwide resolution—which means that determination of its truth or falsity will resolve an issue that is *central to the validity of each one of the claims in one stroke*.

Id. at 350 (emphasis added). The Court derived its test—that the common question must in essence be outcome-determinative—not from the wording of Rule 23(a)(2), but from a law review article by the late Professor Richard Nagareda. *See* Richard Nagareda, *Class Certification in the Age of Aggregate Proof*, 84 N.Y.U. L. Rev. 97 (2009).

Justice Ginsburg, writing for four Justices, dissented. She accused the majority of "blend[ing] Rule 23(a)(2)'s threshold [commonality] criterion with the more demanding [predominance] criteria of Rule 23(b)(3), and thereby elevat[ing] the (a)(2) inquiry so that it is no longer 'easily satisfied.'" *Id.* at 375. The dissent was troubled that the practical effect of the majority's opinion was to add a "predominance" requirement to classes brought under Rule 23(b)(1) or (b)(2), even though only Rule

23(b)(3), by its terms, requires a showing of predominance.

Dukes has been widely understood to raise the threshold standard for commonality, and a number of federal courts have cited the case in rejecting class certification on commonality grounds. *See, e.g., D.L. v. District of Columbia*, 713 F.3d 120 (D.C. Cir. 2013); *M.D. ex rel. Stukenberg v. Perry*, 675 F.3d 832 (5th Cir. 2012). A majority of federal courts have also declined to limit *Dukes* to its facts, concluding that it applies to class actions brought under (b)(1)(A), (b)(1)(B), (b)(2), or (b)(3) regardless of plaintiffs' underlying substantive claims. Some courts, however, have distinguished *Dukes, see, e.g., Parsons v. Ryan*, 289 F.R.D. 513, 521 (D. Ariz. 2013), and class actions continue to be certified notwithstanding the Court's heightened standard for commonality. *See* Robert H. Klonoff, *Class Actions Part II: A Respite From the Decline*, 92 N.Y.U. L. Rev. 971 (2017). Ultimately, the decision has not curtailed class actions to the degree that many commentators and plaintiffs' attorneys had feared.

C.   WHETHER MORE THAN ONE COMMON LEGAL OR FACTUAL ISSUE IS NECESSARY

The language of Rule 23(a)(2) presents a threshold issue: By its use of the plural ("questions"), it appears to provide that a court may not find commonality satisfied unless there is *more than one* common question of law or fact. By contrast, Rule 20(a) (permissive joinder), Rule 24(b) (permissive intervention), and Rule 42(a) (consolidation) all make it clear through the use of the singular ("question") that only a single common legal or factual question is required. Nonetheless, it is well established that Rule 23(a)(2) is satisfied if a proposed class action involves even a single common question of law or fact. As the Supreme Court stated in *Dukes*, " '[e]ven a single [common] question' will do." 564 U.S. at 359 (citation omitted; brackets in *Dukes*).

D.   LAW *OR* FACT

It is also evident from Rule 23(a)(2) that the commonality requirement can be satisfied by presentation of a common question of law *or* fact. This means that common questions of law, as well as fact, will satisfy the rule. Thus, many courts have found commonality satisfied where all of the plaintiffs are suing under the same legal theory or theories. Some courts, however, have resisted finding commonality based solely on questions of law, such as whether a statute of limitations barred the class members' claims, or whether punitive damages would be available, holding instead that such questions do not satisfy Rule 23(a)(2). *Dukes* arguably supports this latter interpretation of Rule 23(a)(2), given that the Court held (as noted above) that disparate factual questions among putative class members precluded a finding of commonality.

§ 3.9 TYPICALITY

A. LACK OF CONSENSUS ON MEANING

Rule 23(a)(3) provides, as a prerequisite to class certification, that "the claims or defenses of the representative parties [must be] typical of the claims or defenses of the class." This requirement first appeared in the 1966 amendments to Rule 23. The 1938 version of Rule 23 did not contain a typicality requirement, but simply required adequacy of representation: "one or more [representatives], as will fairly insure the adequate representation of all." The Advisory Committee Notes to the 1966 amendments provide no guidance regarding the intent of Rule 23(a)(3). Courts have thus struggled to interpret the typicality requirement, resulting in confusion and a lack of consensus.

Some courts have stated that the typicality requirement has no independent meaning and should be ignored. But even those courts do not agree as to *why* this is the case. Some say that typicality is the same as commonality; others say that it is the same as adequacy of representation; others say that Rule 23(a)(3) merely repeats the requirement that the class representative be a member of the class that he or she purports to represent; and still others say that typicality is just another label for determining whether individual questions predominate over common questions. As noted in § 3.8, the Supreme Court has recognized that adequacy, typicality, and commonality "tend[ ] to merge" and that these requirements "serve as guideposts for determining whether ... maintenance of a class action is economical and whether the named plaintiff's claim and the class claims are so interrelated that the interests of the class members will be fairly and adequately protected in their absence." *Amchem Prods., Inc. v. Windsor*, 521 U.S. 591, 626 n.20 (1997) (citation and internal quotation marks omitted); *accord Dukes*, 564 U.S. at 349 n.5.

Despite this confusion, a number of courts have applied the canon of construction dictating that portions of a statute or rule should not be rendered meaningless, and thus have attempted to give independent significance to the typicality requirement. As a result, courts have occasionally invoked Rule 23(a)(3) as a reason to deny class certification.

B.   GENERAL APPROACH BY COURTS GIVING SEPARATE MEANING TO TYPICALITY

A number of cases state that the core of typicality is a comparison of the claims and defenses of the representative with those of the class. This comparison involves many inquiries: Is the class representative challenging the same alleged misconduct as the unnamed class members? Is he or she advancing the same legal theory based on the same type of injuries? Is the class representative's claim subject to unique defenses or other factual or legal flaws not present in the claims of unnamed class members? Ultimately, the inquiry is designed to ensure that a representative, in pressing his or her claims, is also pressing the claims of the other class members.

Courts that focus on comparing the representative's claim with those of the other class members nearly always hold that a representative's claims need not be identical to those of unnamed class members, but only substantially similar. Factual differences do not destroy typicality unless they cast serious doubt on the representative's ability to prosecute the claims of the other class members. For example, in *Marcus v. BMW of North America, LLC*, 687 F.3d 583 (3d Cir. 2012) (also discussed above in the context of heightened ascertainability, *see* § 3.1), the putative class alleged consumer fraud, breach of warranty, and breach of contract in connection with allegedly defective Bridgestone "run-flat" tires equipped on various BMW models. The defendants argued that Marcus, the class representative, was not typical of the class in part because he had leased only one model of BMW with one kind of run-flat tire, whereas other members of the class had purchased or leased different models with different kinds of run-flat tires. The district court rejected that argument and found typicality satisfied. The Third Circuit agreed, explaining that the district court did not abuse its discretion in finding that the alleged defect in the run-flat tires "will show itself in a substantially similar way across the various tire models and sizes at issue." 687 F.3d at 599. Moreover, there was no "indication that BMW's ... representations differed significantly depending on the model-year BMW or specification of [run-flat tire]." *Id*. Thus, the court concluded that, while factual differences existed between Marcus's claim and those of other class members, those differences "d[id] not prejudice his ability to protect absent class members' interests fairly and adequately." *Id*.

C.   UNIQUE DEFENSES

An important inquiry under typicality is whether the class representative is subject to unique defenses that threaten to divert the focus of the litigation away from the classwide claims. The concern is that the entire class will be bound by an adverse ruling that may turn on a defense specific to the representative. To destroy typicality, however, such a defense must be *unique*—or at least limited to a small segment of the class. A defense that can be asserted against the entire class—for example, that *every* class member's claim is barred by the statute of limitations—does not raise a typicality problem. Furthermore, a purportedly unique defense must be supported by the record. Purely speculative defenses will not render a representative atypical.

Some courts are reluctant to view unique defenses as an impediment to class certification, reasoning that to do so would be to improperly decide the merits of the case at the certification stage. Other courts, however, hold that there is no need to resolve the merits of the defense: As long as the defense— meritorious or not—is likely to occupy a considerable amount of trial time to the detriment of the class as a whole, then a typicality problem exists. In addition, as noted above and in *Dukes*, assessment of class certification requirements may "entail some overlap with the merits." *See* § 5.2.

Courts agree that a unique defense must be serious to justify disqualification of someone as a class representative. The defense must, in other words, be likely to become a significant issue at trial. For example, the Third Circuit in *Marcus* also addressed the defendants' argument that Marcus was atypical because New York law applied to his claims—providing him with unique defenses not available to those class members whose claims were governed by New Jersey law. The court concluded that such unique defenses were not serious enough to defeat typicality, explaining that the defendants "failed to demonstrate how any defenses unique to Marcus's claims [would] become a major focus of the litigation." 687 F.3d at 599–600.

Examples of class representatives with unique defenses that could defeat typicality are:

- A representative in an employment discrimination suit who, according to the defendant employer, was terminated not because of race but because he was caught stealing money from the company and covering up the theft by falsifying records.

- A representative in a securities fraud suit who purchased large volumes of the company's stock *after* the alleged fraud was disclosed.

- A representative in a mass tort property damage case whose property value actually increased when the defendant opened its neighboring manufacturing plant.

- A representative in a consumer protection case who admitted to friends that he knew about the alleged dangers of a product *before* purchasing it.

In each of these scenarios, the representative would be subject to substantial cross-examination on these issues, and the negative facts could jeopardize the outcome of the case for the entire class. Each situation must be evaluated on its own facts, however, and courts differ as to how rigidly they approach the issue. For instance, some courts hold that a representative who is subject to a possible statute of limitations defense cannot satisfy typicality, while other courts refuse to view a statute of limitations defense as disqualifying.

D.   PLAINTIFF SEEKING RECOVERY AGAINST ONLY ONE OF SEVERAL DEFENDANTS

Ordinarily, the class representatives as a group must have a viable suit against every defendant named in the complaint in order to satisfy the typicality requirement. For example, if the sole class representative bought illegally overpriced airline tickets from only one of ten defendants in a case, that person normally would not be typical of the class as a whole. There are, however, cases holding that this requirement need not be satisfied when the defendants are alleged to have engaged in a conspiracy to injure the class, or where they are linked in some special way (for instance, by being part of a common organization or otherwise acting in concert). *See* § 12.1.

E.   FACTUAL DISPARITIES DEFEATING TYPICALITY

Some courts apply a typicality analysis in holding that factual differences from one class member to another defeat class certification. For example, if the various class representatives allege different injuries from a chemical exposure (*e.g.*, some claim breathing problems, others claim headaches, and still others claim property damage), some courts hold that no class member's claim is "typical." Other courts, however, find no typicality problem in these circumstances, reasoning that mere differences in damages do not defeat typicality. Such courts hold that as long as the class members are all challenging the same alleged misconduct and are relying on the same legal theories, typicality is satisfied. For instance, in one case involving an alleged fraudulent scheme against life insurance policyholders, the court found that typicality was satisfied even though the class members alleged a wide variety of fraudulent sales practices. The court reasoned that the claims arose from the same fraudulent course of conduct and involved similar legal theories. *In re Prudential Ins. Co. Am. Sales Practices Litig. Agent Actions*, 148 F.3d 283 (3d Cir. 1998) (involving review of a classwide settlement).

One possible approach to factual disparities (and thus to potential typicality problems) is to form subclasses. If each subclass has at least one representative with facts typical of the subclass as a whole, then the typicality concerns will have been resolved. In some instances, however, courts hold that there are too many factual differences even *within* a proposed subclass to declare any member's claims or defenses "typical." Subclasses are discussed in § 5.2.

§ 3.10   ADEQUACY OF REPRESENTATION

A. OVERVIEW

Rule 23(a)(4) requires that, before a class may be certified, a court must find that "the representative parties will fairly and adequately protect the interests of the class." This requirement—which applies to both the class representatives and class counsel—is based on fundamental principles of due process: A ruling cannot bind absent class members if the representatives were inadequate. *Hansberry v. Lee*, 311 U.S. 32 (1940). Rule 23(a)(4) requires only *adequate* class representatives and counsel; it does not require the best possible representatives and counsel.

A court's initial determination of adequacy is not necessarily definitive. The court has a continuing duty to monitor the adequacy of the class representatives and class counsel. Moreover, Rule 23(d)(1)(B)(iii) allows the court to give notice to class members of "the members' opportunity to signify whether they consider the representation fair and adequate," thus giving class members a role in supervising the adequacy of representation.

Rule 23(a)(4) is not the only subdivision of Rule 23 that addresses adequacy. As discussed below (§ 3.8) Rule 23(g), added in 2003, specifically addresses the criteria for appointing class counsel.

In addition, the Private Securities Litigation Reform Act of 1995 (PSLRA), which applies only to securities class actions, provides a statutory process for appointing a class representative. Securities class actions are discussed in detail in Chapter 11.

B.   COUNTERINTUITIVE FEATURE THAT CHALLENGES TO ADEQUACY ARE NORMALLY RAISED BY DEFENDANTS

The law governing adequacy of representation reveals an unusual feature: In most cases the *defendants* are the ones who seek to challenge adequacy. But do defendants really *want* to exclude inadequate representatives or class counsel? Or would they prefer weak, ineffective representatives and class counsel? (The same tension exists with respect to typicality: Do defendants really want to exclude atypical representatives who, for example, are subject to unique defenses?) It is undoubtedly true that, in some cases, a defendant's motivation is not to secure the substitution of adequate plaintiffs and counsel, but to obtain dismissal of the class suit altogether. On the other hand, defendants have an important interest in ensuring that, if a class action goes forward, the class members are represented by adequate named plaintiffs and counsel. If defendants secure a favorable verdict with inadequate representatives, the class members will have a strong argument that they are not bound by the judgment. *See* § 8.4. Thus, the absence of adequate representation can be a no-win situation for defendants: If defendants lose, the entire class benefits, but if defendants win, they risk having their success destroyed through attacks on the judgment based on inadequate representation.

Nonetheless, while defendants may have legitimate reasons for challenging adequacy, courts sometimes view such challenges with skepticism, reasoning that defendants' real goal is not to protect absent class members but rather to see that no class is certified. Other courts, by contrast, do not question the sincerity of defendants' challenges.

Many courts give conclusive weight to a defendant's *failure* to contest adequacy. Other courts, however, conduct an independent review of adequacy despite defendant's failure to contest the issue.

C.   ADJUDICATING THE ADEQUACY OF CLASS REPRESENTATIVES

The adequacy of class representatives is an issue for the trial court and is reviewed only for abuse of discretion. It encompasses numerous components, discussed below, although many courts focus solely on whether class representatives suffer from a conflict of interest and thus do not scrutinize other indicia of adequacy (*e.g.*, knowledge of the case or good moral character). Most courts require serious deficiencies before finding that a class representative is inadequate.

When a case involves multiple representatives, Rule 23(a)(4) is satisfied if even one representative is adequate; there is no requirement that every representative satisfy Rule 23(a)(4), although a proposed class representative who fails to satisfy the adequacy requirements cannot continue to serve in that role.

D. VIGOROUS PROSECUTION

A number of courts state that a class representative must vigorously prosecute the claims of the class. This means, for example, that he or she must be committed to the claim, believe in its merit, prosecute the case in a timely manner, and supervise the conduct of class counsel. Also, a class representative must have the necessary time and resources to devote to the case and must not be hampered by severe and disabling physical or mental problems (unless such injuries are the basis of the class's claim). A representative's failure to attend important court hearings or respond to critical discovery may provide strong evidence of inadequacy. Likewise, a representative's failure to move promptly for class certification may raise adequacy concerns. In addition, the size of a representative's claim may bear on adequacy: If a representative has only a small stake in the outcome, he or she generally will be less inclined to commit the time and resources necessary to be vigorous and effective. (Of course, this principle cannot be applied too expansively or it would be impossible to find adequate representatives in "negative-value" cases.) No particular factor is dispositive; instead, courts evaluate the totality of the circumstances. Few courts actually reject class representatives on this basis.

E.   KNOWLEDGE OF THE CASE

Numerous courts indicate that a class representative must have at least some knowledge of the facts, parties, and basic issues in the case and must stay in contact with class counsel. This requirement is meant to ensure that the class representative is an active participant, not a mere figurehead in a lawyer-driven suit. On the other hand, many courts recognize that class representatives cannot be expected to have precise knowledge of all the factual or legal issues involved, particularly when the case is complicated or highly technical. Thus, courts frequently find that a representative is competent if he or she has some basic knowledge of the case. Such courts recognize that clients necessarily rely on counsel to understand the relevant factual and legal intricacies. Cases actually finding inadequacy on this ground are rare and generally involve representatives who cannot even articulate the claims or grievances at issue and have little or no knowledge of the parties, remedies sought, or responsibilities of class representatives.

F.   HONESTY, GOOD CHARACTER, AND CREDIBILITY

Several courts state that a class representative must have good moral character. For instance, a representative who gives materially false testimony or otherwise acts dishonestly in the litigation at issue may be found inadequate, whereas minor inconsistencies in memory or testimony are permitted. The issue is less clear when misconduct occurred in an unrelated case or circumstance, although serious misconduct in another context may render a representative inadequate. Depending on the circumstances, a prior criminal record may or may not render a class representative inadequate. Again, few courts have disqualified class representatives on this ground.

G.   LACK OF CONFLICTS

A class representative should not have interests that significantly conflict with those of the other class members. For example, if the representative has a financial interest in a company that was allegedly involved in the claimed wrongdoing, the plaintiff's failure to sue that company along with the other defendants may raise serious adequacy concerns. Likewise, adequacy issues would be triggered with respect to a class representative who is a relative of the opposing party or the opposing party's counsel. In some circumstances, conflicts of interest may also arise if the representative is related to class counsel. In all instances, however, the issue must be decided based on the particular facts.

Many cases addressing adequacy (as well as typicality, *see* § 3.9) have focused on potential conflicts between the class representative and unnamed class members. Indeed, this is by far the most common reason for rejecting class representatives. As indicated above, many courts focus solely on alleged conflicts in ruling on adequacy and do not even consider issues of knowledge or character.

It is easy to understand why a representative with serious conflicts must be deemed inadequate. For example, in a discrimination case, a person seeking to represent a class of African-American employees who were terminated from their jobs might have a fatal conflict of interest if he also claims that his termination was based on age discrimination. To win his age discrimination case, he might need to show that he was replaced by a younger African-American man, and that an older white man was also passed over for the job. Such evidence, while advancing the representative's own age discrimination claim, would undercut the unnamed class members' claims of race discrimination. Similarly, in a securities fraud suit, a conflict might exist if a named plaintiff sold—rather than purchased—stock at a time when the defendant corporation was falsely painting a rosy picture of the company's future prospects. These types of conflicts may also subject the class representative to the argument that he or she should be disqualified on typicality grounds because of unique defenses. *See* § 3.9.

Likewise, a class representative who has a personal relationship with class counsel (*e.g.*, counsel's parent, child, or spouse) might be more concerned about maximizing counsel's fees than maximizing the recovery for individual class members. For example, in *Eubank v. Pella Corp.*, 753 F.3d 718 (7th Cir. 2014), the Seventh Circuit overturned a class settlement on adequacy grounds in part because lead class counsel was the lead class representative's son-in-law, and informed consent was not sought from class members). The court reasoned that, "the larger the fee award to class counsel, the better off [the class representative's] daughter and son-in-law would be financially . . . (which sharpened the conflict of interest) by a lot." *Id.* at 724.

A related type of potential conflict occurs when the named plaintiffs' claims differ from those of the class. For example, in *Amchem Products, Inc. v. Windsor*, 521 U.S. 591 (1997), and again in *Ortiz v. Fibreboard Corp.*, 527 U.S. 815 (1999), the Supreme Court made clear that class representatives who allegedly suffered injury from exposure to asbestos could not represent class members who had been exposed but had not yet suffered injury. The Court noted that the goal of the class representatives—to maximize recovery for those who had already suffered injury— conflicted with the goal of those who had not yet suffered injury: to preserve the maximum amount possible to compensate for potential future injuries.

Conflicts of interest may also arise under the terms of class action settlements (*see* § 9.1). For example, in 2013 the Ninth Circuit overturned a class settlement on adequacy grounds because the settlement awarded "incentive payments" to the class representatives. *Radcliffe v. Experian Info. Solutions Inc.*, 715 F.3d 1157 (9th Cir. 2013). Although the court noted that incentive payments do not always create conflicts of interest, it emphasized that the payments at issue were *conditioned on support for the settlement* and significantly exceeded what unnamed class members could expect to receive for their injuries. Thus, the court reasoned, "these circumstances created a patent divergence of interests between the named representatives and the class." *Id.* at 1161.

Courts have indicated that "minor conflicts" will not demonstrate inadequacy. Rather, "the conflict must be a 'fundamental' one going to the specific issues in controversy." *Valley Drug Co. v. Geneva Pharms., Inc.*, 350 F.3d 1181, 1189 (11th Cir. 2003) (citations omitted).

H.   UNIQUE DEFENSES

The existence of unique defenses is relevant not only to typicality (*see* § 3.9) but also to adequacy. If a representative must devote attention to defenses unique to the representative's own case, then that is time taken away from representing the interests of the class as a whole.

I.   ABILITY TO FINANCE THE CLASS ACTION

A few courts have held that a class representative's inability to finance the litigation renders the representative inadequate. Most courts, however, do not strike class representatives on this ground. This is especially true when class counsel is able and willing to fund the litigation. The issue turns in part on the applicable code of ethics. In some states, it is unethical for an attorney to advance litigation costs without any expectation of repayment, while in other states such conduct is permissible. *See* discussion in § 13.1.

When a court deems a class representative's financial resources relevant, it generally looks to whether the representative has sufficient resources to pay for class notice and other reasonable costs. The issue of a named representative's financial resources is sometimes a subject of pre-certification discovery, a topic discussed in § 5.3.

J.   MEMBERSHIP IN THE CLASS

It is fundamental that a class representative must be a member of the class that he or she seeks to represent. As explained above (§ 3.3), the textual basis (if any) of this requirement is unclear. Many courts, however, have identified Rule 23(a)(4) as the authority for this requirement on the ground that someone who lacks the characteristics of other class members and has not suffered the same injuries cannot adequately represent those absent class members.

K.   ADEQUACY OF CLASS COUNSEL

Although successful challenges to the adequacy of class counsel are rare, they do occur. In recent years, some courts have started to take a closer look at the issue. For example, in *Creative Montessori Learning Centers v. Ashford Gear, LLC*, 662 F.3d 913 (7th Cir. 2011), the Seventh Circuit held, contrary to the district court, that a showing of "egregious" misconduct by counsel was not required. Rather, the proper standard is whether class counsel's conduct "creates a *serious doubt* that counsel will represent the class loyally." *Id.* at 918 (emphasis added).

Courts examine a variety of factors in assessing adequacy of counsel. Rule 23(g)—enacted in 2003 and discussed below—focuses specifically on the criteria to be taken into account in ensuring that class counsel is adequate.

Qualifications. Courts look at the qualifications, experience, and reputation of counsel, particularly in handling class actions or other complex cases, or in handling other cases involving the same subject matter (such as other antitrust cases). It is rare for a class attorney to have such meager qualifications as to be found inadequate under Rule 23(a)(4) or Rule 23(g). Frequently, lawyers lacking significant class action experience will affiliate with more experienced counsel to assist in the representation.

Performance. Courts also look at the performance of counsel in the litigation at issue. An attorney who has repeatedly missed deadlines, failed to pursue discovery in a vigorous manner, filed deficient pleadings or briefs, or otherwise exhibited lackluster performance may be found inadequate. A few courts take the view that Rule 23(a)(4) mandates an exemplary level of performance by class counsel, given that the interests of numerous unnamed class members are impacted. Other courts, however, merely seek to ensure that counsel's performance is minimally competent.

Involvement of Class Representatives. An attorney representing a class may be found inadequate if he or she does not keep the class representatives informed of important matters and does not allow them to review and comment on key court filings. For instance, a class representative's failure to review the complaint before it is filed bears not only on the adequacy of the class representative but also on the adequacy of counsel.

Unlawful or Unethical Conduct. Courts further examine whether counsel has committed legal or ethical violations, either in the case at issue or in other cases. Courts are particularly unwilling to tolerate attorneys who encourage or elicit false testimony or who destroy relevant evidence. Some courts also disqualify counsel who advance litigation costs in violation of governing ethical rules. (As noted above, these rules vary from jurisdiction to jurisdiction.)

Conflicts of Interest. Courts also examine whether class counsel have conflicts of interest with respect to the litigation. For example, class counsel must not have a financial or other relationship with any defendant and must not be simultaneously serving as counsel for any of the defendants in any other case. A close relationship between class counsel and a class representative—such as a family relationship or significant business relationship—may also render both counsel and the representative inadequate. Likewise, class counsel may be inadequate if he or she is a member of the putative class at issue. Class counsel may also have a conflict when he or she attempts to represent two separate classes in suits against the same defendant or attempts to represent two potentially conflicting groups in the same case, such as holders of present tort claims (with existing physical injuries) and holders of future claims (involving exposure to a substance but no existing physical injury). *See Ortiz v. Fibreboard Corp.*, 527 U.S. 815 (1999); *Amchem Prods., Inc. v. Windsor*, 521 U.S. 591 (1997).

Duty of Counsel to Educate Representative and Identify Inadequate Representatives. A few courts have held that class counsel has a duty, throughout a class action, to ensure that class representatives understand their obligations and perform them properly. If class representatives are not performing adequately, class counsel must bring these problems to the court's attention. Failure to adhere to these duties may render class counsel inadequate.

Rule 23(g). Rule 23(g) addresses court appointment of class counsel. It recognizes the critical role that class counsel plays in ensuring fair treatment of class members. Rule 23(g)(1) states that "[u]nless a statute provides otherwise, a court that certifies a class must appoint class counsel." Codifying the case law, Rule 23(g)(4) specifies that class counsel "must fairly and adequately represent the interests of the class." Rule 23(g)(1)(A) provides the criteria that the court must consider in appointing class counsel: (i) counsel's work "in identifying or investigating potential claims in the action"; (ii) "counsel's experience in handling class actions, other complex litigation, and the types of claims asserted in the action"; (iii) "counsel's knowledge of the applicable law"; and (iv) "the resources that counsel will commit to representing the class." In addition, Rule 23(g)(1)(B) permits the court to "consider any other matter pertinent to counsel's ability to fairly and adequately represent the interests of the class." Rule 23(g)(1)(C) provides that in selecting counsel the court may, *inter alia*, order potential class counsel to "provide information on any subject pertinent to the appointment" and may require counsel "to propose terms for attorney's fees and nontaxable costs."

Rule 23(g)(3) provides that, prior to appointing counsel, the court may designate interim counsel. When only one applicant seeks appointment as class counsel, the court must still find that counsel satisfies the criteria of Rule 23(g)(1) and (4). Under Rule 23(g)(2), if more than one adequate applicant seeks appointment, the court "must appoint the applicant best able to represent the interests of the class." Rule 23(g)(1)(D) also provides that, in appointing class counsel, the court may include provisions regarding attorneys' fees and nontaxable costs consistent with Rule 23(h) (which sets forth the rules governing attorneys' fees and nontaxable costs in class actions).

Courts have rarely rejected class counsel under Rule 23(g), and the cases provide little insight as to whether the rule has significantly altered how courts assess adequacy of counsel. Some courts have continued to find class counsel adequate with only minimal scrutiny, offering only superficial reasoning to support findings of adequacy. *See, e.g., Wiener v. Dannon Co., Inc.*, 255 F.R.D. 658, 672 (C.D. Cal.

2009). Moreover, although Rule 23(g)'s language is mandatory—providing that "the court . . . *must* consider [the criteria set forth in subsection (1)(A)]" (emphasis added)—some courts simply acknowledge that they were "guided" by Rule 23(g) without further explanation. *E.g., In re Cree, Inc., Sec. Litig.*, 219 F.R.D. 369, 373 (M.D.N.C. 2003). Furthermore, in many cases defendants do not even contest the adequacy of proposed counsel under Rule 23(g).

A few courts, however, have rigorously scrutinized the qualifications of counsel based on the Rule 23(g) criteria. For instance, one court discussed an applicant's adequacy in great detail, and then appointed a different attorney as "lead counsel" while retaining the original applicant as "co-counsel." *LeBeau v. United States*, 222 F.R.D. 613, 618–19 (D.S.D. 2004).

L.   ADDITIONAL ADEQUACY CONCERN APPLICABLE TO BOTH CLASS REPRESENTATIVES AND CLASS COUNSEL: FAILURE TO BRING CERTAIN CLAIMS IN ORDER TO IMPROVE LIKELIHOOD OF CLASS CERTIFICATION

Assume that a case raises a number of potential causes of action. Some can be litigated without significant individual issues. Others, however, raise myriad individualized questions. An example of the latter would be a fraud claim raising individualized issues of reliance (*see* § 4.4). If class counsel and the representative(s) choose not to bring claims that are not suitable for class certification, they risk being challenged on adequacy grounds. In the view of some courts, *res judicata* could potentially bar class members from later bringing these omitted claims. (*Res judicata* applies to claims that were *or could have been* brought in an earlier suit.) Some courts have found adequacy concerns in such circumstances because class members may lose the chance to bring potentially viable claims. In recent years this argument has resonated with some courts. As the Eleventh Circuit pointed out in *Cooper v. Southern Co.*, 390 F.3d 695, 721 (11th Cir. 2004), omitting claims to enhance the likelihood of class certification raises concerns about whether "the named plaintiffs would adequately represent interests of other putative class members." In *Dukes*, the Supreme Court suggested that similar concerns may arise under issue preclusion (or collateral estoppel). 564 U.S. at 363. *See* § 4.3.

Other courts, however, have held that because the omitted claims could not have been brought on a classwide basis, class members are free to bring those claims individually. For that reason, the class representatives and counsel are not inadequate for failing to assert them as part of the class action. As one court stated, "[c]lass representatives must press all claims which can be prosecuted on a class basis, but they need not and should not press for certification of claims that are unsuitable for class treatment." *Sullivan v. Chase Inv. Servs., Inc.*, 79 F.R.D. 246, 265 (N.D. Cal. 1978).

M.   SOLUTIONS TO INADEQUATE REPRESENTATION

Courts have taken a variety of approaches to addressing inadequacy of class representatives and class counsel. If an adequacy problem arises before a class action is certified, the court may either deny class certification or permit the substitution of an adequate representative or adequate counsel. Alternatively, the court may narrow the class to encompass only those individuals who would be adequately represented, or may divide the putative class members into subclasses with separate representatives. If an adequacy problem arises after certification, the court may likewise allow substitution of new representatives or counsel, narrow the class, or, in extreme cases, decertify the class. In no event should a court allow the case to proceed in the absence of at least one adequate representative and one adequate attorney for each subclass in the case.

In situations where some putative class members have already suffered injury and others have only been exposed to a dangerous condition (a situation common in, *e.g.*, asbestos cases), some courts have approved of dividing the injured and exposure-only claimants into subclasses. *See, e.g., In re Nat'l Football League Players Concussion Injury Litig.*, 821 F.3d 410, 432 (3d Cir. 2016) (rejecting adequacy challenge and upholding district court's use of subclasses for injured and exposure-only claimants).

Two circuit court cases exemplify the various judicial approaches to remedying adequacy issues during the proceedings. In *Birmingham Steel Corp. v. TVA*, 353 F.3d 1331 (11th Cir. 2003), the Eleventh Circuit held that the district court abused its discretion in decertifying the class based on a representative's inadequacy without providing an opportunity for a new class representative to be substituted. The court emphasized that, at the time of the finding of inadequacy, "discovery had been completed, numerous pretrial motions had been resolved, and the case was ready for trial." *Id.* at 1342. It is unclear whether the outcome would have been the same had the adequacy concerns arisen earlier in the case. By contrast, the Seventh Circuit upheld decertification without giving class counsel time to find a new representative, concluding that there was no evidence that any class member "ha[d] any interest beyond that of a curious onlooker in pursuing [the] litigation." *Culver v. City of Milwaukee*, 277 F.3d 908, 913 (7th Cir. 2002).

N.   COLLATERAL ATTACKS ON ADEQUACY

Courts and commentators are sharply divided over whether class members must raise adequacy issues in the class action itself or are permitted to raise the issues in a collateral attack. These issues are discussed in § 8.5.

CHAPTER 4

CLASS CERTIFICATION REQUIREMENTS: RULE 23(b)

In addition to satisfying the four threshold requirements for certification and the four requirements of Rule 23(a), a class action must also satisfy the criteria of at least one of the four categories of Rule 23(b): (b)(1)(A), (b)(1)(B), (b)(2), or (b)(3). These Rule 23(b) categories can be difficult to apply. The case law is often conflicting and confusing, and the text of Rule 23 fails to provide clear guidance.

As an initial matter, the student or practitioner should be aware that a court is not restricted to one category, and may certify a class under multiple subdivisions of Rule 23(b)—for instance Rule 23(b)(2) and Rule 23(b)(3). In other words, the subdivisions are not mutually exclusive. *See, e.g., Markocki v. Old Republic Nat'l Title Ins. Co.*, 254 F.R.D. 242, 252 (E.D. Pa. 2008) (certifying class under all four subsections of Rule 23(b)); *George v. Kraft Foods Global, Inc.*, 251 F.R.D. 338, 353 (N.D. Ill. 2008) ("Since both Rule 23(b)(1) and (b)(2) offer a sound basis for certification, we see no need to choose between them. As other courts have done from time to time, we therefore will certify the class under both[.]").

Most class actions are brought and certified under Rule 23(b)(3). Class actions are also frequently certified under Rule 23(b)(2). Rule 23(b)(1)(A) and Rule 23(b)(1)(B) are utilized much less frequently. This chapter discusses all four types of class actions.

In reviewing each subdivision's requirements, it is important to keep in mind the distinction between classes that are "mandatory" and those that are not. Class actions certified under Rule 23(b)(3) provide potential class members with notice and the opportunity to "opt out" of the class, requirements that the Supreme Court has held to be necessary in order to satisfy due process in some circumstances. *See Wal-Mart Stores, Inc. v. Dukes*, 564 U.S. 338, 361–67 (2011); *Phillips Petroleum Co. v. Shutts*, 472 U.S. 797, 812 (1985). Accordingly, (b)(3) classes are not mandatory. On the other hand, classes certified under Rule 23(b)'s remaining subdivisions are considered mandatory. Because there is no opportunity to opt out of the litigation, the result of a class action certified under Rules 23(b)(1)(A), (b)(1)(B), or (b)(2) will be binding on *all* class members, regardless of whether they choose to be part of the class action.

§ 4.1 RULE 23(b)(1)(A) CLASSES

Rule 23(b)(1) is divided into two subsections, (b)(1)(A) and (b)(1)(B), each of which has different purposes and requirements. A class that meets the requirements of *either* (b)(1)(A) or (b)(1)(B) may proceed as a (b)(1) class action, assuming that the threshold requirements and those set forth in Rule 23(a) have been satisfied (*see* Chapter 3). In addition, courts have sometimes certified classes under both (b)(1)(A) and (b)(1)(B). *See, e.g., Feret v. Corestates Fin. Corp.*, No. 97–6759, 1998 WL 512933, at *13 (E.D. Pa. Aug. 18, 1998) (deeming an ERISA class action "appropriate for certification under both clauses of Rule 23(b)(1)").

A.   THE PURPOSES OF RULE 23(b)(1)(A) CLASSES

Rule 23(b)(1)(A) focuses on the party opposing the class—typically the defendant. (By contrast, Rule 23(b)(1)(B) is a mirror-image provision that focuses on protecting the interests of class members.) Rule 23(b)(1)(A) authorizes a class action if:

> [P]rosecuting separate actions by or against individual class members would create a risk of ... inconsistent or varying adjudications with respect to individual class members that would establish incompatible standards of conduct for the party opposing the class[.]

The purpose of Rule 23(b)(1)(A) is thus to protect a party who is facing multiple lawsuits (or the threat of multiple suits) from being subjected to a series of contradictory court orders. One example cited in the Advisory Committee Notes is "litigation of ... landowners' rights and duties respecting a claimed nuisance," a situation that "could create a possibility of incompatible adjudications."

To illustrate, if a factory is sued for nuisance by numerous neighbors seeking different forms of relief, the landowner could be subjected to incompatible adjudications. Some neighbors may be seeking shutdown of the plant; others may be seeking only that certain air quality standards be met; and still others may be seeking entirely different forms of relief.

Another example of the need for (b)(1)(A) classes is cited in the Advisory Committee Notes: "Separate actions by individuals against a municipality to declare a bond issue invalid or condition or limit it." Here, too, absent a Rule 23(b)(1)(A) class, the municipality could be subject to inconsistent adjudications. For instance, some courts might order the municipality to revoke the bond issue; others might order the municipality to impose conditions (and those conditions might conflict from one case to another); and still other courts might approve the bond issue. A (b)(1)(A) class would prevent the municipality from having to face those potentially inconsistent adjudications.

Rule 23(b)(1)(A) classes are often certified in cases involving the Employee Retirement Income Security Act (ERISA), 29 U.S.C. §§ 1001 *et seq.* For example, in *In re Merck & Co., Inc. Securities, Derivative & ERISA Litigation*, MDL No. 1658, 2009 WL 331426 (D.N.J. Feb. 10, 2009), the court certified a class under (b)(1)(A), stating that "[t]he risk of establishing inconsistent standards under ERISA is particularly strong" where the law provides for suits to enforce fiduciary duties owed to the plan (as opposed to the individual plaintiffs). *Id.* at *12.

Although one of the purposes of a (b)(1)(A) class is to protect the party opposing the class, most courts do not require that the opposing party acquiesce to class certification. In other words, most (but not all) courts will certify a (b)(1)(A) class to protect a defendant against inconsistent adjudications even if the defendant *opposes* class certification.

B. REQUIREMENTS FOR CERTIFICATION UNDER RULE 23(b)(1)(A)

To qualify under Rule 23(b)(1)(A), the parties seeking class certification must establish a realistic probability that the party opposing the class will face separate actions that will risk exposing that party to inconsistent adjudications. As the Advisory Committee Notes state: "The class action device can be used effectively to obviate the actual or virtual dilemma which would thus confront the party opposing the class." To qualify under Rule 23(b)(1)(A), the risk of separate actions may not be hypothetical or speculative. Furthermore, some courts have held that in situations where many potential claimants have small individual claims (thus making suits other than class actions cost-prohibitive), the separate actions requirement of Rule 23(b)(1)(A) is *not* satisfied because, apart from the class action suit, the defendant does not in fact face a likelihood of separate actions. *E.g.*, *Eisen v. Carlisle & Jacquelin*, 391 F.2d 555, 564 (2d Cir. 1968).

Notably, some courts hold that no threat of incompatible standards of conduct exists if inconsistent trial court rulings are likely to be resolved by the appellate courts.

C.   CERTIFICATION UNDER RULE 23(b)(1)(A) IN CASES SEEKING MONETARY DAMAGES

Even if a litigant faces numerous related suits, this does not necessarily mean that the defendant faces a risk of inconsistent adjudications. Most courts hold that Rule 23(b)(1)(A) applies only to actions seeking declaratory or injunctive relief, not to actions seeking only compensatory damages. These courts reason that having to pay damages to some plaintiffs but not others does not subject the defendant to inconsistent standards of conduct. For instance, in *In re Dennis Greenman Securities Litigation*, 829 F.2d 1539, 1545 (11th Cir. 1987), the court held that (b)(1)(A) certification was improper because the class members, all of whom were suing an allegedly dishonest stockbroker, were seeking only monetary damages. *Accord, e.g., Babineau v. Fed. Express Corp.*, 576 F.3d 1183, 1195 (11th Cir. 2009).

On the other hand, some courts hold that an action seeking compensatory damages may be certified under Rule 23(b)(1)(A), as long as the putative class also seeks injunctive or declaratory relief. Of course, the injunctive or declaratory remedy must expose the party opposing the class to varying adjudications and incompatible standards of conduct. In cases where a proposed (b)(1)(A) class seeks both kinds of relief, some courts have used an analysis similar to that historically applied in Rule 23(b)(2) cases, discussed in § 4.3, asking whether monetary damages constitute the primary relief sought (in which case certification under (b)(1)(A) is generally inappropriate). *See, e.g., Corley v. Entergy Corp.*, 222

F.R.D. 316, 321 (E.D. Tex. 2004) (noting that "[m]any courts . . . have concluded that class certification is inappropriate [under Rule 23(b)(1)(A)] if the plaintiffs seek primarily monetary relief"); *see also id.* at 321 n.7 (listing cases).

A few older cases permitted Rule 23(b)(1)(A) class actions to be maintained for compensatory damages when faced with mass tort claims, reasoning that inconsistent damages awards could lead to uncertainty regarding how the defendant should conduct itself in the future. *See, e.g., In re Fed. Skywalk Cases*, 93 F.R.D. 415, 423 (W.D. Mo. 1982) (certifying Rule 23(b)(1)(A) class for liability for compensatory and punitive damages), *vacated on other grounds*, 680 F.2d 1175 (8th Cir. 1982). Subsequent Supreme Court precedent, however, has cast serious doubt on the validity of these cases. As discussed in § 6.1, the Supreme Court has questioned whether certification of a "mandatory" class is ever appropriate where the plaintiffs seek monetary damages. *Wal-Mart Stores, Inc. v. Dukes*, 564 U.S. 338, 361–67 (2011).

Even classes seeking declaratory relief are sometimes improper for certification under (b)(1)(A) because they are, at bottom, requests for damages. For example, in *McDonnell Douglas Corp. v. U.S. Dist. Court*, 523 F.2d 1083 (9th Cir. 1975), plaintiffs sought class certification under Rule 23(b)(1)(A) in relation to an airplane crash. The complaint requested damages and a declaration of liability. The Ninth Circuit held that the claim for damages did not raise the possibility of inconsistent adjudications, and that the prayer for declaratory relief—a request for a finding of liability—was in substance nothing more than a request for damages. Thus, plaintiffs' reliance on (b)(1)(A) was misplaced.

D. CERTIFICATION OF MEDICAL MONITORING CLASSES UNDER RULE 23(b)(1)(A)

Some courts have applied Rule 23(b)(1)(A) to medical monitoring cases. Medical monitoring is a process whereby a class of individuals who have been exposed to a dangerous condition seek to have the defendant provide them with periodic medical checkups (or establish a fund to use to pay for such checkups) to determine whether any dangerous symptoms later develop. In some cases, medical monitoring is brought as a separate cause of action. In others, it is sought as an element of damages.

Some courts have held that Rule 23(b)(1)(A) classes are appropriate in medical monitoring cases because separate judicial orders in individual cases could result in different types of medical monitoring regimens, making it difficult or impossible for a defendant to comply. Other courts, however, have refused to certify (b)(1)(A) classes in medical monitoring cases because the plaintiffs did not show how separate actions could result in incompatible standards of conduct imposed upon the defendant.

For example, in *Zinser v. Accufix Research Institute, Inc.*, 253 F.3d 1180 (9th Cir. 2001), the Ninth Circuit rejected certification of a medical monitoring class of pacemaker implantees under (b)(1)(A) because it concluded that the medical monitoring claimants sought primarily monetary damages. The court also noted that "[a]ny administrative difficulty [defendant] potentially might face from slightly different medical monitoring programs required by different courts for differently situated potential claimants does not rise to the level of requiring of [defendant] *inconsistent* courses of conduct." *Id.* at 1195 (emphasis in original).

E.   OTHER KINDS OF CASES INVOLVING RULE 23(b)(1)(A)

In addition to the cases discussed above, Rule 23(b)(1)(A) has been applied in cases by patent owners against alleged patent infringers; in actions for declaratory relief against government agencies; in actions by professional athletes against their players' league challenging proposed mergers with rival teams; and in actions by employees against their employers for recovery of benefits.

One interesting case under (b)(1)(A) involved a suit by Hispanic prisoners challenging the constitutionality of a policy barring alien prisoners from transferring to minimum-security facilities. In certifying the class, the court reasoned that individual lawsuits could have created conflicting rules as to the permissibility of such transfers. *Franklin v. Barry*, 909 F. Supp. 21 (D.D.C. 1995).

§ 4.2 RULE 23(b)(1)(B) CLASSES

A. OVERVIEW OF RULE 23(b)(1)(B)

Rule 23(b)(1)(B) authorizes class actions when:

> [P]rosecuting separate actions by or against individual class members would create a risk of . . . adjudications with respect to individual class members that, as a practical matter, would be dispositive of the interests of the other members not parties to the individual adjudications or would substantially impair or impede their ability to protect their interests[.]

The Advisory Committee Notes state, in part:

> [Rule 23(b)(1)(B)] takes in situations where the judgment in a nonclass action by or against an individual member of the class, while not technically concluding the other members, might do so as a practical matter. . . . This is plainly the case when claims are made by numerous persons against a fund insufficient to satisfy all claims[.]

As the Advisory Committee Notes reveal, the purpose of (b)(1)(B) is to protect the members of the putative class. It is therefore the mirror image of Rule 23(b)(1)(A), which is designed to protect those who oppose the class. This explains why the two classes are designated (b)(1)(A) and (b)(1)(B), with the other two being designated as (b)(2) and (b)(3). Under the most common usage of (b)(1)(B), in the "limited fund" cases discussed below, class certification is designed to avoid depletion of finite resources by those who are first to secure a judgment.

B.   *STARE DECISIS* EFFECT INSUFFICIENT TO SATISFY RULE 23(b)(1)(B)

To obtain certification under Rule 23(b)(1)(B), the party seeking certification must show a risk of prejudice to putative class members in the absence of a class action. Courts generally hold, however, that the possibility that an action will have a precedential (or *stare decisis*) effect on later cases (and thereby indirectly threaten the class) is not a sufficient reason to invoke Rule 23(b)(1)(B). The rationale behind these cases is that were Rule 23(b)(1)(B) to apply simply because of *stare decisis* effects, the other subdivisions of Rule 23(b) would be rendered superfluous. Because every class must share common issues pursuant to Rule 23(a)(2), any individual class member's suit could conceivably have a *stare decisis* effect on other class members' claims in the absence of a class action. Under that reasoning, any case satisfying commonality would satisfy Rule 23(b)(1)(B), a conclusion that the drafters of Rule 23 could not have contemplated.

C.   REQUIREMENTS FOR "LIMITED FUND" TREATMENT

As noted above, the most common use of Rule 23(b)(1)(B) is in so-called limited fund cases. Limited fund cases are those in which all of the parties seeking recovery must obtain damages from a finite source of assets that will be exhausted before all expected claims are paid. Examples of limited funds include trust funds, bank accounts, insurance policies, and assets of an estate. However, in an important 1999 decision, the Supreme Court restricted the situations in which limited fund cases may be properly certified, with the result that courts are now unlikely to certify limited fund classes that do not comport with a relatively narrow historical understanding of Rule 23(b)(1)(B)'s purpose.

In *Ortiz v. Fibreboard Corp.*, 527 U.S. 815 (1999), the Supreme Court articulated the standards that govern whether a class action qualifies for certification under the "limited fund" doctrine. *Ortiz* involved a large national class of persons with asbestos-related claims amounting to potentially billions of dollars. The defendant, Fibreboard Corporation, had a net worth of approximately $235 million. Although Fibreboard had exhausted much of its insurance coverage because of massive asbestos claims during the 1980s, it claimed to have insurance coverage remaining through two carriers on policies that were issued in the 1950s. That coverage was being disputed by the insurance carriers in litigation in California state court.

In the early 1990s, Fibreboard made efforts to settle hundreds of thousands of potential asbestos claims. The corporation approached a group of asbestos-plaintiffs' lawyers, with the goal that those attorneys would bring a "limited fund" class action under Rule 23(b)(1)(B) consisting of all asbestos claims, and that Fibreboard would then enter into a classwide settlement. Fibreboard wanted a (b)(1)(B)

class because that subdivision does not provide for
opt outs, thereby ensuring that there would be a cap
on its liability. Fibreboard's insurance carriers,
having lost at the trial level in the California
coverage litigation, joined in the settlement
negotiations in 1993. As negotiations over a "global
settlement" continued, plaintiffs' counsel began to
settle cases that were already then pending (the so-
called inventory claims), with fifty percent of the
settlement funds being conditioned on Fibreboard's
either achieving a "global" settlement or prevailing in
its California insurance cases. On the eve of an
appellate argument in the California insurance
coverage cases, the negotiating parties agreed to a
$1.535 billion settlement, with virtually all of the
money coming from Fibreboard's insurance carriers
(and with Fibreboard retaining all but $500,000 of its
net worth). Days later, plaintiffs' counsel filed an
action in the Eastern District of Texas seeking
certification of a class that essentially consisted of all
asbestos claimants everywhere who had not yet filed
suit against Fibreboard. Over the objections of
several intervening class members, the district court
certified a Rule 23(b)(1)(B) class, and the Fifth
Circuit affirmed.

The Supreme Court reversed. The Court first noted
that "limited fund" class actions in equity had three
characteristics that the Advisory Committee must
have considered in drafting (b)(1)(B): (1) the fund
available to satisfy all claims is inadequate to pay the
claims; (2) "the whole of the inadequate fund [is]
devoted to all the overwhelming claims"; and (3) the

claimants to the fund are "treated equitably among themselves." 527 U.S. at 838–39.

With respect to the first element, the Court criticized the district court for simply accepting the parties' settlement agreement without making an independent determination that a "limited fund" in fact existed. While not ruling out the possibility that a settlement amount could form the basis of a "limited fund" determination, the Court noted that the settlement figure at issue could not be relied upon because of the conflicting interests of class counsel, who had also negotiated settlements of inventory cases (not included within the class) that were tied to the success of a global settlement. As the Court noted, "[c]lass counsel thus had great incentive to reach any agreement in the global settlement negotiations that they thought might survive" court approval. *Id*. at 852.

With respect to the second element, the Court stated that classic "limited fund" cases ensured claimants the "best deal," and did not result in the defendant being better off under the class action than if individual suits had been filed. The Court found it troubling that Fibreboard would be able to emerge from the settlement with virtually all of its net worth intact. The Court, however, did not base its holding on this part of the test, and specifically reserved the question of whether a defendant could retain any of its net worth in a (b)(1)(B) settlement. *Id*. at 859–61.

Finally, when assessing the third element, the Court deemed the class action settlement inequitable because it treated claimants with claims of differing values identically. The Court noted that, under the terms of the disputed insurance coverage, claimants exposed to asbestos after 1959 could end up receiving much less were they forced to litigate, since the major insurance policy expired in 1959. Lumping these claimants together with the pre-1959 claimants and giving them an equal share of the limited fund was an inequitable allocation of the fund. The Court also criticized the fact that holders of present claims (those with actual physical injuries) and those with future claims (exposure without present physical injury) were lumped together without separate counsel and subclasses to protect their respective interests. *Id.* at 856 ("As we said in *Amchem*, 'for the currently injured, the critical goal is generous immediate payments,' but '[t]hat goal tugs against the interest of exposure-only plaintiffs in ensuring an ample, inflation-protected fund for the future.") (citation omitted).

The Court identified, but did not decide, several additional arguments made by those objecting to the proposed settlement, including (1) the denial of due process and Seventh Amendment jury trial rights stemming from the inability of class members to opt out of the settlement; and (2) potential Article III standing issues involving "exposure-only" class members who had not yet suffered physical injury.

As a result of *Ortiz*, the vast majority of courts have refused to certify mass tort cases under Rule 23(b)(1)(B). *See, e.g., In re Telectronics Pacing Sys., Inc.*, 221 F.3d 870, 872–73 (6th Cir. 2000); *Zinser v. Accufix Research Inst., Inc.*, 253 F.3d 1180, 1196–97

(9th Cir. 2001); *In re Simon II Litig.*, 407 F.3d 125, 127–28 (2d Cir. 2005). In a case involving Hurricane Katrina, the Fifth Circuit underscored *Ortiz's* focus on the impropriety of treating differently situated class members uniformly. *In re Katrina Canal Breaches Litig.*, 628 F.3d 185, 191–94 (5th Cir. 2010). In that case, the court reversed certification of a settlement class under (b)(1)(B) where class members had suffered highly disparate injuries "ranging from property damage to personal injury and death," and "no method [was] specified for how these different claimants [would] be treated *vis-a-vis* each other." *Id.* at 193–94.

D.   RULE 23(b)(1)(B) AND PUNITIVE DAMAGES

The prospect of significant punitive damage awards in factually related cases may be a ground for certification under Rule 23(b)(1)(B). Punitive damages present a special problem because, as a remedy, they are intended not to compensate the plaintiff(s) to whom they are awarded, but to punish the defendant(s). Punitive damages awarded by juries often exceed the compensatory damages that a plaintiff can recover, although recent Supreme Court precedent has attempted to limit "excessive" punitive awards on due process grounds. *See, e.g., State Farm Mut. Auto. Ins. Co. v. Campbell*, 538 U.S. 408, 425 (2003) (stating that "few [punitive damage] awards exceeding a single-digit ratio between punitive and compensatory damages, to a significant degree, will satisfy due process").

Courts tend to focus on two issues with respect to punitive damages and Rule 23(b)(1)(B). First, if litigants in individual lawsuits will each be able to claim significant punitive damage awards, even the wealthiest defendants likely will not have assets sufficient to pay all of the awards. Second, if litigants individually sue a defendant in related but separate suits, some courts may be reluctant to authorize repeated awards of punitive damages against a defendant who has already sustained a series of punitive damage awards for the same misconduct.

Courts have developed two theories under Rule 23(b)(1)(B) to deal with punitive damages and the issues above. Under the first theory, certification of a punitive damages class is appropriate to protect claimants because, were the claims litigated individually, the assets of the defendant might not be great enough to satisfy multiple, large punitive damage awards. This first theory also encompasses potential due process limits on multiple awards stemming from the same conduct.

The second theory, which has been called the "limited generosity" theory, invokes certification under Rule 23(b)(1)(B) out of a concern that late-coming plaintiffs will be less likely to obtain awards of punitive damages against a defendant who has already been subjected to punitive damages for the same conduct (sometimes referred to as "overkill").

In general, plaintiffs have had only mixed success in asserting either theory. The Supreme Court's decision in *Ortiz*, which stated that courts should be reluctant to stray from the "historical limited fund model," makes it even less likely that many courts will adopt these or other creative limited fund theories. 527 U.S. at 842.

In re Simon II Litigation, 211 F.R.D. 86 (E.D.N.Y. 2002), *rev'd*, 407 F.3d 125 (2d Cir. 2005), illustrates the caution exercised by most courts in the wake of *Ortiz*. There, the district court certified a nationwide class of smokers under (b)(1)(B) solely on claims for punitive damages out of concern that "the first plaintiffs may recover vast sums while others who arrive later are left with a depleted fund against which they cannot recover." 211 F.R.D. at 190. Relying on *Ortiz*, the Second Circuit reversed, holding that "[t]he fund . . . is not easily susceptible to proof, definition, or even estimation, by any precise figure," and "the record . . . does not evince a likelihood that any given number of punitive awards to individual claimants would be constitutionally excessive, either individually or in the aggregate, and thus overwhelm the available fund." 407 F.3d at 138.

Even before *Ortiz*, only a handful of courts had certified (b)(1)(B) punitive damages classes, and most of those that did so were reversed on appeal. *See, e.g.*, *In re N. Dist. of Cal. "Dalkon Shield" IUD Prods. Liab. Litig.*, 521 F. Supp. 1188, 1193 (N.D. Cal. 1981) (certifying (b)(1)(B) class on both limited fund and limited punishment theories), *rev'd*, 693 F.2d 847, 852 (9th Cir. 1982) (rejecting both rationales and decertifying the class); *In re Fed. Skywalk Cases*, 93 F.R.D. 415, 425 (W.D. Mo. 1982) (certifying (b)(1)(B) class because "[o]nly a single class-wide adjudication of the issues of liability for and amount of punitive damages can protect the interest of every victim in receiving his or her just share of any punitive damage award"), *vacated*, 680 F.2d 1175, 1183 (8th Cir. 1982).

One notable exception to the cautious approach illustrated above, however, was the *Exxon Valdez* litigation, where the district court certified a Rule 23(b)(1)(B) punitive damages class under the "limited punishment" theory described above. *In re Exxon Valdez*, 236 F. Supp. 2d 1043, 1060 (D. Alaska 2002); *see also In re Exxon Valdez*, 229 F.3d 790, 795–96 (9th Cir. 2000). In that case, defendant Exxon itself sought certification under the limited punishment theory, successfully persuading the district court that it should face a single classwide trial on damages and liability. Although the amount of the jury's punitive damage award was the subject of numerous subsequent appeals, culminating in a Supreme Court decision, *Exxon Shipping Co. v. Baker*, 554 U.S. 471 (2008), the procedures by which the damages were determined were not. Indeed, the fact that punitive damages had been determined via a mandatory (b)(1)(B) class was not at issue before the Supreme Court, which held, *inter alia*, that the amount of the punitive damage award was excessive under federal maritime law.

E.   OTHER TYPES OF RULE 23(b)(1)(B) CASES

Rule 23(b)(1)(B) is not restricted solely to limited fund cases. As the Advisory Committee Notes point out, "[s]imilar problems . . . can arise in the absence of a fund either present or potential." For example, "[a] negative or mandatory injunction secured by one of a numerous class may disable the opposing party from performing claimed duties toward the other members of the class or materially affect his ability to do so." In such a situation, adjudication as to one or more class members would significantly affect the rights and interests of other class members, rendering a (b)(1)(B) class action appropriate. Additional examples include suits in which a class of individuals claims that the defendant breached a contract, suits seeking to enjoin a nuisance, and so-called ERISA "stock drop" cases. *See, e.g., In re Merck & Co., Inc. Sec., Derivative & ERISA Litig.*, MDL No. 1658, 2009 WL 331426, at *10–11 (D.N.J. Feb. 10, 2009) (noting that certification under Rule 23(b)(1)(B) is not restricted to limited fund cases, and certifying a class under (b)(1)(B) because, if plaintiffs were to proceed individually, certain outcomes in one case "would be, as a practical matter, dispositive of the interests of the other [plaintiffs] in that particular regard").

F.   COMPARISONS BETWEEN RULE 23(b)(1)(B) AND OTHER JOINDER DEVICES

Courts and commentators have noted the functional similarities between the certification of a class under Rule 23(b)(1), compulsory joinder under Rule 19 (*see* § 15.2), and interpleader under Rule 22 (*see* § 15.4). Indeed, the Advisory Committee Notes to Rule 23(b)(1) state that "the considerations stated under clauses (A) and (B) are comparable to certain of the elements which define the persons whose joinder in an action is desirable as stated in Rule 19(a), as amended."

As with interpleader under Rule 22, Rule 23(b)(1)(B) focuses on prejudice to absent parties in the case of a limited fund. Moreover, like Rule 19(a), Rule 23(b)(1)(B) focuses on impairment of the interests of nonparties.

G.   PREFERENCE BETWEEN MANDATORY AND OPT-OUT CLASSES

In many instances, a class may qualify for certification under Rule 23(b)(1)(A)—or (b)(1)(B)—as well as other subdivisions of Rule 23(b). The choice between subdivisions can be of great significance because it may determine whether class members receive notice and the right to opt out of class membership. *See* § 6.1. The rule applied by most courts is that, if an action can qualify under both Rule 23(b)(1) and Rule 23(b)(3), the action is generally certified under (b)(1), and an inquiry under (b)(3) will not be undertaken. By using this approach, courts avoid burdening litigants with the (often costly) notice requirements that go along with certification under (b)(3). For example, in *George v. Kraft Foods Global, Inc.*, 251 F.R.D. 338 (N.D. Ill. 2008), the district court certified an ERISA class under all of Rule 23's subsections except (b)(3) because the class did not seek primarily monetary damages. The court thereby avoided the complications associated with providing notice to future plan members who were within the definition of the certified class. *Id.* at 351–53.

As noted above, however, and discussed further in § 6.1, it is important to keep in mind that, in cases where plaintiffs are seeking monetary relief, certification of mandatory classes may raise due process issues because of the absence of notice and opt-out rights for all putative class members. *See generally* Robert H. Klonoff, *Class Actions for Monetary Relief Under Rule 23(b)(1)(A) and (B): Does Due Process Require Notice and Opt-Out Rights?*, 82 Geo. Wash. L. Rev. 798 (2014).

H.   OPTING OUT OF A RULE 23(b)(1) CLASS

Despite the fact that certification under Rule 23(b)(1)(A) or (b)(1)(B) establishes a mandatory class (*see* § 4.1), courts have occasionally permitted claimants to opt out of Rule 23(b)(1) classes because of due process concerns. In certain circumstances, however, such as limited fund class actions, opt-outs may very well defeat the entire purpose of certifying a case as a class action. The issue of opt-out rights in (b)(1) and (b)(2) (*i.e.*, traditionally "mandatory") class actions is addressed in § 6.1.

§ 4.3   RULE 23(b)(2)

A. OVERVIEW

Rule 23(b)(2) authorizes a class action if:

[T]he party opposing the class has acted or refused to act on grounds that apply generally to the class, so that final injunctive relief or corresponding declaratory relief is appropriate respecting the class as a whole[.]

Rule 23(b)(2) was conceived to facilitate awards of injunctive or declaratory relief against defendants whose actions affected an entire class of individuals. As the 1966 Advisory Committee Notes indicate, Rule 23(b)(2) was envisioned primarily as a device for civil rights cases to enjoin unlawful discrimination against a class. Although most courts were willing to certify civil rights cases as class actions even prior to Rule 23(b)(2), a few courts had taken the view that civil rights cases were not appropriate for class certification. Since Rule 23(b)(2)'s enactment in 1966, numerous courts have utilized that subdivision to certify civil rights class actions.

As the Advisory Committee Notes also indicate, however, Rule 23(b)(2) was not intended exclusively for civil rights cases. The Notes refer to patent suits and suits alleging unlawful pricing practices as examples. Additional examples include due process, First Amendment, and other constitutional challenges (in cases not involving discrimination claims); suits seeking enforcement under federal or state statutory entitlement programs; and mass tort suits seeking injunctive relief.

As discussed in this section, the Supreme Court's decision in *Dukes* had a major impact on the interpretation and application of Rule 23(b)(2).

B.   GENERAL REQUIREMENTS

By its terms, Rule 23(b)(2) contains two requirements. Both must be satisfied before a Rule 23(b)(2) class can be certified.

First, the party opposing the class must have "acted or refused to act on grounds that apply generally to the class." This requirement is rather vague, and courts have been satisfied with a practice that is generally applicable to a class as a whole. In fact, a defendant's conduct challenged by a Rule 23(b)(2) action need not even be directed at, or cause damage to, every member of the class. According to the Advisory Committee Notes, "[a]ction or inaction is directed to a class within the meaning of [Rule 23(b)(2)] even if it has taken effect or is threatened only as to one or a few members of the class, provided it is based on grounds which have general application to the class." As one court explained, Rule 23(b)(2) "does not require [a court] to examine the viability or bases of class members' claims for declaratory and injunctive relief, but only to look at whether class members seek uniform relief from a practice applicable to all of them." *Rodriguez v. Hayes*, 591 F.3d 1105, 1125 (9th Cir. 2010).

Second, Rule 23(b)(2) provides that the "final injunctive relief or corresponding declaratory relief" must be "appropriate respecting the class as a whole." As the Advisory Committee Notes point out, the injunctive or declaratory relief must "settl[e] the legality of the behavior with respect to the class as a whole." Moreover, the Advisory Committee Notes state—in language that had been critical to some courts prior to *Dukes*—that Rule 23(b)(2) "does not extend to cases in which the appropriate final relief relates exclusively or predominantly to money damages." Monetary damages in the (b)(2) context will be discussed in subsection D below.

The Tenth Circuit summarized the two basic 23(b)(2) requirements as follows:

Rule 23(b)(2) imposes two independent but related requirements. In the first place, the defendants' actions or inactions must be based on grounds generally applicable to all class members. The second requirement is more restrictive. The latter half of Rule 23(b)(2) requires that final injunctive relief be appropriate for *the class as a whole.* The rule therefore authorizes an inquiry into the relationship between the class, its injuries, and the relief sought, and we have interpreted the rule to require that a class must be amenable to uniform group remedies. Put differently, Rule 23(b)(2) demands a certain cohesiveness among class members with respect to their injuries, the absence of which can preclude certification.

Shook v. Board of Cnty. Comm'rs of Cnty. of El Paso, 543 F.3d 597, 604 (10th Cir. 2008) (Gorsuch, J.) (emphasis in original) (citation and internal quotation marks omitted).

In 2020, the Second Circuit rendered an important opinion restricting Rule 23(b)(2). In *Berni v. Barilla S.p.A,* 964 F.3d 141 (2d Cir. 2020), a putative class of past purchasers of defendant's pasta claimed that defendant deliberately misrepresented the quantity of pasta in its packages. Under a class settlement, defendant agreed to an injunction requiring defendant to include a minimum "fill line" on all packages, to specify the weight of pasta contained in the package, and to provide language that the product is sold by weight, not volume. That was the sole relief provided to the class (although defendant also agreed to pay fees to plaintiffs' counsel and incentive payments to the class representatives). The Second Circuit overturned the settlement, holding that class members had "at most, alleged a past harm," and that they were "not likely to encounter future harm of the kind that makes injunctive relief appropriate," given that most members of the class were unlikely to buy the product in the future. And those who did purchase the product again would do so with the information that they claimed to have lacked. Thus, the proper remedy in such a case was damages under Rule 23(b)(3), not injunctive relief.

C.   WHETHER THE PARTY SEEKING CERTIFICATION MUST DEMONSTRATE PREDOMINANCE OR SUPERIORITY

Historically, most courts have declined to read into Rule 23(b)(2) any requirements not evident in its text. Most importantly, unlike Rule 23(b)(3) (discussed in § 4.4), neither the text of Rule 23(b)(2) nor the Advisory Committee Notes provide that common legal or factual questions among the claimants must predominate over individual questions. Consistent with the language of Rule 23(b)(2), a number of courts have held that plaintiffs seeking class certification under (b)(2) need not satisfy this sort of predominance inquiry.

For instance, in *Walters v. Reno*, 145 F.3d 1032 (9th Cir. 1998), the Ninth Circuit upheld the district court's certification of a class consisting of approximately 4,000 undocumented immigrants who had been adjudicated as deportable without constitutional due process under a provision of the Immigration and Naturalization Act of 1990. In upholding certification of the class pursuant to Rule 23(b)(2), despite the government's objection that certification would lead to thousands of individualized administrative proceedings, the Ninth Circuit stated:

> The government's dogged focus on the factual differences among the class members appears to demonstrate a fundamental misunderstanding of [Rule 23(b)(2)]. Although common issues must predominate for class certification under Rule 23(b)(3), no such requirement exists under 23(b)(2). It is sufficient if class members complain of a pattern or practice that is generally applicable to the class as a whole.

Id. at 1047.

The Third Circuit, however, has taken a different approach. In *Barnes v. American Tobacco Co.*, 161 F.3d 127 (3d Cir. 1998), the court of appeals approved a district court's decertification of a Rule 23(b)(2) class consisting of potentially thousands of Pennsylvania smokers. The plaintiffs sought relief in the form of a court-supervised medical monitoring fund that would pay for medical examinations designed to detect latent disease caused by smoking. While acknowledging that Rule 23(b)(2) does not require that common issues predominate over individual issues, the court nonetheless invoked a "cohesiveness" requirement to deny certification under Rule 23(b)(2). Indeed, it noted that a (b)(2) class "may require more cohesiveness" than a (b)(3) class because (b)(2) classes do not permit opt-outs—that is, they are mandatory. *Id.* at 142–43. Referring to the many individual issues in the case, the court concluded that "a class action [would] devolve into a lengthy series of individual trials." *Id.* at 142, 149. *Barnes* illustrates the fact that, even under Rule 23(b)(2), courts will often focus explicitly on whether a class action would be efficient in light of any individualized issues likely to arise. *See also, e.g., Gates v. Rohm & Haas Co.*, 655 F.3d 255, 269–70 (3d Cir. 2011) (noting some similarity between Rule 23(b)(3)'s predominance requirement and "the cohesiveness requirement of Rule 23(b)(2)").

The *Barnes* approach has been embraced by other courts. For example, as the Seventh Circuit stated in *Lemon v. International Union of Operating Engineers*, 216 F.3d 577, 580 (7th Cir. 2000), "Rule 23(b)(2) operates under the presumption that the interests of the class members are cohesive and homogeneous such that the case will not depend on adjudication of facts particular to any subset of the class nor require a remedy that differentiates materially among class members." *See also Maldonado v. Ochsner Clinic Found.*, 493 F.3d 521, 524 (5th Cir. 2007) (affirming district court's denial of (b)(2) certification, and noting that "[t]he difficulty in specifying exactly what Appellants seek from an injunction highlights the fact that individualized issues here overwhelm class cohesiveness" (citation omitted)).

In any event, as discussed in § 3.8, the result of the Supreme Court's *Dukes* opinion is arguably to transform the standard for commonality under Rule 23(a)(2) into a predominance requirement applicable to all class actions, whether certified under (b)(1), (b)(2), or (b)(3). Thus, *Dukes* has clearly made it more difficult for courts to certify (b)(2) classes that involve individualized issues.

Courts are also divided over whether (b)(2) contains a manageability requirement akin to that contained in Rule 23(b)(3) (as part of (b)(3)'s superiority requirement (*see* § 4.4)). Some courts have held that issues of manageability and judicial economy are not relevant under (b)(2) because that subdivision, unlike (b)(3), does not explicitly require consideration of manageability. *E.g., Elliott v. Weinberger*, 564 F.2d 1219 (9th Cir. 1977); *Forbush v. J.C. Penney Co., Inc.*, 994 F.2d 1101, 1105 (5th Cir. 1993). Other courts, however, have held that, because the purpose of a class action is to achieve efficiency, a court may assess manageability and efficiency in determining whether to certify a class under (b)(2). *E.g., Shook v. El Paso Cnty. Bd. of Cnty. Comm'rs*, 386 F.3d 963 (10th Cir. 2004) (Gorsuch, J.); *Lowery v. Circuit City Stores, Inc.*, 158 F.3d 742 (4th Cir. 1998).

The Supreme Court weighed in on the issue in *Dukes*, indicating that inquiries into predominance and superiority are unnecessary in the (b)(2) context:

> [P]redominance [and] superiority ... are missing from (b)(2) not because the Rule considers them unnecessary, but because it

considers them unnecessary *to a (b)(2) class*.
When a class seeks an indivisible injunction
benefitting all its members at once, there is no
reason to undertake a case-specific inquiry into
whether class issues predominate or whether [a]
class action is a superior method of adjudicating
the dispute. Predominance and superiority are
self-evident.

564 U.S. at 362–63 (emphasis in original). Thus,
according to *Dukes*, by its very nature a (b)(2) class
assumes overarching common questions that make
class adjudication appropriate.

D.   THE ISSUE OF WHETHER MONETARY RELIEF CAN BE SOUGHT IF IT IS "INCIDENTAL" TO DECLARATORY OR INJUNCTIVE RELIEF

Dukes was a critical opinion not only on
commonality but also on Rule 23(b)(2). Unlike the
commonality issue, which divided the Court five to
four, the Court's (b)(2) ruling was unanimous. The
issue in *Dukes* was whether (b)(2) certification was
proper when, in addition to declaratory and
injunctive relief, the class sought monetary relief in
the form of backpay.

Prior to *Dukes*, courts took several approaches in
analyzing the permissibility of monetary claims
under (b)(2), but no federal circuit had held that
backpay was an impermissible remedy under (b)(2).
Most circuits followed the Fifth Circuit's restrictive
approach in *Allison v. Citgo Petroleum Corp.*, 151
F.3d 402 (5th Cir. 1998), which allowed monetary

claims under (b)(2) only if the claims were "incidental" to the declaratory or injunctive relief sought. *Id.* at 415. Under the *Allison* approach, "incidental damages should be only those to which class members automatically would be entitled once liability to the class (or subclass) as a whole is established," and liability for such damages "should not require additional hearings to resolve the disparate merits of each individual's case." *Id.* Even under *Allison*, however, backpay was permissible under (b)(2) because the court deemed the remedy to be "equitable" in nature, and therefore akin to declaratory or injunctive relief. This rationale was consistent with numerous other cases allowing equitable remedies in (b)(2) cases. Indeed, the Fifth Circuit later held (in a race discrimination case construing *Allison*) that damages stemming from allegedly discriminatory insurance pricing were "incidental" because they could be calculated mechanically through a formula or grid. *In re Monumental Life Ins. Co.*, 365 F.3d 408, 419 (5th Cir. 2004).

The Second Circuit, in *Robinson v. Metro-North Commuter Railroad*, 267 F.3d 147 (2d Cir. 2001), adopted a more expansive view of Rule 23(b)(2), holding that a district court should assess the appropriateness of (b)(2) certification in light of "the relative importance of the remedies sought, given all of the facts and circumstances of the case." *Id.* at 164 (citation and internal quotation marks omitted). Under this so-called *ad hoc* test, backpay could be recovered, but so could other types of potentially significant damages, even if they were more than "incidental." The Second Circuit seized upon the language of the Advisory Committee Notes, which state that Rule 23(b)(2) "does not extend to cases in which the appropriate final relief relates exclusively or predominantly to money damages." According to the Second Circuit, the issue was whether the injunctive or declaratory relief was "predominant[ ]" in terms of the benefit to the class. *Id.* at 164. The Ninth Circuit en banc adopted a similar approach in *Dukes*, holding that a class may seek monetary damages under (b)(2) as long as such damages are not "superior [in] strength, influence or authority to injunctive or declaratory relief." 603 F.3d 571, 616 (9th Cir. 2010) (en banc) (citation and internal quotation marks omitted), *rev'd*, 564 U.S. 338 (2011).

The Supreme Court in *Dukes* rejected the Second and Ninth Circuits' reliance on the "exclusively or predominantly" standard set forth in the Advisory Committee Notes. The Court noted that "it is the Rule itself, not the Advisory Committee's description of it, that governs." 564 U.S. at 363. It also rejected *Allison*'s conclusion that backpay was recoverable under (b)(2) because it was equitable in nature—a conclusion that every federal circuit to address the issue had embraced. According to *Dukes*, "[t]he Rule does not speak of 'equitable' remedies generally but of injunctions and declaratory judgments." *Id.* at 365. Thus, reasoned the *Dukes* Court, "individualized monetary claims belong in Rule 23(b)(3)." *Id.* at 362. Noting that (b)(3)—but not (b)(2)—affords the protections of notice and opt-outs, *Dukes* left open the possibility that the assertion of *any* monetary claims under (b)(2), even if incidental, would violate the

class members' due process rights. *Id.* at 363. The
Court did not decide the issue, however, because it
found that claims for backpay could not be
characterized as "incidental" given the
"individualized" nature of such relief. *Id.* at 365–66.

The Supreme Court has not yet provided a
definitive answer to the question left open in *Dukes*:
whether a class seeking "any forms of 'incidental'
monetary relief" can be properly certified under
(b)(2). The lower federal courts, however, appear to
have heeded the Supreme Court's cautionary
language in *Dukes*, and have carefully distinguished
between those claims appropriate for certification
under (b)(2) and those appropriate for certification
under (b)(3). Some class actions that might have been
certified under (b)(2) prior to *Dukes*, including a
number of civil rights class actions, have instead
been certified (if at all) under (b)(3). *See, e.g., Ellis v.
Costco Wholesale Corp.*, 657 F.3d 970 (9th Cir. 2011)
(overturning district court's certification under (b)(2)
of a class of women alleging sex discrimination,
"remand[ing] for the district court to apply the legal
standard established in [*Dukes*]"); *Moore v.
Napolitano*, 926 F. Supp. 2d 8 (D.D.C. 2013) ((b)(3)
certification of class alleging racial discrimination in
promotion of U.S. Secret Service agents); *Kerner v.
City & Cnty. of Denver*, No. 11–cv–00256, 2013 WL
1222394 (D. Colo. Mar. 25, 2013) ((b)(3) certification
of class alleging racial discrimination in government
hiring practices). Other courts have taken a similar
"hybrid" approach, certifying claims for classwide
injunctive or declaratory relief under (b)(2) and
claims for monetary relief or individualized equitable

relief under (b)(3). *See, e.g., Butler v. Suffolk Cnty.*, 289 F.R.D. 80 (E.D.N.Y. 2013); *In re Motor Fuel Temp. Sales Practices Litig.*, 292 F.R.D. 652 (D. Kan. 2013). For further discussion of this issue, *see* Robert H. Klonoff, *Class Actions Part II: A Respite from the Decline*, 92 N.Y.U. L. Rev. 971 (2017).

E.   MEDICAL MONITORING UNDER RULE 23(b)(2)

Certification of a medical monitoring class pursuant to Rule 23(b)(1)(A) is discussed in § 4.1. In some instances, potential medical monitoring classes also seek certification under Rule 23(b)(2). For purposes of (b)(2), the critical question for some courts is whether medical monitoring constitutes monetary or injunctive relief. Such courts are likely to view a request for money to pay for medical monitoring as monetary relief, but may view a request for a court-supervised program as a claim for injunctive relief. Some courts, however, view a medical monitoring claim as primarily one for damages, even if the class is requesting a court-supervised program. These courts are concerned that permitting (b)(2) classes for medical monitoring would enable the class members to circumvent the more exacting requirements of (b)(3).

F.   NOTICE AND OPT-OUT RIGHTS

In contrast to Rule 23(b)(3), Rule 23(b)(2) does not mandate that class members be notified that a class has been certified, and it does not give (b)(2) class members a right to opt out of the class. Nonetheless, courts have occasionally ordered notice and opt-out rights in (b)(2) classes as a matter of discretion. Rule 23(b)(2)'s approach to notice and opt-out rights, as well as the potential due process issues raised by a mandatory class seeking monetary damages, are discussed in § 6.1.

G. CLASSES APPROPRIATE FOR CERTIFICATION UNDER BOTH RULE 23(b)(2) AND RULE 23(b)(3)

As noted in § 4.2, when a class qualifies for certification under both Rule 23(b)(1) and Rule 23(b)(3), courts usually prefer certification under (b)(1) as opposed to (b)(3), because (b)(3) contains notice and opt-out requirements that inevitably lead to fewer people being bound by the outcome. Courts generally prefer (b)(2) classes over (b)(3) classes for the same reasons. Some courts, however, have stated that the issue of certification under (b)(2) versus (b)(3) must be decided on a case-by-case basis after considering, among other things, the fairness to putative class members under each approach.

Relevant to this inquiry is the manner in which class counsel and class representatives configure the suit in order to seek certification under a particular subsection of Rule 23(b). This configuration may also bear on adequacy of representation under Rule 23(a)(4), in addition to the (b)(2) versus (b)(3) determination. For instance, if class representatives and counsel decline to pursue otherwise valid claims for monetary damages in order to increase the likelihood of certification under (b)(2), class members—without the ability to opt out of the mandatory (b)(2) class—may later find themselves unable to pursue individualized damages due to claim preclusion (*res judicata*) or issue preclusion (collateral estoppel). *See* § 3.10. The Supreme Court in *Dukes* discussed these concerns:

> [The] predominance test ... creates perverse incentives for class representatives to place at risk potentially valid claims for monetary relief. [The plaintiffs' strategy of excluding claims for compensatory damages from their complaint] made it more likely that monetary relief would not "predominate." But it also created the possibility ... that individual class members' compensatory-damages claims would be *precluded* by litigation they had no power to hold themselves apart from.... That possibility underscores the need for plaintiffs with individual monetary claims to decide *for themselves* whether to tie their fates to the class representatives' or go it alone—a choice Rule 23(b)(2) does not ensure that they have.

564 U.S. at 364 (emphases in original). Consequently, as the quotation above suggests, courts analyzing whether to certify a class under (b)(2) or (b)(3) may need to consider not only the claims being presented by representatives and counsel, but also any claims that were omitted.

Some courts, rather than looking only at whether to certify under (b)(2) or (b)(3), also consider the possibility of certifying a "hybrid" class, *i.e.*, a class with some claims certified under (b)(2) and other claims certified under (b)(3). The Fifth Circuit rejected such an approach in *Allison v. Citgo Petroleum Corp.*, 151 F.3d 402 (5th Cir. 1998), based on the facts of that case. The Eleventh Circuit, however, endorsed the possibility of a "hybrid" approach in *Williams v. Mohawk Industries, Inc.*, 568 F.3d 1350 (11th Cir. 2009). There, the court of appeals reversed the district court's denial of class certification and remanded for reconsideration as to whether plaintiffs could "maintain a class action for compensatory relief [under] (b)(3), and a hybrid class for injunctive relief [under (b)(2)]." 568 F.3d at 1352 (citations omitted). Indeed, as noted above, several courts have taken this approach in the wake of *Dukes*, certifying claims for classwide injunctive or declaratory relief under (b)(2) and certifying claims for monetary relief or individualized equitable relief under (b)(3).

H.   DEFENDANT CLASSES
UNDER RULE 23(b)(2)

Courts are sharply divided over whether class actions can be filed *against* a class under Rule 23(b)(2). The various approaches are discussed in § 12.1.

I.   WHETHER RULE 23(b)(2) CONTAINS
A "NECESSITY" REQUIREMENT

Many courts in (b)(2) cases have considered situations in which, because of the nature of injunctive or declaratory relief sought, the outcome of a lawsuit will impact all class members regardless of whether the court certifies the case as a class action. A good example would be an action against a city challenging the constitutionality of a city ordinance when the city acknowledges that the result of the litigation will bind it with respect to all citizens. In light of the city's acknowledgment, it is unclear whether a class action serves any purpose. Arguably, whether an individual plaintiff or a class obtains a ruling that the ordinance is unconstitutional, the ordinance will be invalid as to any citizen. Likewise, if a single plaintiff seeks a declaratory judgment that a statute or contract has a particular meaning, a class action may not be necessary for similarly situated individuals to benefit from the ruling. *Res judicata* and collateral estoppel are relevant in this context and will be explored further in the class action context in § 8.4. Many defendants have thus attempted to invoke the doctrine of "necessity" as a reason to deny class certification: If a class suit is not necessary to achieve the desired result, then there is no reason to proceed with a class action.

This argument has no basis in the text of Rule 23 and has generally been unsuccessful. A number of courts hold that, if the requirements of Rule 23 are otherwise met, lack of necessity cannot be a reason to deny class certification. *See, e.g., Disability Rights Council of Greater Wash. v. Wash. Metro Area Transit Auth.*, 239 F.R.D. 9, 23 (D.D.C. 2006) ("As numerous courts have observed, whether certification is 'necessary' is not a question Rule 23 directs the courts to consider." (citations omitted)). Additionally, in some instances it will not be clear whether the defendant would voluntarily comply with its duties to all class members in the absence of a classwide judgment. Where the defendant refuses to concede that it will treat all class members uniformly, the defendant cannot plausibly argue that a class action is unnecessary.

The Third Circuit recently summarized courts' various approaches to the necessity doctrine in *Gayle v. Warden Monmouth County Correctional Institution*, 838 F.3d 297, 308–12 (3d Cir. 2016) (rejecting formal necessity requirement and instead requiring " 'rigorous analysis' of the appropriateness of (b)(2) relief" (citation omitted)).

§ 4.4 RULE 23(b)(3)

A. OVERVIEW

When Rule 23 was revised in 1966, many scholars viewed Rule 23(b)(3) with particular skepticism. Rule 23(b)(3) replaced the old "spurious" class action (*see* § 2.4), with a new, untested "opt-out" class. Although the new (b)(3) purported to contain specific criteria for evaluating whether class certification was appropriate, those criteria were—and remain— somewhat vague and difficult to apply.

Rule 23(b)(3) states that a class action is maintainable if:

> [T]he court finds that the questions of law or fact common to class members *predominate* over any questions affecting only individual members, and that a class action is *superior* to other

available methods for fairly and efficiently adjudicating the controversy.

(Emphases added). Rule 23(b)(3) thus requires that a court undertake two inquiries: (1) Do the common questions of law or fact "predominate" over questions affecting only individual class members?; and (2) Is class treatment "superior" to alternative methods available for adjudicating the controversy? In articulating Rule 23(b)(3)'s purposes, the Advisory Committee Notes state:

> In the situations to which this subdivision relates, class action treatment is not as clearly called for as in those described above [(b)(1) and (b)(2)], but it may nevertheless be convenient and desirable depending upon the particular facts. Subdivision (b)(3) encompasses those cases in which a class action would achieve economies of time, effort, and expense and promote uniformity of decision as to persons similarly situated, without sacrificing procedural fairness or bringing about other undesirable results.

B. DEFINING "PREDOMINANCE"

The "predominance" inquiry—touched on briefly above in the (b)(2) context—arises because a court, in assessing the need for a class action, should consider the extent to which classwide adjudication of the common questions would advance the case overall. This analysis involves weighing and evaluating both the common and individualized questions in the case. Neither Rule 23(b)(3) nor the Advisory Committee

Notes define "predominance," and courts and commentators have struggled in determining how to apply the concept. Although courts and commentators agreed (at least prior to *Dukes*) that the predominance criterion is more rigid than commonality, *see* § 3.8, there is disagreement over what, precisely, is encompassed by predominance. Moreover, given that class certification is most commonly sought under Rule 23(b)(3), the predominance requirement may present the single biggest hurdle for parties seeking certification of a class action.

Some courts have stated that, although adjudication of common questions need not resolve the entire litigation, common questions predominate only if resolving those questions at least signals the beginning of the end of the litigation. Other courts have applied a more lenient standard, finding that common questions may predominate if the litigation as a whole is materially advanced by resolving the common questions. Still other courts consider the extent to which individualized proof or arguments must still be made after resolution of the common questions. Under this latter approach, "[w]here, after adjudication of the classwide issues, plaintiffs must still introduce a great deal of individualized proof or argue a number of individualized legal points to establish most or all of the elements of their individual claims, such claims are not suitable for class certification under Rule 23(b)(3)." *Klay v. Humana, Inc.*, 382 F.3d 1241, 1255 (11th Cir. 2004).

By contrast, some courts have resisted attempts to define the predominance inquiry in terms of quantity or quality of common questions. Instead, they have determined that the dispositive issue should be, in essence, a gut-level decision by the trial court based upon consideration of how the case would actually be litigated. *See, e.g., Powers v. Hamilton Cnty. Pub. Defender Comm'n*, 501 F.3d 592, 619 (6th Cir. 2007) ("[The] predominance requirement is met if [a] common question is at the heart of the litigation.").

At least one court has held that, in assessing predominance, the court is not limited to contested issues. Thus, for example, even if a defendant concedes classwide questions of liability, those questions may be counted in weighing whether common questions outweigh individual questions. *In re Nassau Cnty. Strip Search Cases*, 461 F.3d 219 (2d Cir. 2006). According to the Second Circuit, "[e]liminating conceded issues from Rule 23(b)(3)'s predominance calculus would undermine the goal of efficiency by requiring plaintiffs who share a 'commonality of the violation and the harm,' nonetheless to pursue separate and potentially numerous actions because, ironically, liability is so clear." *Id.* at 228 (citation omitted).

In a case reflecting a relatively demanding predominance standard, the Seventh Circuit held that the very nature of a particular remedy— rescission of mortgages—made it unsuitable for class treatment. Common issues did not predominate, the court held, where putative class members sought, *inter alia*, the right to rescind their mortgages because defendants had allegedly violated the Truth in Lending Act. *Andrews v. Chevy Chase Bank*, 545 F.3d 570 (7th Cir. 2008). The court explained: "If the class certification only serves to give rise to hundreds or thousands of individual proceedings requiring individually tailored remedies, it is hard to see how common issues predominate." *Id.* at 577. Indeed, some courts have deemed predominance unsatisfied after identifying "significant individualized issues . . . without carefully *weighing* those individualized issues against the common issues." Robert H. Klonoff, *The Decline of Class Actions*, 90 Wash U. L. Rev. 729, 792 (2013) (emphasis added).

Predominance issues tend to arise frequently in antitrust class actions. Such disputes often revolve around plaintiffs' ability to offer common proof of injury, as opposed to "highly individualized, fact-intensive inquir[ies] that necessarily require[ ] consideration of factors unique to each potential class member." *Blades v. Monsanto Co.*, 400 F.3d 562, 571 (8th Cir. 2005); *but see In re Scrap Metal Antitrust Litig.*, 527 F.3d 517, 535 (6th Cir. 2008) (applying a more lenient approach and stating that "even where there are individual variations in damages, the requirements of Rule 23(b)(3) are satisfied if the plaintiffs can establish that the defendants conspired to interfere with the free-market pricing structure").

C. CALCULATION OF INDIVIDUAL DAMAGES AND THE PREDOMINANCE INQUIRY

The determination of damages suffered by each class member is one area in which individualized questions often exist. For many years, courts had almost uniformly held that individualized damages, standing alone, did not defeat class certification.

The Supreme Court's 2013 decision in *Comcast Corp. v. Behrend*, 569 U.S. 27 (2013), drew considerable attention to individualized damages and the issue of predominance. There, the Court overturned certification of an antitrust class action under (b)(3), holding that the plaintiffs fell "far short of establishing that damages are capable of measurement on a classwide basis"; as a result, plaintiffs could not "show Rule 23(b)(3) predominance," because "[q]uestions of individual damage calculations will inevitably overwhelm questions common to the class." *Id.* at 34. The plaintiffs, however, had *conceded* that, under the particular circumstances of the case, certification would be improper without classwide proof of damages. Indeed, the dissent highlighted the plaintiffs' concession and on that basis argued that the majority opinion "should not be read to require, as a prerequisite to certification, that damages . . . be measurable on a class-wide basis." *Id.* at 41 (Ginsburg & Breyer, J.J., dissenting). *Comcast* is discussed further in § 5.2.

After *Comcast* was decided, defendants pressed for a broad reading of the Court's decision, arguing that the need to calculate and prove individualized damages necessarily defeated predominance. A majority of post-*Comcast* courts, however, have rejected such arguments, concluding that the Supreme Court's decision did not foreclose certification of class actions involving individualized damages. *See, e.g., In re Urethane Antitrust Litig.*, 768 F.3d 1245, 1257–58 (10th Cir. 2014) ("*Comcast* did not rest on the ability to measure damages on a class-wide basis."); *In re IKO Roofing Shingle Prods. Liab. Litig.*, 757 F.3d 599 (7th Cir. 2014) (distinguishing *Comcast* and noting that, were " 'commonality of damages' essential[,] . . . then class actions about consumer products [would be] impossible").

In 2016, the Supreme Court addressed the issue again and made clear that individualized damages do not automatically defeat predominance. The Court stated: "When one or more of the central issues in the action are common to the class and can be said to predominate, the action may be considered proper under Rule 23(b)(3) even though other important matters will have to be tried separately, *such as damages. . . .*" *Tyson Foods, Inc. v. Bouaphakeo*, 136 S. Ct. 1036, 1045 (2016) (emphasis added).

To calculate individual damages in class actions, courts have adopted a number of devices, such as using special masters or magistrates or employing separate juries to decide damages issues. But these devices are generally used only in the settlement context. The use of special masters or magistrates over a party's objection raises Seventh Amendment right to jury trial issues. In addition, the practice of using multiple juries has recently been questioned in some contexts on Seventh Amendment "reexamination" grounds. *See* § 5.6. The Supreme Court in *Dukes* rejected an approach that sought to utilize depositions and special masters to ascertain an average level of damages and then apply that figure to each member of the class. The Court labeled that approach "Trial by Formula." 564 U.S. at 367. For further discussion of issues relating to classwide proof, *see* § 5.6.

D.   SUBMISSION OF A TRIAL PLAN

A relevant consideration under Rule 23(b)(3) is whether plaintiffs have proposed a viable plan to try the case. As the Advisory Committee Notes to the 2003 amendments point out, "[a]n increasing number of courts require a party requesting class certification to present a 'trial plan' that describes the issues likely to be presented at trial and tests whether they are susceptible of classwide proof." Examples of such cases include *Wachtel v. Guardian Life Insurance of America*, 453 F.3d 179 (3d Cir. 2006), which quoted the Advisory Committee Notes with approval, and *Feder v. Electronic Data Systems Corp.*, 429 F.3d 125 (5th Cir. 2005), in which the court noted that a trial plan must be developed before certification when the case raises "potential trial complications." *Id*. at 139. Although this point is often discussed in the context of Rule 23(b)(3)'s "superiority" requirement, the existence of a trial plan bears on both superiority and predominance.

E.   SPECIAL ISSUES REGARDING
FRAUD AND RELIANCE

Plaintiffs often seek Rule 23(b)(3) certification in cases involving fraud or other torts sounding in fraud. The problem in such cases is that, because each member of the plaintiff class has been exposed to differing representations, individual questions of reliance may predominate over common questions. Defendants routinely contend that resolving the issue of reliance depends on proving the specific representations made to each plaintiff, the information available to each plaintiff at the time of the representations, and whether each plaintiff actually—and reasonably—relied on the representations. The difficulties surrounding fraud claims are discussed in the Advisory Committee Notes:

> [A] fraud perpetrated on numerous persons by the use of similar misrepresentations may be an appealing situation for a class action, and it may remain so despite the need, if liability is found, for separate determination of the damages suffered by individuals within the class. On the other hand, although having some common core, a fraud case may be unsuited for treatment as a class action if there was material variation in the representations made or in the kinds or degrees of reliance by the persons to whom they were addressed.

Most courts hold that the existence of individualized reliance issues in a fraud case weighs against class certification. Indeed, the Fifth Circuit, in *Castano v. American Tobacco Co.*, 84 F.3d 734 (5th Cir. 1996), articulated a bright-line rule: "[A] fraud class action cannot be certified [under (b)(3)] when individual reliance will be an issue." *Id.* at 745.

Several other courts have concluded that the presence of individualized reliance issues is fatal to class certification. A few courts, however, have taken the view that individualized reliance issues do not defeat class certification.

The Second Circuit, in *McLaughlin v. American Tobacco Co.*, 522 F.3d 215 (2d Cir. 2008), considered the issue of reliance in the context of tobacco litigation. The district court had certified a class of current and former smokers who sued a group of cigarette manufacturers under the Racketeer Influenced and Corrupt Organizations Act (RICO), alleging that the defendants had deceived them into believing that "light" cigarettes were healthier than "full-flavored" cigarettes. The Second Circuit reversed, finding that individual questions of reliance (as well as individual questions with respect to causation, injury, and damages) predominated. *Id.* at 234. Observing that "under RICO, *each* plaintiff must prove reliance, injury, and damages," *id.* at 219–20 (emphasis in original), the court went on to find that the class members' reliance on defendants' allegedly misleading advertising was not susceptible to classwide proof. "[P]roof of misrepresentation," the court stated, "even widespread and uniform misrepresentation—only satisfies half of the equation; the other half, reliance on the misrepresentation, cannot be the subject of general proof." *Id.* at 223. Importantly, however, the court rejected the Fifth Circuit's "blanket rule that a 'fraud class action cannot be certified when individual reliance will be an issue.'" *Id.* at 224 (quoting *Castano*, 84 F.3d at 745). And, going one step further, the Second Circuit endorsed the Advisory Committee Notes' proposition that fraud claims may in some circumstances be suitable for class treatment, even outside of the securities context. *Id.* at 225.

By contrast, in *Jenson v. Fiserv Trust Co.*, 256 F. App'x 924 (9th Cir. 2007), the Ninth Circuit upheld class certification in a fraud case, noting that "common issues do not necessarily fail to predominate simply because reliance must be shown." *Id.* at 926. In *Jenson*, the court found that reliance could be "infer[red]" where the defendant told each prospective investor that it would get a high yield from the investment. *Id.*; *see also Arenson v. Whitehall Convalescent & Nursing Home, Inc.*, 164 F.R.D. 659, 666 (N.D. Ill. 1996) (emphasizing that "individual issues of reliance do not [automatically] thwart class actions" (citation and internal quotation marks omitted)).

Likewise, although courts have often refused to certify RICO class actions due to individualized reliance issues, the Tenth Circuit in *CGC Holding Co., LLC v. Broad & Cassel*, 773 F.3d 1076 (10th Cir. 2014), affirmed certification of a (b)(3) class alleging civil RICO claims. The court noted that, [u]nder certain circumstances, . . . it is beneficial to permit a commonsense inference of reliance applicable to the entire class," and held that such an inference was permissible given that "the behavior of plaintiffs and the members of the class cannot be explained in any way other than reliance upon the defendant's conduct." *Id.* at 1089–90. The court emphasized, however, that its holding was "limited to transactional situations—almost always financial transactions." *Id.* at 1091 n.9.

Some plaintiffs have avoided reliance issues by suing under consumer protection statutes that permit recovery for fraudulent conduct without proof of reliance. *See, e.g., Yokoyama v. Midland Nat'l. Life Ins. Co.*, 594 F.3d 1087, 1094 (9th Cir. 2010) (holding that Hawaii's Deceptive Practices Act, under which the plaintiffs brought suit, did not require proof of individual reliance, and therefore that the district court erred in denying class certification on that basis). Other plaintiffs have argued that reliance issues should not foreclose class certification when the alleged misrepresentations were uniform as to each member of the class.

F.   SECURITIES CASES: SPECIAL SITUATIONS WHERE A COURT MAY PRESUME RELIANCE

In securities fraud cases, the predominance inquiry often turns on reliance, and courts have held that reliance may be *presumed* in certain circumstances. Courts have historically relied heavily on two seminal Supreme Court cases: *Basic v. Levinson*, 485 U.S. 224 (1988), and *Affiliated Ute Citizens v. United States*, 406 U.S. 128 (1972). In 2011, the Court decided *Erica P. John Fund, Inc. v. Halliburton Co.*, 563 U.S. 804 (2011) (*Halliburton I*), which, *inter alia*, solidified the principles set forth in *Basic*—namely, the availability of a rebuttable presumption of reliance in securities fraud cases (sometimes called the "fraud-on-the-market" theory). The Court reaffirmed *Basic*'s presumption of reliance

in *Stoneridge Investment Partners LLC v. Scientific-
Atlanta*, 552 U.S. 148 (2008). In 2014, the Court
confronted the question whether the "fraud-on-the-
market" theory should be overruled, and declined to
do so. *Halliburton Co. v. Erica P. John Fund, Inc.*,
573 U.S. 258 (2014) (*Halliburton II*). A detailed
discussion of reliance in the securities fraud
context—including a complete discussion of
Halliburton I and *II*, *Stoneridge Investment*, and
their predecessors—is contained in § 11.3.

It should be emphasized that, outside of the
securities context, courts have been reluctant to
presume reliance under *Basic*, *Affiliated Ute*, or other
doctrines developed in securities fraud cases. For
example, in *McLaughlin*, 522 F.3d 215 (discussed
above), the plaintiffs attempted to rely on a
"variation" of the *Basic* presumption in seeking class
certification of their fraud claims against cigarette
manufacturers under RICO. The Second Circuit
squarely rejected that attempt, relying in part on the
major differences between the cigarette and
securities markets. *Id*. at 223–25.

G.   PREDOMINANCE AND MASS TORTS

"Mass torts" are discussed comprehensively in
§ 11.1, but the subject is intertwined with the
analysis of predominance under Rule 23(b)(3).
Indeed, many of the most important (b)(3) cases in
recent years have been mass tort cases, such as cases
involving exposure to asbestos or injuries caused by
allegedly defective products. As discussed in § 11.1
several courts have raised concerns about permitting

class certification in mass tort cases. These concerns, as they relate to predominance, often find their roots in potential issues such as the need for individualized causation and defendants' assertion of individualized defenses to each putative class member's claim.

H. RULE 23(b)(3) PREDOMINANCE AND CHOICE-OF-LAW CONCERNS IN MULTI-JURISDICTIONAL CLASS ACTIONS

As discussed in detail in § 7.1, classes that consist of members from multiple states (or from different countries) implicate the predominance inquiry by creating potentially difficult choice-of-law issues. This is because—especially in light of CAFA—many Rule 23(b)(3) class actions involving state-law claims are litigated in federal court pursuant to diversity jurisdiction. In those cases, the applicable state law may vary from class member to class member. Under *Erie Railroad Co. v. Tompkins*, 304 U.S. 64 (1938), and *Klaxon Co. v. Stentor Electric Manufacturing Co.*, 313 U.S. 487 (1941), a federal court in a diversity case must apply the choice-of-law rules of the state in which the court sits. In cases where the classes at issue consist of claimants from all fifty states and the District of Columbia, there conceivably could be, depending on the applicable choice-of-law rules, up to fifty-one different sources of law governing the claims (all fifty states plus the District of Columbia). This would be true, for example, when the applicable choice-of-law rules require that a court in a nationwide class action apply the law of the place of injury. Applying so many laws can be an onerous task, particularly in the context of a jury trial.

Numerous courts have found that the need to apply many different laws causes individual questions to predominate over common questions, thus defeating class certification under (b)(3). Some courts, however, have certified classes notwithstanding the presence of such issues. *See* § 7.1.

I. SUPERIORITY IN RULE 23(b)(3) CLASSES: ALTERNATIVE METHODS FOR RESOLVING THE DISPUTE

In addition to predominance, Rule 23(b)(3) requires that a court addressing a motion for class certification assess whether class treatment is "superior to other available methods for fairly and efficiently adjudicating the controversy." As the wording of (b)(3) indicates, courts must consider alternative methods of litigating the dispute, including the various methods discussed in Chapters 14–16. Such alternative methods include:

- Individual actions;

- Compulsory or permissive joinder under Rules 19 and 20, respectively;

- Intervention of nonparties under Rule 24;

- Consolidation under Rule 42(a);

- Multi-jurisdictional coordination, such as coordinated pretrial proceedings through the Judicial Panel on Multidistrict Litigation;

- Deference to another judicial forum (federal or state court), or deference to an administrative forum; or

- Use of a test case or bellwether approach, whereby a small number of putative class members try their cases individually with or without the defendant's agreement that, if the plaintiffs prevail, the defendant will not relitigate common questions when the remaining claimants bring suit.

The issue in each instance is whether some device other than a class action can resolve the cases fairly and efficiently, without the complexities inherent in a class action.

J.   ASSESSING SUPERIORITY IN RULE 23(b)(3) CLASSES USING ENUMERATED FACTORS

In assessing superiority, courts consider a wide variety of factors. These include the four factors listed in the text of subdivision (b)(3) itself:

(A) the class members' interests in individually controlling the prosecution or defense of separate actions;

(B) the extent and nature of any litigation concerning the controversy already begun by or against class members;

(C) the desirability or undesirability of concentrating the litigation of the claims in the particular forum; and

(D) the likely difficulties in managing a class action.

No single factor is determinative, and as the Advisory Committee Notes make clear, the court may consider other factors when making a superiority determination. The following sections discuss the four factors listed in Rule 23(b)(3), as well as other factors that courts have considered.

(1) Rule 23(b)(3)(A): Interest in Individual Control of the Litigation

The first superiority factor listed in Rule 23(b)(3) is the "class members' interests in individually controlling the prosecution or defense of separate actions." Class actions are often justified on the ground that they permit the aggregation of claims of similarly wronged individuals where each injured person's limited damages would otherwise render individual litigation cost prohibitive. Courts have labeled such situations "negative-value" suits.

Litigants, however, occasionally try to certify class actions when each putative class member is alleged to have suffered significant damages. Courts are generally more reluctant to certify such classes (as opposed to classes in which the relief sought by individual class members is less substantial) because, given the large individual claims at stake, each putative class member has a greater interest in controlling the litigation. Furthermore, given that each individual case could result in an award of substantial damages, it may be economically viable for individual plaintiffs to obtain separate counsel. Similarly, statutes that permit the award of attorneys' fees may also militate against a finding of superiority, given that the ability to recover legal costs may often make individual litigation economically viable.

Ultimately, the inquiry under (b)(3)(A) is very case-specific. As the Advisory Committee Notes explain:

> [T]he court should inform itself of any litigation actually pending by or against the individuals. The interests of individuals in conducting separate lawsuits may be so strong as to call for denial of a class action. On the other hand, these interests may be theoretic rather than practical; the class may have a high degree of cohesion and prosecution of the action through representatives would be quite unobjectionable, or the amounts at stake for individuals may be so small that separate suits would be impracticable. The burden that separate suits would impose on the party opposing the class, or upon the court calendars, may also fairly be considered.

Accordingly, the court must make a practical, realistic assessment as to whether, among other things, the class members would prefer to litigate separately or collectively.

(2) Rule 23(b)(3)(B): Extent and Nature of Pending Litigation

Rule 23(b)(3)(B) requires a certifying court to consider "the extent and nature of any litigation concerning the controversy already begun by or against class members." The rule does not specify, however, whether the presence of other litigation is a factor in *favor* of class treatment or *against* it. Accordingly, the rule has been interpreted to call for a variety of different—and sometimes contradictory—assessments. For example, some courts have viewed the presence of similar litigation as showing the superiority of a class action (because the cases can be heard together). Other courts, however, have viewed the *absence* of similar litigation as favoring superiority (because individuals do not have enough at stake to bring their own separate claims).

Conversely, the absence of similar suits has been used as a reason to deny certification on superiority grounds. As the Fifth Circuit noted in *Castano*, "[o]ur specific concern is that a mass tort cannot be properly certified without a prior track record of trials from which the district court can draw the information necessary to make the predominance and superiority [analysis] required by [R]ule 23." 84 F.3d at 747. On the other hand, some courts have held that the *presence* of similar suits causes the suit at issue to fail the superiority test (because the individual suits demonstrate that the plaintiffs already have sufficient incentives to sue without the need for class treatment).

Moreover, as explicitly set forth in Rule 23(b)(3)(B), the "nature" of the other pending litigation will factor into the superiority analysis. If the other pending lawsuits are themselves class actions, courts are much less likely to find that a new class action would be superior. On the other hand, even the pendency of a multi-jurisdictional class action will not necessarily deter a court from certifying a smaller class, particularly if the larger class has not yet been certified.

The forum of the related case may also be relevant. For example, in *Gregory v. Finova Capital Corp.*, 442 F.3d 188 (4th Cir. 2006), the plaintiffs sought certification of a securities fraud class action against a bankrupt defendant. In holding that the existing bankruptcy forum was superior, the Fourth Circuit noted that "[i]t would be inefficient and needlessly duplicative to allow the class action to go forward when the adversary proceeding will likely adjudicate this controversy in the normal course of [the defendant's] bankruptcy." *Id.* at 191.

(3) Rule 23(b)(3)(C): Desirability or Undesirability of Concentrating the Litigation in the Particular Forum

Rule 23(b)(3)(C) requires that a court considering class certification assess "the desirability or undesirability of concentrating the litigation of the claims in the particular forum." Courts sometimes reject certification under this subdivision if parties, witnesses, and evidence are dispersed throughout the nation. Courts have also frequently held, however, that concentration of the claims in a single forum was desirable, despite dispersion of parties, witnesses, and evidence—either because the key events complained of occurred in the forum state, or because inconvenience to at least some parties and witnesses was inevitable regardless of the forum chosen for the litigation.

(4) Rule 23(b)(3)(D): Manageability Issues

Rule 23(b)(3)(D) requires that a court consider "the likely difficulties in managing a class action." Of the four superiority factors specifically listed in Rule 23(b)(3), this factor has received the most attention from litigants and courts.

A key focus under (b)(3)(D) involves how to identify and provide notice to members of the class. By virtue of the notice requirements imposed on Rule 23(b)(3) classes by Rule 23(c)(2), *see* § 6.1, a court must sometimes attempt to notify large classes dispersed throughout the country, with little or no information to assist it in doing so. The difficulty of notifying any significant percentage of the putative class may counsel against certification.

Although courts are reluctant to certify classes whose members would be difficult to communicate with or identify, the sheer size of a class does not necessarily result in the denial of certification. For example, in *In re Domestic Air Transportation Antitrust Litigation*, 137 F.R.D. 677 (N.D. Ga. 1991), the district court certified a class involving an estimated 12.5 million unidentified purchasers of airline tickets during a four-year period. The district court concluded that a class action was the only fair approach because the individual claims were so small that, in the absence of a class action, most claims would not be pursued.

On the other hand, some courts have found that sheer numbers may make a class unmanageable. For instance, in *In re Hotel Telephone Charges*, 500 F.2d 86 (9th Cir. 1974), the Ninth Circuit held that a putative class of 40 million hotel guests was "beyond [a court's] capacity to manage or effectively control." 500 F.2d at 91 (citations and internal quotation marks omitted).

As noted above, choice-of-law concerns with respect to multi-jurisdictional class actions impact a court's predominance inquiry under Rule 23(b)(3). These same concerns also affect a court's manageability inquiry pursuant to Rule 23(b)(3)(D). This is because the existence of a class in which members' claims will be litigated pursuant to many different jurisdictions' laws makes the litigation much more difficult to administer. Similarly, as noted above, although certification generally should not be denied solely on the ground that class members will have to prove their damages on an individualized basis, potential difficulties in calculating damages may be a factor in assessing manageability—particularly if there are other manageability concerns as well.

One important limitation on manageability should be noted. As discussed in § 9.1, when a class is being certified solely for settlement, a court need not inquire into whether the case, if *tried*, would present serious manageability problems, given that there will not be a trial. *Amchem Prods., Inc. v. Windsor*, 521 U.S. 591, 593–94 (1997).

K. ASSESSING SUPERIORITY UNDER RULE 23(b)(3) USING FACTORS OTHER THAN THOSE ENUMERATED

Courts are not limited to the four factors enumerated in Rule 23(b)(3) and have thus considered a variety of other factors in analyzing superiority. These additional factors have included whether an alternative regulatory mechanism exists and whether a class action would achieve significant judicial efficiencies. *See, e.g., In re Phenylpropanolamine (PPA) Prods. Liab. Litig.*, 214 F.R.D. 614, 622 (W.D. Wash. 2003) (finding defendants' refund and product replacement programs superior to class litigation); *but see, e.g., Turner v. Murphy Oil USA, Inc.*, 234 F.R.D. 597, 610 (E.D. La. 2006) (declining to consider defendant's private settlement program as part of the superiority inquiry because "[t]he analysis is whether the class action format is superior to other methods of *adjudication*, not whether a class action is superior to an out-of-court, private settlement program" (emphasis in original)).

It should be noted that some courts have declined to find superiority satisfied where the case involved potentially significant statutory damages but little or no actual harm to the plaintiffs themselves. *See, e.g., Leysoto v. Mama Mia I., Inc.*, 255 F.R.D. 693, 699 (S.D. Fla. 2009) (refusing to certify a putative class whose members had admittedly suffered no actual economic injury, and stating that the "sole benefit of certification would be the *threat* [to defendant] of

ruinous damages for the purposes of settlement"
(emphasis added)).

CHAPTER 5

LITIGATING A CLASS ACTION

Litigating a class action is a multi-step process that begins with a complicated array of strategic decisions. Once those initial decisions have been made, the parties must then marshal their evidence to address the critical issue of class certification. Discovery is ordinarily central to this evidence-gathering function. If a class is certified, the parties must then address the multitude of case management and trial-related tasks necessitated by a class action. As a practical matter, the certification decision is usually dispositive; the vast majority of cases in which a class is certified ultimately settle before trial. Nonetheless, in recent years, a number of major class actions have gone to trial. Moreover, even in a case that is almost certain to settle at some point, it is important to understand the litigation-related issues: The parties' bargaining positions (and thus any ultimate settlement) will depend heavily on those parties' perceptions of what is likely to happen should the case go to trial.

This Chapter addresses the various strategic and legal issues that attorneys and parties must face in litigating a class action.

§ 5.1 STRATEGIC CONSIDERATIONS IN CLASS ACTION LITIGATION

At the outset of a class action, both the plaintiff and the defendant must consider a variety of strategic issues. These initial decisions will frequently determine the ultimate outcome of the litigation. These decisions, of course, will be informed by the class action rule (Federal Rule 23 or its state counterpart), the relevant case law, and any applicable local rules.

A.   PLAINTIFF'S PERSPECTIVE

Whether to Pursue a Class Action. A threshold decision facing plaintiffs and plaintiffs' counsel is whether to pursue a class action at all. In some instances, many of the benefits of a class action can be obtained by multidistrict litigation (*see* Chapter 14), joinder of multiple plaintiffs (*see* § 15.1), consolidation (*see* § 15.6), the use of a test case with potential *res judicata* (claim preclusion) or collateral estoppel (issue preclusion) effects, or other approaches. In other cases, a class action has distinct advantages—in particular, the dramatic increase in bargaining power that often comes with class certification. Certification may allow the plaintiff class to insist upon more favorable settlement terms than those that could be obtained in individual lawsuits.

Significantly, this bargaining advantage is accompanied by a substantial expansion of the responsibilities entrusted to plaintiffs' counsel. When a class is certified, plaintiffs' counsel becomes a fiduciary to all potential members of the class and cannot make decisions solely on what is best for the named plaintiffs. Thus, settling on behalf of individual plaintiffs becomes more difficult once a putative class action is certified.

Additionally, would-be class counsel must anticipate the increased scope of his or her potential legal, ethical, and financial responsibilities if a class is certified. Among other considerations, counsel should be mindful of the factors set forth in Rule 23(g) that courts evaluate when appointing class counsel (*see* § 3.8), as well as Rule 23(g)(4)'s broad mandate that "[c]lass counsel must fairly and adequately represent the interests of the class." In particular, attorneys representing a class owe fiduciary duties to the class members, and must take care that any conflicting interests among class members are accounted for—usually either by separate representation of the different interests or by narrowing the class definition to avoid the conflict. *See* § 13.1. The cost of providing notice to the class is another practical consideration, as notice may be required by both Rule 23 and due process. Notice requirements are discussed further in § 6.1.

Whom to Sue. Plaintiffs must make an initial determination as to which defendant(s) to include in the case. The issue cannot be decided based on the simplistic rationale that more defendants are always better because more money will be available. Rather, plaintiffs must evaluate the strategic implications of adding defendants. Each additional defendant creates potential individualized issues that could be used by the defendant(s) to defeat class certification. Also, multiple defendants may utilize their collective resources to overwhelm the putative class and make the case difficult to prosecute effectively.

Where to Sue. This decision is often critical. The conventional wisdom is that plaintiffs' attorneys prefer state court, while defense attorneys prefer federal court. The perception is that state court judges (many of whom are elected) are more willing than federal judges to certify sprawling class actions, especially against out-of-state defendants. For that reason, the business community overwhelmingly supported legislative efforts (culminating in the Class Action Fairness Act (CAFA)) to shift most multistate class actions to federal court, whereas the plaintiffs' trial bar overwhelmingly opposed such efforts.

Even if CAFA does not grant a defendant a federal forum in a particular case, plaintiffs' presumptive preference for state court should not be absolute, and plaintiffs' counsel must analyze the precise circumstances involved. For example, selecting a state court may mean giving up potentially viable federal causes of action, given that the assertion of a federal claim will allow the defendant to remove the case to federal court.

If plaintiffs' counsel selects state court, he or she must be careful to structure the case so that the defendant cannot successfully remove the case based on diversity jurisdiction or other grounds. Structuring a massive class action to avoid federal jurisdiction is now particularly challenging in light of CAFA. *See* § 8.3.

Additionally, in a post-CAFA world, the choice of where to bring suit has taken on added complexity. Broadly stated, there are two basic ways in which plaintiffs' counsel can try to secure the forum perceived to be most favorable to the class members' interests. First, counsel may still pursue a state court forum by structuring the class suit so as to come within one or more of CAFA's exemptions (discussed in § 8.3). These exemptions, however, are relatively narrow. Second, counsel may opt to forgo state court in the first instance, and instead focus on whether the law of a particular federal circuit is more hospitable to the lawsuit's ultimate chances of success. Realistically, plaintiffs may have no choice but to litigate in federal court. As noted, CAFA now allows most multistate class actions to be removed to federal court, and other cases may satisfy federal jurisdictional criteria on other grounds, such as supplemental jurisdiction (*see* § 8.3) or federal question jurisdiction. Thus, it may be more fruitful for plaintiffs to focus on selecting a federal district court within a circuit whose law is most favorable on the key issues.

In choosing a forum, it is important for parties to consider both the applicable procedural and substantive laws. For example, Mississippi state procedural rules do not provide for a class action device as such, so the decision to stay in Mississippi state court as a practical matter means mass joinder (at best) rather than a class action. Also, state-specific restrictions on class certification may, in a particular case, render a federal forum more attractive than a state forum. *See* § 8.6.

Which Claims to File. As with deciding which defendants to sue, it is not necessarily true that more claims are better. Some claims are particularly susceptible to classwide determination, while other claims are often laden with individualized issues. For example, numerous courts have declined to certify fraud cases because of individual issues of reliance. *See* § 4.4 above. Accordingly, when other viable claims exist, plaintiffs' counsel may decide to omit a fraud claim from the complaint to avoid the potential adverse ramifications from a class certification standpoint. Of course, plaintiffs' counsel must consider whether the omission of viable claims will raise adequacy of representation concerns, particularly in light of potential *res judicata* and collateral estoppel issues. *See* § 3.10.

In addition, following the Supreme Court's establishment of a more rigorous pleading standard (often referred to as a "plausibility" standard) in *Bell Atlantic Corp. v. Twombly*, 550 U.S. 544 (2007), and *Ashcroft v. Iqbal*, 556 U.S. 662 (2009), plaintiffs must focus carefully on how they plead the claims that they select. As discussed in § 5.1, defendants may elect to challenge plaintiffs' complaint at the outset, adding increased importance to plaintiffs' compliance with the Court's mandate that they allege sufficient facts to "raise a right to relief above the speculative level." *Twombly*, 550 U.S. at 555. While a detailed discussion of pleading standards following *Twombly* and *Iqbal* is beyond the scope of this text, prospective plaintiffs and class counsel would be well advised to consider them carefully when drafting the class complaint. *See, e.g., Matrixx Initiatives, Inc. v. Siracusano*, 563 U.S. 27 (2011) (applying the pleading standards established by *Twombly* and

Iqbal in the class action context); *Twombly,* 550 U.S. 544 (involving a putative class action).

How to Define the Class. This issue must likewise be decided by weighing the pros and cons of various alternatives. Although a broad class may have pecuniary or tactical advantages, it is not always true that a broader class is better. An expansive nationwide class action might entail so many individualized issues—such as complicated choice-of-law issues—that it would be destined to fail as a class action. In addition, under CAFA, the scope of the class may affect plaintiffs' ability to remain in state court. Also, a more limited statewide class, in which only one state's law controls, may have a better chance of surviving commonality, predominance, and superiority. Likewise, a class that is defined more narrowly in terms of the number of people and time periods involved may have a greater chance of being certified than an unwieldy class involving hundreds of thousands (or even millions) of people.

Which (and How Many) Representatives to Select. Careful consideration must be given to the selection of class representatives. The threshold decision regarding how many representatives to utilize is a difficult one. On the one hand, having more than one representative helps to ensure that the class action may continue if one of the representatives is found to be inadequate or atypical (or if that representative's claims become moot during the pendency of the action). On the other hand, the presence of multiple representatives may give defense counsel the opportunity to demonstrate conflicts among the class representatives (and thus conflicts among the class members), or to show why individual questions with regard to each representative (and thus each class member) would predominate over common questions. The use of multiple representatives also adds to the difficulty of preparing plaintiffs for depositions and trial.

The qualifications of the class representatives must be carefully scrutinized. Counsel must ensure that the representatives do not have characteristics that could trouble the court—such as unsavory backgrounds or prior disapproval from other courts, particularly in the class action context. Potential conflicts of interest may exist as well. Furthermore, the representatives must be individuals who will invest the time and effort necessary to learn the basic facts of the case and be effective witnesses.

When to Move for Class Certification. As discussed in § 5.2, many jurisdictions—both federal and state— have specific rules dictating when a plaintiff must move for class certification. In the absence of such a rule, plaintiffs' counsel faces a tactical decision between moving for class certification early in the case or waiting until a later point in time, after substantial discovery has occurred. This tactical decision will depend in part on whether, absent discovery, the defendant is likely to possess evidence showing the presence of individualized questions, such as evidence showing that class members suffered various types of injuries at different points in time. If discovery will aid the defendant in making a better showing against the suitability of class certification, then the plaintiffs may well prefer to seek an early ruling on certification. On the other hand, plaintiffs may determine that their chances for obtaining class certification will depend heavily on the ability to marshal strong evidence to support the Rule 23 requirements. In that situation, plaintiffs may choose to hold back on moving for class certification until they have had a chance to pursue thorough discovery.

B.   DEFENDANT'S PERSPECTIVE

Defense counsel face an equally challenging series of strategic decisions. Many of these decisions mirror those faced by plaintiffs' counsel.

Whether to Seek a Different Forum. Like plaintiffs' counsel, defense counsel must carefully analyze the pros and cons of a particular forum. Thus, defense counsel must evaluate whether, if the case is filed in state court, legal grounds exist for removing the case to federal court under CAFA (*see* § 8.3), supplemental jurisdiction (*see* § 8.2), or otherwise. If such grounds exist, counsel must then decide whether, as a strategic matter, the defendant would be better off in state or federal court. Defense counsel must also decide whether a particular venue is preferable and, if so, whether legal arguments can be made to support that choice of venue. And, of course, defense counsel must decide whether a case filed in state court presents an unusual situation in which the defendant might be better off litigating in state court.

Whether to Challenge the Viability of the Complaint or Class Certification at the Outset. One of the most difficult issues facing defense counsel is whether to seek dismissal of the case at the outset or first obtain a ruling on class certification. A dismissal on the merits prior to certification binds only the class representative. If a defendant's position on the merits is extremely strong, defense counsel may in a rare case choose to litigate the certification issue first—or even acquiesce to certification—so that a favorable decision on the merits will bind the entire class.

On the other hand, a decision certifying a class could have potentially disastrous consequences for the defendant, particularly if there is a significant risk that the defendant will lose the case at trial. In that event, a better option may be to seek dismissal on the merits before litigating the certification issue. If the motion to dismiss is successful, defense counsel can use the ruling as persuasive precedent in any future class or individual suit raising similar questions. If the motion is unsuccessful, the defendant can still contest class certification.

If a putative class action appears vulnerable to a pre-discovery dismissal, defense counsel may wish to consider filing a motion to dismiss under Rule 12(b)(6) for failure to state a claim upon which relief can be granted. Defendants have also occasionally sought to attack class allegations under Rule 12(f), which empowers courts to "strike from a pleading an insufficient defense or any redundant, immaterial, impertinent, or scandalous matter."

Whether to Challenge Class Certification Prior to the Initiation of Class Discovery. As discussed in

§ 5.3, it is theoretically possible to challenge class allegations prior to any discovery. Defense counsel must decide whether to attempt to defeat class allegations on the pleadings or instead develop an evidentiary record after full discovery. If the class certification issues turn on factual matters, then an attack on the pleadings will not prevail. Moreover, if an initial motion challenging the class allegations on the pleadings is unsuccessful, that ruling could make the trial court skeptical when the defendant later challenges class certification after discovery. On the other hand, a successful motion early in the case would eliminate expensive and time-consuming discovery.

How to Attack the Class Certification Issue. Defense counsel must decide whether to attack class certification based on the inability to satisfy Rule 23(b), on deficiencies with respect to class representatives (such as adequacy or typicality problems), or on other (or multiple) grounds. An attack focused exclusively on the class representatives could ultimately lead nowhere because plaintiffs' counsel may simply substitute other representatives. Moreover, if there are other strong grounds for challenging class certification— such as a predominance of individualized issues in a putative (b)(3) class action—focusing on characteristics of the representatives could be viewed as nitpicking and could undermine the force of the predominance challenge. On the other hand, challenging the class representatives could be effective if plaintiffs' counsel has few clients and has apparently chosen the best ones to serve as representatives. In that circumstance, successfully challenging the representatives could, as a practical matter, end the entire lawsuit.

§ 5.2 THE CLASS CERTIFICATION DECISION

A. OVERVIEW

As explained in earlier sections, the ruling on class certification is frequently the most important decision in the case. Despite this importance, however, there are few rules governing motions to certify a class. This section discusses the rules and practices relating to the certification decision.

B.   TIMING OF CERTIFICATION DECISION

Prior to the 2003 amendments, Rule 23(c)(1) directed that the certification decision should be made by the court "[a]s soon as practicable after commencement of an action brought as a class action." Amended Rule 23(c)(1)(A) changes that language to state that "the court must—at an early practicable time—determine by order whether to certify the action as a class action." The Advisory Committee Notes indicate that the pre-2003 standard "neither reflect[ed] prevailing practice nor capture[d] the many valid reasons that may justify deferring the initial certification decision." For example, extensive, time-consuming discovery may be necessary before the decision can be made. In addition, the parties may need time, prior to the certification decision, to address how the proposed class action would actually be tried. The Advisory Committee Notes caution, however, that the court should "not unjustifiably delay[ ]" the certification decision.

The appellate courts generally leave the timing of the certification decision to the discretion of the trial courts. Many trial courts, however, have adopted time frames in their local rules specifying when motions for class certification must be made, typically thirty to ninety days after filing of the complaint. Some courts have strictly applied these time frames and have refused to consider untimely class certification motions. Other courts hold that these time limits may be extended for good cause.

There is no rule of thumb regarding how long a trial court should take to rule on class certification. Some courts decide the issue relatively promptly, while others take many months (or even years) to decide the question.

The timing of class certification affects a variety of important litigation issues. An early ruling on certification helps define the structure of the litigation, the parties, the subsequent motion practice, and the approach to settlement negotiations. Additionally, the denial of class certification usually means that the clock begins running again on the statute(s) of limitations applicable to the unnamed class members' claims. *See* § 8.1.

The timing of the certification decision also affects the defendant's decision whether—and when—to bring a motion to dismiss on the merits. Courts are split over the advisability of ruling on dispositive motions prior to ruling on class certification. Some courts hold that dispositive motions prior to certification are permissible and will rule on these motions prior to certification. Other courts, while not entirely prohibiting the resolution of dispositive motions prior to certification, discourage the practice. The disadvantage to the defendant of bringing a motion on the merits prior to certification is that, even if the motion is successful, it will bind only the named plaintiffs, not any of the unnamed class members. *See* § 5.1.

C. RAISING THE CERTIFICATION ISSUE

In general, the named plaintiff raises the issue of class certification in a motion to the court (usually accompanied by briefs, declarations, and exhibits). The plaintiff has the burden of establishing that a class action is proper and that the requirements of Rule 23 are satisfied.

The defendant, however, need not wait for the plaintiff to raise the issue of class certification. *See, e.g., Vinole v. Countrywide Home Loans, Inc.*, 571 F.3d 935 (9th Cir. 2009) (affirming district court's grant of defendant's motion to deny class certification). The defendant may raise the issue through a motion to deny class certification or a motion to strike the class allegations. When the defendant makes such a motion, the motion is frequently accompanied by a motion to dismiss or a motion for summary judgment.

As discussed in § 5.3, the trial court has discretion regarding whether to permit discovery on class certification issues.

D.   COURT'S OBLIGATION TO RULE

The general rule is that, absent certification by the trial court, a suit may not properly proceed as a class action. One exception that has arisen on rare occasion is when a complaint seeks classwide relief and the court grants such relief, even absent a formal motion for class certification. Given the rigorous analysis required for class certification under Rule 23, however, the validity of case law invoking such an exception is questionable. In all events, courts will not permit an action to proceed as a class action when the plaintiff's complaint does not seek classwide relief. In other words, a court may not *sua sponte* convert an action brought in an individual capacity that does not seek classwide relief into a class action. Likewise, a court may not grant classwide remedies that are not sought in the complaint.

E.   APPROPRIATENESS OF INQUIRY INTO THE MERITS

Rule 23 defines in detail the requirements for class certification, but it says nothing about whether those requirements must be satisfied by evidence (as opposed to merely by pleading). Prior to an important 2001 Seventh Circuit decision, *Szabo v. Bridgeport Machines, Inc.*, 249 F.3d 672 (7th Cir. 2001), authored by Judge Easterbrook, most courts permitted plaintiffs to seek class certification based on the pleadings or only minimal evidentiary support. Courts generally declined to resolve factual disputes at the class certification stage. In *Szabo*, the Seventh Circuit determined that the prevailing approach of looking primarily at the pleadings stemmed from a misreading of the Supreme Court's decision in *Eisen v. Carlisle & Jacquelin*, 417 U.S. 156 (1974).

The issue in *Eisen* was whether a court had discretion to shift the cost of class notice from the plaintiff (who normally incurred the cost) to the defendant based on the court's assessment that the plaintiff was likely to prevail on the merits. After conducting a hearing and finding that plaintiffs were likely to prevail on the merits, the district court had ordered defendants to pay 90 percent of the cost of notifying millions of class members. In rejecting that approach, the Supreme Court stated: "We find nothing in either the language or history of Rule 23 that gives a court any authority to conduct a preliminary inquiry into the merits of a suit in order to determine whether it may be maintained as a class action." *Id*. at 177. Numerous courts interpreted this language to mean that they could not address the merits of a case in addressing class certification, even if an element of class certification overlapped with the merits.

Another Supreme Court case, however, pointed in a different direction. In *General Telephone Co. v. Falcon*, 457 U.S. 147 (1982), a Title VII case, the Court stated: "Sometimes the issues are plain enough from the pleadings to determine whether the interests of the absent parties are fairly encompassed within the named plaintiff's claim, and *sometimes it may be necessary for the court to probe behind the pleadings before coming to rest on the certification question*." *Id.* at 160 (emphasis added). The Court noted that a class could be certified only after "rigorous analysis." *Id.* at 161.

By the mid-1990s, and especially in light of *Falcon*, some courts began to retreat from a strict construction of *Eisen*, opining that courts should look beyond the pleadings as part of a rigorous analysis. *See, e.g., Castano v. Am. Tobacco Co.*, 84 F.3d 734, 737, 744 (5th Cir. 1996); *In re Am. Med. Sys., Inc.*, 75 F.3d 1069, 1079 (6th Cir. 1996). Even those courts, however, generally looked only to see if there was *some* evidence to support class certification and did not take it upon themselves to resolve conflicting testimony going to the merits.

In *Szabo,* however, the Seventh Circuit endorsed not only rigorous review of the evidence, but also (in some circumstances) the *resolution* of conflicting evidence bearing on the merits. As the Seventh Circuit explained, "nothing in . . . *Eisen* . . . prevents the district court from looking beneath the surface of a complaint to conduct the inquiries identified in [Rule 23] and exercise the discretion it confers." *Id.* at 677. The court thus held that, "[b]efore deciding whether to allow a case to proceed as a class action . . . a judge should make whatever factual and legal inquiries are necessary under Rule 23." *Id.*

Prior to the Supreme Court's 2013 decision in *Amgen v. Connecticut Retirement Plans & Trust*

Funds, 568 U.S. 455 (2013) (discussed in detail below), virtually every federal circuit to rule on the issue followed the *Szabo* court's analysis. The most extensive discussion of the issue was contained in *In re Hydrogen Peroxide Antitrust Litigation*, 552 F.3d 305 (3d Cir. 2008). Citing *Szabo* and other case law, the Third Circuit made clear that "the court must resolve all factual or legal disputes relevant to class certification, even if they overlap with the merits— including disputes touching on elements of the cause of action." *Id*. at 307.

In *Wal-Mart Stores, Inc. v. Dukes*, 564 U.S. 338 (2011), the Supreme Court briefly discussed the issues raised in *Szabo* and *Hydrogen Peroxide*. By 2011, when the Court rendered its decision, the proposition that *Eisen* did not preclude courts from rigorously examining the evidence was so clear that the Supreme Court summarily dismissed the pre-*Szabo* reading of *Eisen* as "mistaken[ ]" and constituting "the purest dictum." *Id*. at 2552 n.6. The Court stated that "[t]he class determination generally involves considerations that are enmeshed in the factual and legal issues comprising the plaintiffs' cause of action." *Id*. at 351 & n.6. Thus, *Dukes* appeared to uphold the *Szabo/Hydrogen Peroxide* approach to merits inquiry at the class certification stage. The Court did not squarely decide, however, whether courts were required to *resolve* disputes between plaintiffs' evidence and defendant's evidence, because it found that plaintiffs' evidence, standing alone, did not support commonality.

In 2013, however, the Supreme Court returned to the issue in far more depth. In *Amgen v. Connecticut Retirement Plans & Trust Funds*, 568 U.S. 455 (2013), the Court cautioned against "put[ting] the cart before the horse" by focusing on the merits at the class certification stage. *Id.* at 460.

The case involved securities fraud claims brought against Amgen, a pharmaceutical company, alleging that it publicly made material representations regarding several products. Amgen argued that, because materiality is an essential element of the "fraud-on-the-market" theory (*see* § 11.3), the plaintiffs should have to proffer evidence of materiality to show that common questions predominated over individual questions. The Court rejected that argument, holding that such evidence going to the merits was not required by Rule 23. The Court reasoned that "Rule 23(b)(3) requires a showing that *questions* common to the class predominate, *not that those questions will be answered, on the merits, in favor of the class.*" *Id.* at 459 (second emphasis added).

Moreover, the Court in *Amgen* cautioned generally that "Rule 23 grants courts no license to engage in free-ranging merits inquiries at the certification stage," noting that the purpose of a certification ruling "is not to adjudicate the case; rather, it is to select the 'metho[d]' best suited to adjudication of the controversy 'fairly and efficiently.' " *Id.* at 466, 460. Thus, the Court emphasized, "[m]erits questions may be considered to the extent—but only to the extent—that they are relevant to determining whether the

Rule 23 prerequisites for class certification are satisfied." *Id.* at 466.

Following *Amgen*, several circuits have emphasized (in contrast with cases such as *Szabo* and *Hydrogen Peroxide*) that the class certification stage is generally not the time to decide the merits. For example, in *Suchanek v. Sturm Foods, Inc.*, 764 F.3d 750, 758 (7th Cir. 2014), the Seventh Circuit cited *Amgen* and stated that "Rule 23 allows certification of cases that are fated to lose as well as cases that are sure to win." In *Rikos v. Proctor & Gamble Co.*, 799 F.3d 497, 505, 523 (6th Cir. 2015), the Sixth Circuit criticized the defendant for "misconstru[ing] Plaintiffs' burden at the class certification stage," and held that the district court erred in considering evidence proffered by the defendant at the certification stage, because that evidence "affect[ed] only the merits of th[e] case, not predominance." Similarly, in *Alcantar v. Hobart Service*, 800 F.3d 1047, 1053 (9th Cir. 2015), the Ninth Circuit held that "the district court erred in denying class certification because it evaluated the merits rather than focusing on whether the questions presented—meritorious or not—were common to the class." And in *Williams v. Jani-King of Philadelphia*, 837 F.3d 314, 322 (3d Cir. 2016), the Third Circuit refused to address one of the defendant's questions presented on appeal because that question required the court "to weigh in on the merits of the Plaintiffs' claims" at the class certification stage.

F.   THE CERTIFICATION HEARING

(1)   Need for a Hearing on Class Certification

Rule 23 does not require a hearing when determining class certification, and some courts have held that parties are not entitled to a hearing unless they can show prejudice in the absence of a hearing. Nonetheless, courts generally hold some type of hearing before ruling on class certification issues, especially when a court determines that it must look beyond the pleadings. Some cases emphasize the need for a hearing before *denying* class certification. Courts have also noted the need for a hearing when factual disputes exist.

Even if a hearing is held, the litigants are not always allowed to submit evidence. Whether an evidentiary hearing will be ordered (and, if so, what evidence will be allowed) depends upon the particular case. In many cases, oral argument (or even just written briefing) will suffice, particularly when the pertinent facts are undisputed. On the other hand, if the facts are complicated or hotly disputed, an evidentiary hearing may be essential.

(2)   Burden of Proof and Procedures at the Hearing

At the hearing, the party seeking certification bears the burden of establishing that all the requirements of Rule 23 are met. Conclusory allegations will not satisfy this burden. Rather, courts require an adequate statement of facts indicating that each of the requirements of Rule 23 is met. Although some courts state that all doubts should be resolved in favor of certification, most courts are more demanding in assessing whether the requirements of Rule 23 are met.

With respect to procedures at the hearing, the *Manual for Complex Litigation (4th)* advises that the hearing should not be a mini-trial on the merits. The court has broad discretion to control the nature of the hearing by limiting the number of witnesses and prescribing other procedures. Factual issues can often be narrowed by the submission of uncontradicted declarations, stipulations, and answers to requests for admission.

(3) Expert Testimony at the Class Certification Stage (*Comcast*)

The Supreme Court's 2013 decision in *Comcast Corp. v. Behrend*, 596 U.S. 27 (2013), is discussed in Chapter 4 in the context of individualized damages and Rule 23(b)(3) predominance. *See* § 4.4. The decision, however, also addressed the use of expert testimony at the class certification stage. In *Comcast*, the plaintiffs used expert testimony to establish a model for measuring damages on a classwide basis for purposes of satisfying Rule 23(b)(3)'s predominance requirement. The district court found sufficient evidence of a common methodology to measure damages on a classwide basis and certified the class. On appeal, the Third Circuit declined to entertain the defendant's arguments attacking the reliability of plaintiffs' expert damages model, reasoning that those arguments went to the merits of the calculations and were not proper at the class certification stage.

In a 5–4 opinion, the Supreme Court held that the class had been improperly certified. It concluded that the plaintiffs' expert damages model was not geared to the specific theory of liability accepted by the district court, and that the Third Circuit had erred in refusing to address the defendant's arguments challenging the model. The Court reasoned:

> The Court of Appeals simply concluded that respondents "provided a method to measure and quantify damages on a classwide basis," finding it unnecessary to decide "whether the methodology [was] a just and reasonable inference or speculative." Under that logic, at the class-certification stage *any* method of measurement is acceptable so long as it can be applied classwide, no matter how arbitrary the measurements may be. Such a proposition would reduce Rule 23(b)(3)'s predominance requirement to a nullity.

569 U.S. at 35–36. (emphasis in original). Thus, at minimum *Comcast* suggests that district courts must extend their "rigorous analysis" of Rule 23's class certification requirements to expert testimony on matters of classwide proof. It further suggests that plaintiffs may be required to develop their expert proof to a significant degree as part of the class certification process. The Court's opinion has been subject to varying interpretations, and has received significant attention from scholars and commentators. *See, e.g.*, Alex Parkinson, Comcast

Corp. v. Behrend *and Chaos on the Ground*, 81 U.
Chi. L. Rev. 1213 (2014); Joseph Krebs, Comcast v.
Behrend: *The Class Action Channel Is Still
Scrambled*, 16 Duq. Bus. L.J. 83 (2013).

(4) Expert Testimony at the Class Certification Stage (*Daubert*)

In *Daubert v. Merrill Dow Pharmaceuticals, Inc.*,
509 U.S. 579 (1993), the Supreme Court recognized
that trial courts must perform a gatekeeping function
by ensuring that scientific expert testimony is both
relevant and reliable. The Court subsequently held
that *Daubert* applies not only to scientific expert
testimony, but also to other expert testimony
involving technical or specialized knowledge. *Kumho
Tire Co. v. Carmichael*, 526 U.S. 137 (1999).

Whether *Daubert* and *Kumho Tire* apply with full
force at the class certification stage is open to some
debate, but the trend favors applying *Daubert*, at
least to the extent necessary to perform the required
"rigorous analysis" at the class certification stage.
The leading case on this point is *American Honda
Motor Co., Inc. v. Allen*, 600 F.3d 813 (7th Cir. 2010)
(per curiam), in which the Seventh Circuit concluded
that, "when an expert's report or testimony is critical
to class certification, . . . a district court must
conclusively rule on any challenge to the expert's
qualifications or submissions prior to ruling on a
class certification motion." *Id.* at 815–16. *Accord, e.g.*,
In re Blood Reagents Antitrust Litig., 783 F.3d 183,
187 (3d Cir. 2015) ("[A] plaintiff cannot rely on
challenged expert testimony, when critical to class

certification, to demonstrate conformity with Rule 23 unless plaintiff also demonstrates, and the trial court finds, that the expert testimony satisfies the standard set out in *Daubert*.").

Some courts, however, have rejected the *American Honda* approach. For instance, the Eighth Circuit in *In re Zurn Pex Plumbing Products Liability Litigation*, 644 F.3d 604 (8th Cir. 2011), held that the district court acted properly in conducting a "focused" and limited inquiry, as opposed to a full-scale *Daubert* review. Some district courts have gone so far as to declare *Daubert* inapplicable at the class certification stage.

The Supreme Court has not ruled on the issue, but it did note in *Dukes* that "[w]e doubt" that the district court was correct in concluding that "*Daubert* [does] not apply to expert testimony at the [class] certification stage. . . ." 564 U.S. at 354.

(5) Reasons for the Certification Ruling

The determination of whether an action may be maintained as a class action is left to the discretion of the trial court and may be reversed only for abuse of discretion. Rule 23 does not on its face require that the certification order be accompanied by findings and conclusions. (The only exception is that a court certifying a Rule 23(b)(3) class must "find[ ]" that the predominance and superiority requirements are satisfied.) Nonetheless, as the *Manual for Complex Litigation (4th)* points out, "the court should enter findings of fact and conclusions, addressing each of the applicable criteria of Rule 23. Failure to do so may result in reversal or remand for further proceedings after interlocutory appeal under Rule 23(f)." § 21.21. Indeed, the Fifth Circuit has stated that "when certifying a class a district court must detail with sufficient specificity how the plaintiff has met the requirements of Rule 23." *Vizena v. Union Pacific R.R. Co.*, 360 F.3d 496, 503 (5th Cir. 2004). In addition, the Third Circuit has held that the class certification order or accompanying memorandum must provide "a clear and complete summation of the claims, issues, or defenses subject to class treatment." *Wachtel v. Guardian Life Ins. Co. of Am.*, 453 F.3d 179, 184 (3d Cir. 2006).

G.   CERTIFICATION OPTIONS

(1) Conditional Certification

As discussed in § 5.3, prior to the 2003 amendments, Rule 23(c)(1) provided that an order certifying a class "may be conditional." The 2003 amendments deleted this language. According to the Advisory Committee Notes, "[a] court that is not satisfied that the requirements of Rule 23 have been met should refuse certification until they have been met." Despite the deletion of language permitting conditional certification, one court has indicated that the 2003 amendments do not foreclose the use of conditional certification in the context of a class settlement. *Denney v. Deutsche Bank Sec., Inc.*, 443 F.3d 253 (2d Cir. 2006). *Denney* raised the question whether conditioning certification solely for settlement purposes was proper. In concluding that it was, the court stated: "[C]onditional certification survives the 2003 amendment to Rule 23. . . . [I]f the requirements of Rule 23(a) and (b) are met, certification may be granted, conditionally or unconditionally." *Id.* at 270.

Most courts agree that, while the amended rule prohibits a court from certifying a class when there is doubt about whether the requirements for certification are met, it does allow the court to modify its ruling in the face of changed circumstances. Specifically, Rule 23(c)(1)(C) allows a court to alter or amend a certification order, provided that the court makes the change before rendering a final judgment in the case. The Advisory Committee Notes point out, for example, that the class definition may need to be altered (and new notice and opt-out rights may be required), or the court may decide that decertification is necessary.

A party seeking revocation or modification of a class certification ruling must normally show newly discovered facts or an intervening change in the law. The court may modify its certification decision *sua sponte*, but usually will do so only if a significant change in the facts or law warrants such a modification.

(2) Use of Subclasses

Rule 23(c)(5) permits the use of subclasses to resolve problems relating to the Rule 23 requirements. Whether to permit subclasses normally rests within the discretion of the trial court, although in some circumstances subclasses may be required—such as when a case involves claims of exposure to a harmful substance by both those who have already suffered physical injuries as a result and those who have not. *Ortiz v. Fibreboard*, 527 U.S. 815 (1999).

It is fundamental that each subclass must satisfy all of the requirements for certification (the three threshold requirements, the four requirements of Rule 23(a), and the requirements of at least one subdivision of Rule 23(b)). The proponent of class certification bears the burden of showing that the class action may be properly divided into subclasses.

Subclasses are often used to resolve difficulties that arise within classes after certification, and may also be used prior to certification of a larger class. In addition, subclasses are often required when it appears that the class representatives and class members have potentially conflicting factual or legal positions. Subclasses have also been used when there are claims or theories of damages unique to certain class members. The *Manual for Complex Litigation (4th)* points out that "[s]ubclassing sometimes represents a workable solution for differences in substantive law and for choice of law difficulties." § 21.23.

On occasion, the use of subclasses may complicate rather than remedy the problems in a class action. For instance, multiple subclasses may lead to confusion and conflicts among the classes, their representatives, and their counsel, requiring greater judicial supervision (and possibly resulting in serious manageability problems). Moreover, if too many subclasses are created, plaintiffs may have difficulty showing that each subclass satisfies the numerosity requirement.

(3) Issue Certification and Bifurcation

Rule 23(c)(4) provides that, "[w]hen appropriate, an action may be brought or maintained as a class action with respect to particular issues." The court may grant partial certification under Rule 23(c)(4) either *sua sponte* or upon the motion of one of the parties. The court may separate claims or issues within a complaint, certifying some as a class action and leaving others as individual claims or issues. Courts may also certify part of the action as a Rule 23(b)(3) class action with opt-out rights and another portion of the same action as a Rule 23(b)(1) or Rule 23(b)(2) class action, neither of which requires opt-out rights. Courts have also bifurcated the issues of liability and damages by certifying a class action for purposes of liability, leaving the individual class members to pursue their damage claims separately following a determination as to the defendant's liability. The decision whether to bifurcate a class action is within the discretion of the trial court after conducting an inquiry into the factual and legal aspects of the case.

The requirements of Rule 23(a) must, of course, be met for the court to permit partial certification under Rule 23(c)(4). That means that numerosity, commonality, typicality, and adequacy of representation must all be satisfied.

A crucial issue Rule 23(c)(4) is whether the "predominance" requirement of Rule 23(b)(3) must be satisfied. Most courts have squarely held that (b)(3) predominance need not be shown. *See, e.g., Martin v. Behr Dayton Thermal Products LLC*, 896 F.3d 405, 413 (6th Cir. 2018) (certifying a (c)(4) class in an environmental tort case and explaining that (c)(4) does not require a showing of overall predominance); *Gunnells v. Healthplan Servs., Inc.*, 348 F.3d 417, 439–45 (4th Cir. 2003) (explaining easier burden under (c)(4)); *Gates v. Rohm & Hass Co.*, 655 F.3d 255, 273 (3d Cir. 2011) (also rejecting view that overall predominance is required under (c)(4)); *In re Nassau Cnty. Strip Search Cases,* 461 F.3d 219 (2d Cir. 2006) (to the same effect). *See also* Principles of the Law of Aggregate Litigation § 2.02(a)(1) (2010) (urging issue class certification where "the court determines that resolution of the common issue would materially advance the resolution of multiple civil claims by addressing the core of the dispute in a manner superior to other realistic procedural alternatives, so as to generate significant judicial efficiencies"). These authorities have reasoned that, were (b)(3) predominance required, (c)(4) would be superfluous because a plaintiff seeking only an issue class would still have to satisfy the more demanding criteria of (b)(3).

At one time, the Fifth Circuit took a contrary view and indicated that full (b)(3) predominance was required for an issue class. *Castano v. Am. Tobacco Co.*, 84 F.3d 734 (5th Cir. 1996). The *Castano* court stated that (c)(4) was simply a "housekeeping rule," and that "a cause of action, as a whole, must satisfy the predominance requirement of (b)(3)[.]" *Id.* at 745– 46 n.21. Subsequent Fifth Circuit cases, however, have retreated from *Castano*. *See, e.g., In re Deepwater Horizon*, 739 F.3d 790, 806 & n.65 (5th Cir. 2014) (noting that "the district court anticipated that 'issues relating to damages' could and would be 'severed and tried separately' from other issues relating to liability, in accordance with this court's previous case law and Rule 23(c)(4)"); *Steering Comm. v. Exxon Mobil Corp.*, 461 F.3d 598, 603 (5th Cir. 2006) (indicating that bifurcation might provide "a remedy for the obstacles preventing a finding of predominance" but not reaching the issue because plaintiff did not rely on (c)(4)). Indeed, in 2018, a sister circuit noted, after carefully studying the Fifth Circuit's case law, "that any potency the [*Castano*] view once held [in that Circuit] has dwindled." *Martin*, 896 F.3d at 412 (6th Cir. 2018).

In ordering a bifurcation or partial certification, the trial court will normally try the common issues first, followed by trials of the individualized issues. Because of such bifurcation, the court should examine whether issue certification raises Seventh Amendment concerns. *See* § 5.6. For a discussion of the Seventh Amendment and issue certification, *see* Robert H. Klonoff, *The Decline of Class Actions*, 90 Wash. U. L. Rev. 729, 812–15 (2013).

One important case upholding issue certification (without citing Rule 23(c)(4)) is *Mejdrech v. Met-Coil Sys. Corp.*, 319 F.3d 910 (7th Cir. 2003). In an opinion by Judge Posner, the court upheld certification of two issues in a case alleging groundwater contamination by a noxious solvent (TCE): (1) "whether [defendant] leaked TCE in violation of law," and (2) "whether the

TCE reached the soil and groundwater beneath the homes of the class members." *Id.* at 911. The court recognized that, after the resolution of these common issues, "[t]he individual class members [would] still have to prove the fact and extent of their individual injuries." *Id.* at 911–12. But the existence of those individual issues did not prevent the certification of the two classwide issues.

(4) Multiple or Competing Classes

It is not uncommon for multiple class actions to be filed in various federal courts or in both state and federal courts. Sometimes the same class lawyers are involved; sometimes the various suits are pursued by different lawyers. In some instances, the definitions and scope of the various cases are the same; in others, they differ substantially. The *Manual for Complex Litigation (4th)* contains a number of possible options for courts faced with such multiple class actions, including: asking the Judicial Panel on Multidistrict Litigation (*see* Chapter 14) to centralize the federal cases before one federal judge for pretrial proceedings; coordinating with other judges (both state and federal) on class certification, discovery, and motions (*see* § 14.4); defining the class to exclude members of an already-certified state court class; allowing an already-certified state court class to go forward without certifying a federal court class action; and expanding the federal case to take into account the claims and parties involved in other putative class actions.

When one of multiple class actions is resolved, either by trial or settlement, that resolution may have *res judicata* implications for other pending class actions involving overlapping class members. *See* § 8.5.

(5) Decertification

After certification, a court retains the power to decertify a class prior to a final decision on the merits. Indeed, courts have occasionally decertified classes years into a lawsuit. For instance, decertification may be warranted if unanticipated complexities are revealed during discovery, or if the class representatives prove to be inadequate and no substitutes are readily available. Of course, decertification means that the parties and the court have wasted substantial resources on the case. Thus, courts should not rely on the possibility of decertification as a reason to avoid scrutinizing the appropriateness of class certification at the outset.

§ 5.3 DISCOVERY IN CLASS ACTIONS

This section addresses discovery in the class action context. Class discovery occurs at two stages: (1) at the pre-certification stage in connection with whether to certify a class; and (2) in connection with the merits of the lawsuit. In each of these contexts, several important issues arise.

A. DISCOVERY ON CLASS CERTIFICATION ISSUES

(1) Overview

The determination of whether a class should be certified is frequently the most important issue in the case. A plaintiff who fails to secure class certification may find that the case is financially impracticable to pursue on an individual basis. By the same token, a defendant who fails to defeat class certification may be forced to settle the case for a substantial sum or face the risk of economic devastation (and perhaps bankruptcy). In many instances, the most crucial aspect of resolving whether class certification will be granted is the evidence that each side marshals. Discovery, of course, is crucial to this evidence-gathering process. Aggressive, thorough discovery is frequently decisive in class certification battles.

(2) Granting or Denying Class Certification Without Discovery

It is useful at the outset to discuss the circumstances in which courts may rule on class certification without discovery. Although pre-certification discovery often provides a court with important information bearing on the Rule 23(a) and (b) criteria, the decision whether to permit *any* discovery prior to the certification decision rests within the trial court's discretion. In some instances, a court may deny any discovery because it believes that it can determine, based solely on the pleadings, whether the requirements of Rules 23(a) and (b) are satisfied. *See, e.g., Pilgrim v. Universal Health Card, LLC,* 660 F.3d 943, 949 (6th Cir. 2011) (upholding dismissal of class action allegations, noting that "we cannot see how discovery or for that matter more time would have helped [plaintiffs]").

For example, if plaintiffs seek certification for personal injuries and property damage on behalf of millions of people throughout the nation, a court may determine from the face of the complaint that the individualized questions—including choice-of-law issues, plaintiff-specific medical issues, causation issues, and so forth—are so pervasive that common questions cannot predominate. Alternatively, the requirements of Rule 23 may be so clearly satisfied on the face of the pleadings that a court may grant class certification without discovery. This could be the case, for example, in a securities fraud suit involving alleged misstatements in a prospectus by a major Fortune 500 company in which there are no apparent issues of individualized reliance and the defendant does not challenge the adequacy of the class representatives or class counsel. Likewise, class certification may be granted or denied without discovery when the opposition to certification is based solely on legal—as opposed to factual—arguments, such as an argument that class actions are barred by a specific statute pertaining to the claims at issue.

In most instances, courts will not grant or deny class certification without first allowing discovery. In circumstances where the viability of class claims depends heavily on facts outside of the pleadings, some appellate courts have held that the failure to allow any discovery constitutes an abuse of discretion. Nonetheless, there is also authority supporting class certification rulings that are made without discovery. The *Manual for Complex Litigation (4th)* states that "[d]iscovery may not be necessary when claims for relief rest on readily available and undisputed facts or raise only issues of law (such as a challenge to the legality of a statute or regulation)." § 21.14. The *Manual* goes on to note, however, that "[s]ome discovery may be necessary . . . when the facts relevant to any of the certification requirements are disputed" or "when the opposing counsel contends that proof of the claims or defenses unavoidably raises individual issues." *Id.*

In some instances, parties may choose to rely almost entirely on evidence gathered outside of formal discovery. It is not uncommon for parties to submit extensive expert declarations and other supporting material, even when little formal discovery has taken place. More often, however, the record will include both declarations and materials obtained during class certification discovery.

(3) Conditional Certification or Deferral of Certification Pending Discovery

When the court finds that the pleadings are not adequate to decide the class certification issue, the usual approach is to defer ruling on the issue until discovery has been conducted. A few courts have taken a different approach: conditionally certifying the class, while preserving the opportunity to reexamine the initial determination if discovery reveals information suggesting the inappropriateness of class certification. These courts rely on the pre-2003 version of Rule 23(c)(1), which permitted "conditional certification" and provided that the ruling could be amended before a decision on the merits. Most courts recognized, however, even prior to the 2003 amendments, that a class should not be even conditionally certified unless a *prima facie* showing had been made that the case satisfied Rules 23(a) and (b). The 2003 amendments to Rule 23(c) delete the language permitting "conditional" certification, thus making clear that premature certification is inappropriate. As the Advisory Committee Notes to the amendment explain, "[a] court that is not satisfied that the requirements of Rule 23 have been met should refuse certification until they have been met." As discussed in § 5.2, however, even after the 2003 amendments, there is some authority authorizing conditional certification.

The 2003 amendment retains the language that a certification order "may be altered," but sets the cutoff at "final judgment," rather than a "decision on the merits," to avoid ambiguity (*e.g.*, to confirm that alteration may be made even after liability, if remedial proceedings are still pending).

(4) Discovery of Merits Issues Before Class Certification

Merits discovery is discussed later in this chapter. But one merits discovery issue is relevant to the discussion herein: the permissibility of merits discovery before a ruling on class certification. This issue has taken on increasing complexity in light of the emphasis by a number of courts on the need to perform a rigorous analysis of the Rule 23 requirements at the class certification stage. *See* § 5.2. Courts have recognized that, in making class certification rulings, the inquiry almost invariably touches upon the merits of an action, particularly when class issues are inextricably linked with merits issues. For example, without information regarding the nature of different class members' claims, defendants normally cannot contest the plaintiffs' contention that common questions exist and that the named representatives' claims are typical of those of the class. Thus, as the Supreme Court confirmed in *Wal-Mart Stores, Inc. v. Dukes*, 564 U.S. 338 (2011), discovery related to the substantive nature of the plaintiffs' claims may often be necessary to determine whether the requirements of Rule 23 are satisfied. *See* § 5.3. On the other hand, as noted in § 5.2, the Supreme Court sent a strong message in *Amgen, Inc. v. Connecticut Retirement Plans & Trust Funds*, 568 U.S. 455 (2013), that the class certification stage is usually not the time to focus on the merits.

This overlap between class certification and merits discovery poses case management challenges for courts. For instance, in *In re Rail Freight Surcharge Antitrust Litigation*, 258 F.R.D. 167 (D.D.C. 2009), defendants argued for "phased discovery [to] facilitate[ ] early resolution of the class certification issue and reduce[ ] the burden of the subsequent merits discovery," *id.* at 169, while plaintiffs asserted that "class certification and merits evidence are indistinguishable." *Id.* at 171. The court adopted a compromise approach that frontloaded some, but not all, merits discovery.

Courts are sometimes able to distinguish between issues that are relevant solely to certification (or, perhaps, to both certification and the merits) and issues that are entirely merits-based. But this does not mean that courts universally forbid pure merits discovery before certification. In fact, courts occasionally open up all discovery even prior to certification. Many courts, however, bifurcate class and merits discovery when the merits of the claims are not relevant at the certification stage. Some courts also reason that merits discovery could end up being wasteful: Absent certification, the case may not go forward at all, or it may go forward with the issues greatly narrowed. The *Manual for Complex Litigation (4th)* takes a cautious approach with respect to pre-certification merits discovery. It notes that "[a]llowing some merits discovery during the precertification period is generally more appropriate for cases that are large and likely to continue even if not certified." § 21.4. By contrast, the *Manual* states that, "in cases that are unlikely to continue if not certified, discovery into aspects of the merits unrelated to certification delays the certification decision and can create extraordinary and unnecessary expense and burden." *Id.* Ultimately, the decision whether to bifurcate class and merits discovery must be made on a case-by-case basis. As the Advisory Committee Notes to the 2003 amendments state, "[a]ctive judicial supervision may be required to achieve the most effective balance that expedites an informed certification determination without forcing an artificial and ultimately wasteful division between 'certification discovery' and merits discovery.' "

One tactical issue factors heavily into the debate about certification discovery versus merits discovery: One or both parties may want to use certification discovery as an opportunity to preview the opponent's case (or even to secure damaging substantive admissions). As a related matter, the parties may view certification discovery as an opportunity to obtain information, at an early stage of the case, that could facilitate a prompt, favorable settlement. Because of such strategic considerations, it would be overly simplistic to state that plaintiffs always want class discovery and defendants always oppose it (or vice versa). In some cases, defendants may be the ones who are aggressively pursuing discovery and plaintiffs may be the ones who are resisting; in other cases, the positions may be reversed.

(5) Types of Pre-Certification Discovery

Depositions are frequently appropriate at the class certification stage, particularly when the person deposed is a proposed class representative or a defendant (or corporate representative) with critical information. In some instances, however, courts may require that a party initially seek discovery through other means (*e.g.*, interrogatories, document requests, and requests for admission) and pursue depositions only upon a showing of good cause. Obviously, the limitations imposed will depend in part on the complexity of the case, the size of the putative class, the nature of the relief sought (*i.e.,* damages, injunctive relief, or declaratory relief), and the scope and amount of relief at stake. Limitations on discovery may also reflect the "maturity" of the litigation. For instance, if the case involves a novel or untested theory or claim, a court may be more flexible in allowing discovery. On the other hand, if there is extensive information in the public domain as a result of prior trials or other proceedings involving similar claims and issues, a court may impose greater restrictions.

(6) Limitations on the Scope of Class Certification Discovery

Trial courts have wide discretion over the scope of discovery. In general, discovery regarding class certification issues is governed by Rules 26 through 37 of the Federal Rules of Civil Procedure, the same rules that govern discovery in all federal civil cases. As with discovery generally, "[u]nless otherwise limited by court order," parties to a class action "may obtain discovery regarding any nonprivileged matter that is relevant to any party's claim or defense and proportional to the needs of the case. . . ." Fed. R. Civ. P. 26(b)(1). If a court limits discovery to class certification issues, that limitation necessarily circumscribes the scope of what is relevant and proportional.

Class certification discovery may be relevant to a number of issues, such as numerosity, the adequacy or typicality of the class representatives, the appropriateness of the class definition, predominance and superiority under Rule 23(b)(3), and other matters addressed by the requirements for class certification. In applying the relevancy and proportionality standards to class certification discovery, some courts have considered (1) the court's needs; (2) the amount of time discovery would require; and (3) the probability that discovery would be helpful in resolving the issue of class certification. Courts also look at whether the discovery would be unduly burdensome.

The goal of trial courts in overseeing class discovery is to define discovery that is sufficiently broad to allow the parties to address the class certification requirements, but also is tailored to protect both sides from burdensome or privileged requests. Some common types of class discovery include: depositions of class representatives to probe their backgrounds, their familiarity with the case, and the existence of any unique or individualized defenses; depositions of corporate officials on the issue of Rule 23(b)(3) superiority to ascertain the existence of other similar lawsuits and the results in such cases; depositions of experts proffered to demonstrate or refute the existence of common issues; and discovery regarding plaintiffs' proposed trial plan for the case.

A court may restrict the scope of discovery in a variety of ways, particularly when the discovery sought would be expensive or burdensome. Such restrictions include the following:

Geographic and Time Restrictions. A common restriction is to limit discovery to a particular geographic area (for instance, limiting discovery in a suit involving toxic spill to those geographic areas where the named plaintiffs lived). Similarly, courts may restrict discovery by limiting the time frame for which information can be sought.

The Number of People Against Whom Discovery Is Sought. Another common restriction is to limit discovery to a set number of people, a percentage of the group of targeted individuals, or a random sampling of the group. A court may also limit the discovery to particular classifications of people, such as limiting plaintiffs' discovery in an employment discrimination case to immediate supervisors of the named plaintiffs.

The Defined Class. Although courts generally allow discovery consistent with the breadth of the class definition, this is not true when the class definition is unreasonably broad. In that event, a court might limit discovery to a class that is at least potentially viable. For example, if a plaintiff files a putative nationwide class and the court is convinced at the outset that *at most* a statewide class would be warranted, the court might restrict discovery to claims and plaintiffs within a particular state.

Financial Issues. Courts are cautious about allowing wholesale discovery concerning the named plaintiffs' finances. Some courts, however, have permitted such discovery when it is relevant to whether the named plaintiffs possess the financial resources necessary to provide adequate representation for the class. Of course, this rationale is subject to recognition that, as a practical matter, class counsel, not the representative, usually funds the case.

Courts are also cautious in allowing pre-certification discovery into the contingent fee or other fee arrangements between the named plaintiffs and their counsel or the arrangements for payment of costs and expenses. Here too, however, discovery may be allowed when the information sought can be linked to the adequacy of class counsel or another Rule 23 requirement.

Other Limitations. Courts also commonly restrict class certification discovery by imposing strict schedules for completing discovery; limiting the number of depositions, interrogatories, and document requests; and limiting the length of depositions. In addition, as noted above, courts may restrict the types of discovery devices that can be used (*e.g.*, prohibiting depositions except in limited circumstances).

(7) Discovery of Names of Absent Class Members

Names Sought by Plaintiff. Plaintiffs frequently seek the identities of putative class members when such information is in the possession of defendants. For example, in an employment discrimination case, the defendant employer presumably can identify every member of a particular minority group who was laid off during a given period. The names of putative class members are certainly relevant at the notice stage. Rule 23(c)(2)(B) requires that the court "direct to class members the best notice that is practicable under the circumstances, including individual notice to all members who can be identified through reasonable effort."

The Supreme Court has indicated that courts may, in some circumstances, require a defendant to help identify the class members to whom notice must be sent by compiling a list of names and addresses. *Oppenheimer Fund, Inc. v. Sanders*, 437 U.S. 340 (1978). At the pre-certification stage, however, defendants are likely to contend that plaintiffs do not need to obtain the *identities* of class members but only information about the *numbers* of class members. Courts often refuse to allow discovery of the class members' identities at the pre-certification stage, sometimes out of concern that plaintiffs' attorneys may be seeking such information to identify potential new clients, as opposed to using the information to establish the appropriateness of certification.

Names Sought by Defendant. Courts are likewise reluctant to require plaintiffs, at the pre-certification stage, to provide defendants with the names and addresses of putative class members. Because discovery of putative class members is susceptible to being used by defendants to harass and embarrass potential class members, courts have frequently imposed limits on the scope of such discovery. Some courts have also noted concerns that, if given names of potential class members, defendants might approach those individuals and attempt to compromise or settle their claims outside the context of the case. Although defendants have frequently tried to justify the need for names by pointing to the Rule 23 criteria, courts have generally not been receptive to arguments that the identification of unnamed class members is relevant to such issues as numerosity, typicality, commonality, and adequacy of representation.

Other courts, by contrast, have been more lenient in permitting such discovery, particularly when the defendant is willing to receive the information pursuant to a protective order that limits (1) the persons who may receive the information, and (2) the uses that may be made of it.

(8) Pre-Certification Discovery Directed to Absent Class Members

Although the issue of discovery directed to absent class members usually arises at the merits discovery phase following class certification, it also may arise prior to certification. While such discovery is not *per se* unavailable prior to class certification, courts generally disfavor it. Courts must balance the competing interests of the absent class members in remaining passive and those of the defendant in acquiring information to defeat class certification.

Courts considering the scope of discovery against absent class members generally will permit such discovery only if: (1) the defendant demonstrates a clear need for the information to litigate class issues; (2) the court is satisfied that the discovery requests are narrowly tailored to their purpose; (3) the discovery requests are tendered in good faith and are not unduly burdensome; and (4) the information is not available from the representative parties.

Some courts prefer document requests and interrogatories over depositions because the former are often less intrusive. Accordingly, the party seeking discovery will in many instances bear a heavier burden to justify depositions.

The type of plaintiff involved may affect a court's willingness to allow pre-certification discovery from absent class members. For instance, a court may be more inclined to allow such discovery when the absent class members are organized groups and businesses rather than individuals with small claims and limited means. One approach that some courts have adopted is to allow focused discovery from a sample of absent class members.

(9) Expert Discovery and Judicial Gatekeeping

As discussed above, under *Daubert v. Merrill Dow Pharmaceuticals, Inc.*, 509 U.S. 579 (1993), and *Kumho Tire Co. v. Carmichael*, 526 U.S. 137 (1999), trial courts must perform a gatekeeping function to ensure that scientific and other expert testimony related to technical or specialized knowledge is relevant and reliable. Courts have taken different positions, however, as to the propriety of conducting a *Daubert* challenge at the class certification stage.

See § 5.2. A court's approach to *Daubert* may dictate the extent to which it is willing to permit expert-related discovery.

B.   POST-CERTIFICATION MERITS DISCOVERY IN CLASS ACTIONS

(1)   General Principles

Although full-blown post-certification merits discovery is normally allowed against class representatives, courts generally limit merits discovery against absent class members. Courts are sensitive to the fact that an absent class member's role is very different from that of a class representative. The latter expects to be subjected to considerable discovery, including document requests, interrogatories, and (in many cases) depositions. Absent class members, by contrast, normally assume that their role in the case will be largely passive, at least in the early stages of the case. Nonetheless, if the trial court concludes that discovery of absent class members would be relevant to the issues for trial and is not being sought for harassment purposes, the court has discretion to order such discovery. Indeed, given the stakes in some class action trials, many courts are willing to allow at least some merits discovery against absent class members.

The *Manual for Complex Litigation (4th)* provides several examples of limitations on discovery directed to absent class members, including restricting discovery to only a sample of class members, requiring the use of questionnaires as opposed to potentially more burdensome interrogatories, or severely limiting the number of interrogatories. And, as is often the case with pre-certification discovery, courts often prefer written discovery over depositions.

(2) Discovery of the Unnamed Class Members' Individual Claims

One difference between merits discovery and certification discovery is that, at some point (if the class claims are successful after a classwide trial), individual class members will have to prove their membership in the class as well as their entitlement to damages. Obviously, at that stage of the case, defendants have a compelling argument for seeking discovery from all participating class members (who, at this point, are no longer absent but are coming forward to share in the recovery).

(3) Penalties for Noncompliance with Discovery Requests

Noncompliance with discovery by unnamed class members—particularly when specifically authorized by the court—has occasionally resulted in sanctions. The Seventh Circuit has held that unnamed class members who fail to respond to discovery are subject to all of the sanctions allowed under the Federal Rules of Civil Procedure, including dismissal of their claims with prejudice. *Brennan v. Midwestern United Life Ins. Co.*, 450 F.2d 999 (7th Cir. 1971). A few courts, however, have held that unnamed class members are not parties and thus cannot be sanctioned under Rule 37.

(4) Stay of Discovery Pending Dispositive Motions

If a defendant has filed a dispositive motion, such as a motion to dismiss for failure to state a claim, the defendant may be able to convince the court to stay all discovery pending a ruling on the motion. It is within the discretion of the court, however, to decide whether discovery should continue pending the court's ruling on a dispositive motion.

§ 5.4 ORDERS CONTROLLING CLASS PROCEEDINGS

Rule 23(d) gives the court discretion to issue orders controlling class actions. The Advisory Committee Notes state that this subdivision "is concerned with the fair and efficient conduct of the action." Specifically, Rule 23(d) allows the court to issue orders:

- relating to the course of proceedings;

- requiring notice to class members;

- imposing conditions on the representative parties or intervenors;

- requiring amendment of pleadings to eliminate allegations as to class representation; and

- addressing similar procedural matters.

Rule 23(d)(1) contains five separate subdivisions, which are discussed below. It should be noted at the outset, however, that courts frequently enter orders authorized by Rule 23(d) without identifying the particular subdivision and often without identifying Rule 23(d) at all.

A.   RULE 23(d)(1)(A)

Rule 23(d)(1)(A) states that the court "may issue orders that . . . determine the course of proceedings or prescribe measures to prevent undue repetition or complication in presenting evidence or argument." The court's power under this rule is often exercised in conjunction with other federal rules, such as Rule 16, which governs pretrial conferences.

Among other things, courts have stayed proceedings and excluded intervenors under 23(d)(1)(A). For instance, courts have stayed actions where similar actions are pending before several courts in order to await the outcome of the other litigation. Courts have also temporarily stayed actions in an effort to encourage alternative forms of resolution. In addition, courts have directed that a class be closed to future intervenors in order to simplify the litigation in accordance with the spirit of Rule 23.

Prior to the adoption of the 2003 amendments to Rule 23, the general rule was that the class representatives controlled the decision to appoint lead counsel for the class. In some circumstances, however, courts used their power under (d)(1) to appoint lead counsel. Now, Rule 23(g) requires that the court appoint class counsel. *See* § 3.10.

B.   RULE 23(d)(1)(B)

Rule 23(d)(1)(B)(i) (addressed in § 6.1) provides courts with the power to require that notice be given of any step in the litigation. Additionally, Rule 23(d)(1)(B)(ii) allows the court to "require . . . giving appropriate notice to some or all class members of . . . the proposed extent of the judgment." Rule 23(d)(1)(B)(iii) adds the following to the list of subjects on which the court can order notice: "the [class] members' opportunity to signify whether they consider the representation fair and adequate, to intervene and present claims or defenses, or to otherwise come into the action."

C.   RULE 23(d)(1)(C)

Rule 23(d)(1)(C) enables a court to issue orders that "impose conditions on the representative parties or on intervenors." The Advisory Committee Notes state that this subdivision "reflects the possibility of conditioning the maintenance of a class action, *e.g.*, on the strengthening of the representation . . . and recognizes that the imposition of conditions on intervenors may be required for the proper and efficient conduct of the action." Under this subdivision, the court has the full spectrum of judicial sanctions available for noncompliance with its orders.

Some courts have required that the representative divide one class action into multiple class actions as a condition of maintaining the suit on a classwide basis. This authority is related to the court's power to create subclasses and is often exercised at the class certification stage. *See* § 5.2. The court, however, cannot require that individuals consolidate their individual actions into a class action.

Courts sometimes condition the maintenance of a class action upon strengthening class representation. For instance, a court may order intervention of another class member when concerns exist about the adequacy of the existing class representatives. Likewise, a court may require appointment of additional counsel when it has concerns about the adequacy of existing counsel.

As Rule 23(d)(1)(C) itself contemplates, courts also impose conditions on intervenors in class actions. Such conditions are the same as those imposed on intervenors in ordinary litigation, such as setting a final date for intervention or limiting the extent of participation by intervenors to particular issues. Courts may also impose conditions on communications between class counsel and potential class members. *See* § 13.1.

D.   RULE 23(d)(1)(D)

Rule 23(d)(1)(D) authorizes the court to issue orders "requir[ing] that the pleadings be amended to eliminate allegations about representation of absent persons and that the action proceed accordingly." This subdivision is often invoked in conjunction with a decision under Rule 23(c)(1) denying class certification. When the court denies certification, it may order the class allegations stricken from the complaint and permit the action to proceed only in the plaintiff's individual capacity. The court may also order that the class allegations be amended to reduce the size of the class or to divide the class into subclasses. Additionally, the court may order separate trials of individual issues that are not capable of being handled on a classwide basis.

E.   RULE 23(d)(1)(E)

Rule 23(d)(1)(E) authorizes the court to issue orders that "deal with similar procedural matters." Although this rule allows flexibility in controlling the conduct of class actions, courts generally interpret the words "similar procedural" to indicate that such orders must not alter the ability of parties to present their claims. Permissible powers under Rule 23(d)(1)(E) clearly overlap with those under Rules 23(d)(1)(A) through (d)(1)(D), and courts often do not indicate that they are relying on Rule 23(d)(1)(E).

§ 5.5 SUMMARY JUDGMENT

Interesting issues have arisen when a case raises both class certification and summary judgment issues. At the most basic level, if a court grants summary judgment after class certification is granted and notice is sent to the class, that ruling binds the entire class. On the other hand, if the court grants summary judgment *before* a class is certified, that ruling applies only to the named plaintiffs, not to a non-existent class. But what if the court grants summary judgment after class certification is granted but *before* notice has been sent to the class? Does the summary judgment ruling apply to the entire putative class or only to the named plaintiffs?

In *Schwarzschild v. Tse*, 69 F.3d 293 (9th Cir. 1995), the district court faced this precise situation; it granted class certification and then granted defendants' summary judgment motion before notice of class certification had been sent to the class. In a split decision, the Ninth Circuit held that the defendants' victory applied only to the named plaintiffs. By obtaining summary judgment prior to class notice, the defendants had forfeited their right to have notice of class certification sent to the class. As the court reasoned, "when defendants obtain summary judgment before the class has been properly certified *or before notice has been sent*, they effectively waive their right to have notice circulated to the class. . . ." *Id.* at 297 (emphasis added). *Accord, e.g., Faber v. Ciox Health, LLC*, 944 F.3d 593, 602 (6th Cir. 2019) (citing cases).

§ 5.6 TRIAL STRUCTURE AND EVIDENTIARY ISSUES

Although most class actions settle prior to trial, anecdotal evidence suggests that, in recent years, relatively more cases are going to trial. *See* Robert H. Klonoff, *Class Actions in the Year 2026: A Prognosis*, 65 Emory L.J. 1569 (2016) (citing numerous class actions that went to trial, resulting in both plaintiff and defense verdicts).

In general, the trial court is given broad discretion in fashioning the course of trial proceedings in class actions. Some of the tools used by trial courts in managing class actions are bifurcation (such as dividing the trial into liability and damages phases), Rule 23(d) orders, and the appointment of special masters. Some class action trials, however, have raised significant issues under the Seventh Amendment and the Due Process Clause. This section discusses various trial-related issues.

A.   THE SEVENTH AMENDMENT

(1) Overview

The Seventh Amendment to the U.S. Constitution went largely unmentioned in class action litigation for many years after the 1966 amendments to Rule 23. More recently, however, the Seventh Amendment has become a major issue in some cases, and several court rulings have called into question whether large, bifurcated class actions can be litigated consistent with Seventh Amendment protections.

The Seventh Amendment provides:

In Suits at common law, where the value in controversy shall exceed twenty dollars, the right of trial by jury shall be preserved, *and no fact tried by a jury shall be otherwise reexamined in any Court of the United States, than according to the rules of the common law.* (Emphasis added).

The section of the Seventh Amendment italicized above is known as the Reexamination Clause. The Reexamination Clause was included in the Seventh

Amendment out of concern that jury verdicts from local trial courts would be overturned by appellate courts that would not confine themselves to issues of law but would undertake a *de novo* review of the facts. (Although the Seventh Amendment does not apply to state courts, many states have comparable right-to-jury-trial protections.)

(2) Bifurcated Trials and the Reexamination Clause

As discussed in this section, some courts have utilized bifurcated trials to adjudicate common, classwide issues first, leaving the individual issues to be resolved in subsequent trials. For example, assume a negligence action against a pharmaceutical company for the production of an allegedly defective drug consumed by thousands of potential class members. A common issues trial might be warranted to determine whether the drug causes a particular illness or whether the company misrepresented the side effects of the medication. On the other hand, even if those issues were decided in favor of the class, individual trials would still be required to determine such issues as whether the particular class member in fact used the drug; whether he or she followed the instructions on the package; whether his or her illness was caused by some other source; and so forth.

In the type of bifurcated case described above, a series of juries is frequently used. When large numbers of class members are involved, it is not feasible to assign a single jury to sit through months—or potentially years—of separate trials.

Defendants have expressed concern, however, that this bifurcated procedure requires multiple juries to reexamine the same issues in violation of the Seventh Amendment. Although the Supreme Court has not addressed this precise issue in the context of a class action, a number of federal circuit courts have done so, and several have questioned the constitutionality of various bifurcated jury trials in class actions.

An early opinion raising Seventh Amendment concerns in a class action was *Alabama v. Blue Bird Body Co., Inc.*, 573 F.2d 309 (5th Cir. 1978). In *Blue Bird*, the Fifth Circuit suggested that a trial that bifurcated liability and damages might require examination of overlapping issues by two juries in violation of the Seventh Amendment. For nearly two decades following *Blue Bird*, however, the Reexamination Clause was rarely invoked in class action litigation.

Beginning in 1995, a number of decisions addressed the issue. The first, *In re Rhone-Poulenc Rorer Inc.*, 51 F.3d 1293 (7th Cir. 1995), brought the Reexamination Clause to the forefront of class action litigation. *Rhone-Poulenc* involved a nationwide class of hemophiliacs who contracted HIV from contaminated blood transfusions in the early 1980s. Under the district court's proposed trial plan, an initial jury trial would determine certain common issues, such as whether defendants were negligent. If any defendants were found negligent, individual class members would then be permitted to file their own suits around the country, with the later juries being instructed on the first jury's findings. The

Seventh Circuit held that this plan violated the Reexamination Clause. The court reasoned that issues to be decided by subsequent juries (such as comparative negligence and proximate causation) would overlap with issues decided by the first jury. For example, comparative negligence involves comparing the plaintiff's negligence to the negligence of the defendant, something the first jury would have already done. The court found that these Seventh Amendment problems (in conjunction with other problems identified by the court (*see* § 10.4)) warranted the issuance of a writ of mandamus.

Subsequently, the Fifth Circuit in *Castano v. American Tobacco Co.*, 84 F.3d 734 (5th Cir. 1996), found similar Seventh Amendment problems in a proposed bifurcated class action. *Castano* was a nationwide class action (involving potentially millions of individuals) against the nation's largest tobacco companies. The plaintiffs alleged, among other things, that the defendant tobacco companies negligently failed to inform consumers that nicotine is addictive and that the defendants had manipulated nicotine levels. The district court certified the class and found that manageability concerns—raised by the existence of myriad individualized comparative negligence issues—could be addressed through bifurcated proceedings. Although most of the Fifth Circuit's opinion reversing the district court addressed the deficiencies of the proposed class action under Rule 23(b)(3) (*see* § 11.1), the court also addressed the Seventh Amendment. Relying on both *Blue Bird* and *Rhone-Poulenc*, the court stated that, contrary to the Seventh

Amendment, a second jury's consideration of comparative negligence with respect to individual class members would permit that jury to revisit the first jury's core finding as to negligence.

(3) Criticism of the *Rhone-Poulenc* and *Castano* Approach

Rhone-Poulenc, *Castano*, and other similar cases have raised fundamental questions about the viability of large, bifurcated class actions involving multiple juries. Not all courts, however, have agreed with the Seventh Amendment analysis in *Rhone-Poulenc* and *Castano*.

In *In re Copley Pharmaceutical, Inc., "Albuterol" Products Liability Litigation,* 161 F.R.D. 456 (D. Wyo. 1995), the district court certified a nationwide class action against a pharmaceutical company. Under the court's bifurcated trial plan, the first trial would focus solely on common issues, such as the defendant's negligence, while the second phase, if necessary, would focus on individual issues, such as causation and damages. The *Copley Pharmaceutical* court sharply criticized the *Rhone-Poulenc* decision, reasoning that its approach would essentially prohibit bifurcated trials in class actions. The court pointed out that the Advisory Committee expressly endorsed the use of bifurcated trials in its notes accompanying Rule 23(c)(4). *Accord, e.g., Valentino v. Carter-Wallace, Inc.,* 97 F.3d 1227, 1232 (9th Cir. 1996) (rejecting *Rhone-Poulenc* approach).

In *Robinson v. Metro-North Commuter Railroad Co.,* 267 F.3d 147 (2d Cir. 2001), the Second Circuit, while not expressly criticizing the *Rhone-Poulenc* approach to the Seventh Amendment, suggested that Seventh Amendment reexamination concerns in a bifurcated class action could be avoided by ensuring that the first jury makes precise, detailed findings that can be applied by later juries. And the Third Circuit has noted that "the Seventh Amendment prohibition is not against having two juries *review* the same evidence but rather against having two juries *decide* the same essential issues." *In re Paoli R.R. Yard PCB Litig.*, 113 F.3d 444, 452 n.5 (3d Cir. 1997) (emphasis added).

(4) Other Seventh Amendment Issues

Although most attention has focused on the Seventh Amendment's Reexamination Clause, the basic guarantee of a jury trial for suits at common law may also be implicated in the class action context. In *Cimino v. Raymark Industries, Inc.*, 151 F.3d 297 (5th Cir. 1998), for example, the Fifth Circuit disapproved of a district court's plan to decide over two thousand asbestos-related tort cases using extrapolated data from a much smaller number of cases tried by a jury. The Fifth Circuit held that the use of extrapolated data denied the defendants their Seventh Amendment right to have a jury determine issues of causation separately for each claimant.

In *Ortiz v. Fibreboard Corp.*, 527 U.S. 815 (1999), the Supreme Court, without deciding the issue, expressed concerns that a mandatory settlement-only class action violated absent class members'

Seventh Amendment rights by resolving their claims regardless of their consent.

B. DUE PROCESS: AGGREGATE AND STATISTICAL PROOF

An important due process issue involves the permissibility of proving damages on an aggregate basis through the use of expert or statistical evidence. This is sometimes referred to as "extrapolation," where data for a sample of class members is extrapolated to the class as a whole. Plaintiffs sometimes contend that such forms of classwide proof are necessary to allow large, complicated cases to proceed as class actions, where requiring individualized proof would effectively bar plaintiffs from moving forward as a class. Defendants, however, frequently argue that such aggregate proof violates due process (as well as the Seventh Amendment and applicable state law).

Historically, courts have taken various views on the propriety of dispensing with proof on a plaintiff-by-plaintiff basis. Some courts have condemned the use of aggregate proof as a violation of due process, while others have upheld the approach in certain kinds of complex cases.

In *In re Fibreboard Corp.*, 893 F.2d 706 (5th Cir. 1990), the Fifth Circuit rejected aggregate statistical proof in the context of thousands of asbestos cases. Under the trial plan proposed by the district court, plaintiffs and defendants were each to choose fifteen illustrative plaintiffs, whose individual claims would be tried along with those of the eleven class representatives. Then, based upon the forty-one cases plus expert testimony, the jury would determine total damages suffered by the remaining 2,990 class members. The Fifth Circuit invalidated the trial plan and, in so doing, indicated that such aggregated proof raised due process and Seventh Amendment concerns. The court rejected plaintiffs' theory that "statistical measures of representativeness and commonality [would] be sufficient for the jury to make informed judgments concerning damages." *Id.* at 710. It also rejected the argument that this approach was "the only realistic way of trying these cases," and that "the difficulties faced by the courts as well as the rights of the class members to have their cases tried [cried] powerfully for innovation and judicial creativity." *Id.* at 712. The court noted that such arguments were "compelling," but that "they are better addressed to the representative branches—Congress and the State Legislature." *Id.*

The Fifth Circuit took a similar approach in a subsequent post-trial phase of *In re Fibreboard*, in which the same district court again tried to determine classwide damages through the use of a sample of class members. The appellate court specifically found that the district court's trial plan violated the defendant's Seventh Amendment right to a jury trial on each plaintiff's claim. *Cimino v. Raymark Indus.,* 151 F.3d 297 (5th Cir. 1998).

By contrast, in *Hilao v. Estate of Marcos*, 103 F.3d 767 (9th Cir. 1996), the Ninth Circuit upheld proof of damages on an aggregate basis. The case was a class action under the Alien Tort Claims Act by victims of Ferdinand Marcos's regime in the Philippines. The complaint alleged that the class members and their deceased relatives had been tortured or executed or had "disappeared" as a result of actions by Philippine military or paramilitary groups. The case was certified as a class and went to trial. On the issue of remedies, the district court determined damages for more than 9,000 claims based on approximately 130 randomly selected claims. An expert witness then determined an average award for each type of claim (torture, execution, disappearance) and multiplied the amount by the number of class members in each category. On appeal, the Ninth Circuit rejected defendant's due process and related challenges to the calculation of aggregated damages for the class. The court noted that the approach was "justified by the extraordinarily unusual nature of [the] case." *Id.* at 786. It pointed out that "the time and judicial resources required to try the nearly 10,000 claims in this case would alone make resolution of [the] claims impossible," *id.*, and the "similarity in the injuries suffered by many of the class members would make such an effort, even if it could be undertaken, especially wasteful." *Id.*

In 2011, the Supreme Court weighed in on the issue in *Wal-Mart Stores, Inc. v. Dukes*, 564 U.S. 338 (2011). In *Dukes*, an employment discrimination case, the Ninth Circuit had relied on *Hilao* in refusing to strike down a tentative trial plan that envisioned aggregate proof of classwide damages using economic models. The Supreme Court

unanimously rejected the Ninth Circuit's holding,
reasoning:

> The Court of Appeals believed that it was
> possible to replace [individualized adjudication]
> with Trial by Formula. A sample set of the class
> members would be selected, as to whom liability
> for sex discrimination and the backpay owing as
> a result would be determined in depositions
> supervised by a master. The percentage of
> claims determined to be valid would then be
> applied to the entire class, and the number of
> (presumptively) valid claims thus derived would
> be multiplied by the average backpay award . . .
> to arrive at the entire class recovery. . . . We
> disapprove that novel project. . . . [A] class
> cannot be certified on the premise that Wal-
> Mart will not be entitled to litigate its statutory
> defenses to individual claims.

564 U.S. at 367.

Following *Dukes*, there was concern among
plaintiffs' attorneys about the continued viability of
aggregate statistical proof in class actions. In 2016,
however, the Supreme Court returned to the issue in
Tyson Foods, Inc. v. Bouaphakeo, 136 S. Ct. 1036
(2016).

Tyson Foods was a state-law class action and Fair
Labor Standards Act (FLSA) collective action
brought by workers at a pork-processing facility
alleging entitlement to overtime for time spent
"donning" and "doffing" protective gear and walking
to and from their work areas. The defendant had not

preserved the relevant records, so the plaintiffs relied on an expert statistical model calculating the average donning and doffing time for class members based on a representative sample. At trial, plaintiffs' expert conceded that there was substantial variance among class members' donning and doffing times given their different jobs, equipment, and protective gear. Another plaintiffs' expert conceded that some class members did not suffer injury, because they did not work more than forty hours per week. The jury found for the plaintiffs, and the Eighth Circuit affirmed.

In a 6–2 decision written by Justice Kennedy, the Supreme Court held that, because such statistical proof would have been admissible in an individual case (because the defendant had failed to keep proper records), it was admissible in the aggregate trial. The Court rejected the defendant's (and several amici's) sweeping arguments for a "categorical exclusion" of statistical proof in class actions, noting that such a result "would make little sense." 136 S. Ct. at 1046. The Court explained that statistical proof may be "the only practical means to collect and present the relevant data establishing a defendant's liability" and noted that such aggregate statistical proof is used in various other areas of law. *Id.*

Some commentators have viewed *Tyson Foods* as a narrow decision that will not impact the use of statistical proof in most class actions. Other commentators, however, view *Tyson Foods* as significant precedent for plaintiffs seeking to use aggregate statistical proof in class actions. *See* Robert G. Bone, Tyson Foods *and the Future of*

Statistical Adjudication, 95 N.C. L. Rev. 607 (2017) (articulating the latter viewpoint). Because this issue has arisen most frequently in the mass torts area, it is also mentioned in that context in § 11.1.

CHAPTER 6

NOTICE, OPT-OUT RIGHTS, AND COMMUNICATIONS WITH CLASS MEMBERS

This chapter discusses three core issues in class action law and practice: (1) whether class members are entitled to notice that the class has been certified (as well as notice of other important events in the litigation); (2) whether the class members are entitled to opt out (*i.e.*, remove themselves from the class) and pursue their own individual actions; and (3) whether (and under what circumstances) communications with class members are proper. These issues have generated considerable controversy and a significant body of case law. Notice and opt-out rights are closely related to the due process requirements for binding absent class members, and thus should be considered together with the discussion of *res judicata* and collateral estoppel in Chapter 8 of this text. *See* § 8.4.

§ 6.1 CLASS NOTICE AND OPT-OUT RIGHTS

A. NOTICE AND OPT-OUT RIGHTS IN RULE 23(b)(3) CLASS ACTIONS

Unlike classes under Rules 23(b)(1) and (b)(2), which generally are not subject to notice of certification or a right to opt out, class actions certified under Rule 23(b)(3) are subject to specific notice and opt-out requirements. Rule 23(c)(2)(B) provides that, in class actions maintained under Rule 23(b)(3), the court "must direct to class members the best notice practicable under the circumstances, including individual notice to all members who can be identified through reasonable effort." The notice shall advise each member "that the court will exclude from the class any class member who requests exclusion, stating the time and manner for requesting exclusion."

In *Eisen v. Carlisle & Jacquelin*, 417 U.S. 156 (1974), the Supreme Court addressed the notice requirements of Rule 23(c)(2)—the predecessor to amended Rule 23(c)(2)(B)—in a class action maintained under Rule 23(b)(3). In *Eisen,* the class certified by the district court included millions of buyers and sellers of small quantities of securities. Instead of requiring individual notice to all class members who could be reasonably identified, the district court adopted a less ambitious plan of requiring notice only to (1) all firms that were members of the New York Stock Exchange, (2) approximately 2,000 identifiable class members, and (3) 5,000 class members selected at random, coupled with publication notice in several national newspapers. Relying on Rule 23(c)(2), but also looking to due process case law for guidance, the Supreme Court rejected that approach. The Court held that individual notice was required for the 2,250,000 class members whose names and addresses were known or easily ascertainable. The Court relied upon the language of Rule 23(c)(2), as well as the Advisory Committee Notes to Rule 23, both of which support the view that the notice requirements of Rule

23(c)(2) are not discretionary and are designed to satisfy due process. The Court rejected the high cost of providing individual notice to 2.25 million class members as a reason for departing from the express language and intent of Rule 23(c)(2). The Court also rejected the argument that adequate representation, not notice, is the "touchstone of due process in a class action." *Id.* at 176. It noted that "Rule 23 speaks to notice as well as to adequacy of representation and requires that both be provided." *Id.* Accordingly, the Court concluded that "Rule 23(c)(2) requires that individual notice be sent to all class members who can be identified with reasonable effort." *Id.* at 177.

Consistent with *Eisen*, the lower courts have required notice in Rule 23(b)(3) actions to all class members whose identities can be determined with reasonable effort. If some class members cannot be identified through reasonable effort, a class may still be certified, although the inability to identify a substantial percentage of the class may be a reason for denying class certification.

In some cases, such as consumer cases involving potentially millions of consumers who purchased a product, individual notice to class members is not possible because their names and addresses are not reasonably ascertainable. In such instances, other forms of notice, such as the use of newspapers, television, radio, or the Internet, may be used. Indeed, these other forms of notice may sometimes be ordered as extra protection even when individual notice is ordered.

B.   METHODS FOR PROVIDING NOTICE IN RULE 23(b)(3) CLASS ACTIONS

Historically, when a class member can be identified, individual notice by first-class mail has generally been required. Occasionally, courts will allow bulk mailings or mailings to "occupant." Several courts have held that a class member need not actually receive the mailing to be bound, so long as the method chosen was reasonably calculated to provide notice. Courts have occasionally upheld notices that contained typographical errors or that omitted apartment numbers. Although the Supreme Court in *Phillips Petroleum Co. v. Shutts*, 472 U.S. 797 (1985), stated that "[t]he plaintiff must receive notice," *id.* at 812, the Court has not squarely addressed the circumstances in which a class member may be bound when notice has been sent out in good faith but not received.

For class members who cannot be identified through reasonable efforts, the usual method of notice is through newspaper or journal publications. The publications selected should be those that class members are likely to read. This would include newspapers with wide circulation, publications targeted to class members' geographic area(s), and publications targeted at the particular backgrounds of the class members (such as financial publications when the class members are accountants or financial specialists). Other methods of notice include television, radio, the Internet, and bulletins (such as at the class members' place(s) of employment).

In recent years, electronic forms of notice have become increasingly prevalent. Notice is now frequently given via e-mail, websites, and social media such as Facebook. Some public interest organizations, such as Public Citizen, have even posted videos on YouTube notifying class members of settlements. *See, e.g.*, http://youtube.com/watch?v=ZluS3tutxZU (last visited July 30, 2020) (providing notice of settlement in Paxil litigation).

Recognizing this recent trend, amended Rule 23(c)(2)(B) provides that notice in (b)(3) class actions "may be by United States mail, *electronic means, or other appropriate means*." (Emphasis added). This amendment clarifies that, contrary to the pre-Internet *Eisen* decision, electronic notice may in some circumstances be the most effective form of notice. To reinforce the purpose of the amendment, the Advisory Committee Notes to the amended rule state: "Instead of preferring any one means of notice, . . . the amended rule relies on courts and counsel to focus on the means or combination of means most likely to be effective in the case before the court. The court should exercise its discretion to select appropriate means of giving notice."

It should also be noted that, as an alternative to separate mailings (or individual electronic notice), a court may sometimes order notice as part of a defendant's own mail distribution, such as an enclosure with bills or monthly statements.

For further discussion of the expanding role of technology in class actions, *see* Robert H. Klonoff,

Class Actions in the Year 2026: A Prognosis, 65
Emory L.J. 1569, 1650–54 (2016).

C.   TIMING OF RULE 23(c)(2) NOTICE

Rule 23(c)(2) does not specify when notice should
be sent, leaving the decision to the trial court's
discretion. The rule does make clear, however, that
individual notice in Rule 23(b)(3) cases should allow
time for class members to decide whether to opt out
of the class. Also, as the *Manual for Complex
Litigation (4th)* points out, "[i]f the certification order
is amended to eliminate previously included class
members," notice may be "necessary to inform
affected individuals who might have relied on the
class action to protect their rights." § 21.311.

Occasionally, there may be a reason for delaying
notice. As the *Manual* points out, "[w]hen the parties
are nearing settlement, . . . a reasonable delay in
notice might increase incentives to settle and avoid
the need for separate class notices of certification and
settlement." *Id.*

D.   FORM AND CONTENT OF
RULE 23(c)(2) NOTICE

Rule 23(c)(2)(B) sets forth the content of the notice
required in Rule 23(b)(3) class actions:

The notice must concisely and clearly state in
plain, easily understood language:

(i)   the nature of the action;

(ii) the definition of the class certified;

(iii) the class claims, issues, or defenses;

(iv) that a class member may enter an appearance through counsel if the member so desires;

(v) that the court will exclude from the class any member who requests exclusion, stating when and how members may elect to be excluded;

(vi) the time and manner for requesting exclusion; and

(vii) the binding effect of a class judgment on class members under Rule 23(c)(3).

The notice should also provide information about the case in order to permit each class member recipient to make an informed decision about whether to opt out. As the *Manual for Complex Litigation (4th)* notes, the notice should identify the parties, class representatives, and counsel involved, specify the parties' positions and relief sought, and explain the benefits and risks to class members of remaining in the case versus opting out. In addition, the notice should be written evenhandedly and should not attempt either to encourage or discourage participation in the class action. The Federal Judicial Center's website provides several examples of class action notices. *See* http://www.fjc.gov/content/30125 3/illustrative-forms-class-action-notices-introduction (last visited July 30, 2020).

Before the notice is sent to class members, it is normally submitted to the court for review and approval. Rarely does the court itself actually draft the notice. The requirement that the notice be understandable to class members (*see* Rule 23(c)(2)(B)) may in some circumstances necessitate sending the notice in more than one language.

E.   THE COST OF PROVIDING NOTICE IN RULE 23(b)(3) CLASS ACTIONS

The general rule is that the named plaintiff—not the defendant—should administer the Rule 23(c)(2) notice and pay for it. As noted in § 13.1, however, class counsel is entitled to advance the costs of notice, and under some ethical codes class counsel can absorb those costs without requiring reimbursement from class representatives.

Class counsel, however, is not always required to perform all tasks incident to sending notice, such as ascertaining the identities of class members. Rule 23(d) gives the court discretion to "make appropriate orders" for the fair conduct of the action. Courts have relied upon this rule to require that the defendant perform tasks incident to providing notice when the court determines that the defense can do so with less difficulty or expense than plaintiffs' counsel. When the court orders the defendant to perform notice-related tasks, such as identifying members of the class, the court has discretion to impose the cost on the party ordered to do the task, or to shift the cost to the party that benefits.

In *Oppenheimer Fund, Inc. v. Sanders*, 437 U.S. 340 (1978), the Supreme Court addressed the allocation of costs incurred in sending class notice.

The plaintiffs in that case moved for class certification, but before certification was granted, the plaintiffs moved to redefine the class to reduce its size. The district court denied plaintiffs' motion to redefine the class, which the defendants had opposed, but placed the cost of notifying the originally defined class on the defendants. The Supreme Court repudiated the district court's approach, holding that the cost should have been placed on the plaintiffs. The Court held that the district court erred in finding that the defendants should bear the cost of notice, even though the district court had found that the cost was minor in relation to the defendants' assets. While recognizing that the ability of a party to pay may in some circumstances be a valid consideration in determining who should bear the cost of notice, the Court stated that ability to pay was not the definitive test. Rather, "the test in this respect normally should be whether the cost is substantial; not whether it is 'modest' in relation to ability to pay." *Id.* at 361. The Court also rejected the argument that shifting the expense to the defendants was justified because they kept some of their records on computer tapes, which made it difficult for plaintiffs to retrieve the information. The Court pointed out that there was no indication of a bad faith effort to conceal information from the plaintiffs. The Court also noted that in its earlier decision in *Eisen v. Carlisle & Jacquelin*, 417 U.S. 156 (1974), it had rejected the notion that a district court could conduct a preliminary hearing on the merits to determine which side should pay for the notice.

Following *Oppenheimer*, lower courts have generally imposed the costs of notice on plaintiffs. In exceptional circumstances, however, courts have shifted the cost of providing notice to the defendant when the defendant performs the tasks involved in the ordinary course of business and when the burden on the defendant would not be substantial. For instance, courts have sometimes required telephone companies to include class action notices in monthly billing statements to customers. Courts have also sometimes shifted notice costs to the defendant when the plaintiff is indigent or when the defendant has engaged in wrongful conduct, such as deliberately failing to maintain proper records. Of course, even if the plaintiff (or, more realistically, plaintiff's counsel) must initially incur the costs of notice, he or she may be able to recoup those costs if the case succeeds on the merits.

Although the Supreme Court has not taken up the issue again since *Oppenheimer*, several Justices have expressed concern about the due process implications of taking into account a defendant's wealth in deciding who should pay for class notice. *DTD Enterprises Inc. v. Wells*, 558 U.S. 964 (2009) (Kennedy, J.). In a denial of a petition for writ of *certiorari* Justice Kennedy, joined by Chief Justice Roberts and Justice Sotomayor, noted that "impos[ing] the onerous costs of class notification on a defendant simply because of the relative wealth of the defendant and without any consideration of the underlying merits of the suit" raises "a serious due process question." Justice Kennedy's suggestion that the merits could be considered in deciding whether to shift the cost of notice to the defendant arguably conflicts with *Eisen*, discussed in § 5.2.

F.   ABILITY TO OPT OUT OF A RULE 23(b)(3) CLASS

In addition to requiring notice in Rule 23(b)(3) classes, Rule 23(c)(2)(B) also requires that Rule 23(b)(3) class members be given an opportunity to opt out. Apart from meeting the mechanical and timing requirements set forth in the notice itself, a class member need not meet any standard in order to opt out. For example, the class member need not provide an explanation for his or her decision to opt out.

Opt-out rights serve two related functions. First, a class member's failure to opt out is treated as implied consent to the jurisdiction of the court and implied consent to be bound by the court's judgment, at least if the class has been adequately represented. Second, opt-out rights provide procedural protection to class members who desire to pursue their claims individually.

Courts usually allow thirty to sixty days for a class member to opt out of the class. Opt-out papers returned by class members are usually filed with the court (although other procedures, such as a special address, may be adopted if the class is large and the opt-out process would be administratively cumbersome for the court). Courts have discretion to allow opt outs that were not filed in a timely manner, although normally a court should require good cause for deviating from the deadline set forth in the notice.

It is important to recognize that there is no requirement under Rule 23 or due process that notice actually *reach* every class member. For example, in *Juris v. Inamed Corp.*, 685 F.3d 1294 (11th Cir. 2012), the Eleventh Circuit rejected an absent class member's argument that her individual claims against a silicone breast implant manufacturer should remain viable because she did not have an opportunity to opt out of the classwide settlement. The court stated that notice is adequate to satisfy due process where "the notice afforded reaches a *critical mass* of putative class members, such that the facts underlying certification are contested and approached in a sufficiently adversarial manner. . . ." *Id.* at 1318 (emphasis added).

G.   NOTICE IN RULE 23(b)(1) AND RULE 23(b)(2) CLASS ACTIONS

The notice provisions of Rule 23(c)(2)(B) do not apply to class actions certified under Rule 23(b)(1) or 23(b)(2). The only notice expressly required by Rule 23 for (b)(1) and (b)(2) classes is notice of a proposed settlement pursuant to Rule 23(e).

Courts agree that notice of class certification in Rule 23(b)(1) and Rule 23(b)(2) class actions is not required as a matter of due process when only injunctive or declaratory relief is sought. Since courts generally assume that a (b)(1) or (b)(2) class is homogeneous and lacks conflicts of interest, and since Rule 23(a)(4) requires that such classes be adequately represented, courts have usually found no unfairness in dispensing with notice. On the other hand, when the class seeks damages as well as injunctive or declaratory relief, such as in a discrimination action, some courts have held that due process requires notice and a right to opt out in order to bind class members' individual monetary claims. *See* § 6.1.

In the past, courts that ordered notice in Rule 23(b)(1) or Rule 23(b)(2) classes usually relied upon Rule 23(d)(1)(B)(i), which provides that:

> [T]he court may issue orders that: ... (B) require—to protect class members and fairly conduct the action—giving appropriate notice to some or all of the members of ... any step in the action.

Notice under Rule 23(d)(1)(B)(i) is discretionary. Such notice may be advisable to identify and elicit conflicting interests among class members or to give unnamed class members the opportunity to monitor the adequacy of the class representatives or class counsel. When notice is ordered under Rule 23(d)(1)(B)(i), courts are not bound by the notice requirements of Rule 23(c)(2)(B) and may specify the type of notice appropriate for the particular issue, such as ordering notice only by publication. Also, courts are not required to impose the costs of (d)(1)(B)(i) notice on the plaintiffs and may, in their discretion, impose such costs on the defendant.

The 2003 amendments to Rule 23 explicitly give courts discretion to order notice in (b)(1) and (b)(2) class actions. *See* Rule 23(c)(2)(A) ("For any class certified under Rule 23(b)(1) or (2), the court may direct appropriate notice to the class."). The Advisory Committee Notes to the amendments state that the discretion to order notice in a (b)(1) or (b)(2) class "should be exercised with care." According to the Notes, notice is generally less important in (b)(1) and (b)(2) actions because opt outs are not permitted, and the costs of notice may "cripple actions that do not seek damages." The Notes further point out that, when notice *is* ordered in a (b)(1) or (b)(2) class action, courts should exercise "discretion and flexibility" in the method of notice. "Informal methods," such as "[a] simple posting in a place visited by many class members, directing attention to a source of more detailed information, may suffice."

H.   OPT-OUT RIGHTS IN RULE 23(b)(1) AND RULE 23(b)(2) CLASSES

Rules 23(b)(1) and (b)(2) do not, by their terms, allow for opt outs. For this reason, (b)(1) and (b)(2) classes are frequently referred to as "mandatory" (non-opt-out) classes. *See* § 4.1. Courts agree that due process does not require opt outs when only non-monetary relief is sought. The more difficult question is whether notice and opt-out rights are required, even in a (b)(1) or (b)(2) class action, when a significant component of the claim is for damages.

In *Phillips Petroleum Co. v. Shutts*, 472 U.S. 797 (1985), the Supreme Court stated that notice and opt-out rights were required in suits "wholly or predominately" for money damages, *id.* at 812, but left open whether notice and opt-out rights were required in (b)(1) or (b)(2) actions that included monetary claims.

In an important post-*Shutts* decision, the Ninth Circuit held, in the context of an antitrust settlement under (b)(1) and (b)(2), that class members could not be barred from bringing individual damages actions even though such claims had been settled as part of a mandatory class. *Brown v. Ticor Title Ins. Co.*, 982 F.2d 386 (9th Cir. 1992). The court reasoned that due process required notice and opt-out rights before monetary claims could be settled. The Supreme Court granted *certiorari* in the case but ultimately dismissed the writ on procedural grounds. *Ticor Title Ins. Co. v. Brown, cert. dismissed as improvidently granted*, 511 U.S. 117 (1994).

The Supreme Court granted review in a later case to decide the issue, but ended up again dismissing the writ as improvidently granted. *Adams v. Robertson, cert. dismissed as improvidently granted*, 520 U.S. 83 (1997). And, while the issue was raised by the petitioner in *Ortiz v. Fibreboard Corp.*, 527 U.S. 815 (1999) (*see* § 4.2), the Supreme Court in *Ortiz* did not reach the due process issues but instead held that the class settlement violated Rule 23(b)(1)(B). Nor did the Court resolve the issue in *Dukes*, although the Court did state that "the serious possibility [that due process may require notice and opt-out rights even when the monetary claims do not predominate] provides [an] additional reason not to read Rule 23(b)(2) to include the [backpay claims at issue]." 564 U.S. at 363.

In short, the Supreme Court has addressed the topic of notice and opt-out rights in (b)(1) and (b)(2) actions but has not provided definitive guidance. For an in-depth discussion of the issue in the context of Rule 23(b)(1)(A) and (b)(1)(B) class actions, *see* Robert H. Klonoff, *Class Actions for Monetary Relief Under Rule 23(b)(1)(A) and (b)(1)(B): Does Due Process Require Notice and Opt-Out Rights?*, 82 Geo. Wash. L. Rev. 798 (2014).

Because of these lurking due process issues, some courts in (b)(1) and (b)(2) actions permit opt outs, relying on (1) their authority under Rule 23(d)(2) to issue notice to the class or (2) their authority under Rule 23(d)(5) to issue appropriate procedural orders. Other courts certify "hybrid" classes—mandatory classes for non-monetary claims and opt-out classes for damages claims. *See* § 4.3. Still other courts permit mandatory classes even when claims for money are involved because the monetary component is not substantial or does not depend on class members' individualized circumstances.

I. OTHER NOTICES PURSUANT TO RULE 23(d)(1)

Rule 23(d)(1)(B) may be used for many notice purposes beyond simply notifying class members of (b)(1) or (b)(2) certification. For instance, the *Manual for Complex Litigation (4th)* suggests that (d)(1)(B) may be used to notify class members if a previously certified class has been decertified or if the scope of a previously certified class has been narrowed. Rule 23(d)(1)(B) may also be used to supplement, correct, or modify prior notices. (The *Manual* indicates that the party responsible for an error in a prior notice should bear the cost of a corrective notice.)

J. NOTICE TO ABSENT CLASS MEMBERS OF A PROPOSED SETTLEMENT, DISMISSAL, OR COMPROMISE UNDER RULE 23(e)

Rule 23(e)(1)(B) provides that "[t]he court must direct notice in a reasonable manner to all class members who would be bound by [a proposed settlement, dismissal, or compromise]." Unlike Rule 23(c)(2)(B) notice, which applies only to classes certified under Rule 23(b)(3), Rule 23(e)'s notice provision contains no such limitation and thus applies to classes under (b)(1), (b)(2), and (b)(3).

Notice is required in cases when a proposed settlement, dismissal, or compromise occurs *after* certification as well as in cases in which certification and the proposal occur at the same time. Rule 23(e) does not articulate the contents or method of providing notice, leaving such matters to the court's discretion. Certain items, however, are common in a settlement notice. According to the *Manual for Complex Litigation (4th)*, the notice should define the class and any subclasses, and contain the terms of the proposal (including attorneys' fees), information about the hearing (*e.g.*, date, time, and place), procedures for distributing any settlement proceeds, any special benefits awarded to class representatives, options open to class members (and deadlines for acting upon them), methods for objecting to the proposal, and ways of seeking additional information about the proposal.

Although Rule 23 does not specify whether individual notice of a settlement is required, the Advisory Committee Notes to the 2003 Amendments state:

> Reasonable settlement notice may require individual notice in the manner required by Rule 23(c)(2)(B) for certification notice to a Rule 23(b)(3) class. Individual notice is appropriate, for example, if class members are required to take action—such as filing claims—to participate in the judgment, or if the court orders a settlement opt-out opportunity under Rule 23(e)(3) [discussed in § 9.1].

Thus, litigators who are devising notice of a settlement need to consider whether individual notice is required. The ALI takes the position that individual notice of settlement should not be required when the small size of the claims makes such notice economically unjustified. *Principles of the Law of Aggregate Litigation* § 3.04(b) at 204.

One issue that previously divided courts was whether Rule 23(e) applied to settlements, dismissals, or compromises with named plaintiffs *prior* to certification. Some courts held that actions commenced under Rule 23 should be treated as class actions for purposes of dismissal, settlement, or compromise from the moment the action is commenced. As a result, these courts held that notice of a pre-certification settlement, dismissal, or compromise with the named plaintiffs must be given to all putative class members. Other courts, however, held that Rule 23(e) notice was not required in pre-certification settlements, dismissals, or compromises absent evidence of collusion between the parties or the risk of prejudice to the putative class. The 2003 amendments resolved this issue by not requiring notice when only the class representatives are bound by a settlement, dismissal, or compromise. *See* § 9.1. The ALI takes issue with the approach of the 2003 amendment and would require court approval for pre-certification settlement, dismissal, or compromise of named plaintiffs' claims. *Principles of the Law of Aggregate Litigation* § 3.02(b) at 193.

K.   NOTICE OF DECERTIFICATION

Assume that a class is certified and notice is provided to the class members. If the class is later decertified, must notice of the decertification be provided? The Seventh Circuit addressed this issue in *Culver v. City of Milwaukee*, 277 F.3d 908 (7th Cir. 2002). There, the court held that such notice was required. The court noted that the filing of a class action tolls the statute of limitations (*see* § 8.1) but that the statute starts to run again upon decertification. "Unless [class members] are notified that the suit is dismissed, they may fail to file their own suits and . . . find themselves time barred without knowing it." *Id.* at 914. The court qualified its ruling by stating that notice was not required if the class would not be prejudiced (*e.g.,* when the class likely "learn[ed] of [the decertification] through other channels.") *Id.* at 915. A post-*Culver* case within the

Seventh Circuit has held that notice of decertification is not required for mandatory classes in which notice was not required at the time of certification, at least when the initial certification was not highly publicized. *Clarke v. Ford Motor Co.*, 228 F.R.D. 631 (E.D. Wis. 2005).

§ 6.2 COMMUNICATIONS WITH CLASS MEMBERS

A.   COMMUNICATIONS WITH POTENTIAL CLASS MEMBERS BEFORE A CLASS ACTION IS FILED

Courts have no authority to regulate communications with potential class members until a class action suit is actually filed. Before filing, only the relevant rules of professional conduct regulate attorney contact with potential class members. *See* § 13.1.

B.   COMMUNICATIONS WITH POTENTIAL CLASS MEMBERS BETWEEN FILING AND CLASS CERTIFICATION

(1) Reasons for Contacting Class Members

Plaintiffs, defendants, and their respective counsel have an interest in contacting potential class members after the lawsuit has been filed, but before the case has been certified as a class action. Plaintiffs and their counsel may seek to inform potential class members of the existence of the lawsuit, obtain information concerning the underlying facts from individuals who may be similarly situated to the class representatives, recruit additional class representatives, and obtain financial contributions for prosecuting the action. Defendants and their counsel may seek to obtain information concerning the underlying facts—such as conflicts among the class members—to bolster their opposition to class certification. They may also want to communicate with potential class members to obtain individual settlements or to encourage opt outs. The proper timing and content of communications with potential class members are subjects of significant debate, particularly given the serious potential for abuse when large numbers of unrepresented persons are the intended targets.

(2) Use of Rule 23(d) to Regulate Communications with Class Members

Rule 23(d)(1)(C) provides that the court may enter appropriate orders "impos[ing] conditions on the representative parties or on intervenors," and Rule 23(d)(1)(E) "deal[s] with similar procedural matters." Courts have regulated communications with potential class members using Rule 23(d) to protect against: (1) solicitation of class members in violation of the ethical rules; (2) improper solicitation of funds from persons who are not formal parties; (3) unauthorized communications by counsel or parties that misrepresent the status, purpose, or impact of the litigation; and (4) attempts to persuade class members to opt out of the class. Because of these concerns, many courts prior to 1981 routinely prohibited or limited contacts between counsel and absent class members. In 1981, the Supreme Court took up the issue in *Gulf Oil Co. v. Bernard*, 452 U.S. 89 (1981), discussed below.

(3) The *Gulf Oil* Decision

In *Gulf Oil*, the Supreme Court invalidated a district court's protective order banning all communications between the parties (or their counsel) and potential or actual class members, without the court's prior approval. The district court made no findings of fact and did not write an opinion in support of its order. Without deciding whether the order violated the First Amendment as a prior restraint on free speech, the Supreme Court held that the order was an abuse of the district court's discretion under Rule 23(d). The Court noted that, while a trial court had discretion "to enter appropriate orders governing the conduct of counsel and parties," such "discretion [was] not unlimited." *Id.* at 100. Rather, orders restricting communications must be "based on a clear record and specific findings that reflect a weighing of the need for a limitation and the potential interference with the rights of the parties." *Id.* at 101. In addition, the balancing test "should result in a carefully drawn order that limits speech as little as possible, consistent with the rights of the parties under the circumstances." *Id.* at 102. Under the *Gulf Oil* facts, the Court found that, among other things, the district court's order impeded the ability of plaintiffs' counsel to inform potential class members of the existence of the lawsuit. Although the Court based its holding on Rule 23(d), it did note that the district court's order involved "serious restraints on expression." *Id.* at 104.

(4) Developments After *Gulf Oil*

In light of *Gulf Oil*, most courts have invalidated local rules containing communication bans similar to the one struck down by the Supreme Court. A few courts have also continued to ban blanket restrictions of communications as unconstitutional prior restraints of free speech, the issue not reached by the Supreme Court in *Gulf Oil*.

Consistent with *Gulf Oil*, the *Manual for Complex Litigation (4th)* states that "[m]ost judges are reluctant to restrict communications between the parties or their counsel and potential class members, except when necessary to prevent serious misconduct." § 21.12. The *Manual* also notes that, although there is no formal attorney-client relationship between plaintiffs' counsel and potential class members prior to class certification, "an attorney acting on behalf of a putative class must act in the best interests of the class as a whole." *Id.* Thus the court has authority to intervene in instances in which communications with class members are abusive. *Id.* Plaintiffs' counsel should be free, however, to supply information, respond to inquiries, and obtain information necessary to represent the putative class. *Id.*

(5) Application of *Gulf Oil* to Defense Communications

Some courts have distinguished between communications by plaintiffs' counsel and those by defense counsel, holding that *Gulf Oil* does not protect the communications by the defense. Such courts reason that the Supreme Court in *Gulf Oil* was trying to protect the ability of plaintiffs' counsel to represent the class effectively. By contrast, a defendant's stated reason for contacting class members is generally to obtain information to defend the lawsuit, a need that can be satisfied through discovery. Other courts, however, use the *Gulf Oil* balancing test to evaluate all communications with potential class members, whether initiated by plaintiffs or defendants, and prohibit communications that are misleading or are designed to prevent participation in the class action. Some post-*Gulf Oil* courts have regulated defendants' attempts to contact potential class members about settlement before a class is certified. Most courts, however, permit defendants to discuss settlement with unnamed class members prior to certification as long as defendants do not provide false or misleading information or attempt to influence potential class members' decisions regarding whether to opt out of the class. Of course, as the *Manual for Complex Litigation (4th)* notes, "[e]thics rules restricting communications with individuals represented by counsel may apply to restrict a defendant's communications" with named plaintiffs. § 21.12.

(6) Correcting Misleading or Otherwise Improper Communications

If a court determines that a communication by counsel is misleading or otherwise improper, it has authority under Rule 23(d)(1) to issue a corrective or clarifying notice. *See* § 6.1.

C. COMMUNICATIONS WITH CLASS MEMBERS AFTER CLASS CERTIFICATION

A basic rule of legal ethics is that, in representing a client, an attorney may not communicate regarding the subject matter of the representation with a party who is known to be represented by an attorney, absent the consent of that attorney. One issue that sometimes arises in class actions is whether this rule applies to unnamed class members after a class is certified. Most courts hold that upon certification of a class, an attorney-client relationship arises between plaintiffs' counsel and all members of the class. *See* § 13.1. Accordingly, once a class is certified, defense counsel must obtain the consent of class counsel before contacting class members. This principle applies even during the opt-out period following certification, in order to avoid undue influence on class members' opt-out decisions.

Because there is often an ongoing business relationship between a defendant and class members (for example, when class members are current employees or business affiliates of the defendant), courts have allowed post-certification communications between defendants and class members concerning day-to-day business operations.

In such cases, defendants are generally prohibited from discussing the pending lawsuit.

CHAPTER 7

MULTI-JURISDICTIONAL AND STATE COURT CLASS ACTIONS

Nationwide or other multi-jurisdictional class actions enable a court to adjudicate potentially millions of class members' claims in a single proceeding. As a result, such class actions may be more efficient for the parties and the judicial system than a series of smaller class actions. In addition, nationwide class actions may allow the parties to achieve a uniform national result, as opposed to a series of potentially conflicting rulings. Yet courts are generally cautious in certifying such classes because of potentially difficult issues under Rule 23 and the Due Process Clause. This chapter addresses those issues.

In light of the Class Action Fairness Act (CAFA), most multistate class actions are now heard in federal court. *See* § 8.3. Nonetheless, a significant number of class actions are still litigated in state court. For that reason, this chapter also surveys how various state courts approach class action issues.

§ 7.1 NATIONWIDE AND OTHER MULTI-JURISDICTIONAL CLASS ACTIONS

A. STANDARDS FOR CERTIFYING A MULTI-JURISDICTIONAL CLASS

The decision to certify any class, including a nationwide or other multi-jurisdictional class, is committed to the discretion of the trial court. In exercising that discretion, however, the court must recognize that the consequences of certifying—or not certifying—such a class may be profound. Certification of a multi-jurisdictional class results in only one action to adjudicate claims that could involve millions of class members. On the other hand, not certifying such a class could potentially leave millions of people without an effective remedy.

Because of the high stakes involved in adjudicating a nationwide or other multi-jurisdictional class action, some defendants have argued that such classes are never appropriate for certification. In *Califano v. Yamasaki*, 442 U.S. 682 (1979), the Supreme Court "decline[d] to adopt [such an] extreme position." *Id.* at 702. The Court emphasized, however, that a district court should take special care to ensure that a nationwide class is indeed appropriate.

In certifying a multi-jurisdictional class, a trial court must examine the threshold certification requirements and all of the requirements of Rule 23(a) and (b), as discussed in earlier chapters in this text. One important inquiry unique to such class actions is whether the claims are in fact multi-jurisdictional in scope. For example, in *State of Alabama v. Blue Bird Body Co.*, 573 F.2d 309 (5th Cir. 1978), the Fifth Circuit decertified a nationwide class in an antitrust action because the proof offered by plaintiffs to support a nationwide antitrust conspiracy was limited to a particular state, and there was no evidence of a single conspiracy that was national in scope.

An additional issue in multi-jurisdictional class actions is whether such a suit would frustrate other ongoing class action cases. Although it is not fatal that a multi-jurisdictional class could, in effect, swallow up smaller classes around the country, the court must determine whether one large class is the superior method for litigating the issues. Courts often refrain from certifying multi-jurisdictional classes out of deference to more limited suits already underway, such as class actions limited to a single state.

For example, in *In re American Medical Systems, Inc.*, 75 F.3d 1069 (6th Cir. 1996), the Sixth Circuit granted mandamus and reversed a district court order certifying a national class of penile implant claimants, partly because there were "previously-filed cases at more advanced stages of litigation." *Id.* at 1088. The court noted that the certification order "threaten[ed] to throw preexisting cases into disarray," and "[t]he waste of judicial resources due to duplicative proceedings [was] plain and [was] not correctable on appeal." *Id.* Numerous courts, however, have certified multi-jurisdictional class actions notwithstanding the existence of other more limited class actions involving the same issues.

B.   PROCEDURAL AND MANAGEABILITY ISSUES

(1) Overview

As discussed in § 4.4, Rule 23(b)(3)(D) requires that a court consider "the likely difficulties in managing a class action." Two manageability issues are of particular concern in the context of multi-jurisdictional class actions: (1) due process constraints on binding out-of-state class members to a proceeding; and (2) choice-of-law issues precipitated by the scope of the proposed class.

(2) Due Process Constraints on Multi-Jurisdictional Classes

A nationwide or other multi-jurisdictional class action will, by definition, involve claims of absent class members who neither reside in, nor have any connection with, the state in which the case was brought. If these class members from distant states were individual *defendants*, due process would bar them from being bound by the forum court's judgment unless the defendants had "minimum contacts" with the forum state. *International Shoe Co. v. Washington*, 326 U.S. 310 (1945). Although individual plaintiffs in non-class cases are not subject to a "minimum contacts" inquiry, since they are the ones who have *chosen* the particular forum, that rationale does not necessarily apply in multi-jurisdictional class actions. The unnamed class members almost certainly had no input concerning where the class action was brought.

The Supreme Court addressed these concerns in *Phillips Petroleum Co. v. Shutts*, 472 U.S. 797 (1985). *Shutts* involved a state court class action brought under a Kansas class action rule similar to Federal Rule 23. The suit was brought on behalf of thousands of royalty owners who claimed that they were entitled to interest on delayed royalty payments for natural gas produced by Phillips Petroleum. The class members resided throughout the United States and in several foreign countries, and the leases from which the natural gas was produced related to land located in multiple states. Less than one percent of the leases were on land located in Kansas, and only a small percentage of class members had any connection to Kansas. After the state trial court certified the class pursuant to Kansas' equivalent to Rule 23(b)(3), several thousand class members exercised their opt-out rights, and more than one thousand additional class members were excluded because notice could not be delivered. After finding the defendant, Phillips Petroleum, liable, the trial court applied Kansas substantive law in computing damages, regardless of where the individual plaintiffs or natural gas leases were situated, and regardless of whether the class members could have obtained similar damage awards in their home states. The Kansas trial court reasoned that, absent compelling circumstances (which it found did not exist), the law of the forum (*i.e.*, Kansas) controlled all claims. The trial court also justified its choice-of-law selection by noting that the class members had indicated a desire for Kansas law to apply by failing to opt out of the class.

The defendant objected to class certification and to the use of Kansas law to compute damages. It argued that, because most of the class members were not from Kansas, they lacked minimum contacts with the forum state, and thus were free to re-litigate the same issues if they were unhappy with the outcome.

Both the trial court and the Kansas Supreme Court rejected these arguments. The U.S. Supreme Court granted *certiorari* to decide two questions affecting multi-jurisdictional class actions: (1) whether due process permits non-resident plaintiffs lacking minimum contacts to be included in a class; and (2) whether due process is violated if a court uses the substantive law of the forum state instead of conducting a more focused choice-of-law analysis.

With respect to the first issue, the Court held that the Due Process Clause does not require that absent class members in a class action receive the same procedural protections as out-of-state defendants. The Court observed that an absent class member is not subject to burdens that are typically imposed on a civil defendant: They do not need to hire separate attorneys, usually do not have to litigate any counterclaims or cross-claims, and rarely are liable for court costs or fees. Indeed, the Court observed that "an absent class action plaintiff is not required to do anything." *Id.* at 810. The Court thus held that a forum state may exercise jurisdiction over the claim of an absent class member, even though that person does not possess the minimum contacts required for personal jurisdiction over a defendant. The Court went on to hold, however, that certain procedural due process protections must still be provided. Specifically, in order to be bound, the class members must receive notice of the action (and an opportunity to be heard, in person or through counsel) and must be given "an opportunity to remove [themselves] from the class by executing and returning an 'opt-out' or 'request for exclusion' form to the court." *Id.* at 812.

Additionally, due process requires that the named plaintiff adequately represent the interests of the class as a whole. The Court rejected the contention that due process requires absent plaintiffs to affirmatively opt *into* a class as opposed to being included in the class unless they have affirmatively opted *out*. Moreover, in an important footnote, the Court stated that it was not deciding whether the same safeguards apply to classes seeking primarily non-monetary relief. *Id.* at 811 n.3.

On the second issue, the Supreme Court held that it was a violation of due process for the trial court to apply Kansas law to the entire nationwide class given that (1) most class members had no relationship to Kansas, and (2) Kansas law differed materially from the laws of the various other states involved. The Court initially explained that the law of the forum *could* be applied "if it is not in conflict with that of any other jurisdiction connected to [the] suit." *Id.* at 816. When there is a conflict, however, a forum's substantive law may be applied only if the forum has significant contacts with the transaction giving rise to the controversy, so that using the law of the forum is not arbitrary or fundamentally unfair. Noting that the laws of other states connected to the underlying transaction differed significantly from those of Kansas, and that Kansas had no interest in the vast majority of claims, the Court reasoned that the application of Kansas law to every claim in the case was "sufficiently arbitrary and unfair as to exceed constitutional limits." *Id.* at 822. The Court also stated that the class members' purported "desire for Kansas law" was of "little relevance."

It is important to underscore that *Shutts*, by its terms, does not necessarily prohibit the application of a single state's law to a multistate class action. The question of what specific law(s) should apply depends on the choice-of-law rules of the state where the court is located. *See* § 4.4. *Shutts* merely insists that the application of the selected laws not be arbitrary or unfair.

In 2017, the Supreme Court decided *Bristol-Myers Squibb Co. v. Superior Court of California*, 137 S. Ct. 1773 (2017). Following a series of cases beginning with *Daimler AG v. Bauman*, 571 U.S. 117 (2014) (addressing general jurisdiction), the Court took a narrow view of specific jurisdiction in the context of a mass action. The case involved a suit in California state court by more than 600 plaintiffs (most of whom were not California residents) against Bristol-Myers Squibb Company (BMS) asserting state-law claims based on injuries allegedly caused by BMS's blood-thinning drug, Plavix. BMS is incorporated in Delaware and has its headquarters in New York, but it conducts substantial business in California. BMS did not develop the drug or create a marketing strategy for it in California, and California sales of the drug were just over one percent of BMS's nationwide sales revenue. BMS argued lack of personal jurisdiction, but the California courts rejected that argument. The California Supreme Court applied a " 'sliding scale' " approach, stating that " 'the more wide ranging the defendant's forum contacts, the more readily is shown a connection between the forum contacts and the claim.' " *Bristol-Myers*, 137 S. Ct. at 1778–79. The United States

Supreme Court reversed in an 8–1 decision, with only Justice Sotomayor dissenting. The Court found that there was no basis for specific jurisdiction: "What is needed—and what is missing here [for the non-California plaintiffs]—is a connection between the forum and the specific claims at issue." *Id*. at 1781. The Court noted that "[t]he relevant plaintiffs are not California residents and do not claim to have suffered harm in that State." *Id*. at 1782. Moreover, "all of the conduct giving rise to the nonresidents' claims occurred elsewhere." *Id*.

The Court indicated that *Shutts* was not to the contrary:

> The Kansas court [in *Shutts*] exercised personal jurisdiction over the claims of nonresident class members, and the defendant, Phillips Petroleum, argued that this violated the due process rights of these class members because they lacked minimum contacts with the State. According to the defendant, the out-of-state class members should not have been kept in the case unless they affirmatively opted in, instead of merely failing to opt out after receiving notice.

> Holding that there had been no due process violation, the Court explained that the authority of a State to entertain the claims of nonresident class members is entirely different from its authority to exercise jurisdiction over an out-of-state defendant. Since *Shutts* concerned the due process rights of *plaintiffs*, it has no bearing on the question presented here.

> . . . Indeed, the Court stated specifically that its "discussion of personal jurisdiction [did not] address class actions where the jurisdiction is asserted against a *defendant* class. *Shutts, supra,* at 812 n.3.

Bristol-Myers, 137 S. Ct. at 1782–83 (emphases and second alteration in original).

In finding for the defendant, the majority rejected what it called plaintiffs' "parade of horribles," *id.* at 1783, noting:

> Our decision does not prevent the California and out-of-state plaintiffs from joining together in a consolidated action in the States that have general jurisdiction over BMS. BMS concedes that such suits could be brought in either New York or Delaware. . . . Alternatively, the plaintiffs who are residents of a particular State—for example, the 92 plaintiffs from Texas and the 71 from Ohio—could probably sue together in their home States. In addition, since our decision concerns the due process limits on the exercise of specific jurisdiction by a State, we leave open the question whether the Fifth Amendment imposes the same restrictions on the exercise of personal jurisdiction by a federal court. *See Omni Capital Int'l, Ltd. v. Rudolf Wolff & Co.,* 484 U.S. 97, 102 n.5 (1987).

Bristol-Myers, 137 S. Ct. at 1783–84.

Justice Sotomayor dissented. She had previously taken issue with the Court's approach to general jurisdiction in (among other cases) *Daimler AG,* which limited general jurisdiction over a corporation to states where the defendant was "at home," 571 U.S. at 122, generally its state of incorporation and the state where it has its principal place of business.

In *Bristol-Myers*, Justice Sotomayor stated that "the Court takes its first step toward a similar contraction of specific jurisdiction by holding that a corporation that engages in a nationwide course of conduct cannot be held accountable in a state court by a group of injured people unless all of those people were injured in the forum state." 137 S. Ct. at 1784 (Sotomayor, J., dissenting). She noted that the company's "advertising and distribution efforts were national in scope," that the company contracted with a California-based distributor, that the company's conduct was the same as to all plaintiffs, and that the exercise of jurisdiction over BMS was "reasonable." *Id.* at 1786 (Sotomayor, J., dissenting). She further noted that the case was likely to have profound consequences with respect to the ability to litigate mass actions:

> First, and most prominently, the Court's opinion in this case will make it profoundly difficult for plaintiffs who are injured in different States by a defendant's nationwide course of conduct to sue that defendant in a single, consolidated action. The holding of today's opinion is that such an action cannot be brought in a State in which only some plaintiffs were injured. Not to worry, says the majority: The plaintiffs here could have sued Bristol-Myers in New York or Delaware; could

"probably" have subdivided their separate claims into 34 lawsuits in the States in which they were injured; and might have been able to bring a single suit in federal court (an "open . . . question"). Even setting aside the majority's caveats, what is the purpose of such limitations? What interests are served by preventing the consolidation of claims and limiting the forums in which they can be consolidated? The effect of the Court's opinion today is to eliminate nationwide mass actions in any State other than those in which a defendant is " 'essentially at home.' " *See Daimler AG*, 571 U.S. at 127. Such a rule hands one more tool to corporate defendants determined to prevent the aggregation of individual claims, and forces injured plaintiffs to bear the burden of bringing suit in what will often be far flung jurisdictions.

Second, the Court's opinion today may make it impossible to bring certain mass actions at all. After this case, it is difficult to imagine where it might be possible to bring a nationwide mass action against two or more defendants headquartered and incorporated in different States. There will be no State where both defendants are "at home," and so no State in which the suit can proceed. What about a nationwide mass action brought against a defendant not headquartered or incorporated in the United States? Such a defendant is not "at home" in any State. Especially in a world in which defendants are subject to general jurisdiction in only a handful of States, the effect of today's opinion will be to curtail—and in some cases eliminate—plaintiffs' ability to hold corporations fully accountable for their nationwide conduct.

The majority chides [plaintiffs] for conjuring a "parade of horribles," but says nothing about how suits like those described here will survive its opinion in this case. The answer is simple: They will not.

137 S. Ct. at 1789 (Sotomayor, J., dissenting).

Justice Sotomayor recognized that the case involved a lawsuit brought by hundreds of individual plaintiffs, as opposed to a class action brought by representative plaintiffs:

The Court today does not confront the question whether its opinion here would also apply to a class action in which a plaintiff injured in the forum State seeks to represent a nationwide class of plaintiffs, not all of whom were injured there. *Cf. Devlin v. Scardelletti*, 536 U.S. 1, 9–10 (2002) ("Nonnamed class members . . . may be parties for some purposes and not for others"); *see also* Diane P. Wood, *Adjudicatory Jurisdiction and Class Actions*, 62 Ind. L. J. 597, 616–17 (1987).

Bristol-Myers, 137 S. Ct. at 1789 n.4 (Sotomayor, J., dissenting).

When applied alongside *Daimler AG, Bristol-Myers* is likely to have a significant impact on plaintiffs' ability to bring a mass action in their chosen forum when the suit involves claimants from multiple states. To assert general jurisdiction, the defendant must be "at home" in the forum. To assert specific jurisdiction, plaintiffs will have to demonstrate a substantial connection between the defendant and the forum (in *Bristol-Myers*, the Court found no connection between California and the claims of the non-Californians). In a pharmaceutical case, for example, minimum contacts might be demonstrated if significant clinical trials and testing occurred in the forum state.

The majority left open the possibility that the result could be different in federal court because the applicable due process standard is the Fifth Amendment rather than the Fourteenth Amendment (citing *Omni Capital*). But the Fifth Amendment inquiry focuses on whether Congress has authorized nationwide service of process, *BNSF Ry. Co. v. Tyrrell*, 137 S. Ct. 1549, 1555–56 (2017), something that is not common.

The question whether *Bristol-Myers* applies in the class action context was squarely addressed by the Seventh Circuit in *Mussat v. IQVIA, Inc.*, 953 F.3d 441 (7th Cir. 2020). In *Mussat*, the plaintiff received unsolicited faxes from the defendant and brought a nationwide putative class action alleging violations of the Telephone Consumer Protection Act (TCPA). Defendant argued that, under *Bristol-Myers*, the case could not be brought as a nationwide class because the district court lacked personal jurisdiction over the non-Illinois class members. The district court agreed, but the Seventh Circuit reversed, holding that *Bristol-Myers* "[did] not apply to the case of a nationwide class action filed in a federal court under a federal statute." *Id.* at 443. The court pointed out that *Bristol-Myers* itself did not involve a class action and that, indeed, "the Supreme Court . . . expressly reserved whether its holding extended to the federal courts at all." *Id.* at 448. In examining the issue, the Seventh Circuit noted that both subject matter jurisdiction and venue focus only on the named representatives, and that there was "no reason why personal jurisdiction should be treated any differently[.]" *Id.* at 447. The court further noted that "[t]he rules for class certification support a focus on the named representative for purposes of personal jurisdiction." *Id.* at 448. Thus, the court held that "there is no need to locate each and every one of them (the nonparties) and conduct a separate personal-jurisdiction analysis of their claims" in this case. *Id.*

It is very likely that other circuits will address this issue. (Several district courts have addressed the issue, with conflicting approaches, but the Seventh Circuit is the first appellate court to decide the question.) Defendants will no doubt continue to raise the *Bristol-Myers* argument in multistate class actions, notwithstanding *Mussat*. If a circuit conflict develops, it will be up to the Supreme Court to resolve the conflict.

(3) Post-*Shutts* Choice-of-Law Issues in Multi-Jurisdictional Class Actions

In light of *Shutts*, a court in a multi-jurisdictional Rule 23(b)(3) class action may not resolve choice-of-law determinations by arbitrarily selecting one state's law to apply to all class members. As noted in § 4.4, federal courts in diversity cases must apply the law of the state whose law would govern if the case were being tried in state court. In some nationwide tort suits, for example, this could mean that the laws of as many as fifty states (plus the District of Columbia) could apply within a single lawsuit. This is true regardless of whether the nationwide class action is litigated in federal or state court.

Numerous courts have addressed choice-of-law issues in multi-jurisdictional class actions. The Supreme Court in *Amchem Products, Inc. v. Windsor*, 521 U.S. 591 (1997), recognized that choice-of-law concerns could weigh against certification. Likewise, in *Castano v. American Tobacco Co.*, 84 F.3d 734 (5th Cir. 1996), the Fifth Circuit stated that, "[i]n a multistate class action, variations in state law may swamp any common issues and defeat predominance." *Id.* at 741.

Similar concerns were expressed by the Seventh Circuit in *In re Rhone-Poulenc Rorer Inc.*, 51 F.3d 1293 (7th Cir. 1995). *Rhone-Poulenc* involved a nationwide class of hemophiliacs who contracted HIV from contaminated blood transfusions in the early 1980s, prior to the discovery of HIV/AIDS, and claimed that various medical corporations were liable for negligence. Plaintiffs asserted that, had the defendants done more to avoid the then-known risk of Hepatitis B, they would have avoided transmitting the AIDS infections as well. In certifying the class, the district court attempted to avoid choice-of-law issues by holding that a single body of negligence law would apply to all class members. As one of several grounds for decertifying the class, the Seventh Circuit ruled that, because of the novelty of the negligence issues, differences in the laws among the states (even in "nuance") could not be ignored.

In *In re Bridgestone/Firestone, Inc.*, 288 F.3d 1012 (7th Cir. 2002), the Seventh Circuit held that the district court erred in applying the laws of Tennessee and Michigan, the headquarters of Firestone and Ford, respectively, to claims by a putative nationwide class involving alleged defects in certain Firestone tires and Ford Explorers. According to the court, applicable choice-of-law rules required that the law of each class member's place of injury should govern. Because the class included members from all fifty states, the District of Columbia, and various U.S. territories, the court held that the need to apply so many laws to numerous causes of action rendered the suit unmanageable.

More recently, in *Pilgrim v. Universal Health Card, LLC*, 660 F.3d 943 (6th Cir. 2011), the Sixth Circuit upheld the district court's decision granting defendants' motion to deny class certification—without affording plaintiffs any discovery—because the laws of the 50 states were involved. And in *Johnson v. Nextel Communications, Inc.*, 780 F.3d 128 (2d Cir. 2015), the Second Circuit overturned class certification on the ground that neither predominance nor superiority was satisfied where the laws of twenty-seven different states applied.

Most recently, in *Hale v. Emerson Electric Company*, 942 F.3d 401 (8th Cir. 2019), the Eighth Circuit examined the certification of a nationwide class of consumers alleging deceptive advertising by vacuum manufacturer Emerson Electric. Since "every part of the challenged transaction took place in a class member's home state," the laws of each consumer's home state would apply, and nationwide class certification was thus improper. *Id.* at 403.

By contrast, some courts have been receptive to certifying nationwide classes despite variations in state law. For example, in *Klay v. Humana, Inc.*, 382 F.3d 1241 (11th Cir. 2004), the Eleventh Circuit concluded that, even though the laws of all fifty states were implicated, "groupability" rendered any relevant differences in state law negligible. The court reasoned: "[I]f the applicable state laws can be sorted into a small number of groups, each containing materially identical legal standards, then certification of subclasses embracing each of the dominant legal standards can be appropriate." *See also In re U.S. Foodservice Inc. Pricing Litig.*, 729 F.3d 108, 127 (2d Cir. 2013) (upholding certification of class alleging breach of contract under the laws of multiple states, in part on the ground that all relevant jurisdictions had adopted the Uniform Commercial Code; the court noted that "the crucial inquiry is not whether the laws of multiple jurisdictions are implicated, but whether those laws differ in a material manner that precludes the predominance of common issues"); *In re Copley Pharm., Inc., "Albuterol" Prods. Liab. Litig.*, 161 F.R.D. 456, 465 (D. Wyo. 1995) (upholding certification of nationwide products liability class action and noting that such classes are not "*per se* unmanageable"); *In re Worlds of Wonder Sec. Litig.*, No. C 87 5491 SC, 1990 WL 61951, at **4–5 (N.D. Cal. Mar. 23, 1990) (relying on the law of a defendant's principal place of business, even as to class members residing in other states).

Moreover, courts have been more willing to certify classes involving the laws of multiple states in the context of a class that is certified for purposes of settlement. *See, e.g., In re Prudential Ins. Co. Am. Sales Practice Litig. Agent Actions*, 148 F.3d 283 (3d Cir. 1998) (concluding that choice-of-law issues did not present "insuperable obstacles" in nationwide class action settlement); *Sullivan v. DB Investments*, 667 F.3d 273, 301–02 (3d Cir. 2011) (noting that settlement classes may often be certified despite variations in state law "because the concern for manageability that is a central tenet in the certification of a litigation class is removed from the equation").

In 2019, the Ninth Circuit addressed this issue in depth in an en banc decision arising in the settlement class context. A three-judge panel had held that certification of a settlement class was improper because the laws of multiple states applied. *In re Hyundai & Kia Fuel Economy Litig.*, 881 F.3d 679 (9th Cir. 2018). Subsequently, the en banc court (in an 8–3 decision) reversed the panel. *In re Hyundai & Kia Fuel Economy Litig.*, 926 F.3d 539 (9th Cir. 2019) (en banc). The case involved a nationwide putative class action alleging misstatements about the fuel economy of certain automobiles. Before certifying the class, the federal district court stated that it would need to conduct an "extensive choice of law analysis" if the case were going to trial, but that "those issues do not prevent the Court from certifying the class for settlement purposes." 881 F.3d at 700. In a split decision, the panel disagreed, stating that the "district court's reasoning that the settlement context relieved it of its obligation to undertake a choice of law analysis . . . is wrong as a matter of law." 881 F.3d at 702.

In reversing the panel, the en banc court noted that, "subject to constitutional limitations and the forum state's choice-of-law rules, a court adjudicating a multistate class action is free to apply the substantive law of a single state to the entire class." 926 F.3d at 561. Accordingly, the court found that "California courts [are free to] apply California law 'unless a party litigant timely invokes the law of a foreign state,' in which case it is 'the foreign law proponent' who must 'shoulder the burden of demonstrating that foreign law, rather than California law, should apply to class claims.' " *Id.* To meet that burden, the objectors to the class settlement in *Hyundai* were required to show that "(1) the law of the foreign state 'materially differs from the law of California,' meaning that the law differs 'with regard to the particular issue in question'; (2) a 'true conflict exists,' meaning that each state has an interest in the application of its own law to 'the circumstances of the particular case'; and (3) the foreign state's interest would be 'more impaired' than California's interest if California law were applied." *Id.* at 562.

The en banc court noted that "no objector presented an adequate choice-of-law analysis or explained how, under the facts of this case, the . . . three elements were met." *Id.* The court added that "no objector argued that differences between the consumer protection laws of all fifty states precluded certification of a settlement class." *Id.* Accordingly, the en banc court affirmed the district court's approval of the settlement.

The dissent disagreed with the en banc majority's analysis, arguing that the district court had failed to "discharge its threshold responsibility to determine what substantive body of law applied to the plaintiffs' claims before it certified the class." *Id.* at 575. According to the dissent, the en banc majority committed the same error by "pretermitting any discussion of state law variations that might affect a predominance analysis." *Id.* at 576.

One additional question in multistate class actions is whether CAFA will impact the reach of *Shutts.* *Shutts* upheld the ability of state courts to certify nationwide classes. As explained in § 8.3, CAFA has had the effect of shifting most multistate class actions to federal court. Thus, to the extent that *Shutts* unleashed a wave of multistate or nationwide class actions in state court, CAFA has reversed that trend.

CAFA does not, however, address the due process or choice-of-law issues raised by *Shutts.* (Proposals during the consideration of CAFA to address choice-of-law issues were rejected.) Thus, federal courts, like state courts, will still have to ensure that the choice of state law to apply is neither arbitrary nor unfair. Prior to CAFA, federal courts in diversity cases (like their state court counterparts) applied the choice-of-law rules of the state in which the court was located, as required by *Klaxon Co. v. Stentor Electric Manufacturing Co.*, 313 U.S. 487 (1941). Post-CAFA, federal courts have continued to apply that approach.

§ 7.2 STATE COURT CLASS ACTIONS

A.   IMPORTANCE OF STATE COURT CLASS ACTIONS

The primary focus of this text is on federal class actions. As exemplified by *Shutts,* however, the vast majority of states allow class actions to be brought in state courts. State court class actions are worthy of focus in this text for at least two related reasons.

First, because various federal appellate courts have restricted certain kinds of class actions, state courts have become more attractive to plaintiffs. Many litigants believe that state courts are usually more receptive to class actions than are federal courts. One explanation for this receptivity is that most state court judges are elected and thus are motivated to make decisions that are politically popular. Of course, as noted in § 8.3, CAFA has shifted the majority of multistate class actions to federal court.

Second, even after CAFA, state court class actions are important because some class actions involving state law issues may *only* be brought in state court. CAFA by no means eliminates state courts altogether as important venues for some significant class actions.

B. OVERVIEW OF STATE CLASS ACTION RULES

Because of the continuing importance of state court class actions, even after CAFA, it is instructive to survey some of the key differences between state and federal court class actions. A state-by-state survey of state court class action rules, however, is beyond the scope of this text. Rather, this text simply highlights some of the general areas in which class action rules and procedures may differ from one state to another. Students and practitioners analyzing state court class actions should consult the rules and case law applicable to the particular state at issue.

States Adopting the 1966 Version of Rule 23. About two-thirds of the states pattern their class action rules on the 1966 version of Federal Rule 23. Many of these states look closely at federal case law in construing similarly worded state law rules. Other Rule 23 states, however, do not always follow federal case law, particularly when the thrust of federal case law is to restrict the availability of class actions. A number of state courts take the view that class actions should be certified whenever possible.

Among states that pattern their rules after Federal Rule 23, some do not have categories similar to (b)(1) and (b)(2), and thus allow certification only under standards similar to those of (b)(3). Moreover, states use a variety of criteria to determine whether a class action is "superior" to other methods of adjudication. The Michigan rule, for example, explicitly requires courts to consider, in addition to the (b)(3) criteria, (1) whether the claims of individual class members are insufficient in amount to warrant separate lawsuits, and (2) whether the amounts likely to be recovered by individual class members are large enough to justify a class action. In California, while the class action rule is much more succinct than Federal Rule 23, case law makes clear that the requirements are similar to those under Rules 23(a) and (b).

States Not Adopting the 1966 Version of Rule 23. Some states have not adopted a rule similar to Federal Rule 23. Those states take various approaches. For example, Mississippi and Virginia do not have specific rules authorizing class actions. In Virginia, class action-type suits may be brought only to the extent allowed by judicial decisions. In Mississippi, class actions do not exist, either by rule or by case law.

The remaining states take a variety of approaches. A few states, including Nebraska and Wisconsin, pattern their class action statutes after the 1849 "Field Code," a code first enacted in New York that attempted to simplify civil procedure. Class actions under Field Code statutes differ from those under Rule 23. For example, Field Code states do not have different categories of class suits corresponding to

Rules 23(b)(1), (b)(2), or (b)(3), but instead look to whether there is a "community of interest" among the class members. Taken literally, this requirement could foreclose class treatment, for example, in a contract suit where the class members signed separate contracts with the same defendant. Nonetheless, some Field Code states have stated that their requirements are similar in application to those of Federal Rule 23.

North Carolina patterns its class action rule after the 1938 version of Rule 23. The North Carolina rule does not, however, refer specifically to "true," "hybrid," and "spurious" classes. *See* § 2.3.

Approaches to Notice and Opt-Outs. The vast majority of states require notice to the members of a putative class who can be reasonably identified, at least in Rule 23(b)(3)-type class actions. Some states, however, do not require notice (except for notice to out-of-state class members in (b)(3)-type cases) but leave the decision to the discretion of the trial court. These courts reason that the Supreme Court's requirement of best practicable notice in Federal Rule 23(b)(3) actions, as set forth in *Eisen v. Carlisle & Jacquelin*, 417 U.S. 156 (1974) (*see* § 6.1), was based on Federal Rule 23, not on federal due process, and that the due process notice requirements in *Shutts* (*see* § 7.1) apply only to out-of-state class members.

With respect to opt-outs, most states follow the Rule 23 approach and permit both opt-out classes and mandatory classes. Some states, however, have "opt-in" provisions for certain kinds of class actions.

Under these provisions, unless a potential class member takes affirmative steps to join the class, he or she will not be part of the case and will not be bound by the judgment.

CHAPTER 8

SPECIAL CIVIL PROCEDURE ISSUES

Previous chapters have discussed several concepts unique to class actions, such as numerosity, commonality, typicality, adequacy of representation, notice, and opt-out rights. There are, however, a number of basic procedural principles that apply in both class and non-class cases but have special ramifications in the class action context. These include issues relating to statutes of limitations, subject-matter jurisdiction, issue and claim preclusion, and federal relations with state courts. This chapter addresses these issues.

§ 8.1   STATUTE OF LIMITATIONS ISSUES IN CLASS ACTIONS

A.   OVERVIEW OF "TOLLING" PRINCIPLES IN CLASS ACTIONS

The filing of a class action has important statute-of-limitations ramifications for prospective class members. In general, the filing of such a suit "tolls" the statute of limitations period (*i.e.,* stops it from running) for the entire class until class certification is denied. This is true regardless of whether the putative class member was even aware that a class action existed at the time it was pending.

The Supreme Court first announced a limited version of this tolling principle in *American Pipe & Construction Co. v. Utah*, 414 U.S. 538 (1974), stating that "the commencement of the original class suit tolls the running of the statute for all purported members of the class who make timely motions to intervene after the court has found the suit inappropriate for class action status." *Id.* at 553. The Court reasoned that, when a class action is filed, the principal goals of limitations periods—putting defendants on notice of claims and discouraging plaintiffs from sleeping on their rights—are satisfied. The Court also reasoned that its approach was consistent with Rule 23, which is based on the premise that class members should rely on class representatives to press the claims of the entire class.

Nine years later, in *Crown, Cork & Seal Co., Inc. v. Parker*, 462 U.S. 345 (1983), the Court expanded the tolling rule to apply to all members of the putative class, including those who file separate suits, and not simply those who file timely motions to intervene after the denial of class certification.

For tolling to apply, the plaintiff must establish that his or her cause of action was within the definition of the class upon which the plaintiff relies for tolling. For example, a plaintiff suing for personal injuries based on a toxic spill would not be able to rely upon a prior class action that was limited solely to class members claiming property damage. *See, e.g., Raie v. Cheminova, Inc.*, 336 F.3d 1278, 1282–83 (11th Cir. 2003) (class action complaint alleging primarily products liability claims, and not explicitly including wrongful death claims, would not toll statute of limitations for individual wrongful death claims).

B.   WHEN TOLLING CEASES

When a putative class action is first filed, no one can say with certainty whether class certification will ultimately be granted or denied. For tolling purposes, however, courts presume at the outset that class certification will be granted. If class certification is denied, putative class members are expected either to seek to intervene in the case or to file separate actions. Accordingly, when certification is denied, the limitations period begins to run again.

One issue raised by *American Pipe* is ascertaining *when* certification is "denied" for purposes of when the limitations period begins to run again. Does it mean when class certification is denied by the trial court? Or is it when the denial of certification is ultimately upheld by the court of last resort? In *Armstrong v. Martin Marietta Corp.*, 138 F.3d 1374 (11th Cir. 1998) (en banc), the Eleventh Circuit held that tolling ends when the *trial court* denies certification, even though there is still a remote possibility that the ruling will be reversed on appeal. The court explained that because the trial court's denial of certification is a discretionary ruling that is generally upheld on appeal, continued tolling after the trial court's ruling is not necessary to protect the class members' reasonable reliance on the pendency of the class action.

It is worth noting, however, that *Armstrong* was decided before Rule 23(f) became effective later that year. Indeed, the *Armstrong* court itself suggested that if the then-pending Rule 23(f) became law, it might reconsider its holding. *See id.* at 1390 n.34 ("If

[Rule 23(f)] passes, and if it significantly increases the frequency of interlocutory appeals of class certification orders ... then we may revisit the decision taken today, and might for instance allow continued tolling of statutes of limitations during the pendency of an appeal."). Since the adoption of Rule 23(f), courts have split on whether tolling ends after the district court's denial of class certification or continues until after the appellate court's denial of a Rule 23(f) petition (or review of the appeal on the merits). *See In re Vivendi Universal, S.A. Sec. Litig.*, 281 F.R.D. 165, 168–69 (S.D.N.Y. 2012) (noting split).

C.   LIMITATIONS ON THE *AMERICAN PIPE* TOLLING RULE

There are a number of limitations on the *American Pipe* rule. Three of the most significant ones are discussed here.

First, in *China Agritech, Inc. v. Resh*, 138 S. Ct. 1800 (2018), the Supreme Court resolved a circuit split about whether tolling should be extended when a subsequent class action is filed after the denial of class certification. In that case, a third securities fraud class action was brought against China Agritech on behalf of purchasers after class certification had been denied in two separate cases. All three actions were governed by the Private Securities Litigation Reform Act, *see* § 11.3. The third class action was filed a year and a half after the statute of limitations had expired, but plaintiffs (who were not named plaintiffs in the earlier actions) argued that the *American Pipe* tolling rule permitted the late filing. The Court unanimously rejected that argument, holding that *American Pipe* does not allow a "follow-on" class action when the statute of limitations has expired. *Id.* at 1804. The Court reasoned that the purpose of *American Pipe* is to ensure "efficiency and economy of litigation," and that such a purpose would not be accomplished if tolling were applied to successive class actions. *Id.* at 1811.

China Agritech does not necessarily mean that tolling is foreclosed in *every* situation in which class certification has been previously denied. Justice Sotomayor, who concurred only in the judgment, held out the possibility that, outside of the securities law context, there could be circumstances justifying *American Pipe* tolling even for successive class actions. As she noted, "[i]nstead of adopting a blanket no-tolling-of-class-claims-ever rule outside the [Private Securities Litigation Reform Act] context, the Court might hold, as a matter of equity, that tolling only becomes unavailable for future class claims where class certification is denied for a reason that bears on the suitability of the claims for class treatment." *Id.* at 1814. On the other hand, "[w]here . . . class certification is denied because of the deficiencies of the lead plaintiff as class representative, or because of some other nonsubstantive defect, tolling would remain available." *Id.* The majority's sweeping language, however, will make it difficult for plaintiffs to rely on Justice Sotomayor's more nuanced approach.

Second, some courts have held that *American Pipe* does not apply to state-law claims. Put another way, when state-law claims are involved, the issue of tolling is determined by state law, not federal law. As the Seventh Circuit has noted, "[w]hen state law supplies the period of limitations, it also supplies the tolling rules." *Hemenway v. Peabody Coal Co.*, 159 F.3d 255, 265 (7th Cir. 1998) (looking to Indiana law to determine "whether the filing of a class action satisfies the period of limitations for all class members"). Under this approach, if a claim would be time-barred under state law notwithstanding the pendency of a class action, the fact that the case was brought in federal court does not change that result. *But see. e.g., Adams Pub. Sch. Dist. v. Asbestos Corp.*, 7 F.3d 717, 719 (8th Cir. 1993) (suggesting that "federal interests" may be sufficiently strong to justify application of *American Pipe* rule even in diversity cases).

Finally, the Supreme Court has held that *American Pipe* does not apply to statutes of repose in federal securities class actions. *See California Public Employees' Retirement System v. ANZ Securities, Inc.*, 137 S. Ct. 2042 (2017). The Court reasoned that statutes of repose were designed to give complete peace to defendants.

D.   APPLICATION OF *AMERICAN PIPE* TO OPT-OUTS

As noted above, when class certification is denied, the clock starts to run again, and the individual plaintiffs must file their own claims before the limitations period expires. By contrast, if a timely filed class action is certified, then the statute of limitations is not an issue for any class member who remains in the class. An issue arises, however, with respect to a class member who opts out of the class after receiving notice that certification has been granted. In that situation, courts hold that tolling ceases for that individual at the time of opt out and the clock thus starts to run again. Most courts hold that, prior to that time, that individual obtains the benefit of *American Pipe* tolling because the class representatives are deemed to have been pursuing his or her rights.

E.   AMENDING INDIVIDUAL ACTIONS TO ASSERT CLASS CLAIMS

An issue related to *American Pipe* is whether otherwise time-barred class claims will be deemed timely on the ground that they "relate back" to the filing of an individual claim. Federal Rule of Civil Procedure 15(c)(1)(B) provides, in pertinent part, that "an amendment of a pleading relates back to the date of the original pleading when the ... amendment asserts a claim or defense that arose out of the conduct, transaction, or occurrence set out—or attempted to be set out—in the original pleading."

A typical scenario is as follows: Plaintiff files an individual employment discrimination claim. After the statute of limitations has expired for similarly situated employees who did not sue, plaintiff then attempts to modify his or her case to make it a class action suit, even though the putative class members would be time-barred if they pursued their claims individually. In general, courts analyze this situation by evaluating whether the original complaint provided the defendant with notice that a class action could be pursued. If the defendant was aware, prior to the expiration of the statute of limitations, that classwide relief might be sought, or if the complaint itself describes a class that shares grievances similar to those of the plaintiff, courts are frequently willing to allow the class claims to relate back to the filing of the individual claim. On the other hand, when the individual complaint provides no such notice of classwide claims, courts generally hold that untimely class claims cannot be revived.

§ 8.2 JURISDICTIONAL ISSUES: GENERAL CONCEPTS

As noted in § 5.1, many plaintiffs' lawyers prefer to litigate class actions in state court. Defense lawyers, by contrast, usually prefer a federal forum. If a case filed in state court raises questions under federal law, the defendant can remove the case to federal court. And even if a case filed in state court contains only state-law claims, the defendant may nonetheless have grounds to remove the case to federal court based on diversity of citizenship. Before CAFA, defense counsel often faced two major impediments in removing cases to federal court based on diversity of citizenship: (1) establishing the jurisdictional amount (under 28 U.S.C. § 1332(a)(1), only cases in which the amount in controversy exceeds $75,000 are removable); and (2) establishing complete diversity of citizenship (*i.e.*, that no plaintiff shares the same citizenship with any defendant). Although CAFA has relaxed these requirements in certain circumstances (*see* § 8.3), an understanding of these historically critical diversity requirements is essential to appreciating the genesis and importance of CAFA. Moreover, some cases may be removable under traditional diversity criteria even if they do not satisfy CAFA's requirements.

A.   DETERMINING CITIZENSHIP FOR DIVERSITY PURPOSES

The federal diversity statute, 28 U.S.C. § 1332, requires (in addition to the $75,000 amount-in-controversy requirement) complete diversity of citizenship. It is well established that, in the class action context, the court should consider only the citizenship of the named plaintiffs and not the citizenship of the unnamed class members. *See Supreme Tribe of Ben Hur v. Cauble*, 255 U.S. 356 (1921). This principle is important. If the citizenship of each class member had to be considered, establishing complete diversity would be impossible in class actions that are nationwide in scope. Even the *Cauble* rule however, has posed serious impediments for defendants seeking to remove class actions to federal court.

Under *Cauble*, plaintiffs seeking to litigate in state court must scrutinize the citizenship of the named plaintiffs and defendants to guard against removal to federal court based on diversity. This means that, if the key defendant is not a citizen of the same state as the named plaintiffs, then the risk of removal exists.

Frequently, plaintiffs' lawyers include in-state as well as out-of-state defendants in the lawsuit, leading to claims by defendants that the in-state defendants were improperly joined and that their citizenship should be disregarded for diversity purposes. Defendants frequently argue, for example, that the defendant who would otherwise destroy diversity was "fraudulently joined" in the case and should be disregarded for diversity purposes. For instance, in a products liability suit by a Missouri plaintiff against a Michigan automobile manufacturer and a Missouri automobile dealership, the manufacturer may claim that the dealership was fraudulently joined to defeat diversity. Ordinarily, the fraudulent joinder doctrine applies in one of two circumstances: (1) when there is no possibility that the plaintiff can establish a cause of action against the non-diverse defendant, or (2) when there is outright fraud in the pleading of jurisdictional facts (for example, when the complaint falsely alleges the citizenship of a particular defendant).

In some circumstances, plaintiffs will name a defendant who is liable, if at all, to only a small portion of the class. In such cases some defendants have argued that there is fraudulent joinder and that the residency of the particular defendant must be disregarded. The Eleventh Circuit faced that situation in *Triggs v. John Crump Toyota, Inc.*, 154 F.3d 1284 (11th Cir. 1998). In that case, defendants contended that 98 percent of the class members had no conceivable claim against the non-diverse defendant. Defendants thus argued that the non-diverse defendant had been fraudulently joined to defeat diversity. The court rejected that argument, holding that if the named plaintiff has a potential claim against the defendant, diversity cannot be defeated on a fraudulent joinder theory merely because most unnamed class members have no claim against that defendant.

Because fraudulent joinder arguments are difficult to win, plaintiffs' lawyers traditionally had considerable success joining in-state defendants in large, multistate class actions, thereby preventing defendants from successfully removing such cases to federal court. As discussed below, CAFA has modified the rule of complete diversity in certain class actions, permitting removal based on minimal diversity (*i.e.*, any plaintiff or class member with citizenship that differs from that of any defendant).

B.   AGGREGATION OF CLAIMS FOR PURPOSES OF JURISDICTIONAL AMOUNT

Before CAFA, plaintiffs tried to use the $75,000 jurisdictional amount as a vehicle to preclude diversity jurisdiction, while defendants argued that the requirement was not an impediment. Specifically, plaintiffs' counsel took the position that the $75,000 amount-in-controversy requirement needed to be satisfied for *each* class member. By contrast, defense counsel seeking to remove the case to federal court looked for ways to argue that the amount in controversy *exceeded* $75,000, either on an individual class member basis or through some theory of aggregating class members' claims. With respect to aggregation, the question arose whether a court could add up the claims of prospective class members to establish the jurisdictional amount. For example, if the damages claimed for each class member in an 8,000-member class are $10, then the jurisdictional amount would be established if the claimed damages could be aggregated ($80,000).

The Supreme Court addressed this issue in *Zahn v. International Paper Co.*, 414 U.S. 291 (1973). In *Zahn*, the Court held that, to satisfy the amount-in-controversy requirement, each class member in a class action must claim individual damages exceeding the jurisdictional amount. Thus, as a general rule, the claims of the individual class members cannot be combined to ascertain whether the amount-in-controversy exceeds $75,000; rather, *each* class member's claim must exceed $75,000. Even before CAFA, however, several arguments could still be made, notwithstanding *Zahn*, in cases that appeared to involve less than $75,000 per plaintiff.

First, defense lawyers have argued when appropriate that, in addition to seeking compensatory damages, each plaintiff is also seeking punitive damages, and that the total amount of damages awarded to each plaintiff could reasonably exceed $75,000. Whether this argument has merit depends on the particular facts (as well as the applicable substantive law regarding punitive damages).

Second, defense lawyers have argued that, when equitable relief is sought in addition to damages, courts should assess the value of equitable relief sought by the putative class in determining whether the $75,000 jurisdictional amount is satisfied. Again, the success of this argument depends on whether, under the particular facts and governing law, it is reasonable to contend that the equitable relief sought, in combination with damages, is "worth" greater than $75,000 per class member.

Third, *Zahn* itself identifies an exception to its general rule, known as the "common fund" exception. This exception applies when several plaintiffs are enforcing a common or undivided interest. In that event, the amounts sought by each plaintiff may be aggregated for purposes of determining the jurisdictional amount. Circumstances in which the common fund exception applies, however, are rare. They generally involve a single piece of property or a single insurance policy. In that situation, the rights of a particular plaintiff cannot be determined without implicating the rights of others, and it is therefore appropriate to assess the value of the entire fund or piece of property in determining the jurisdictional amount.

Finally, another argument pursued in the wake of *Zahn* is that, if at least one named plaintiff can meet the jurisdictional amount requirement, the other class members need not do so. This argument is based on the "supplemental jurisdiction" statute (enacted in 1990), 28 U.S.C. § 1367, which in certain circumstances allows a court, as a matter of discretion, to extend subject matter jurisdiction over related parties when those parties cannot independently establish jurisdiction. This situation would apply if at least one class representative seeks relief worth greater than $75,000. (A few cases have also permitted courts to allocate attorneys' fees available to the putative class solely to the named representatives, thereby permitting supplemental jurisdiction even when the representatives have only small-value monetary claims.) Before the U.S. Supreme Court's resolution of the issue in *Exxon Mobil Corp. v. Allapattah*, 545 U.S. 546 (2005) (discussed below), the courts were sharply divided on how to analyze the supplemental jurisdiction statute.

Courts holding that section 1367 overruled *Zahn* relied upon, among other things, section 1367(a), which states that a federal court "shall have supplemental jurisdiction" if the additional claims "form part of the same controversy" as the claims over which the district court has "original jurisdiction." These courts reasoned that there was original jurisdiction as long as the class representative and the defendant were from different states and the class representative's own claims exceeded $75,000. Thus, the court could exercise supplemental jurisdiction over the other class members' claims. These courts also relied on section 1367(b), which excludes from section 1367(a)'s reach "claims against persons made parties under Rule 14, 19, 20, or 24," but does not list Rule 23.

Courts holding that section 1367 did not overrule *Zahn* reasoned, among other things, that section 1367 was inapplicable when original jurisdiction over the action did not exist, and under *Zahn*, original jurisdiction did not exist unless *all* class members had claims exceeding $75,000. Those courts also relied on section 1367's legislative history, which indicates that section 1367 was not intended to affect jurisdictional requirements in class actions based solely on diversity.

The Supreme Court resolved this issue (in a 5–4 decision) in *Exxon Mobil Corp. v. Allapattah*, 545 U.S. 546 (2005). In *Allapattah*, the Court held that "where the other elements of jurisdiction are present and at least one named plaintiff in the action satisfies the amount-in-controversy requirement, § 1367 [authorizes] supplemental jurisdiction over the claims of other plaintiffs in the same Article III case or controversy, even if those claims are for less than the jurisdictional amount specified in the statute setting forth the requirements for diversity jurisdiction." *Id.* at 2615. The Court based its decision on the plain language of section 1367(a), as well as on the fact that section 1367(b) did not include class actions among the exceptions to section 1367(a). (The Court adopted the same analysis for cases joined under Rule 20. *See* § 15.1.) Because the Court deemed the language of section 1367 to be clear, it found no merit in contrary arguments based on the legislative history.

The Court noted that its ruling was not mooted by CAFA, which permits class members' claims to be aggregated under a new $5 million amount-in-controversy rule for certain class actions (*see* § 8.3). According to the Court, "many proposed exercises of supplemental jurisdictions, even in the class action context, might not fall within CAFA's ambit." *Id.* at

2628. For example, the class may not satisfy CAFA's $5 million threshold.

By the same token, many cases will satisfy CAFA but not section 1367. Thus, as is common in many consumer cases, if every member of the class, including the representatives, has a claim below $75,000, then there would be no plaintiff who satisfied original jurisdiction, thereby foreclosing any theory of supplemental jurisdiction. Yet CAFA might apply.

In short, when analyzing removal of class actions to federal court, both CAFA and section 1367 are potentially relevant, depending on the facts and circumstances of the case.

§ 8.3   THE CLASS ACTION FAIRNESS ACT

A.   OVERVIEW

Congress enacted the Class Action Fairness Act (CAFA), Pub. L. No. 109–2, 119 Stat. 4, in 2005 in response to concerns that state courts were not treating class action defendants fairly. In particular, corporate defendants, politicians, and others were concerned that, because of strict jurisdictional rules, defendants were frequently stuck litigating major class actions in state court. Because state courts were viewed as less friendly to defendants than federal courts, critics of these jurisdictional rules urged Congress to enact legislation that would shift large and important class actions from state court to federal court. Opponents of such legislation defended the role of state courts in adjudicating class actions and expressed concern that the proposals were nothing but disguised efforts to eliminate most class actions. In addition, some federal and state judges worried that such legislation would jeopardize important principles of federalism and overload the federal courts. Despite these objections, however, CAFA passed with strong bipartisan support.

B. EXPANDED FEDERAL JURISDICTION OVER CLASS ACTIONS

CAFA expands the original jurisdiction of federal district courts over multistate class actions involving state-law claims. Specifically, CAFA grants federal courts jurisdiction over class actions on the basis of diversity when three criteria are met: (1) there are 100 or more putative class members, (2) there is "minimal diversity" between the parties, and (3) the amount in controversy exceeds $5 million in the aggregate. 28 U.S.C. § 1332(d)(2), (d)(5)(B). In amending section 1332, Congress intended to make more multistate class actions removable to federal court while retaining state courts' jurisdiction over class actions that are primarily small and local. CAFA's broad grant of jurisdiction is subject to several exceptions discussed below. Empirical studies have confirmed that CAFA has indeed shifted a significant number of class actions from state court to federal court.

Courts have wrestled with how to handle complaints drafted by plaintiffs attempting to preserve state court jurisdiction post-CAFA. While it is well settled that plaintiffs are the masters of their own complaints, and thus may select the forum, the parties, the claims, and the relief sought, some courts have concluded that plaintiffs should not be able to defeat CAFA removal by cleverly crafting their complaints. *Compare, e.g., Bell v. Hershey Co.*, 557 F.3d 953, 956 (8th Cir. 2009) ("The enactment of CAFA did not alter the proposition that the plaintiff is the master of the complaint."), *with, e.g., Freeman v. Blue Ridge Paper Prods., Inc.*, 551 F.3d 405, 406–09 (6th Cir. 2008) (holding that CAFA conferred jurisdiction where five individual state court class actions were filed by plaintiffs from a single state against a single defendant for the same injuries over a sequential time period for $4.9 million each, and reasoning that there was "no colorable basis" for dividing the suit "other than to frustrate CAFA").

Conversely, defendants seeking removal under CAFA may not pick and choose from both CAFA and traditional jurisdictional requirements to cobble together federal jurisdiction. For instance, in *Yocupicio v. PAE Group, LLC*, 795 F.3d 1057 (9th Cir. 2015), the Ninth Circuit held that federal jurisdiction was not proper where the suit involved both class and non-class claims, and the class claims did not meet CAFA's amount-in-controversy requirement while the non-class claims did not meet the traditional requirement of complete diversity.

C. ESTABLISHING "MINIMAL" DIVERSITY

Under CAFA, minimal diversity exists if any of three prerequisites is satisfied: (1) "any member of a class of plaintiffs is a citizen of a State different from any defendant"; (2) "any member of a class of plaintiffs is a foreign state or a citizen or subject of a foreign state and any defendant is a citizen of a State"; or (3) "any member of a class of plaintiffs is a citizen of a State and any defendant is a foreign state or a citizen or subject of a foreign state." 28 U.S.C. § 1332(d)(2). Notably, the statute looks to the citizenship of "any member" of the class in determining minimal diversity, not just to the citizenship of the class representatives.

Returning to an earlier example (§ 8.2), in a products liability suit by a Missouri class representative against a Michigan automobile manufacturer, minimal diversity would exist even if the plaintiff also named a Missouri automobile dealership as a second defendant. Thus, under CAFA, assuming the other requirements of the statute are met, a plaintiff cannot defeat diversity simply by naming an in-state defendant.

D.   AGGREGATING CLAIMS

With respect to cases that meet the other requirements of the statute, CAFA overrules *Zahn* and permits individual class members' claims to be aggregated to satisfy the jurisdictional amount, provided that the total sought is greater than $5 million, exclusive of interest and costs. For most large, multistate class actions, satisfying this jurisdictional amount will not be an issue because plaintiffs' counsel cannot dispute, based on the class definition and prayer for relief, that the amount in controversy greatly exceeds $5 million.

In those cases in which plaintiffs' counsel contemplate smaller recoveries, they can attempt to avoid federal jurisdiction by simply capping the relief requested in the complaint at or below $5 million. This same practice was used frequently before CAFA to cap individual class member claims at or below $75,000. Such a strategy, however, has proven ineffective when the particular facts and circumstances of the case indicate that a recovery of greater than $5 million may in fact be possible. In *Standard Fire Insurance Co. v. Knowles*, 568 U.S. 588 (2013), for example, the putative class representative stated in the complaint that " 'Plaintiff and Class stipulate that they will seek to recover total aggregate damages of less than five million dollars.' " *Id*. at 591. The defendant removed the case to federal court under CAFA, but the district court remanded based on the plaintiff's stipulation. After the Eighth Circuit declined to hear the appeal, the Supreme Court unanimously reversed, reasoning:

> The District Court in this case found that [the sum potentially at issue if the case were certified as a class action] would have exceeded $5 million *but for* the stipulation. And we must decide whether the stipulation makes a critical difference. In our view, it does not. Our reason is a simple one: Stipulations must be binding.... [A] plaintiff who files a proposed class action cannot legally bind members of the proposed class before the class is certified. Because his precertification stipulation does not bind anyone but himself, [the putative class representative]

has not reduced the value of the putative class members' claims.

Id. at 592–93. (emphasis in original; citations and paragraph breaks omitted). Thus, the Court concluded that the stipulation was ineffective to bind unnamed class members. *See also Hammond v. Stamps.com, Inc.*, 844 F.3d 909 (10th Cir. 2016) (holding that CAFA's jurisdictional amount is satisfied if that amount *might* be recovered; such a recovery need not be likely).

If the class has not successfully capped the recovery at or under $5 million, and the amount in controversy is not otherwise clear on the face of the complaint, courts under CAFA have considered evidence relevant to jurisdictional amount and have resolved uncertainty in favor of remand to state court. *E.g., Miedema v. Maytag Corp.*, 450 F.3d 1322 (11th Cir. 2006). The removing defendant need not produce evidence of the amount in controversy in the removal notice itself; rather, a notice of removal must contain only "a short and plain statement of the grounds for removal," including "a plausible allegation that the amount in controversy exceeds the jurisdictional threshold." *Dart Cherokee Basin Operating Co., LLC v. Owens*, 574 U.S. 81, 83–89 (2014). According to the Supreme Court, "[e]vidence establishing the amount is required . . . only when the plaintiff contests, or the court questions, the defendant's allegation." *Id.* at 89.

CAFA's approach to jurisdictional amount provides a solution to federal jurisdiction when the class does not fall within the supplemental jurisdiction statute, as construed in *Allapattah*. *See* § 8.2. As discussed in § 8.2, under the supplemental jurisdiction statute, at least one class representative must satisfy the $75,000 amount-in-controversy requirement. For many types of class actions, such as those involving economic damages for consumer products, class counsel might have difficulty identifying any member of the class with damages greater than $75,000. Under CAFA, however, no individual class member needs to allege damages greater than $75,000. All that is required is that the aggregate damages at issue exceed $5 million.

E. MASS ACTIONS

In addition to cases filed under the state and federal class action rules, CAFA also applies to "mass actions," defined as "any civil action . . . in which monetary relief claims of 100 or more persons are proposed to be tried jointly on the ground that the plaintiffs' claims involve common questions of law or fact." 28 U.S.C. § 1332(d)(11)(B)(i). The rationale for including mass actions under CAFA is that such suits, while not strictly class actions, have led to abuses similar to those that occur in some class actions.

Although mass actions share some similarities to class actions for purposes of CAFA, they are not treated precisely the same. Importantly, there is no aggregation available for mass actions under CAFA, so each plaintiff must satisfy the $75,000 amount-in-controversy requirement under 28 U.S.C. § 1332(a) to establish diversity jurisdiction. Moreover, unlike class actions, although plaintiffs may elect to try their claims together, each plaintiff acts on his or her own behalf, not on behalf of others who are similarly situated.

Section 1332(d)(11)(B)(i) has posed some interpretive challenges for courts. In 2014, for example, the Supreme Court confronted the issue whether unnamed real parties in interest count as claimants for purposes of establishing whether a suit constitutes a mass action under the statute. In *Mississippi ex rel. Hood v. AU Optronics Corp.*, 571 U.S. 161 (2014), the Mississippi Attorney General brought an action in state court on behalf of the state of Mississippi, alleging that the defendants had formed an international cartel relating to liquid crystal display (LCD) screens. The defendants removed the case under CAFA, arguing that the suit constituted a mass action because more than 100 real parties in interest—Mississippi consumers—would benefit from the restitution sought by the plaintiff. The Supreme Court unanimously rejected the defendants' theory, relying on the plain text of § 1332(d)(11)(B)(i) and reasoning that, had Congress intended to encompass "unspecified individuals who have no actual participation in the suit," it would have done so explicitly by referring to "persons (named or unnamed)" as it did elsewhere in the statute. 571 U.S. at 169.

In *Corber v. Xanodyne Pharmaceuticals, Inc.*, 771 F.3d 1218 (9th Cir. 2014), the Ninth Circuit had to apply section 1332(d)(11)(B)(i)'s "proposed to be tried jointly" language. The court held that that language applied to a petition by plaintiffs in several state-court actions to consolidate their cases under a California Rule of Civil Procedure allowing for "the coordination of 'all of the actions for all purposes.' " *Id.* at 1223 (quoting Cal. C.C.P. § 404). The court concluded that the plaintiffs had, "in language or substance, . . . proposed a joint trial," thus qualifying the case as a mass action subject to federal jurisdiction under CAFA. *Id.*

F. EXPANDED REMOVAL TO FEDERAL COURT

In addition to liberalizing original jurisdiction in diversity cases, CAFA makes it easier for class actions (and "mass actions") to be removed from state court to federal court. CAFA—through section 28 U.S.C. § 1453—accomplishes this goal for class actions covered by the statute in a number of ways:

First, prior to CAFA, complete diversity was required for removal, thus imposing a major barrier to its implementation. 28 U.S.C. § 1441(b). After CAFA, only "minimal diversity" (*see* § 8.3) is required for covered class actions. 28 U.S.C. § 1453(b).

Second, prior to CAFA, under section 1446(b) defendants only had one year from the date of filing to remove a class action. For CAFA-covered cases, defendants no longer have a one-year deadline for removal. 28 U.S.C. § 1453(b). (It should be noted that, under the Federal Courts Jurisdiction and Venue Clarification Act of 2011, the one-year requirement no longer applies even in non-CAFA cases if the district court finds that the plaintiff deliberately failed to disclose the amount in controversy to prevent removal. Pub. L. 112–63, 125 Stat. 758 (codified in scattered sections of 28 U.S.C.).)

Third, prior to CAFA, courts held that under section 1446, a defendant could not remove a diversity class action to federal court without the consent of the other defendants. *See, e.g., Emrich v. Touche Ross & Co.*, 846 F.2d 1190, 1193 n.1 (9th Cir. 1988). For CAFA-covered cases, defendants no longer need such consent. 28 U.S.C. § 1453(b).

Fourth, prior to CAFA, under section 1441(b)(2), removal was not allowed if any defendant was a citizen of the state where the class action was originally brought. For CAFA-covered cases, a defendant may remove an otherwise qualifying case to federal court even when one or more of the defendants is a citizen of the forum state. 28 U.S.C. § 1453(b).

Finally, prior to CAFA, under section 1447(d), if a class action was removed to federal court and then remanded to state court, federal appellate interlocutory review of the remand order was generally prohibited. As discussed below (*see* § 8.3), for CAFA-covered cases, the remand order is subject to immediate review, at the discretion of the federal appellate court. 28 U.S.C. § 1453(c)(1).

G.   EXCEPTIONS TO CAFA'S JURISDICTIONAL RULES

CAFA contains several exceptions to its expanded diversity jurisdiction. These exceptions, discussed below, are designed to keep truly local controversies in the state courts.

Home State and Local Controversy Exceptions. Even where the "minimal diversity" and the amount-in-controversy criteria have been met, the federal district court is permitted, or even required, to decline jurisdiction in three circumstances. Two such circumstances fall under the "home state" exception, and the third is called the "local controversy" exception.

Under the home state exception, the district court *may* decline jurisdiction when: (1) more than one third but fewer than two thirds of the proposed plaintiff class members are citizens of the state where the action was originally filed; and (2) "the primary defendants" are also citizens of the forum state. If these two factors are satisfied, the court may decline jurisdiction when, considering the totality of the circumstances and in the interest of justice, abstention appears appropriate. In making this determination, the court must consider six factors relating to, among other things, the nexus between the forum, the claims, and the parties. 28 U.S.C. § 1332(d)(3). In addition, the district court *must* decline jurisdiction when: (1) two thirds or more of the proposed plaintiff class members are citizens of the state where the action was originally filed; and (2) "the primary defendants" are also citizens of the forum state. 28 U.S.C. § 1332(d)(4)(B).

Under the local controversy exception, the district court *must* decline jurisdiction when: (1) more than two thirds of the proposed plaintiff class members are citizens of the state where the action was originally filed; (2) at least one defendant "whose alleged conduct forms a significant basis for the claims asserted" and from whom "significant" relief is sought is also a citizen of the forum state; (3) the principal injuries occurred in the forum state; and (4) a similar class action has not been filed within the preceding three years. 28 U.S.C. § 1332(d)(4)(A).

The above exceptions are not triggered until the removing party has shown that the case meets CAFA's removal criteria. Courts have held that the party seeking remand then bears the burden of proving that an exception applies. *See, e.g., Serrano v. 180 Connect, Inc.*, 478 F.3d 1018, 1023 (9th Cir. 2007).

The home state and local controversy exceptions require a federal court to make a number of important threshold determinations. These exceptions also require the court to determine the meaning of terms left undefined by CAFA, such as "primary defendants," "significant" relief, and "principal injuries"—determinations that have led to considerable litigation.

As an initial matter, the federal court must determine how many putative class members are citizens of the forum state, a fact-intensive exercise. In addition, courts are divided on the impact of a corporate defendant's dual citizenship on federal jurisdiction under CAFA, *see Johnson v. Advance Am.*, 549 F.3d 932, 936 (4th Cir. 2008) (noting disagreement), and the Supreme Court has not addressed the issue. The Supreme Court, however, has clarified how a corporation's principal place of business should be determined for purposes of diversity jurisdiction analysis: namely, the principal place of business is "where a corporation's officers direct, control, and coordinate the corporation's activities" (normally its headquarters). *Hertz Corp. v. Friend*, 559 U.S. 77, 80–81 (2010).

Second, courts have taken various positions on the meaning of "primary defendants" under the home state exception. For example, some courts define primary defendants as those who are directly liable to plaintiffs; under that approach, defendants who are vicariously liable, sued under aiding and abetting theories, or liable through indemnification or contribution, would not be primary defendants. Other courts look for guidance in the CAFA Senate Report, which says that primary defendants are "the real 'targets of the lawsuit'—*i.e.*, the defendants that would be expected to incur most of the loss if liability is found." S. Rep. No. 109–14, at 43–44 (2005). Still other courts define primary defendants as those who are able to bear the cost of liability. Finally, some courts have held that *all* primary defendants must be citizens of the forum state for the home state exception to apply.

Third, courts are divided over how to determine whether a defendant is significant, a requirement under the local controversy exception. Thus, courts differ over what constitutes "significant relief" and conduct that forms a "significant basis" for invoking the local controversy exception. Courts have used both absolute and comparative approaches when determining the significance of a defendant. *See Coleman v. Estes Express Lines, Inc.*, 631 F.3d 1010, 1019 (9th Cir. 2011) (noting disagreement among courts).

A final issue under these exceptions is whether the "principal injuries" provision, section 1332(d)(4)(A)(i)(III), requires that principal injuries resulting from the alleged conduct *and* any related conduct of each defendant must be incurred in the home state. The wording of the statute makes clear that satisfying either prong is sufficient. *See* 28 U.S.C. § 1332(d)(4)(A)(i)(III) (requiring that "principal injuries resulting from the alleged conduct *or* any related conduct of each defendant were incurred in the State in which the action was originally filed" (emphasis added)); *Kaufman v. Allstate N.J. Ins. Co.*, 561 F.3d 144, 158 (3d Cir. 2009) (concluding that, because the statute used the word "or," only one of those requirements must be satisfied).

State Action Exception. CAFA excludes actions brought against "primary defendants" who are states, state officials, or other governmental entities. 28 U.S.C. § 1332(d)(5)(A). The exception is intended to prevent such parties from avoiding legitimate claims by removing class actions to federal court and then arguing that sovereign immunity under the Eleventh Amendment prohibits the court from granting the requested relief. The exception keeps such claims in state courts, which are not so constrained.

Small Class Exception. As noted above, CAFA excludes class actions where the proposed plaintiff class has fewer than 100 members. 28 U.S.C. § 1332(d)(5)(B). This exception permits actions with relatively few claimants to remain in state court.

Securities and Internal Corporate Affairs Exception. CAFA excludes actions relating to: (1) a covered security as defined by the federal securities laws; (2) "the internal affairs or governance of a corporation" or business enterprise under state law; and (3) the rights, duties, and obligations under the federal securities laws. 28 U.S.C. § 1332(d)(9)(A)–(C). This exception is designed to preserve the federal-state jurisdictional lines established by the Securities Litigation Uniform Standards Act of 1988. Pub. L. 105–353, 112 Stat. 3227 (codified at 15 U.S.C. §§ 77p and 78bb).

Third-Party Defendants Exception. Neither the general removal statute, 28 U.S.C § 1441(a), nor the removal provision of the Class Action Fairness Act, 28 U.S.C § 1453(b), permits third-party counterclaim defendants to remove a case to federal court. *Home Depot U.S.A., Inc. v. Jackson*, 139 S. Ct. 1743 (2019). In *Home Depot*, CitiBank brought a debt collection action against defendant Jackson alleging that Jackson was liable for charges made on a Home Depot credit card. Jackson—who was the defendant in the original action—brought a class action suit as a third-party plaintiff against Home Depot and another entity, alleging unlawful referral sales, and deceptive and unfair trade practices in violation of state law. Home Depot removed the case to federal court, and Jackson moved to remand on the ground that "third-party/additional counter defendants" like Home Depot were barred from removal. *Id.* at 1747. The Supreme Court held that removal was impermissible, reasoning that "[b]ecause in the context of these removal provisions the term 'defendant' refers only to the party sued by the original plaintiff . . . neither provision allows such a third party to remove." *Id.* at 1746.

H.   APPELLATE REVIEW

In the ordinary (non-CAFA) case, a party cannot normally seek appellate review of an order remanding a removed case to state court. Thus, subject only to limited exceptions, a federal district court has complete, unreviewable authority to remand a case to state court. By contrast, a ruling declining to remand a case to state court is reviewable by the federal appellate court, generally at the end of the case upon final judgment. Congress, in enacting CAFA, wanted to avoid situations where a single federal judge could circumvent CAFA by engaging in an unreviewable act of remanding a case to state court. Accordingly, Congress provided for discretionary immediate appellate review of remand decisions. Specifically, 28 U.S.C. § 1453(c)(1) gives federal courts of appeal discretion to grant immediate review of an order granting or denying a remand motion. The appeal, if granted, must be completed within 60 days from the date the appeal was filed, subject to one extension of ten days for good cause (upon agreement of all parties).

Despite the statute's reference to when the appeal was "filed," courts construing CAFA have held that the 60-day period for completing the appeal begins when the appeal is *accepted* by the appellate court, not when the appeal is *filed*. *See, e.g., Amalgamated Transit Union Local 1309, AFL-CIO v. Laidlaw Transit Servs., Inc.*, 435 F.3d 1140 (9th Cir. 2006). Focusing on the filing date would have made it impossible in many cases for the appellate court to comply with the 60-day (or even 70-day) period. CAFA provides that if the appeal is not resolved by the end of the 60-day (or 70-day) period, the appeal shall be deemed denied. 28 U.S.C. § 1453(c)(4).

Under CAFA, the application for appeal must be filed in the appellate court "not less than 7 days after entry of the order" granting or denying a remand motion. As written, this language would have led to absurd results: a party could not file an appeal until the seventh day but could do so any time thereafter. Courts addressing this issue have unanimously concluded, however, that "less than" was a typographical error and that Congress meant to allow appeals filed "within" or "not more than" seven days after entry of the order.

Courts have identified several factors to be considered in determining whether to grant discretionary review of a CAFA remand order. These include whether "an important CAFA-related question" is presented; whether the question is "unsettled"; whether the question appears to be "incorrectly decided or at least fairly debatable"; whether the question is "consequential to the resolution of the case"; whether the question is "likely to evade effective review" if left unanswered until after final judgment; whether the question is likely to recur; whether the decision or order at issue is "sufficiently final"; and whether the "balance of the relevant harms" weighs in favor of immediate review. *See Coll. of Dental Surgeons of P.R. v. Conn. Gen. Life Ins. Co.*, 585 F.3d 33, 36–40 (1st Cir. 2009).

§ 8.4 *RES JUDICATA* AND COLLATERAL ESTOPPEL

Class actions are designed to adjudicate, in a single action, the grievances of numerous parties with similar claims. One objective of a class action judgment is to prevent future litigation of *claims* that were, or could have been, litigated in the class action (*res judicata* or claim preclusion). Another goal is to prevent further litigation of *issues* that were determined in, and were necessary to resolve, the class action (collateral estoppel or issue preclusion). This section examines the doctrines of *res judicata* and collateral estoppel in the context of class actions.

A. CLAIM PRECLUSION (*RES JUDICATA*) IN THE CLASS ACTION CONTEXT

(1) Overview

Rule 23(c)(3) requires a court rendering a class action judgment to identify the members of the class. This requirement is necessary to determine who is bound by the judgment for *res judicata* purposes.

The doctrine of *res judicata* in a class action arises when a court enters judgment on the merits, and one or more of the parties identified in that judgment (individual class members, the class as a whole, or the opposing party) pursues a claim in a separate court based on the cause of action adjudicated in the prior judgment. *Res judicata* not only bars claims that were actually litigated during the class action, but also those that could have been litigated.

The difficulty in applying *res judicata* in the class action context stems from determining who is bound by the earlier judgment. Subject to certain exceptions discussed immediately below, in class actions brought under Rule 23 the *res judicata* effect of a judgment extends to the entire certified class. *Res judicata* does not, however, bar an unnamed putative class member from pursuing his or her own claims when class certification is denied.

(2) Class Members Who May Not Be Bound by a Prior Adjudication

There are two important exceptions to the general rule that the *res judicata* effect of a judgment extends to the entire certified class.

The first exception applies when the absent class members are not provided with the required notice and opportunity to opt out of the class. The determination of whether absent class members are provided with requisite notice depends on the type of Rule 23 class action at issue. In Rule 23(b)(3) class actions, best practicable notice and the opportunity to opt out are necessary to bind absent class members (although several lower courts have excused actual notice when notice was attempted but not achieved, such as when an apartment number was inadvertently omitted from an address (*see* § 6.1)). Lower courts are divided over whether, in "mandatory" class actions under Rules 23(b)(1)(A), 23(b)(1)(B) and 23(b)(2), in which monetary relief is sought, due process requires that absent class members be given an opportunity to opt out before they will be bound by a judgment in the class action. The Supreme Court has raised but not decided the issue. *See* § 6.1.

The second exception applies when the appointed class representative(s) and counsel fail to provide fair and adequate representation in the original suit. This factor requires a court to examine the qualifications and performance of both the named representative(s) and their counsel. *See* § 3.10. The adequacy analysis for *res judicata* differs from that by the original court in the sense that the original court may have ruled on adequacy of representation at the outset but may not have revisited the issue in light of the actual performance of the representative(s) and counsel at trial or during pretrial proceedings. For purposes of *res judicata*, a reviewing court may examine, for instance, whether the representatives were inadequate because they did not appeal an adverse ruling. As discussed in § 8.5, however, some courts have identified significant procedural limitations on a court's authority to review, on collateral attack, the adequacy findings of the certifying court. Other courts, by contrast, have permitted collateral attacks on the adequacy of representation, including the Second Circuit in the *Agent Orange* litigation, *see Stephenson v. Dow Chem. Co.*, 273 F.3d 249 (2d Cir. 2001), *aff'd by an equally divided Court*, 539 U.S. 111 (2003). The Supreme Court granted *certiorari* in *Stephenson* to address issues involving collateral attacks on adequacy. Ultimately, however, the Court split four to four (with Justice Stevens not participating) and thus did not issue a precedent-setting ruling. *See* § 8.5.

B.   ISSUE PRECLUSION (COLLATERAL ESTOPPEL) IN THE CLASS ACTION CONTEXT

Issue preclusion, or collateral estoppel, differs from claim preclusion in a basic way: Rather than precluding a subsequent cause of action entirely, it bars a party from raising an issue that was adjudicated in an earlier proceeding. Collateral estoppel can be "mutual" or "non-mutual." When the plaintiff and defendant in the subsequent action were both involved in the initial action, collateral estoppel is "mutual." When only one of the parties in the subsequent action was involved in the initial action, collateral estoppel may still apply, in which case it is "non-mutual." *Parklane Hosiery Co., Inc. v. Shore*, 439 U.S. 322 (1979). Issues involving both mutual and non-mutual collateral estoppel arise in class actions.

One issue is whether a defendant who prevails in an earlier class action can assert collateral estoppel against those class members who opted out of the earlier litigation. Courts have rejected such attempts on the ground that "[a]n opt-out plaintiff is not a party to the class action and ... collateral estoppel cannot bind a person who was neither a party nor privy to a prior suit." *In re Corrugated Container Antitrust Litig.*, 756 F.2d 411, 418–19 (5th Cir. 1985).

Another situation involving opt-out class members arises when the class prevails in the initial class action, and an opt-out class member in a subsequent lawsuit attempts to assert non-mutual collateral estoppel against the defendant. In *Premier Electrical Construction Co. v. National Electrical Contractors Association, Inc.*, 814 F.2d 358 (7th Cir. 1987), the Seventh Circuit refused to permit plaintiffs who opted out of a prior class action to use offensive issue preclusion in their subsequent individual suit against the defendant. To hold otherwise, the court reasoned, would unfairly give the opt-outs the best of all worlds: They would not be bound if the plaintiff class lost, but they could reap the benefits if the class won. According to the court, this sort of "one-way intervention" is precisely what Congress sought to eliminate when it did away with "spurious" classes in 1966. *Id.* at 362; *see* § 2.3.

§ 8.5 FEDERAL RELATIONS WITH STATE COURTS IN THE CLASS ACTION CONTEXT

Class actions frequently proceed on parallel tracks in federal and state court. At times, the same plaintiffs' lawyers may be pressing ahead on both tracks. At other times, two groups of plaintiffs' lawyers may be competing in a race to judgment.

Such parallel litigation leads to several important issues, including: (1) what, if any, preclusive effect a state court ruling has on a parallel federal proceeding; (2) whether collateral attacks may be mounted based on inadequate representation; and (3) what effect a denial of class certification in federal court has on a subsequent state court class action. This section discusses these issues, and also touches on the class action implications of the "*Rooker-Feldman*" doctrine, which provides that lower federal courts may not review state court decisions.

A.   BINDING EFFECT OF STATE COURT SETTLEMENTS OF EXCLUSIVELY FEDERAL CLAIMS

When a state court class action has been settled, and the settlement releases not only state-law claims but also claims that are within the exclusive jurisdiction of the federal courts, the question arises whether a member of the class is free to pursue those federal claims in federal court. Various aspects of this question were addressed by the Supreme Court in *Matsushita Electric Industries Co. v. Epstein*, 516 U.S. 367 (1996), and by the Ninth Circuit on remand in *Epstein v. MCA, Inc.*, 179 F.3d 641 (9th Cir. 1999). In that litigation, there had previously been two class actions against the same defendants, one in federal court (involving claims within the exclusive jurisdiction of the federal courts) and one in state court (involving only state-law claims). The state court plaintiffs settled on a classwide basis with the defendants, releasing all state and federal claims. Notice of the settlement was sent to the class, including the class representatives in the federal action, who did not exercise their right to opt out and did not appear at the settlement hearing. The state court subsequently conducted a hearing and approved the settlement. The defendants in the federal action then argued that the state court settlement was entitled to "full faith and credit" and precluded the plaintiffs' federal claims. The defendants relied on the Full Faith and Credit Act, 28 U.S.C. § 1738, which requires federal courts to give state court judgments the same force and effect that they would receive in a state court in the rendering jurisdiction. The class members who sought to pursue their claims notwithstanding the settlement responded that the federal court should not grant full faith and credit to the state court settlement because it was entered into in violation of the absent class members' right to adequate representation.

The Supreme Court held in *Matsushita* that a federal court is required to give full faith and credit to a state court settlement that releases claims within the exclusive jurisdiction of the federal courts. It reasoned that, because the state court had jurisdiction over the subject matter of the dispute, the fact that the federal claims could not have been litigated in state court did not bar the parties from settling those claims in the state action. The court did not decide whether the claims could nonetheless go forward in federal court because of the plaintiffs' contention that the state court settlement resulted from inadequate representation.

B. COLLATERAL ATTACKS BASED ON ADEQUACY OF REPRESENTATION

On remand from the Supreme Court in *Matsushita*, the Ninth Circuit initially held that the claims could go forward despite *Matsushita* because the representation of the class in the state court case had been inadequate. That decision was arguably in accord with the traditional rule permitting collateral attack based on inadequate representation. The court subsequently reversed itself, however, and held in a split decision that, under the Full Faith and Credit Act, federal courts are precluded from passing judgment on the adequacy of representation in state court if the issue has been fully and fairly litigated—and decided by the state court—in the context of the class settlement.

By contrast, as mentioned above, the Second Circuit, in a decision affirmed by an equally divided Supreme Court (and thus without precedential value), permitted a collateral attack on adequacy. *Stephenson v. Dow Chem. Co.*, 273 F.3d 249 (2d Cir. 2001), *aff'd by an equally divided court*, 539 U.S. 111 (2003). *In Stephenson*, the Second Circuit held that two veterans seeking a remedy for adverse health effects from exposure to Agent Orange could collaterally attack a prior classwide settlement of Agent Orange claims on the ground that the representation of the class had been inadequate. The court so held, even though the representation had been found adequate at the time of the original certification. In particular, the court found that the cutoff for claiming cash benefits contained in the settlement agreement resulted in a disadvantage to veterans whose injuries manifested themselves after the cutoff date and that such veterans, by being put in this situation, had been inadequately represented. According to the court, "[b]ecause these plaintiffs were inadequately represented in the prior litigation, they were not proper parties and cannot be bound by the settlement." 273 F.3d at 261.

In *In re Diet Drugs Products Liability Litigation*, 431 F.3d 141 (3d Cir. 2005), the Third Circuit expressly disagreed with the Second Circuit's decision in *Stephenson*, noting that "where the class action court has jurisdiction over an absent member of a plaintiff class and it litigates and determines the adequacy of the representation of that member, the member is foreclosed from later relitigating that issue." *Id*. at 146. Subsequently, the Second Circuit (in a partial retreat from *Stephenson*) recognized that collateral attack on adequacy grounds is *not* permitted if the precise argument was "considered and rejected by the class action court," but that collateral attack *is* appropriate "if the class action court ruled only in general terms that representation was adequate." *Wolfert v. Transamerica Home First, Inc.*, 439 F.3d 165, 172 (2d Cir. 2006). Ultimately, the Supreme Court will need to provide guidance on this issue.

C.   BINDING EFFECT OF PRIOR FEDERAL COURT DENIAL OF CLASS CERTIFICATION UPON A LATER STATE COURT CLASS ACTION

When a federal court denies class certification, one potential issue is whether a state court is allowed to grant class certification based upon similar claims. This question had divided the courts, with some refusing to give the denial of class certification preclusive effect, *see, e.g., J.R. Clearwater, Inc. v. Ashland Chem. Co.*, 93 F.3d 176 (5th Cir. 1996), and others holding that a ruling denying certification was binding not only on the named representatives but also on the unnamed class members, *see, e.g., In re Bridgestone/Firestone, Inc., Tires Prods. Liab. Litig.*, 333 F.3d 763 (7th Cir. 2003). The Supreme Court resolved the conflict in *Smith v. Bayer Corp.*, 564 U.S. 299 (2011).

In *Smith*, a federal district court, having denied class certification, enjoined a West Virginia state court from considering class certification under the West Virginia equivalent to Federal Rule of Civil Procedure 23. The district court had relied on the "relitigation exception" to the Anti-Injunction Act, a provision that permits a federal court to enjoin a state court proceeding when necessary to "protect or effectuate [the federal court's] judgments." 28 U.S.C. § 2283. The Supreme Court unanimously ruled that the district court exceeded its authority. It did so on two grounds.

First, the Court determined that the issue facing the West Virginia state court was not identical to the one addressed by the federal court. Class actions were more liberally certified in West Virginia (in particular, the "predominance" requirement was easier to satisfy under the state class action rule). Thus, the question facing the state court was not the same as the one decided by the federal court.

Second, the class representative in the state suit (Smith) was only an unnamed class member in the federal suit, and thus was not a "party" in the first suit. The Court determined that "[t]he definition of the term 'party' can on no account be stretched so far as to cover a person like Smith, whom the plaintiff in a lawsuit was denied leave to represent." *Id.* at 313.

§ 8.6 CLASHES BETWEEN FEDERAL RULE 23 AND STATE LAW

In *Shady Grove Orthopedic Associates, P.A. v. Allstate Insurance Co.*, 559 U.S. 393 (2010), a sharply divided Court held that Federal Rule of Civil Procedure 23 controlled over a New York state law purporting to prohibit certain state law statutory damages claims from being litigated on a classwide basis. Consequently, the plaintiff could maintain a class action in federal court under diversity jurisdiction, even where the forum state's law would forbid the same claims from being brought as a class action in state court.

The case began when medical provider Shady Grove Orthopedic Associates brought a putative class action against automobile insurer Allstate Insurance Company for alleged violation of New York's no-fault auto insurance law. Shady Grove sued in federal district court pursuant to CAFA's diversity jurisdiction provision, 28 U.S.C. § 1332(d)(2)(A), seeking statutory interest penalties on overdue payments of insurance benefits owed to plaintiffs. The federal district court dismissed the case on the ground that Section 901(b) of New York Civil Practice Law and Rules (CPLR 901(b)) prohibited class action suits seeking to recover a statutory penalty or minimum recovery, unless otherwise explicitly authorized by the statute.

In the Second Circuit, Shady Grove argued, *inter alia*, that the *Erie* doctrine precluded a federal court from applying a state procedural rule that would limit the use of a procedural device—*i.e.*, the class action—that was otherwise available under the Federal Rules of Civil Procedure. *Shady Grove Orthopedic Associates, P.A. v. Allstate Ins. Co.*, 549 F.3d 137, 141 (2d Cir. 2008). The Second Circuit disagreed and affirmed the district court's judgment.

The question faced by the Supreme Court in *Shady Grove* was whether, if a plaintiff sues in federal court under a state rule such as section 901(b), the case can be certified in federal court as a class action (assuming it otherwise meets Rule 23's criteria), despite the fact that the same claim could *not* be litigated on a classwide basis in state court. The Court's answer was yes—the state claims could be certified as a Rule 23 class action, because the federal rule displaced the state law's prohibition. The majority of the Justices who endorsed that conclusion disagreed on the proper analysis, however, resulting in some uncertainty as to how similar issues should be resolved.

Writing for four Justices, Justice Scalia's plurality opinion concluded that the relevant inquiry was "not the substantive or procedural nature or purpose of the affected state law," but rather "the substantive or procedural nature of the Federal Rule." 559 U.S. at 410. That is, "the validity of a Federal Rule depends entirely upon whether it regulates procedure. If it does, it is authorized by [the Rules Enabling Act] and is valid in all jurisdictions, with respect to all claims, regardless of its incidental effect upon state-created rights." *Id.* (citations omitted). Thus, the state claims at issue could be certified.

The fifth vote in the *Shady Grove* decision was Justice Stevens, who wrote a separate opinion concurring in the judgment. Although Justice Stevens agreed with the plurality that Federal Rule 23 should control in the case at hand, he suggested that "there are some state procedural rules that federal courts must apply in diversity cases because they function as a part of the State's definition of substantive rights and remedies." *Id.* at 416–17 (Stevens, J., concurring).

The dissent, written by Justice Ginsburg, argued that New York's law addressed an "entirely different concern" (*i.e.*, remedies and substance) than Rule 23's concern (*i.e.*, class action certification and conduct), and rejected the notion of an "inevitable collision" between the statutes. *Id.* at 447–49. Thus, in the dissent's view, the class action was prohibited.

In the wake of *Shady Grove*, federal courts faced with a conflict between a state law limiting or prohibiting class actions and Federal Rule of Civil

Procedure 23 have drawn differing conclusions. Courts applying *Shady Grove* have been challenged by at least two issues. First, which opinion controls, the plurality by Justice Scalia, or the concurrence by Justice Stevens? The answer is important, given that the plurality's approach is significantly less hospitable to state laws purporting to curtail class actions in federal court, whereas the concurrence's approach is more case-specific and nuanced. Second, having decided on the correct approach, the court must then decide whether the particular state rule in the case before it has any application in a federal class action.

On the threshold question, courts have largely agreed that Justice Stevens's concurrence—and not Justice Scalia's four-Justice plurality opinion—is the controlling approach. *See, e.g., In re Wellbutrin XL Antitrust Litig.*, 756 F. Supp. 2d 670, 675 (E.D. Pa. 2010); *In re Whirlpool Corp. Front-Loading Washer Prod. Liab. Litig.*, No. 1:08–WP–65000, 2010 WL 2756947, at *2 (N.D. Ohio July 12, 2010), *aff'd*, 678 F.3d 409 (6th Cir. 2012), *vacated*, 569 U.S. 901 (2013). On the substantive question, however, courts have diverged. Although several courts have upheld class action restrictions in state consumer protection laws, notwithstanding Rule 23, a clear consensus has not yet emerged. *Compare, e.g., McKinney v. Bayer Corp.*, 744 F. Supp. 2d 733, 747–49 (N.D. Ohio 2010) (distinguishing *Shady Grove* and applying state class action prohibition in federal court), *with In re OnStar Contract Litig.*, No. 2:07–MDL–01867 2010 WL 3516691, at *4 (E.D. Mich. Aug. 25, 2010) (holding that Rule 23 displaced a state statute limiting class action recovery to state residents, and thus the plaintiffs could pursue a nationwide class action in federal court).

§ 8.7 *"ROOKER-FELDMAN"* DOCTRINE

The *Rooker-Feldman* doctrine, enunciated by the Supreme Court in *Rooker v. Fidelity Trust Co.*, 263 U.S. 413 (1923), and *District of Columbia Court of Appeals v. Feldman*, 460 U.S. 462 (1983), stands for the principle that federal courts other than the U.S. Supreme Court lack jurisdiction to review state court decisions or claims inextricably intertwined with earlier state court judgments. A claim is inextricably intertwined with a state-court judgment where the federal court can grant relief only to the extent that it determines that the state court wrongly decided the case.

In the class action context, *Rooker-Feldman* issues may arise where class members in a resolved state court class action seek redress in federal court for alleged injustices in the state court class action. For example, in *Kamilewicz v. Bank of Boston Corp.*, 92 F.3d 506 (7th Cir. 1996), class members in an Alabama state court class action that had settled sued their own class counsel in federal district court because their recoveries under the settlement ranged from $0.00 to $8.76 while attorneys' fees amounted to several times that amount per class member. The district court dismissed the case for lack of subject matter jurisdiction under *Rooker-Feldman*, concluding that the suit amounted to a "collateral attack on a state court judgment which would require that [the district court] consider issues 'inextricably intertwined' with the state court case." *Id.* at 509. The Seventh Circuit agreed. It explained that, "if the injury which the federal plaintiff alleges resulted from the state court judgment itself, then *Rooker-Feldman* controls, and the lower federal courts lack jurisdiction over the claim." *Id.* at 510. The federal suit against class counsel, it reasoned, was simply "a multi-pronged attack on the [state court's] approval of the settlement regarding the attorney fees issue.... The federal claims are 'inextricably intertwined' with the state court judgment, whether that judgment is right or wrong." *Id.* at 511.

The Supreme Court has cautioned, however, that *Rooker-Feldman* is a very narrow doctrine. In *Lance v. Dennis*, 546 U.S. 459 (2006), the Court emphasized that the doctrine is "confined to cases brought by state-court losers complaining of injuries caused by state-court judgments rendered before the district court proceedings commenced and inviting district court review and rejection of those judgments." *Id.* at 464 (citation and internal quotation marks omitted).

CHAPTER 9

RESOLUTION AND FUNDING OF CLASS ACTIONS

This chapter addresses various issues that arise when a class action settles. It further discusses issues relating to class remedies, attorneys' fees, funding of class actions, and alternative dispute resolution (ADR).

§ 9.1 CLASS ACTION SETTLEMENTS

In non-class litigation, court approval of settlements is generally not required. Different rules apply, however, when a class action is settled. Rule 23(e)(1)(A) states that "[t]he claims, issues, or defenses of a certified class may be settled, voluntarily dismissed, or compromised only with the court's approval." Rule 23(e)(1) provides that "[t]he court must direct notice in a reasonable manner to all class members who would be bound by [a proposed settlement, dismissal, or compromise]." These requirements, along with additional provisions of Rule 23 adopted in 2003, raise a host of important issues.

A. OVERVIEW: INTERESTED PARTICIPANTS

Settlement negotiations in class actions are necessarily more complex than those involving traditional, non-class litigation. Numerous players have important roles, including the class representatives, class counsel, unnamed class members (who may support a settlement, take no position, or object to it), the defendant, defense counsel, insurers (who may be responsible for providing coverage for the claims), and the court. Surprising alliances frequently occur. For instance, it is not uncommon for class counsel and defense counsel to join forces in support of a settlement in the face of strong objections by particular class members. Issues of collusion and conflicts of interest sometimes arise in the settlement context. Understanding the roles of these various participants is important in considering the issues raised in the following sections.

B.   PRE-CERTIFICATION SETTLEMENT WITH ONLY NAMED PLAINTIFFS

Before discussing settlements that seek to bind the class as a whole, this section first examines pre-certification settlements that seek to bind only the named plaintiffs. At first blush, it might seem that such a settlement would not raise any concerns requiring judicial oversight. Prior to the 2003 amendments to Rule 23, however, some courts had held that the 1966 version of Rule 23(e), which barred "dismiss[al] or compromise[ ] without the approval of the court," applied even prior to certification. Those courts recognized that, prior to certification, there is a serious threat that the defendant will offer the named plaintiffs and plaintiffs' counsel an overly generous settlement, thereby resolving the claims of the class representatives and, hopefully, eliminating the threat of a class action. Put another way, the concern is that the named plaintiffs will leverage their status as representatives to enhance their bargaining power and achieve a lucrative settlement. Thus, some courts reasoned that, having filed a putative class claim, the class representatives and counsel cannot walk away from the case and settle only the representatives' claims without court approval. Such courts reasoned that they needed to ensure that the settlement amount (including attorneys' fees) was reasonable. An unusually large individual settlement for a dubious claim could indicate that the representatives and counsel were being paid a premium to agree not to pursue the class action.

Other courts, however, held that court approval was only required when a *certified* class was settled. The rationale of those cases was that, because only the named plaintiffs are bound by a pre-certification settlement, the putative class does not need the protection of court approval.

The 2003 amendments resolved the issue in favor of the latter approach. Rule 23(e) requires court approval only for settlement of "a certified class." The Advisory Committee Notes expressly reference the prior conflict in the case law and make clear that the amended rule does *not* "require court approval of settlements with putative class representatives that resolve[ ] only individual claims."

The *Manual for Complex Litigation (4th)* notes that, despite amended Rule 23(e), courts "should inquire into the circumstances behind [a precertification] dismissal" when "a voluntary dismissal might represent an abuse of the class action process." § 21.61 n.948. This might be the case, for example, when the named representatives receive an unusually large individual settlement that could be viewed as a payoff for agreeing not to prosecute the case as a class action. The ALI's *Principles of the Law of Aggregate Litigation* criticizes the approach of the 2003 amendments and argues that court approval should be required. § 3.02(b) at 193.

C.   NOTICE OF A PRE-CERTIFICATION SETTLEMENT OF INDIVIDUAL CLAIMS

Because the 2003 amendments do not require court approval of a pre-certification settlement, notice of such settlement to the putative class is also not required. Rule 23(e)(1)(B) requires notice only to "class members who would be bound" by a proposed settlement, voluntary dismissal or compromise. Unnamed class members, of course, would not be bound by a settlement solely between named plaintiffs and defendants. The Advisory Committee Notes state categorically that "notice is not required when the settlement binds only the individual class representatives."

The *Manual for Complex Litigation (4th)* points out, however, that notice to the putative class may be necessary in "unusual" cases involving possible "abuse of the class action procedure," § 21.312, such as concern about a representative reaping an unusually large individual settlement for agreeing not to prosecute the case as a class action. Such notice would be given pursuant to Rule 23(d)(1)(B) (*see* § 5.4).

D.   CERTIFICATION FOR
SETTLEMENT PURPOSES

During the 1980s and 1990s, courts began certifying class actions solely for purposes of settlement. Coinciding with that trend, some courts and commentators became increasingly concerned about the fairness of such settlements, debating whether certification for settlement only should be granted under a more lenient standard than certification for trial. These issues reached the Supreme Court in *Amchem Products, Inc. v. Windsor*, 521 U.S. 591 (1997).

In *Amchem*, the issue was whether a class had been legitimately certified for purposes of a global settlement of current and future asbestos-related claims. During negotiations, defendants had insisted that they would not settle the pending claims unless they received protection from future claims. Thus, settlement talks focused on creating an administrative scheme that would dispose of asbestos claims not yet in litigation. Class counsel, who represented the litigants in the thousands of asbestos cases already pending, also undertook to represent the interests of the anticipated future claimants. Objectors challenged the adequacy of class counsel and the named representatives, complaining of conflicts of interest between the pending and future claims. The district court found that the settlement was fair and certified the class for settlement purposes only.

The objectors appealed, arguing that the class of exposed asbestos claimants who had not already sued had not been properly certified under Rule 23. To resolve this issue, the appellate courts had to determine whether the standards for certification of a Rule 23(b)(3) class action for settlement purposes were less demanding than those mandated by Rule 23(b)(3) when a class is to be certified for trial. The argument for a lower standard was that, since the case was not going to trial, the Rule 23(a) and (b) criteria focusing on predominance, manageability, superiority, and commonality in the context of a class action trial were irrelevant. The Third Circuit ruled that settlement was not a proper consideration in applying Rule 23 and held that the certified class of future claimants did not satisfy the mandatory requirements of Rule 23(a) and (b)(3).

Although the Supreme Court affirmed in a 7–2 decision, its reasoning differed somewhat from that of the Third Circuit. Most importantly, the Court indicated that settlement *was* relevant to one aspect of class certification. In a settlement class, "a district court need not inquire whether the case, if tried, would present intractable management problems . . . for the proposal is that there be no trial." *Id.* at 620; *see* Fed. R. Civ. P. 23(b)(3)(D). The other requirements of Rule 23, however—"those designed to protect absentees by blocking unwarranted or overbroad class definitions—demand undiluted, even heightened, attention in the settlement context." *Id.*

The Court rejected the argument that, in the settlement context, satisfying Rule 23(a) and (b) was unnecessary because of Rule 23(e)'s requirements of a fairness determination and class notice. The Court noted that the Rule 23(e) requirements were *in addition* to the other standards under Rule 23 and did not supersede the normal certification inquiry. Applying the Rule 23 criteria (other than manageability), the Court agreed with the Third Circuit's holding that the Rule 23 requirements had not been satisfied by the sprawling settlement class certified by the district court.

Subsequently, in *Ortiz v. Fibreboard Corp.*, 527 U.S. 815 (1999), the Supreme Court, in striking down a proposed limited fund settlement class under Rule 23(b)(1)(B), reiterated that district courts must pay close attention to the requirements of Rule 23(a) and (b) in the settlement context. The Court stated that "[a] settlement's fairness under Rule 23(e) does not dispense with the requirements of Rule 23(a) and (b)." *Id.* at 863–64.

Both *Amchem* and *Ortiz* involved settlements designed to deal with the unique and difficult problems of asbestos litigation. Nonetheless, those opinions have guided the lower courts in evaluating other settlement classes. A number of courts have rejected classwide settlements in light of *Amchem*. *See, e.g., Grand Theft Auto Video Game Consumer Litig.*, 251 F.R.D. 139, 158 (S.D.N.Y. 2008). And many cases—especially mass torts—now settle outside of the class action context, without the protections of Rule 23(e) to ensure fairness to the class. *See* § 16.5. On the other hand, numerous class settlements have been approved notwithstanding *Amchem. See, e.g., In re Nat'l Football League Players Concussion Injury Litig.*, 821 F.3d 410 (3d Cir.), *cert.*

denied sub nom. Gilchrist v. Nat'l Football League,
137 S. Ct. 591, and *cert. denied sub nom. Armstrong
v. Nat'l Football League,* 137 S. Ct. 607 (2016);
Sullivan v. DB Investments, Inc., 667 F.3d 273 (3d
Cir. 2011).

Settlement classes have also been the subject of
possible rule changes, although no change has
actually been adopted. Thus, the Supreme Court
noted in *Amchem* that the Advisory Committee had
proposed an amendment to Rule 23 explicitly
permitting certification of settlement-only classes
"even though the requirements of subdivision (b)(3)
might not be met for purposes of trial." 521 U.S. at
619 (citation and internal quotation marks omitted).
After *Amchem,* however, the Advisory Committee
chose not to go forward with the proposal. In the
process leading up to the 2018 amendments to Rule
23, the Committee decided not to recommend a
proposal similar to the one noted in *Amchem.*

Also worth mentioning is the fact that the
American Law Institute (ALI) has proposed that
certification of settlement-only classes be permitted
under more relaxed standards than litigation
classes—in particular, without the need to satisfy
predominance. *See Principles of the Law of Aggregate
Litigation* § 3.06, at 219.

E.   BINDING EFFECT IN LATER LITIGATION
OF A CONCESSION THAT THE SETTLEMENT
CLASS IS APPROPRIATE FOR CERTIFICATION

Amchem makes clear that, apart from
manageability, the requirements for certification

under Rule 23(b)(3) apply not only to litigation classes but to settlement classes as well. Assume that the parties to a settlement present the proposal to a court, arguing that the case is properly certifiable as a settlement class. If the settlement does not go forward, is the defendant bound by such arguments in opposing certification of a class for litigation purposes? In *Carnegie v. Household International, Inc.*, 376 F.3d 656 (7th Cir. 2004), the court ruled that, under the doctrine of judicial estoppel, a party that urged certification of a settlement class was barred, after the settlement was disapproved, from later arguing against certification of a litigation class. The *Carnegie* decision has been criticized by some commentators, and the ALI rejects it. *See Principles of the Law of Aggregate Litigation* § 3.06(d), at 219. The Advisory Committee Notes to the 2018 amendments also reject the *Carnegie* approach, noting that "[i]f [a] settlement is not approved, the parties' positions regarding certification for settlement should not be considered if certification is later sought for purposes of litigation."

F.   CONSIDERATIONS IN APPROVING SETTLEMENTS

Preliminary Approval. For many years, most courts have followed a two-step process in reviewing a class settlement. First, the court decides whether the settlement is sufficiently within the realm of reasonableness to warrant notice to the class. If the case has not been certified as a class action, then the court also examines whether certification as a settlement class is likely. If the court decides these questions in the affirmative, it grants what is frequently called "preliminary approval." Upon preliminary approval, notice describing the proposed settlement is sent to the class. For a Rule 23(b)(3) settlement, the notice will also typically provide a set time period (and instructions) for class members to follow if they wish to object to the settlement or to opt out of the class. Prior to 2018, this two-step approach was not set forth in Rule 23.

In 2018, however, Rule 23 was amended to codify what had long been the prevailing practice. Under new Rule 23(e)(1)(A), the parties are required to provide the court with "information sufficient to enable it to determine" whether to approve sending notice to the class. And new Rule 23(e)(1)(B) provides that notice may be ordered only if it is "justified by the parties' showing that the court will likely be able to" ultimately grant final approval and certify a class.

The above-quoted language—permitting notice only after a court finds it "likely" that it will ultimately certify a class and grant final approval—is designed to front-load a serious review of the settlement. It is counterproductive for a court to give only a cursory review of a settlement before sending out notice, only to decide later that the settlement is unfair or that class certification is not proper.

Final Approval Criteria: Approach Prior to 2018. Well before the adoption of the 2018 amendments, it was well settled, pursuant to Rule 23(e)(2), that a court may approve a classwide settlement only after conducting a hearing and finding that the settlement is "fair, reasonable, and adequate." Under this process, class members who object to a proposed settlement have the opportunity to present those objections to the district court. The court is free to reject those objections or accept them (either by rejecting the settlement altogether or alerting the parties that changes must be made before the court will give its approval).

Prior to the 2018 amendments, Rule 23 contained no specific guidance on how courts should assess the fairness of class action settlements, although the Advisory Committee Notes referred to *In re Prudential Insurance Co. America Sales Practices Litigation Agent Actions,* 148 F.3d 283, 316–24 (3d Cir. 1998), and to the *Manual for Complex Litigation (4th).* Those authorities provide several factors that courts should consider, including: (1) the nature of the claims and possible defenses; (2) whether the proposed settlement was fairly and honestly negotiated; (3) whether serious questions of law and fact exist, placing the ultimate outcome of the litigation in doubt; (4) whether the value of an immediate recovery outweighs the mere possibility of future relief after protracted and expensive litigation; (5) whether the parties believe that the settlement is fair and reasonable; (6) the defendant's financial viability; (7) the number and objective merit of any objections received from the class members; (8) the risks in establishing damages; (9) the complexity, length, and expense of continued litigation; and (10) the stage of the proceedings.

Each circuit ultimately ended up formulating its own criteria for reviewing the fairness of settlements. While there was overlap among the circuits, there was also a lack of consistency—for instance, some circuits applied nine factors while others applied only four. *See Principles of the Law of Aggregate Litigation* § 3.05(a), at 205–07, 210 (discussing the variety of approaches).

Criteria Under the 2018 Amendments. In crafting amendments to Rule 23, the Advisory Committee noted the wide variety of approaches taken by the circuits with respect to the pertinent fairness criteria. The Committee determined that it would be useful to identify a limited number of core criteria that courts should consider in reviewing any class settlement. The new Rule 23(e)(2), which went into effect on December 1, 2018, instructs courts to consider whether:

(A) the class representatives and class counsel have adequately represented the class;

(B) the proposal was negotiated at arm's length;

(C) the relief provided for the class is adequate, taking into account:

   (i)   the costs, risks, and delay of trial and appeal;

   (ii) the effectiveness of any proposed method of distributing relief to the class, including the method of processing class-member claims;

    (iii) the terms of any proposed award of attorney's fees, including timing of payment; and

    (iv) any agreement required to be identified under Rule 23(e)(3); and

  (D) the proposal treats class members equitably relative to each other.

As the above language reveals, subsections A and B focus on procedural fairness, while subsections C and D focus on the fairness of the settlement's substantive terms.

It is important to note that these criteria do not displace the previously adopted circuit-specific criteria. Instead, they augment those criteria to ensure that district courts consider the critical factors. Over time, however, these Rule 23-based criteria are likely to lead to greater consistency among the circuits.

Presumption of Fairness (or Lack of Such a Presumption). Some courts apply a presumption that a settlement negotiated at arm's length is fair and reasonable. In applying such a presumption, courts have noted the strong policy considerations favoring settlement. *See, e.g., Wal-Mart Stores, Inc. v. VISA U.S.A.,* 396 F.3d 96 (2d Cir. 2005); *see also Principles of the Law of Aggregate Litigation* § 3.05(a), at 208–09.

Other courts, however, have been more skeptical in reviewing class settlements and have not begun their reviews with a presumption of fairness. For instance, in *Reynolds v. Beneficial National Bank*, 288 F.3d 277 (7th Cir. 2002), the Seventh Circuit, in an opinion by Judge Richard Posner, overturned a class settlement on the ground that:

> [T]he [trial] judge should have made a greater effort (he made none) to quantify the net expected value of continued litigation to the class, since a settlement for less than that value would not be adequate. Determining that value would require estimating the range of possible outcomes and ascribing a probability to each point on the range [discounted to present value].

Id. at 284–85. The appellate court was also troubled that "[t]wo classes were absorbed into the settlement even though their claims were sharply different from those of the classes represented by the settlement counsel." *Id.* at 285.

Courts have been particularly skeptical when potential ethical concerns are raised regarding class counsel. For instance, in *Eubank v. Pella Corp.*, 753 F.3d 718 (7th Cir. 2014), the Seventh Circuit overturned a class settlement because of numerous ethical violations by class counsel, including a conflict of interest created by the fact that lead class counsel was the lead class representative's son-in-law. *See also, e.g., Pearson v. NBTY*, 772 F.3d 778, 781 (7th Cir. 2014) (overturning settlement because it provided for attorneys' fees to class counsel of "an outlandish 69 percent" of the total settlement value); *Radcliffe v. Experian Info. Solutions Inc.*, 715 F.3d 1157, 1167 (9th Cir. 2013) (overturning settlement due to inadequacy of class counsel where counsel's agreement with the class representatives provided for incentive payments only if the representatives supported the settlement). For further discussion of the increased judicial focus on ethical violations in the settlement class context, *see* Robert H. Klonoff, *Class Actions in the Year 2026: A Prognosis*, 65 Emory L.J. 1569, 1623–35 (2016).

Side Agreements. In connection with the settlement approval process, Rule 23(e)(3) requires parties seeking settlement approval to "file a statement identifying any agreement made in connection with [the proposed settlement, voluntary dismissal, or compromise.]" This provision was adopted as part of the amendments to Rule 23 in 2003. The Advisory Committee Notes point out that, even prior to the amendment, the parties were required to "disclose all terms of the settlement or compromise that the court must approve under Rule 23(e)(1)." The 2003 amendment was "aim[ed] instead at related undertakings that, although seemingly separate, may have influenced the terms of the settlement by trading away possible advantages for the class in return for advantages to others." The Notes point out that, while the court may request the actual agreements (or summaries thereof), the amendment "should not become the occasion for discovery by the parties or objectors."

Simultaneous Certification and Settlement. Some cases are settled after initially being certified as class actions over the defendant's opposition. Other putative classes, such as in *Amchem*, seek certification and approval of a settlement simultaneously. As the *Manual for Complex Litigation (4th)* points out, "[c]lass actions certified solely for settlement, particularly early in the case, sometimes make meaningful judicial review more difficult and more important." § 21.612. Indeed, some courts have held that more scrutiny should be given to cases certified and settled simultaneously than to cases settled after initially being certified.

In-Kind Settlements. A major factor impacting a court's assessment of fairness is the use of in-kind payments. Class action settlements have increasingly made use of in-kind payments, *i.e.*, non-cash compensation paid by the defendant to the plaintiff class. These in-kind payments often take the form of discount coupons that the class members can redeem when purchasing the defendant's products (so-called coupon settlements). Courts have had the opportunity to consider class action settlements involving discounts on air travel, video games, kitchen appliances, automobiles, and even bar review courses. Some courts and commentators have expressed concern that such settlements, rather than punishing the defendant, offer the defendant a disguised promotional opportunity. As a result, some courts have rejected such settlements, although other courts have approved them. Some coupon settlements have been structured to include an additional cash component or to require minimum payments in the event of low coupon redemption. Significantly, CAFA places major new restrictions on coupon settlements. *See* § 9.2.

Hearing Requirement. Another settlement-related issue is whether a fairness hearing must be held, even if no one lodges an objection to the proposed settlement. As a result of the 2003 amendments, Rule 23(e)(2) now makes clear (consistent with the prevailing practice) that a hearing—but not necessarily live testimony—is required before court approval of *any* class action settlement.

Lack of Court Authority to Alter Terms. Although a court may play a role in encouraging settlements, it does not have the power under Rule 23(e) to rewrite a proposed settlement on its own initiative or at the request of objectors. Put another way, the court cannot force the parties to accept a settlement to which they have not agreed. The court is only authorized to: (1) accept the proposed settlement; (2) reject the settlement and postpone the trial to see if a different settlement can be reached; or (3) try the case. *Evans v. Jeff D.*, 475 U.S. 717 (1986).

After a court preliminarily approves a settlement and notice is sent to the class, the issue sometimes arises whether notice is required if the parties subsequently change the terms of the settlement after the opt-out period or period for objecting expires. Substantial modification of the proposal may prejudice the rights of absent class members who relied on the original terms in deciding not to object or opt out. Courts vary as to whether they will permit amendments at this late stage, but they are more likely to permit amendments that are merely technical in nature or amendments that strengthen (as opposed to weaken) the settlement from the class's perspective.

G.   POST-CERTIFICATION NOTICE OF SETTLEMENT

If a class has previously been certified and notice has been sent out, notice of settlement is still required if the parties reach an agreement. Rule 23(e)(1) states that "[t]he court must direct notice in a reasonable manner to all class members who would be bound" by the settlement. In contrast to the explicit language of Rule 23(c)(2), however, Rule 23(e) does not dictate the method or content of the required notice. Thus, courts have substantial discretion, subject only to due process requirements.

In *Mullane v. Central Hanover Bank & Trust Co.*, 339 U.S. 306 (1950), the Supreme Court stated that, to meet due process standards, notice must be "reasonably calculated, under all the circumstances, to apprise interested parties of the pendency of the action." *Id.* at 314. Although the case was not a class action, its due process standards were incorporated into Rule 23 when the rule was amended in 1966.

Under *Eisen v. Carlisle & Jacquelin*, 417 U.S. 156 (1974), first-class mail to identifiable individuals, combined with publication, fully satisfies the notice requirements of both Rule 23 and the Due Process Clause. *See* § 6.1. Because this method satisfies the higher notice standard of Rule 23(c)(2), it clearly satisfies the lesser standards under Rule 23(e).

In some instances, electronic notice will suffice even under Rule 23(c)(2)(B). As noted in § 6.1, electronic notice has become increasingly common, and the 2018 amendment to Rule 23(c)(2)(B) clarifies that electronic notice may sometimes be an effective (or even the most effective) form of notice. A number of courts have approved notice of class settlements via e-mail, websites, and other electronic means, particularly in cases involving technology or online services where the parties already rely on such means of communication. *See, e.g., Browning v. Yahoo! Inc.*, No. C04–01463, 2007 WL 4105971, at *4 (N.D. Cal. Nov. 16, 2007) ("Email notice was particularly suitable in this case, where settlement class members' claims arise from their visits to Defendants' Internet websites.") (citation omitted). Other courts, however, have deemed e-mail notice inadequate when the defendant has access to class members' mailing addresses. *See, e.g., Karvaly v. eBay Inc.*, 245 F.R.D. 71, 91–93 (E.D.N.Y. 2007) (rejecting notice of settlement via e-mail as an inadequate substitute for traditional first-class mail despite the parties' reliance on Internet communications).

The more difficult issue is whether—and when—notice short of that required under (c)(2) satisfies the lesser standard of Rule 23(e). Because the matter is largely left to the discretion of the trial court, there is no clear answer. Some courts have found that simple publication, or even posting, may suffice, reasoning that the form of notice need not reach every class member. Other courts have taken a more rigorous approach and have required greater efforts to ensure that notice is received by class members who can be reasonably identified. The Advisory Committee Notes to the 2003 amendments point out that, in some circumstances, individual notice in the settlement context may be required "in the manner required by Rule 23(c)(2)(B) for certification notice to a Rule 23(b)(3) class." The Notes explain that "[i]ndividual notice is appropriate, for example, if class members are required to take action—such as filing claims—to participate in the judgment, or if the court orders a settlement opt-out opportunity under Rule [23(e)(4)]" (*see* discussion in the following section). Of course, if the case is certified under (b)(3) at the same time the settlement is approved, then the notice requirements of Rule 23(c)(2)(B) would apply.

As explained in § 6.1, although Rule 23(e) does not specify all of the information that must be included in a notice, certain items—including the settlement's terms and information about the fairness hearing—should normally be included. The Federal Judicial Center provides several examples of notices of class settlements at https://www.fjc.gov/content/301253/ illustrative-forms-class-action-notices-introduction (last visited July 30, 2020).

H.   OPPORTUNITY TO OPT OUT OF A PROPOSED SETTLEMENT AFTER EXPIRATION OF ORIGINAL OPT-OUT PERIOD

Added to Rule 23 in 2003, Rule 23(e)(4) provides that, in a case previously certified under Rule 23(b)(3), "the court may refuse to approve a settlement unless it affords a new opportunity to request exclusion to individual class members who had an earlier opportunity to request exclusion but did not do so." This provision deals with the situation in which the time to opt out has expired before a proposed settlement is reached. Without another opt-out opportunity, class members would be forced to accept the settlement or to try to derail it through objections. They would not be permitted to opt out. Under the 2003 amendments, the court has discretion to condition approval of the settlement on allowing class members another opportunity to opt out. This judicial option to afford another opt-out right is limited to (b)(3) class actions.

Thus far, relatively few courts have actually ordered a second opt-out period. *See, e.g., In re Nat'l Football League Players' Concussion Injury Litig.*, 307 F.R.D. 351, 423 (E.D. Pa. 2015) (second opportunity to opt out not required by due process), *aff'd on other grounds*, 821 F.3d 410 (3d Cir. 2016). And the Second Circuit has indicated that appellate courts will apply a deferential standard when a court refuses to grant a second opt-out right. *Denney v. Deutsche Bank AG*, 443 F.3d 253 (2d Cir. 2006). The American Law Institute has taken a stronger position, proposing that class members should ordinarily have a second period to opt out "[i]n any class action in which the terms of a settlement are not revealed until after the initial period for opting out has expired." *Principles of the Law of Aggregate Litigation* § 3.11, at 253. But neither Rule 23 nor the case law has adopted the ALI's approach.

I.   OBJECTIONS TO SETTLEMENT

Overview. Rule 23(e)(5)(A) states that any class member may lodge objections to a proposed settlement pursuant to Rule 23(e). These objections may result in agreed modifications favorable to the class or they may lead the court to reject the settlement. Of course, the most common outcome is that the district court will simply overrule the objections.

Specificity. Prior to 2018, Rule 23 did not provide guidance regarding the level of specificity required in objecting to a class settlement. For instance, there was nothing to stop an objector from simply filing an objection saying that the settlement was "unfair" and "improper"—objections that obviously offered no insight for the court. In the 2018 amendments, however, Rule 23 was modified in two ways (in new Rule 23(e)(5)(A)) to ensure that objections are not merely conclusory. First, an objection must state "with specificity" the grounds for the objection. Conclusory objections will no longer suffice. Second, the objection must state whether it applies "only to the objector, to a specific subset of the class, or to the entire class[.]" These new requirements are designed to force an objector to do the hard work of crafting potentially legitimate objections, instead of just lodging vague and unspecified criticisms.

Professional Objectors: Pre-2018 Amendments. For many years, courts and scholars have noted the potential for abuse by objectors. A not uncommon practice was for an objector to approach class counsel for a side-payment in exchange for dismissal of an objection. Because even a frivolous appeal could hold up finalization of a settlement for years—given the objector's ability to lodge an appeal in the federal court of appeals and, subsequently, in the Supreme Court—plaintiffs' counsel were often willing to make such payments.

The *Manual for Complex Litigation (4th)* recognized that objections may be made "for improper purposes" that would "benefit only the objectors and their attorneys (*e.g.*, by seeking additional compensation to withdraw even ill-founded objections)." § 21.643. As the *Manual* pointed out, even baseless objections "can be costly and significantly delay implementation of a class settlement." *Id.* Indeed, some attorneys have been censured by courts as "serial" or "professional" objectors. *See, e.g., In re Cathode Ray Tube (CRT) Antitrust Litig.*, 281 F.R.D. 531, 533 (N.D. Cal. 2012) (discussing attorney who "routinely represents objectors purporting to challenge class action settlements, and does not do so to effectuate changes to settlement, but does so for his own personal financial gain"); *In re Initial Pub. Offering Sec. Litig.*, 728 F. Supp. 2d 289, 294 (S.D.N.Y. 2010) (identifying several attorneys as "serial objectors"). The problem of professional objectors was also noted in the academic literature. *See, e.g.,* John E. Lopatka & D. Brooks Smith, *Class Action Professional Objectors: What to Do About Them?*, 39 Fla. St. U. L. Rev. 865 (2012).

Prior to 2018, Rule 23 provided—in what was then Rule 23(e)(5)—that objections could "be withdrawn only with the court's approval." And, as noted, even prior to 2018, Rule 23 required disclosure of side agreements. Yet these provisions did not deter professional objectors from filing baseless appeals to secure side-payments. Most importantly, the disclosure of side agreements to the district court could be circumvented once the objector filed an appeal from the approval of the settlement. At that point, the objector could pursue a side payment without any disclosure obligations.

When the Advisory Committee began looking into proposed changes to Rule 23—several years before the adoption of the 2018 amendments—the problem of professional objectors was cited by judges, attorneys, and scholars as the abuse most in need of a rule change. Those concerns ultimately led to the various amendments to Rule 23 addressing objectors.

2018 Amendments to Deter Baseless and Bad Faith Objectors. As noted above, the 2018 amendments added language to Rule 23 requiring that objections be stated with specificity. The centerpiece of the amendments, however, is a new provision that requires court approval of any payment in connection with the dismissal of any objection, either at the trial level or on appeal. It adopts the process of Federal Rule of Civil Procedure 62.1, which deals with the situation in which a case is on appeal but the appellate court wishes to obtain the views of the trial court. Thus, the amendment addresses a major shortcoming of the prior rule—*i.e.,* that the requirement of disclosure of side agreements to the district court could be circumvented once the objector filed an appeal from the district court's approval of the settlement.

Early signs indicate that the amendment is having some impact. In *In re Foreign Exchange Benchmark Rates Antitrust Litigation,* 334 F.R.D. 62 (S.D.N.Y. 2019), the court was asked to approve a payment of $300,000 to an objector by class counsel (to be paid from counsel's attorneys' fees) in exchange for the objector's dismissal of an appeal raising the objection. While recognizing that legitimate objectors can perform a valuable service, the court noted that the objection at issue "does little more than benefit Objector's counsel and 'perpetuate a system that can encourage objections advanced for improper purposes'" (quoting the Advisory Committee Note to the 2018 amendments). The court further noted that "the amount of the award had nothing to do with the Objector's objection." *Id.* at 64. And it noted that approval of such a request "would serve only to encourage objectors or their attorneys to extract this type of payment, and 'make a living simply by filing frivolous appeals and thereby slowing down the execution of settlements.'" *Id.* Thus, the court declined to approve the requested payment and dismissal.

In *Rougvie v. Ascena Retail Group, Inc.,* No. CV 15–724, 2019 WL 944811 (E.D. Pa. Feb. 21, 2019), although the court found that the 2018 amendments to Rule 23 did not apply to settlements approved in 2017, it expressed optimism about the amended Rule: "This amendment should prove to facilitate objections by good-faith objectors often not represented by counsel while discouraging bad-faith or professional objectors represented by counsel seeking fees." *Id.* at *17.

It is too soon to know whether the amended rule will substantially deter objectors who improperly seek side payments to drop their objections. Obviously, the success of the amendment will turn on whether counsel act with integrity. Nothing can be done if unethical counsel are willing to state (falsely) that no side payments were made for dismissal of an objection when in fact payments were made "under the table." Moreover, when the parties comply with the rule and seek approval of a side payment, courts must be vigilant in rejecting side payments absent a showing that the objections resulted in actual benefits to the class.

Finally, it should be noted that, when a payment has been made to an objector (either by class counsel or the defendant) in exchange for dismissal of the objection, a potential remedy is disgorgement of the payment. In *Pearson v. Target Corp.*, 968 F.3d 827 (7th Cir. 2020), the Seventh Circuit held that disgorgement was a proper remedy when the defendant and class counsel each contributed to pay three objectors a total of $130,000 to dismiss their objections. Normally, the class would have obtained the disgorged funds, but in *Nick Pearson,* it would not have been economically feasible to distribute the funds directly to class members because of the high administrative costs involved. Thus, the court approved distribution of those funds to a *cy pres* recipient, a research and education foundation. Of course, if Rule 23(e)(5), as amended in 2018, works as expected, no payments will be made in the first place because courts will refuse to approve payments to objectors whose objections did not benefit the class.

For an in-depth treatment of professional objectors and the pertinent 2018 amendments, *see* Robert H. Klonoff, *Class Action Objectors: The Good, the Bad, and the Ugly*, 89 Fordham L. Rev. ___ (forthcoming 2020).

Discovery by Objectors. Objectors can gain access to information necessary to challenge a proposed settlement by asking the district court to allow them to take discovery. In rare circumstances, such discovery may even include depositions of counsel involved in settlement negotiations. Of course, it is within the court's discretion to deny discovery by objectors.

Standing to Appeal. One issue that previously divided courts was whether a class member who timely objected to a class settlement at the fairness hearing had the power to bring an appeal without first intervening. The Supreme Court resolved this issue in *Devlin v. Scardelletti,* 536 U.S. 1 (2002). In *Devlin*, an unnamed class member, Devlin, sought to intervene but his motion was denied. Later, Devlin objected to the settlement at the fairness hearing, but the settlement was approved despite his objections. The Fourth Circuit held that since Devlin was not a named representative and had correctly been denied intervention, he lacked standing to challenge the settlement on appeal. The Supreme Court reversed, reasoning that the right to appeal was not restricted to named parties to the litigation. The Court held that "nonnamed class members are parties to the proceedings in the sense of being bound by settlement." *Id.* at 10. As a result, as long as they objected to the settlement in a timely fashion at the district court level, they are allowed to challenge the settlement on appeal without being required to intervene in the case. One open issue under *Devlin* is whether the decision applies only to mandatory classes (*Devlin* itself involved a mandatory class). Some courts have concluded that *Devlin* does not apply to opt-out classes, reasoning that the objectors could have avoided their problem by exiting from the class. Other courts, however, have declined to so limit *Devlin*.

§ 9.2 CAFA SETTLEMENT PROVISIONS

CAFA addresses a variety of settlement issues. The overriding concern expressed by Congress was that courts (particularly state courts) had been approving settlements that rewarded plaintiffs' counsel handsomely but offered little, if any, meaningful recovery to the class. To address this concern, Congress focused on four areas: coupon settlements, net-loss settlements, settlements that favor some class members over others based on geographic location, and notification of appropriate federal and state officials.

A.   COUPON SETTLEMENTS

CAFA regulates fee awards in coupon settlements. Under 28 U.S.C § 1712(a), if a class settlement provides for recovery of coupons to the class, "the portion of any attorney's fee award to class counsel that is attributable to the award of the coupons shall be based on the value to class members of the coupons that are redeemed." This provision is designed to discourage coupon settlements that afford little real value to class members but provide the basis for large attorneys' fees for class counsel. For instance, a coupon good for $500 off the price of a $30,000 automobile almost certainly does not yield $500 in value to each class member. Most class members would never use such a coupon, particularly to buy the very brand of vehicle about which they complained. A secondary market for such coupons (such as eBay) would undoubtedly yield a cash price of far less than $500. Yet, prior to CAFA, class counsel often used the face value of coupons in claiming a percentage of the "fund" as attorneys' fees. *See* § 9.4.

The statute does not define "coupon," thus raising myriad questions. For instance, it is unclear whether a settlement involving gift cards or vouchers would constitute a coupon settlement. *Compare, e.g., Redman v. RadioShack Corp.*, 768 F.3d 622, 635–36 (7th Cir. 2014) (rejecting distinction between "coupons" and "vouchers" and noting that, "from the standpoint of the dominant concerns that animate the provisions of [CAFA] regarding coupon settlements it's a matter of indifference whether the coupon is a discount off the full price of an item or is equal to (or for that matter more than) the item's full price"), *with, e.g., In re Online DVD-Rental Antitrust Litig.*, 779 F.3d 934, 950–52 (9th Cir. 2015) (holding that settlement consisting of $12 Wal-Mart gift cards was not a "coupon settlement" within the meaning of CAFA, in part because class members received "a set amount of money to use on their choice of a large number of products from a large retailer"). Moreover, CAFA does not explain how the actual value of coupons should be calculated, or when the calculation should be made (at the time of settlement, only after the expiration of the redemption period, or at some intermediate point). Presumably, Congress anticipated that courts would rely on expert testimony to determine value; CAFA explicitly permits a court to "receive expert testimony from a witness qualified to provide information on the actual value to class members of the coupons that are redeemed." 28 U.S.C § 1712(d).

B.   NET LOSS SETTLEMENTS

Under 28 U.S.C § 1713, a court may approve a settlement in which a class member receives a "net loss" only upon finding in writing "that nonmonetary benefits to the class member substantially outweigh the monetary loss." Congress passed this provision in response to isolated but highly publicized cases in which class members actually suffered a net loss under a class settlement (after deductions for attorneys' fees). In practice, net loss settlements were extremely rare even before the enactment of 28 U.S.C. § 1713. Moreover, even prior to CAFA, Rule 23(e)(2) provided a tool for addressing such settlements by requiring that a court find, as a condition of approval, that a class settlement is "fair, reasonable, and adequate."

C.   PROHIBITION AGAINST GEOGRAPHIC-BASED DISCRIMINATION IN SETTLEMENTS

Under 28 U.S.C § 1714, "[t]he court may not approve a proposed settlement that provides for the payment of greater sums to some class members than to others solely on the basis that the class members to whom the greater sums are to be paid are located in closer geographic proximity to the court." The source of concern that led Congress to enact this provision is unclear; the legislative history cited no instances of disparate payments based solely on geographic location. In any event, as noted, Rule 23(e)(2) already provided a vehicle for a court to invalidate an unfair settlement by requiring that a court find a class settlement to be "fair, reasonable, and adequate."

D.   NOTICE TO GOVERNMENT OFFICIALS

Under 28 U.S.C § 1715(b), within ten days after a proposed settlement is filed with the court, "each defendant that is participating in the proposed settlement shall serve upon the appropriate State official of each State in which a class member resides and the appropriate Federal official, a notice of the proposed settlement." The notice must contain numerous items including, *inter alia,* the complaint, notice, settlement terms, names of class members (or, if not feasible, an estimate (by state) of the number of class members), and any applicable agreements of counsel and opinions by the court. 28 U.S.C § 1715(b)(1), (8). The purpose of the notice is to allow interested officials to weigh in on the fairness of the proposed settlement. Often, the appropriate federal official to notify is the U.S. Attorney General. The appropriate state official, however, is not always clear. CAFA requires notification of "the person in the State who has primary regulatory or supervisory responsibility with respect to the defendant, or who licenses or otherwise authorizes the defendant to conduct business in the State, if some or all of the matters alleged in the class action are subject to regulation by that person." 28 U.S.C § 1715(a)(2). Multiple officials may fit this description, raising a dilemma for defense counsel.

The penalty for noncompliance with the notice requirement is severe: a class member, at his or her option, may choose not to be bound by the settlement. 28 U.S.C § 1715(e)(1). For that reason, some commentators have urged defense counsel to err on the side of giving notice to all officials who are even arguably within the statutory mandate. The downside is that the amount of material that must be disclosed may, in many cases, be voluminous.

It is not clear whether the notice requirement has led to meaningful participation by government officials. Anecdotal evidence suggests that, in most class settlements, notice to government officials has not had a major impact.

E.   GAPS IN CAFA'S SETTLEMENT PROVISIONS

CAFA's settlement provisions contain several limitations and gaps. Two serious ones are worth noting.

First, the settlement provisions apply only to federal court class actions. Thus, the parties to a settlement—even of a federal case—can settle the case in state court, thereby avoiding CAFA's limitations. For example, if both sides are agreeable to a coupon settlement that would determine fees based on the face value of coupons, the plaintiffs can file a copycat lawsuit in state court, and present the coupon settlement to the state court judge. Because the defendant will not want to remove the case to federal court, CAFA's settlement provisions will not apply, 28 U.S.C. § 1711(2) (limiting term "class action" to cases filed in or removed to federal court), and the parties can settle without CAFA's restrictions. The existing federal case would then be dismissed as *res judicata*. Congress arguably did not anticipate such an easy route to circumvent CAFA, and it could potentially fix the problem by making state cases that would qualify under CAFA subject to the settlement provisions, even if the defendant chooses not to remove the particular case to federal court.

Second, the underlying principle of CAFA's coupon provisions—basing fees on actual "value" to the class—is not carried forth with respect to non-coupon settlements. For example, a common approach to settlement is for defendant to set up a "fund" from which payments claimed by class members are made, with any unclaimed funds reverting to defendant. To illustrate, if a settlement calls for a payment by a computer company of $10 for each defective computer monitor made during a particular period of time (1 million monitors in all), the parties might set up a fund for $10 million, with any unclaimed funds to revert to the defendant. Given the small amounts involved, it is unlikely that many class members will go to the trouble of filing claims. If attorneys' fees are based on the total fund, not the amount actually claimed, then the situation is analytically very similar to fees based on the face amount—rather than the actual value—of coupons in a coupon settlement. Many courts have permitted fees to be based on the entire fund, even if the likelihood is that most of the fund will revert to the defendant. Although the policy of CAFA would appear contrary to such fee awards, CAFA (by its terms) does not forbid them.

§ 9.3 CLASS ACTION REMEDIES

Courts utilize a variety of approaches in allocating remedies among class members. In some instances, individual class members will be required to come forward and prove their damages separately, sometimes in jury or arbitration proceedings. In other instances, particularly when a settlement fund is involved, courts are able to utilize more efficient procedures, such as summary proceedings before a special master or the submission of proof-of-claim forms or other documentation establishing injuries. Certain kinds of cases, such as securities fraud cases, are particularly suitable for simplified administrative procedures. Others, such as discrimination and mass tort cases, are less suitable for summary procedures, and may sometimes require mini-trials or arbitrations.

In many cases, individual adjudication of damages is not feasible, either because of difficulty identifying individual class members or because the damages that would be allocated to each class member are so small that they would be outweighed by the administrative costs of distributing the awards. One device that some courts have used (mainly in settlements) is the fluid recovery or *cy pres* ("as near as possible") approach. Fluid recovery permits the calculation of damages on an aggregate basis and the distribution of funds to benefit the entire class. Two common approaches are used: (1) requiring a defendant to reduce the market price of a good or service (such as taxicab fares) for a period of time to compensate for alleged overcharges; or (2) using the recovery to provide funding for a public interest organization or a project that will benefit the class as a whole (*e.g.*, a contribution to a public interest organization for health research or to a water pollution cleanup fund). Courts using the fluid recovery mechanism often point out that it prevents wrongdoers from being unjustly enriched when damages are too small to be distributed to individual class members in a cost-effective way.

Several federal courts have raised concerns about the use of fluid recovery as a means of resolving manageability difficulties associated with proving individual claims. As the Ninth Circuit has stated, "allowing gross damages by treating unsubstantiated claims of class members collectively significantly alters substantive rights under the [statute in question]." *In re Hotel Tel. Charges*, 500 F.2d 86, 90 (9th Cir. 1974). Other courts, however, have concluded that the propriety of using fluid recovery to award damages should be evaluated on a case-by-case basis. *See, e.g., Simer v. Rios*, 661 F.2d 655 (7th Cir. 1981).

When damages are awarded pursuant to a statutory scheme and are not dependent upon individualized proof, the concerns about circumventing manageability issues by using a *cy pres* approach do not arise. Nonetheless, some courts have still expressed concern that the funds are not going directly to the class members.

The use of fluid recovery is also less controversial when a court uses it solely for the purpose of distributing *unclaimed* damages, rather than as a tool for distributing the damages as a whole. *See, e.g., Six (6) Mexican Workers v. Arizona Citrus Growers*, 904 F.2d 1301 (9th Cir. 1990). In such circumstances, because the fluid recovery affects the interests of only those class members who have not presented claims, courts are generally more receptive to a fluid recovery approach. when only unclaimed damages are involved.

The ALI endorses *cy pres* remedies in class settlements only if certain rigorous criteria are met. In essence, payments should go to individual claimants if feasible. If individual distributions are not viable (because the amounts are too small or class members cannot be identified), then *cy pres* payments are permissible. In that circumstance, however, the court should select a recipient whose interests approximate those of the class. *Principles of the Law of Aggregate Litigation* § 3.07, at 223–24.

Numerous courts have relied on the ALI approach. *See, e.g., In re BankAmerica Corp. Sec. Litig.*, 775 F.3d 1060 (8th Cir. 2015); *Rohn v. Tap Pharm. Prods. (In re Lupron Mktg. & Sales Practices Litig.)*, 677 F.3d 21 (1st Cir. 2012); *Klier v. Elf Atochem N. Am. Inc.*, 658 F.3d 468 (5th Cir. 2011). As the *BankAmerica Corp.* court noted:

> Because the settlement funds are the property of the class, a *cy pres* distribution to a third party of unclaimed settlements funds is permissible only when it is not feasible to make further distributions to class members.... [In that event,] the unclaimed funds should be distributed for a purpose as near as possible to the legitimate objectives underlying the lawsuit, the interests of class members, and the interests of those similarly situated.

775 F.3d at 1064–67 (citation and internal quotation marks omitted). As the above-quoted language reveals, the approach of the ALI and courts following the ALI approach is to presume, where possible, that the money should go to class members. If that is not feasible, then tight controls should be imposed on the selection of the recipient.

Some scholars would go further: they would bar *cy pres* awards on the ground that they are improper devices that do not compensate class members but simply provide a windfall to third-party organizations. *See, e.g.,* Martin H. Redish, Peter Julian & Samantha Zyontz, *Cy Pres Relief and the Pathologies of the Modern Class Action: A Normative and Empirical Analysis*, 62 Fla. L. Rev. 617, 623

(2010) ("*Cy Pres* creates the illusion of class compensation.").

Ultimately, Supreme Court guidance on *cy pres* remedies may be necessary. Indeed, in 2013, Chief Justice Roberts authored a statement regarding the Supreme Court's denial of certiorari in a case involving a *cy pres* remedy. *Marek v. Lane*, 571 U.S. 1003 (2013). He acknowledged the "fundamental concerns surrounding the use of [*cy pres*] in class action litigation" and suggested that the "Court may need to clarify the limits on the use of such remedies" in a future case. *Id.* at 1006.

Most recently, in 2019, the Supreme Court decided a case raising a *cy pres* issue, *Frank v. Gaos*, 139 S. Ct. 1041 (2019). Although the Court ultimately rendered its decision on standing grounds and thus did not reach the *cy pres* issue, *see* § 3.5, Justice Thomas (who believed that there was standing) addressed the *cy pres* question. Justice Thomas was concerned that the settlement was entirely in the form of a *cy pres* settlement and provided "no . . . form of meaningful relief to the class." *Id.* at 1047 (Thomas, J., dissenting). In his view, such a settlement "failed several requirements of Rule 23," including the fact that the named plaintiffs and class counsel were willing to settle the claims without obtaining any relief for the class, but did secure "significant benefits for themselves." *Id.* In Justice Thomas's view, this suggested that the interests of the class were not adequately represented, and the lack of any benefits to the class "rendered the settlement unfair and unreasonable under Rule

23(e)(2)." *Id.* Justice Thomas also questioned whether a class action was the superior method for resolving the dispute when it served only as a "vehicle through which to extinguish the absent class members' claims without providing them any relief." *Id.* He noted that "class members here received no settlement fund, no meaningful injunctive relief, and no other benefit whatsoever in exchange for the settlement of their claims," and that, as a result, "the class action should not have been certified, and the settlement should not have been approved." *Id.* at 1048.

In addition to fluid recovery, other options exist for distributing unclaimed damages, although neither is popular with courts. One is to allow the funds to revert or "escheat" to the government. But that approach would not benefit class members except as members of the public at large. Another is to allow the unclaimed funds to be returned to the defendant. But that approach would result in a windfall for the defendant, thus undermining the goal of deterring future misconduct.

§ 9.4 ATTORNEYS' FEES

A. OVERVIEW OF RULE 23(h)

Rule 23(h), adopted in 2003, specifically authorizes a court in a certified class action to "award reasonable attorney fees and nontaxable costs authorized by law or by agreement of the parties." Under Rule 23(B)(1), a request for attorneys' fees must be made by motion, and under Rule 23(h)(2), "[a] class member, or a party from whom payment is sought, may object to the motion." Under Rule 23(h)(3), the court is permitted, but not required, to hold a hearing, but "must" make findings of fact and conclusions of law in support of a fee award. Rule 23(h)(4) permits the court to refer any issues regarding the amount of fees to a magistrate or special master.

B.   METHODS FOR SETTING
THE AMOUNT OF FEES

Under the "American Rule," each party bears its own costs and attorneys' fees. This rule raises issues in class actions because, if any fee agreement exists at all, it is generally only between class counsel and the class representatives, and such an agreement is usually a contingent-fee agreement. Absent class members almost never have fee agreements with class counsel and thus have no contractual obligation to pay the fees and costs incurred in bringing a class action. Some courts resolve this dilemma by holding that the fee agreements between class counsel and the class representatives may be enforced against the absent class members (without discussion of contract or due process issues). Other courts hold that the absent class members are equitably liable for their *pro rata* share of the attorneys' fees and costs because they derived benefits from the litigation. Typically, the dilemma is only theoretical because fees can be paid out of a settlement fund, with the balance of the fund being used to pay class members. Alternatively, in the settlement context, it is often the case that the defendant will agree to pay attorneys' fees separately on top of the compensation to the class.

Regardless of whether a fee agreement exists, the amount of attorneys' fees in class actions must ultimately be determined by the court. This is true whether the case goes to trial or results in a settlement. Courts have generally used two methods to set class counsel's fees: the percentage-of-the-fund method and the "lodestar" approach. Neither Rule 23(h) nor the Advisory Committee Notes take a position on which approach a court should utilize.

The Percentage Method. The percentage method is traditionally used in common-fund cases, *i.e.*, those in which an attorney creates, preserves, or increases the value of a common fund for the benefit of the class members. Such a fund may be created as a result of a trial verdict or a settlement. The Supreme Court in *dictum* has expressed approval of the percentage method. *Blum v. Stenson*, 465 U.S. 886 (1984). The underlying theory of that method is that the beneficiaries of the fund will be unjustly enriched unless the plaintiffs' attorneys are allowed to recover for their efforts. Under that method, the court's principal focus is on the size of the fund.

Other factors (in addition to the size of the fund) may also be considered. These include the skills of counsel, the complexity of the case, attorney time devoted to the case, awards in comparable cases, and the existence of objections by class members to a potential award.

In most class actions, fee awards fall between twenty-five and thirty percent of the total fund. Courts generally hold that fifty percent is the upper limit of a reasonable award, although there are exceptions for unusually complicated or protracted cases.

Some courts have criticized the percentage method on the ground that the resulting awards are too high. These courts are particularly troubled by situations in which large attorneys' fees are awarded even though the case settled promptly and before the attorneys had invested a significant amount of time.

The Lodestar Method. The lodestar method, devised in 1973 by the United States Court of Appeals for the Third Circuit, *Lindy Bros. Builders v. American Radiator & Standard Sanitary Corp.*, 540 F.2d 102 (3d Cir. 1976), uses a formula to calculate attorneys fee awards, multiplying the number of hours reasonably spent by the class attorneys times a reasonable hourly rate for the work. The multiplication of the number of hours and the hourly rate is known as the "lodestar" of the fee determination. The lodestar may then be increased or decreased through so-called multipliers based upon the particular circumstances. Class attorneys often request upward multipliers because of the risk they took in bringing a contingent-fee case (a "risk" multiplier), the quality of work performed, the complexity of legal and factual issues, and the result obtained. Most courts utilize some form of the lodestar method in fee-shifting cases, *i.e.*, cases in which a statute provides for an award of "reasonable" attorneys' fees for the prevailing party.

In lodestar calculations, attorneys should not be awarded enhancements to the lodestar for "superior performance and results" except under "extraordinary circumstances." *Perdue v. Kenny A.,* 559 U.S. 542, 546 (2010). Normally, the lodestar award is sufficient. *Id.*

The lodestar method has been criticized by some courts on the ground that, by focusing on hours expended, it encourages lawyer inefficiency and provides a disincentive for early settlement. In addition, some courts have noted that the lodestar method gives insufficient consideration to the amount of the award and requires substantial judicial effort to review attorney time sheets (to assess the reasonableness of the work performed). In light of these concerns, a majority of courts in common fund cases have opted for the percentage method over the lodestar method. Some courts utilizing the percentage method, however, permit the use of the lodestar method as a cross-check.

Criteria Set Forth in the Advisory Committee Notes. Although not set out in the text of Rule 23(h), extensive comments on the criteria for determining fees are provided in the Advisory Committee Notes. For instance, the Notes state that the court should carefully scrutinize the results achieved for the class; that the court may wish to defer a fee determination until the actual payout is known; that courts should scrutinize non-monetary settlements with extra care to ensure that the awards provide actual value to the class; and that the court should scrutinize fees closely even if there are no objections to a requested fee. The judiciary's increased focus on misconduct by class counsel in the settlement context (*see* § 9.1) means that settlements providing for large fee awards that are disproportionate to the class members' recovery are scrutinized with care.

Applicability of Benchmarks. Although many courts have utilized a benchmark figure as a guide in awarding attorneys' fees, some courts have rejected the notion of a benchmark. For instance, in *Goldberger v. Integrated Resources, Inc.*, 209 F.3d 43 (2d Cir. 2000), the Second Circuit declined to adopt a benchmark of twenty-five percent of a settlement fund. The court noted that "even a theoretical construct as flexible as a 'benchmark' seems to offer an all too tempting substitute for the searching assessment that should properly be performed in each case." *Id.* at 52.

Fee Caps for Individually Retained Private Attorneys. One issue that several courts have addressed arises when a class action involves not only class counsel but also individually retained private attorneys. Assume, for example, that an individually retained attorney has a fee agreement providing that the attorney will receive 40 percent of any recovery. Subsequently, the case is litigated primarily by class counsel, who obtain a class settlement and seek a fee recovery based on the percentage of the fund. The question is whether those class members who retained their own attorneys are still obligated to pay 40 percent of their recovery to their personal attorneys—on top of the portion of the total fund awarded by the court to pay class counsel for work done on behalf of the entire class. Put another way, does a court have authority to cap privately negotiated fees at some number below the agreed upon 40 percent?

Courts that have addressed this issue have concluded that they indeed have authority to limit fees of individually retained attorneys in these circumstances. *See, e.g., In re Nat'l Football League Players' Concussion Injury Litig.*, 814 F. App'x 678, 683 n.8 (3d Cir. 2020) (finding that "the [district] court . . . did not abuse its discretion in capping the fees for individually retained private attorneys at 22%"); *In re Syngenta AG MIR 162 Corn Litig.*, No. 2:14–md–02591–JWL–JPO (D. Kan. Dec. 31, 2018) at 9–11 & n.6 (slip op.) (capping fees for individually retained private counsel in awarding fees pursuant to a class settlement), *app. pending.*

§ 9.5 THIRD-PARTY
LITIGATION FINANCING

In recent years, third-party litigation financing—the funding of lawsuits by entities other than the parties or their attorneys—has been the subject of extensive debate by scholars, policymakers, and interest groups. That debate has included the issue of funding of class actions and other aggregate litigation.

In the context of individual claims, third-party litigation funding may take the form of a loan representing all or part of a plaintiff's litigation costs in exchange for an agreed share of the ultimate recovery. A more controversial structure may involve high-interest cash loans made directly to plaintiffs (often targeting those of limited means) and secured by the lawsuit or contingency fee. This structure may also involve loans to plaintiffs' law firms secured by the firm's future fee awards.

In the class action context, third-party funding is developing. Traditionally, litigation costs in a class action are advanced by class counsel and recouped from the ultimate recovery, if any (or by a court award using, *e.g.*, the lodestar method, *see* § 9.4). Class counsel assumes the risk that no recovery will be made.

A third-party funder, however, will assume some or all of the risk of financing the litigation in exchange for a percentage of any recovery. Thus, as one scholar points out, "[c]ommercial litigation financing might be attractive to new entrants to the market or as a means of allowing an established firm to penetrate or develop a new segment of the class action market while limiting its risk." Deborah R. Hensler, *Third-Party Financing of Class Action Litigation in the United States: Will the Sky Fall?*, 63 DePaul L. Rev. 499, 508 (2014). This approach may help lawyers who are seeking court permission to serve as class counsel (*see* § 3.10). A lawyer without the resources to finance a class action on his or her own may have difficulty convincing the court that the class will be adequately represented. Third-party financing allows a lawyer to bolster his or her financial ability to litigate a case and thereby to increase the likelihood of qualifying for appointment as class counsel.

Third-party financing has been controversial. For instance, organizations representing U.S. businesses have called for more regulation (and even prohibition) of third-party funding, often citing concerns that such funding will encourage frivolous lawsuits. Third-party funding arrangements are, however, subject to some existing forms of regulation. The longstanding doctrine of champerty in many states prohibits the division of litigation proceeds between parties and nonparties supporting the action. Similarly, most jurisdictions have ethical rules prohibiting or regulating fee splitting between lawyers and nonlawyers. Some states have also passed laws specifically regulating third-party litigation funding. *See, e.g.*, Me. Rev. Stat. Ann. tit. 9–A §§ 12–104, 12–106 (requiring that a prospective funder register with the state, disclose fees and interest rates charged, and certify that it will not exert any influence over the course of the litigation); Ohio Rev. Code Ann. § 1349.55 (similar).

An important question with respect to third-party funding involves whether parties may obtain discovery regarding funders. Such funding arrangements may be relevant to class certification issues—in particular adequacy of representation under Rule 23(a)(4) (*see* § 3.10). For example, in *Natto Iyela Gbarabe v. Chevron Corp.*, No. 14–cv–00173–SI, 2016 WL 4154849 (N.D. Cal. Aug. 5, 2016), the district court granted the defendant's motion to compel production of the named plaintiff's third-party funding agreement, reasoning that the agreement was relevant to adequacy of representation. The plaintiff argued, based on his confidentiality agreement with the third-party funder, that the court alone should review the document in camera. The court disagreed, reasoning that in camera review "would deprive [the defendant] of the ability to make its own assessment and arguments regarding the funding agreement and its impact, if any, on plaintiff's ability to adequately represent the class." *Id.* at *2.

In January 2017, the Northern District of California became the first federal court to announce a rule mandating disclosure of third-party funding in all class action cases. The local civil rules were amended to require disclosure of funders as part of the required joint case management statement "in any proposed class, collective, or representative action." N.D. Cal. Civil LR 3–15.

In 2018, the Advisory Committee on Civil Rules released a memorandum that surveyed rules and laws requiring the disclosure of third-party funding. That study uncovered that, as of November 2017, about half of all federal circuit courts and a quarter of all federal district courts required the disclosure of the identity of litigation funders for recusal purposes. *See* Patrick A. Tighe, *Survey of Federal and State Disclosure Rule Regarding Litig. Funding* (Feb. 7, 2018) http://www.uscourts.gov/sites/default/files/2018-04-civil-rules-agenda-book.pdf (last visited Sept. 18, 2020).

For further scholarly discussion of third-party funding issues, *see* Elizabeth Chamblee Burch, *Financiers as Monitors in Aggregate Litigation*, 48 Ga. L. Advoc. 1 (2014); Deborah R. Hensler, *Third-Party Financing of Class Action Litigation in the United States: Will the Sky Fall?*, 63 DePaul L. Rev. 499 (2014).

§ 9.6 ALTERNATIVE DISPUTE RESOLUTION

Alternative Dispute Resolution (ADR) is a process of private dispute resolution outside of court. It involves procedures such as arbitration, mediation, early neutral evaluation, summary jury trials, mini trials, and negotiation. With the enactment of the Federal Alternative Dispute Resolution Act of 1998, 28 U.S.C. §§ 651–58, federal district courts are now required to authorize the use of ADR in civil proceedings (as well as in adversary proceedings in bankruptcy cases). Although many have argued that class actions can be desirable in the arbitration context, the future of class arbitration procedures has come into question following the Supreme Court's decisions in a series of cases, including *AT&T Mobility, LLC v. Concepcion*, 563 U.S. 333 (2011), *American Express Co. v. Italian Colors Restaurant*, 570 U.S. 228 (2013), and *DIRECTV, Inc. v. Imburgia*, 136 S. Ct. 463 (2015), which are discussed in this section.

To avoid classwide litigation, businesses are now utilizing arbitration provisions in a variety of contexts. Those provisions require arbitration of disputes and prohibit class actions either in court or in arbitration proceedings. Arbitration clauses have become especially common in consumer contracts, but they are also increasingly common in employment agreements and in many other situations.

Arbitration clauses have the imprimatur of federal law. In particular, the Federal Arbitration Act (FAA) embodies a strong federal policy favoring arbitration. Under section 2 of the FAA, agreements to arbitrate "shall be valid, irrevocable, and enforceable, save upon such grounds as exist at law or in equity for the revocation of any contract." Prior to the Supreme Court's opinion in *Concepcion*, a number of courts held that contractual provisions prohibiting classwide arbitration were unconscionable under state law. *See, e.g., Discover Bank v. Superior Court*, 113 P.3d 1100 (Cal. 2005), *abrogated by Concepcion*, 563 U.S. 333. In *Concepcion*, the Court rejected such reliance on state unconscionability law, holding that the FAA's savings clause (section 2) preempted an unconscionability defense.

Concepcion involved a claim by Vincent and Liza Concepcion for $30.22 in sales tax, an amount they claimed was wrongfully charged by AT&T in offering "free" phones. The Concepcions sought to pursue class litigation, but an arbitration clause that AT&T included in the Concepcions's cell phone contract barred both class action litigation and class action arbitration. The district court, relying on *Discover Bank*, denied AT&T's motion to compel arbitration, holding that the arbitration clause was unconscionable under California law. The Ninth Circuit affirmed.

The Supreme Court reversed the Ninth Circuit, holding that such a state law unconscionability defense was preempted by the FAA. The Court noted that "our cases ... have repeatedly described the [FAA] as 'embod[ying] [a] national policy favoring arbitration.'" *Id.* at 345–46 (citations omitted). The Court concluded that "California's *Discover Bank* rule ... interfere[d] with arbitration." *Id.* at 346. The Court also noted that "[a]rbitration is poorly suited to the higher stakes of class litigation." *Id.* at 350.

In his dissent, Justice Breyer (joined by Justices Ginsburg, Sotomayor, and Kagan) rejected the majority's reasoning and noted the important benefits of class actions. Without class arbitration, the dissent noted, small claims such as those raised by the Concepcions would not be pursued at all. *Id.* at 365–66 (Breyer, J., dissenting).

Subsequently, in *CompuCredit Corp. v. Greenwood*, 565 U.S. 95 (2012), a case involving the Credit Repair Organization Act (CROA), consumers contended that the CROA's guarantee of "a right to sue a credit repair organization" meant that the CROA was not subject to the FAA. The issue arose after the defendant moved to compel arbitration of a federal court class action based on an arbitration clause containing a class action waiver. The suit alleged that CompuCredit, in issuing credit cards, misrepresented the credit card's limit and the extent to which the credit card would rebuild the consumer's poor credit history. The Court held that the CROA was not sufficiently clear to exclude the statute from the reach of the FAA. Thus, the arbitration clause was enforceable. Only Justice Ginsberg dissented.

In 2013, the Court decided *American Express.* There, a putative class of merchants, including Italian Colors restaurant, brought an antitrust action against American Express in connection with its card acceptance agreement. The agreement, however, contained a clause requiring arbitration of all claims against American Express and prohibiting arbitration of claims "on a class action basis." 570 U.S. at 231. The district court granted American Express's motion—based on the arbitration clause— to compel individual arbitration under the FAA. The Second Circuit reversed, holding that the class action waiver clause was unenforceable because the merchants had established that arbitrating on an individual basis would be cost-prohibitive, thus preventing the plaintiffs from effectively vindicating their rights under the federal antitrust laws. The Court relied on language from *Mitsubishi Motors Corp. v. Soler Chrysler-Plymouth, Inc.*, 473 U.S. 614, 637 n.19 (1985), suggesting that an arbitration forum would be suspect if it did not allow a litigant to "effectively . . . vindicate its statutory cause of action. . . ." The Supreme Court vacated and remanded in light of an intervening case, but the Second Circuit adhered to its opinion on remand. The Supreme Court again granted certiorari.

In a 5–3 decision (with Justice Sotomayor recused), the Court reversed the Second Circuit and held that the arbitration clause, including the waiver of class arbitration, was enforceable. The majority rejected the Second Circuit's reliance on the high cost of individual arbitrations, reasoning that the "effective vindication" exception in *Mitsubishi Motors* was triggered only where the agreement would operate "as a prospective waiver of a party's *right to pursue* statutory remedies." *American Express*, 570 U.S. at 235 (quoting *Mitsubishi Motors*, 473 U.S. at 637 n.19) (emphasis in original). The majority explained that the higher cost of individual arbitrations did not negate the merchants' right to *pursue* a statutory remedy, and noted that federal law provides no guarantee that claims will be resolved affordably. More generally, the Court emphasized the FAA's mandate that arbitration agreements should be enforced by their terms.

Justice Kagan dissented, joined by Justices Ginsburg and Breyer. The dissent argued that, as a practical matter, the arbitration clause *did* prevent the individual merchants from pursuing statutory remedies. Individual arbitration, the dissent reasoned, would be far more expensive for class members than the value of any potential recovery.

Two years after *American Express*, the Court again addressed the enforceability of an arbitration clause containing a class action waiver. In *DIRECTV*, the plaintiffs maintained that the arbitration clause at issue was unenforceable under California law based on a 2005 California Supreme Court decision. Plaintiffs argued that, unlike the arbitration clause in *Concepcion*, the provision at issue was subject to state law because it stated that it would be ineffective

if "the law of your state" rendered it unenforceable.
136 S. Ct. at 466. The Supreme Court nonetheless
upheld the arbitration clause as enforceable,
reasoning that the phrase "the law of your state"
encompassed only *valid* state law, and that the 2005
California Supreme Court decision on which the
plaintiffs relied was no longer valid in light of
Concepcion. The majority opinion emphasized that
Concepcion was binding on all courts, even though "it
was a closely divided case, resulting in a decision
from which four Justices dissented." *Id*. at 468.

Only Justice Ginsburg dissented in *DIRECTV*. She
expressed concern that *Concepcion* and its progeny
had "resulted in the deprivation of consumers' rights
to seek redress for losses, and . . . insulated powerful
economic interests from liability for violations of
consumer protection laws." 136 S. Ct. at 477
(Ginsburg, J., dissenting).

Concepcion and its progeny have generated
extensive commentary and debate. Numerous
scholars have expressed concern that this case law
will decimate the class action device, as companies
increasingly rely on arbitration clauses containing
class action waivers. *See, e.g.*, Brian T. Fitzpatrick,
The End of Class Actions?, 57 Ariz. L. Rev. 161, 163
(2015). Notwithstanding this criticism, however, the
Supreme Court has continued to reaffirm and expand
its pro-arbitration case law.

One significant development has been in the
employment context. Prior to 2018, there was a
circuit split over whether the enforcement of
arbitration clauses in employment cases (over the

opposition of the employee) was barred by the National Labor Relations Act (NLRA), notwithstanding the general permissibility of such clauses under the FAA. The Supreme Court resolved the circuit split in *Epic Sys. Corp. v. Lewis*, 138 S. Ct. 1612 (2018). Although the Court granted review in three separate cases, it focused on the facts of one case in particular, *Ernst & Young, LLP v. Morris*. In that case, the plaintiff entered into an agreement with the defendant that any disputes would be arbitrated. The plaintiff was given the ability to choose the arbitrator, and the agreement stated that the arbitrator could "grant any relief that could be granted by . . . a court." *Id.* at 1619. Despite that agreement, the plaintiff sued in federal court, claiming that the defendant violated the Fair Labor Standards Act (FLSA) and California law by failing to pay the required overtime compensation. The federal claim was brought as a collective action under 29 U.S.C. § 216(b), *see* § 11.2, and the state-law claim was brought as a Federal Rule 23 class action. The defendant responded with a motion to compel arbitration, which the district court granted. The Ninth Circuit reversed, reasoning that while the FAA generally requires courts to enforce arbitration agreements, "the statute's 'saving clause' . . . removes this obligation" if the agreement violates another federal law. *Id.* at 1620. The court found that enforcement would violate the NLRA by prohibiting employees from engaging in concerted activity of a class or collective action.

The Supreme Court, in a 5–4 decision, reversed the Ninth Circuit. It reasoned that the FAA required arbitration of the claims and that the NLRA did not override the FAA's mandate. According to the Court, the NLRA "secures to employees rights to organize unions and bargain collectively, but it says nothing about how judges and arbitrators must try legal disputes that leave the workplace and enter the courtroom or arbitral forum." 138 S. Ct. at 1619. In the Court's view, the FAA and NLRA "have long enjoyed separate spheres of influence, and neither permits this Court to declare the parties' agreements unlawful." *Id.*

In her dissent on behalf of four Justices, Justice Ginsburg argued that the majority had "ignore[d] the destructive consequences of diminishing the rights of employees to band together in confronting an employer." *Id.* at 1633. According to Justice Ginsburg, the NLRA was not limited to "workers' rights to join unions and to engage in collective bargaining," but instead spoke "more embracively." *Id.* at 1636.

In yet another pro-arbitration ruling, this one in 2019, the Court held that a court cannot compel arbitration on a classwide basis when the agreement is ambiguous on the issue. *Lamps Plus, Inc. v. Varela*, 139 S. Ct. 1407 (2019). After a data breach that disclosed tax information of approximately 1,300 employees of Lamps Plus, respondent Frank Varela, an employee of Lamps Plus, filed a class action on behalf of employees whose tax information had been compromised. Lamps Plus requested individual arbitration, but both the district court and Ninth Circuit rejected the request for individual arbitration and instead authorized classwide arbitration, finding that Varela's agreement was ambiguous on the issue. The Supreme Court granted review. The Court accepted the Ninth Circuit's finding that the agreement was ambiguous but held that an ambiguous agreement is not a sufficient "contractual basis" to compel classwide arbitration. *See id.* at 1419. According to the Court, "more than ambiguity" is required to "ensure the parties actually agreed to arbitrate on a classwide basis." *Id.* at 1415.

Also in 2019, the Supreme Court handed plaintiffs a rare victory in the class arbitration context. *New Prime Inc. v. Oliveira,* 139 S. Ct. 532 (2019). The Court unanimously held that an exclusion in the FAA's coverage—involving "contracts of employment of seamen, railroad employees, or any other class of workers engaged in foreign or interstate commerce"—applied to independent contractors as well as to the specified employees. *Id.* at 534. The Court further held that the issue of whether the exclusion applied was for the court, not the arbitrator, to decide. The opinion is of limited scope, however, because it merely interprets a specific and narrow exclusion and does nothing to help the myriad plaintiffs who do not fall within the exclusion.

Ultimately, *Concepcion, American Express, DIRECTV, Epic Systems,* and *Lamps Plus* are likely to have a significant impact on the ability of many claimants to bring class actions and to arbitrate claims on a classwide basis. Businesses now have a great incentive to include class action waivers in various contracts. In cases involving small claims, the inability to bring class actions—either in court or in arbitration proceedings—will often mean that the claims will never be pursued at all.

CHAPTER 10

APPELLATE REVIEW

As noted throughout this text, the class certification decision is often the most important issue in a class action case. As such, litigants frequently wish to obtain immediate appeal of issues relating to class certification. Absent immediate review, defendants frequently feel compelled to settle when certification is granted, and class representatives (and other class members) frequently give up the litigation altogether when certification is denied. Those plaintiffs and defendants who are willing to continue with the litigation after an adverse certification ruling face potentially serious inefficiencies by having to wait until the end of the case to appeal the certification ruling.

In particular, if certification is granted, the lack of an immediate appeal means that the parties must go through an entire class action trial before the appellate court decides whether a class action should have been certified in the first place. If the appellate court decides that certification was inappropriate, the trial will have been wasted. By the same token, if certification is denied, the parties must wait until the conclusion of the named plaintiff's case before seeking review of the certification ruling. If the appellate court rules that certification should have been granted, then the trial court will have wasted time trying an individual case instead of a class action.

Because of the foregoing considerations, litigants have attempted—with mixed success—to use various mechanisms, discussed below, for obtaining immediate review of class certification rulings. In 1998, Rule 23 was amended to permit appellate courts to allow interlocutory review of decisions granting or denying class certification. This amendment is addressed in detail below. Rule 23(f) renders the various other mechanisms much less significant. Nonetheless, because Rule 23(f) is discretionary and contains strict time limits, a lawyer considering an interlocutory appeal of a class certification ruling should understand these other potential mechanisms. Moreover, these mechanisms provide the historical context for Rule 23(f). Finally, because Rule 23(f) applies only to orders "granting or denying class-action certification" under Rule 23, these other mechanisms may need to be considered for interlocutory appeals of other class action rulings, such as orders involving class notice.

After discussing the appealability of class certification rulings, this chapter examines several miscellaneous appellate issues that sometimes arise in the class action context.

§ 10.1 WHETHER AN ORDER DENYING CLASS CERTIFICATION IS A FINAL DECISION UNDER 28 U.S.C. § 1291

Under 28 U.S.C. § 1291, federal courts of appeals have jurisdiction over appeals from all "final decisions" of federal district courts. In *Coopers & Lybrand v. Livesay*, 437 U.S. 463 (1978), the

Supreme Court held that a trial court's order denying class certification or decertifying a class is not a "final decision" within the meaning of 28 U.S.C. § 1291 and, therefore, is not appealable as a matter of right. The Court rejected appellants' arguments that the certification order was appealable under two previously recognized exceptions to the final judgment rule.

First, appellants argued that the order was appealable as a "collateral order" pursuant to *Cohen v. Beneficial Industrial Loan Corp.*, 337 U.S. 541 (1949). Under that exception, review of a non-final order may be allowed if it (1) conclusively determines disputed questions; (2) resolves an important issue completely separate from the merits of the action; and (3) cannot be effectively reviewed on appeal from a final judgment. The Court found that, in the case of a class certification ruling, these criteria are not satisfied because certification is subject to revision by the trial court; the class issues are intertwined with the merits; and the certification ruling can be reviewed on appeal from a final judgment.

Appellants' second argument in *Coopers & Lybrand* relied upon the "death knell" exception that had been judicially adopted in several circuits. That doctrine assumed that a lawsuit was effectively over when the district court denied class certification in a case in which the individual plaintiffs would not find it economically prudent to pursue their claims in the absence of a class action. In *Coopers & Lybrand,* the Court criticized the "death knell" exception, finding that it was based on policy considerations more appropriately left for Congress and that it unfairly facilitated early appeals only by plaintiffs and not by defendants.

§ 10.2 APPEAL OF DENIAL OF CERTIFICATION UNDER 28 U.S.C. § 1292(a)(1)

Section 1292(a)(1) grants appellate courts jurisdiction over interlocutory orders of the district courts "granting, continuing, modifying, refusing or dissolving injunctions, or refusing to dissolve or modify injunctions." In *Gardner v. Westinghouse Broadcasting Co.*, 437 U.S. 478 (1978), the Supreme Court narrowly interpreted this jurisdictional statute with respect to review of orders denying class certification. Even though plaintiff's complaint sought equitable relief for the entire class, the Court reasoned that the order denying class certification did not entirely dispose of the relief sought, but merely limited its scope. Accordingly, the order was not appealable under section 1292(a)(1).

§ 10.3 APPEAL OF CLASS CERTIFICATION RULING UNDER 28 U.S.C. § 1292(b)

Section 1292(b) permits a district court to certify an otherwise nonappealable order for appellate review when three criteria are met: (1) the "order involves a controlling question of law"; (2) there is "substantial ground for difference of opinion" regarding the order; and (3) "an immediate appeal from the order may materially advance the ultimate termination of the litigation." The district court must state in writing that these criteria are satisfied, and application for an appeal must then be made within ten days after entry of the certification order. If the district court refuses to certify the case for appeal, the court of appeals cannot hear the case unless another legal basis exists for interlocutory review. Even if the district court certifies an order for appeal under section 1292(b), the court of appeals has unreviewable discretion to decline the appeal for any reason (including docket congestion). Isolated examples of 1292(b) review of class certification rulings can be found. *See, e.g.*, *Castano v. Am. Tobacco Co.*, 162 F.R.D. 112 (E.D. La. 1995) (certifying case for approval under 1292(b)), *rev'd*, 84 F.3d 734 (5th Cir. 1996) (accepting review and reversing district court's order certifying tobacco plaintiff class). For the most part, however, courts have been reluctant to use section 1292(b) to achieve interlocutory review of class certification rulings.

§ 10.4 MANDAMUS REVIEW OF CERTIFICATION RULING

The All Writs Act, 28 U.S.C. § 1651, permits an appellate court to grant a petition for mandamus in extraordinary circumstances. Under the mandamus power, the courts of appeals may take jurisdiction and intervene to prevent or correct fundamental injustices by a district court. The mandamus power, however, is rarely warranted. A writ of mandamus is justified only when there is irreparable harm and a clear usurpation of judicial power by the district court.

Litigants have petitioned the appellate courts to exercise this power to intervene when district courts have granted or refused to grant class certification. Although most efforts have not been successful, mandamus has occasionally been granted to undo class certifications.

For example, in *In re Rhone-Poulenc Rorer, Inc.*, 51 F.3d 1293 (7th Cir. 1995), the Seventh Circuit granted a writ of mandamus and ordered the district court to decertify the plaintiff class of HIV-infected hemophiliacs. The court reasoned that the class certification order would probably never be reviewed following final judgment because the defendants would likely be forced to settle with the class members rather than expose themselves to a large classwide judgment. The court was particularly troubled by this pressure to settle because the defendants had previously won twelve of the thirteen individual claims that had been brought. The court also found that mandamus was warranted because of choice-of-law and Seventh Amendment concerns raised by the district court's certification order. *See* §§ 7.1, 11.1.

Likewise, the Sixth Circuit granted mandamus and reversed an order granting class certification in *In re American Medical Systems, Inc.*, 75 F.3d 1069 (6th Cir. 1996). That case was a nationwide class action involving alleged injuries from penile prostheses. The court found that mandamus was warranted because of the district court's failure to look beyond the pleadings and conduct a rigorous analysis into whether Rule 23's requirements were met. The court emphasized that many different models of prostheses were involved, that class members claimed different kinds of malfunctions, that complicated choice-of-law issues existed, and that the district court failed to make factual findings regarding adequacy of representation.

Notwithstanding *Rhone-Poulenc* and *American Medical Systems*, most courts have refused to grant mandamus in the context of class certification rulings.

§ 10.5 APPEAL UNDER RULE 23(f)

Overview of Criteria. As discussed above, the patchwork of potential appellate vehicles has posed difficulties for parties seeking immediate appeal of class certification rulings. As a result, such a ruling often operated, as a practical matter, as a final decision in the case. Plaintiffs whose individual claims could not justify the costs of litigation were effectively barred from continuing their case if they could not obtain immediate review of an order denying class certification. By the same token, if a class was certified, defendants often felt compelled to settle because the risks of an adverse classwide verdict were too great to justify going forward.

To address some of these concerns, Rule 23(f) was added in 1998. It provides:

A court of appeals may permit an appeal from an order granting or denying class action certification under this rule if a petition for permission to appeal is filed with the circuit clerk within 14 days after the order is entered. An appeal does not stay proceedings in the district court unless the district judge or the court of appeals so orders.

There are no specific criteria or limitations in the text of Rule 23(f), and the Advisory Committee Notes state that the courts of appeals have "unfettered discretion whether to permit the appeal, akin to the discretion exercised by the Supreme Court in acting on a petition for certiorari." The Notes suggest that "[p]ermission is most likely to be granted when the certification decision turns on a novel or unsettled question of law, or when, as a practical matter, the decision on certification is likely dispositive of the litigation."

In summarizing the reach of Rule 23(f), the Seventh Circuit has stated that "the more fundamental the question and the greater the likelihood that it will escape effective disposition at the end of the case, the more appropriate is an appeal under Rule 23(f)." *Blair v. Equifax Check Servs., Inc.*, 181 F.3d 832, 835 (7th Cir. 1999). The court noted that "it would be a mistake for us to draw up a list that determines how the power under Rule 23(f) will be exercised." *Id.* at 834.

Rule 23(f) has resulted in a significant number of appellate decisions. The circuit courts have devoted considerable attention to the criteria for granting Rule 23(f) review. These decisions differ somewhat in nuance, and a litigant faced with a Rule 23(f) issue should consult the law of the applicable federal circuit.

By way of illustration, the Eleventh Circuit has identified five guideposts for deciding whether to grant Rule 23(f) review: (1) "whether the district court's ruling is likely dispositive of the litigation by creating a 'death knell' for either plaintiff or defendant"; (2) whether the district court ruling contains "a *substantial* weakness"; (3) "whether the appeal will permit the resolution of an unsettled legal issue that is 'important to the particular litigation as well as important in itself'"; (4) "the nature and status of the litigation," such as "the status of discovery, the pendency of relevant motions, and the length of time the matter already has been pending"; and (5) "the likelihood that future events"—such as the possibility of settlement, bankruptcy of one of the parties, or modification of the class certification ruling—"may make immediate appellate review more or less appropriate." *Prado-Steiman v. Bush*, 221 F.3d 1266, 1274–76 (11th Cir. 2000) (emphasis in original).

One issue that has divided the federal circuits is the weight to be given to the correctness of the decision. Some circuits have held that Rule 23(f) review may be proper to correct a manifestly erroneous decision. Other circuits, however, have held that even a patently erroneous decision is not subject to Rule 23(f) review unless the decision would likely be the death knell of the litigation or review would resolve an important class action legal issue that otherwise would evade review.

A thorough discussion of the various circuit court approaches to Rule 23(f) is contained in the Ninth

Circuit's decision in *Chamberlan v. Ford Motor Co.*, 402 F.3d 952 (9th Cir. 2005).

Scope. Rule 23(f) applies only to a district court order "granting or denying class-action certification under this rule." As the Advisory Committee Notes make clear, "[n]o other type of Rule 23 order is covered by this provision." Thus, for example, an order relating to the scope or content of a class notice, an order restricting communications with class members, or an order allowing or barring certain class discovery would not be reviewable under Rule 23(f) unless such an order was somehow intertwined with an order granting or denying class certification. In addition, one court has held that Rule 23(f) does not apply to collective actions under Section 216(b) of the Fair Labor Standards Act. *Baldridge v. SBC Commc'ns, Inc.*, 404 F.3d 930 (5th Cir. 2005). Collective actions are discussed in § 11.2.

In 2014, the Third Circuit held that discretionary review under Rule 23(f) does not extend to an order granting "preliminary approval" of a proposed settlement and "conditionally certify[ing]" the class "for settlement purposes only." *In re Nat'l Football League Players Concussion Injury Litig.*, 775 F.3d 570 (3d Cir. 2014). *See* § 9.1 (discussing preliminary approval stage). The court reasoned that an order "'preliminarily' or 'conditionally' address[ing] class certification but reserv[ing] the class certification determination for a later time does not qualify as an 'order granting or denying class-action certification'" under Rule 23(f). *Id.* at 584. Would-be appellants, it held, must wait for a definitive ruling on class certification and settlement fairness.

In 2018, Rule 23(f) was amended to codify the *NFL Concussion* decision. It now provides that Rule 23(f) does not authorize interlocutory appeals "from an order under Rule 23(e)(1)," *i.e.,* from an order granting or denying preliminary approval.

Views of the District Court. Unlike review under 28 U.S.C. § 1292(b), review under Rule 23(f) does not require the approval of the district court. Nonetheless, the Advisory Committee Notes point out that the district court "often will be able to provide cogent advice on the factors that bear on the decision whether to permit appeal." According to the Notes, "[t]his advice can be particularly valuable if the certification decision is tentative," but it can be helpful "[e]ven as to a firm certification decision" by "focus[ing] the court of appeals" on the critical issues and possibly "persuad[ing] the disappointed party" not to seek Rule 23(f) review.

Timing of Filing and Responding. Rule 23(f) requires that the application for review be "made within 14 days after the order is entered." Under the 2018 amendment to Rule 23(f), the time for appeal has been lengthened from 14 days to 45 days "if any party is the United States, a United States agency, or a United States officer or employee sued for an act or omission occurring in connection with duties performed on the United States' behalf."

Although Rule 23(f) does not set a time period for responding to a Rule 23(f) petition, Federal Rule of

Appellate Procedure 5, which governs appeals by permission, addresses the issue: "A party may file any answer in opposition or a cross-petition within 10 days after the petition is served." Fed. R. App. P. 5(b)(2).

Absence of Equitable Tolling. In *Nutraceutical Corp. v. Lambert,* 139 S. Ct. 710 (2019), the Supreme Court held that a motion for reconsideration does not toll Rule 23(f)'s 14-day deadline for seeking interlocutory appellate review of class certification decisions. The Court stated that Rule 23(f)—and the federal appellate rule governing extensions of deadlines—"express a clear intent to compel rigorous enforcement of Rule 23(f)'s deadline even where good cause for equitable tolling might otherwise exist." *Id.* at 715.

Rule 23(f) Petitions in Defendant Class Actions. Rule 23(f) is not limited by its terms to plaintiff class actions. Courts have thus applied it to cases brought *against* a class of defendants. *See* § 12.1 (discussing defendant class actions). In *Tilley v. TJX Cos., Inc.,* 345 F.3d 34 (1st Cir. 2003), the First Circuit addressed the Rule 23(f) criteria in the context of a defendant class action. The court held that Rule 23(f) review is warranted in defendant class actions "when one of three circumstances exists: (i) denial of certification effectively disposes of the litigation because the plaintiff's claim would only be worth pursuing as against a full class of defendants; or (ii) an interlocutory appeal would clarify an important and unsettled legal issue that would likely escape effective end-of-case review; or (iii) an interlocutory appeal is a desirable vehicle either for addressing special circumstances or avoiding manifest injustice." *Id.* at 39.

§ 10.6 APPEAL FROM A DENIAL OF CLASS CERTIFICATION WHEN A CLASS REPRESENTATIVE VOLUNTARILY DISMISSES HIS OR HER CLAIMS

In *Microsoft Corp. v. Baker*, 137 S. Ct. 1702 (2017), the Supreme Court held that a class representative could not voluntarily dismiss his or her case with prejudice after the denial of class certification and then appeal the class certification ruling as a final judgment under 28 U.S.C. § 1291. In *Baker*, the class representatives employed that strategy after the Ninth Circuit denied Rule 23(f) review. The Court, in a decision by Justice Ginsburg, rejected the tactic, concluding that it would be an end-run around "Rule 23(f)'s careful calibration—as well as Congress's designation of rulemaking 'as the preferred means for determining whether and when prejudgment orders should be immediately appealable. . . .' " *Id.* at 1714 (citation omitted). The Court further noted that, "even more than the death-knell theory," plaintiffs' approach would "invite[ ] protracted litigation and piecemeal appeals." *Id.* at 1713. In the Court's view, plaintiffs cannot be allowed to "transform a tentative interlocutory order into a final judgment within the meaning of § 1291 simply by dismissing their claims with prejudice. . . ." *Id.* at 1715 (citation omitted).

Justice Thomas, joined by Chief Justice Roberts and Justice Alito, concurred in the result. They agreed with plaintiffs that the dismissal made the judgment final under § 1291, but they asserted that plaintiffs could not appeal because there was no case or controversy under Article III. In light of the dismissals with prejudice, plaintiffs' individual claims could not be revived even if plaintiffs achieved a favorable ruling on class certification.

§ 10.7 INTERVENTION FOR PURPOSES OF APPEAL

When a trial court denies class certification and judgment is later entered in favor of the named plaintiffs on their individual claims, the successful plaintiffs have no need to appeal the denial of certification. Under those circumstances, the issue arises whether a putative class member may intervene in the district court pursuant to Federal Rule of Civil Procedure 24 for purposes of appealing the denial of certification.

The Supreme Court answered in the affirmative in *United Airlines, Inc. v. McDonald*, 432 U.S. 385 (1977). In allowing a class member to appeal after intervening in the case, the Court held that the intervention was timely even though the intervenor did not move to intervene until shortly after final judgment had been entered for the named plaintiffs. The Court reasoned that the intervenor moved promptly after ascertaining that the named plaintiffs would no longer be protecting the interests of the class.

A related issue is whether, after class certification is granted and the case proceeds to judgment, an unnamed class member (or a former class member who opts out) may appeal a final judgment in favor of the defendants—such as an order granting defendants' motion for summary judgment. In *In re Brand Name Prescription Drugs Antitrust Litigation*, 115 F.3d 456 (7th Cir. 1997), the Seventh Circuit held that, in such a situation, neither opt-outs nor unnamed class members may appeal unless they attempted to intervene in the district court.

As discussed in § 9.1, the Supreme Court has made clear that an unnamed class member who makes a timely objection to a class settlement at the district court level is not required to intervene to appeal the settlement. *Devlin v. Scardelletti*, 536 U.S. 1 (2002). Some courts have limited *Devlin* to mandatory classes. It remains unclear whether *Devlin* will affect case law outside the settlement context.

§ 10.8 STANDARD OF REVIEW

Another issue involves the standard of review that applies when an appellate court reviews a district court decision granting or denying class certification. It is well settled that class certification decisions are reviewed under an abuse of discretion standard. In applying the criteria for class certification under Rule 23, however, purely legal questions sometimes arise. Such issues include whether a specific federal statute prohibits the maintenance of class action suits in particular kinds of cases, or whether a "superiority" inquiry should be conducted under Rule 23(b)(2). In those circumstances, a *de novo* standard of review is appropriate.

CHAPTER 11

SPECIAL FOCUS ON MASS TORT, EMPLOYMENT DISCRIMINATION, AND SECURITIES FRAUD CLASS ACTIONS

Although this text cannot focus on every type of suit that may be brought as a class action, it examines three types of cases that have raised significant and controversial issues: mass tort, employment discrimination, and securities fraud class actions.

§ 11.1 MASS TORTS

No area of class action law has generated more judicial and scholarly debate than mass tort class actions. A key element of that controversy arises from the 1966 Advisory Committee Notes, which state:

A "mass accident" resulting in injuries to numerous persons is ordinarily not appropriate for a class action because of the likelihood that significant questions, not only of damages but of liability and defenses of liability, would be present, affecting the individuals in different ways. In these circumstances an action conducted nominally as a class action would degenerate in practice into multiple lawsuits separately tried.

This Note caused a number of early courts to refuse to certify mass tort cases. Later, several courts sought ways to certify mass tort class actions notwithstanding the Advisory Committee's concerns. In recent years, however, courts have again viewed mass tort class actions with skepticism. This subchapter provides a brief historical overview of mass tort class actions and surveys some of the key issues facing courts today.

Preliminarily, it is important to define the term "mass tort." At its broadest, the term can apply to any multi-party lawsuit involving tort claims. In general, the term is used to describe either (1) a mass accident (a single event, such as an airplane crash, involving injuries to many people), or (2) personal injuries on a widespread basis, typically involving allegedly defective products (such as breast implants or other medical devices). Mass tort cases may also involve widespread damage to property or other economic loss. Most of these claims arise under state law rather than federal law.

In its discussion of mass tort cases, the *Manual for Complex Litigation (4th)* identifies various examples of "single incident mass torts": "a hotel fire, the collapse of a structure, the crash of a commercial airliner, a major chemical discharge or explosion, or an oil spill." § 22.1. The term "mass tort" also addresses "dispersed mass torts," which usually involve use of or exposure to allegedly dangerous substances (*e.g.*, "asbestos, Dalkon Shield intrauterine devices, silicone gel breast implants, and diet drugs"). *Id.* In some instances, the exposed victims know of their exposure and have suffered injury. In other instances, exposed class members may know of their exposure but have not developed any injuries. These latter claimants are commonly referred to as "future claimants" or "exposure-only claimants."

As the *Manual* notes, the line between single incident and dispersed mass torts is sometimes difficult to draw. This is because "[e]ven single event torts with a strong local nexus, such as plant emission or a spill of toxic materials, may include latent exposure effects or be affected by individual variables, such as smoking." *Id.*

Nonetheless, some generalization is possible. As a rule, despite the cautionary language in the Advisory Committee Notes with respect to "mass accidents," courts have been more willing to certify "single incident mass torts" than they have been to certify "dispersed mass torts."

A.   JUDICIAL TRENDS IN MASS TORTS CLASS ACTIONS

(1)   Mass Torts in the 1960s and 1970s

Many courts in the 1960s and 1970s relied upon the Advisory Committee Notes in rejecting efforts to certify mass tort cases. In the late 1970s, however, a number of federal trial courts began permitting mass tort class actions, although most of those rulings were reversed on appeal. Two highly publicized examples of cases that were certified and reversed on appeal were (1) the class action involving the collapse of two skywalks at the Kansas City Hyatt Regency, killing 114 people (certified in 1982 and reversed the same year); and (2) a nationwide class of persons claiming injuries from the Dalkon Shield birth control device (certified in 1981 and reversed in 1982).

(2) Mass Torts in the Mid-1980s

In the mid-1980s, the explosion of asbestos suits, as well as the highly publicized Agent Orange litigation, led to a major shift in attitude among many federal courts in favor of certifying mass tort cases. One landmark ruling was *Jenkins v. Raymark Industries*, 782 F.2d 468 (5th Cir. 1986). In that case, the Fifth Circuit upheld the certification under Rule 23(b)(3) of hundreds of claims involving asbestos-related personal injuries. The court noted the prior reluctance of courts to certify mass tort cases, but stated that, in light of the 5,000 pending asbestos cases in that circuit, "[n]ecessity moves us to change and invent." *Id.*

In certifying the class under Rule 23(b)(3), the district court had found that the "state of the art" defense—*i.e.*, that the dangerous nature of asbestos could not reasonably have been known at the time asbestos was placed on the market—predominated over any individual issues. As a result, the district court had permitted the consolidation of approximately 900 cases pending in its district into a class of plaintiffs under Rule 23(b)(3). The Fifth Circuit approved this certification, finding that the predominance and superiority requirements were satisfied. The Fifth Circuit noted that the district court's "plan is clearly superior to the alternative of repeating, hundreds of times over, the litigation of the state of the art issues with, as [the] experienced [district court] judge says, 'days of the same witnesses, exhibits and issues from trial to trial.' " *Id.* at 473.

Other significant appellate court rulings upholding class certification during the mid-1980s included the *School Asbestos* and *Agent Orange* cases. *In re School Asbestos Litig.*, 789 F.2d 996 (3d Cir. 1986); *In re "Agent Orange" Prods. Liab. Litig.*, 818 F.2d 145 (2d Cir. 1987). In *School Asbestos*, the Third Circuit upheld Rule 23(b)(3) certification of an action by school districts in several states seeking recovery of the costs of testing and removing asbestos from school buildings. In so doing, the court noted that "the trend has been for courts to be more receptive to use of the class action in mass tort litigation." 789 F.2d at 1009. In *Agent Orange*, the Second Circuit upheld the certification of a class of former military members and their families seeking damages for injuries caused by exposure to the herbicide Agent Orange.

This receptiveness by appellate courts led plaintiffs to bring a variety of mass tort class actions: cases involving toxic spills, pharmaceutical products, and medical devices, among others. In 1989, for example, certification of a class action in the Dalkon Shield litigation was approved by a federal appellate court (albeit in the settlement context). *In re A.H. Robins Co.*, 880 F.2d 709 (4th Cir. 1989). That case was significant because, as noted above, a different appellate court had overturned an order certifying a class in the Dalkon Shield litigation seven years earlier.

During this shift in favor of certifying mass tort cases, a number of prominent federal district court judges took leading roles in resolving thousands of Agent Orange, asbestos, and Dalkon Shield cases.

(3) Subsequent Judicial Skepticism

Critics of the trend favoring certification of mass tort cases argued that the mere threat of class certification is so devastating that defendants routinely choose to settle rather than risk bankruptcy on the results of a single trial. This view gained momentum in the mid-1990s, when various federal appellate courts issued several significant rulings.

An important ruling (discussed in various places in this text) was the Seventh Circuit's decision in *In re Rhone-Poulenc Rorer Inc.*, 51 F.3d 1293 (7th Cir. 1995). That case involved a nationwide class of hemophiliacs infected by the HIV virus suing drug companies that manufactured blood solids. The district court certified a class action, but the Seventh Circuit granted mandamus and reversed. The court was concerned that defendants were being coerced to settle out of fear of a potential classwide adverse verdict; that difficult choice-of-law questions were presented; and that the bifurcated trial approach envisioned by the trial court would violate defendant's Seventh Amendment jury-trial rights. The court distinguished *Jenkins* as involving a judicial crisis unique to asbestos.

Another significant ruling (also discussed in various places in this text) occurred in *Castano v. American Tobacco Co.*, 84 F.3d 734 (5th Cir. 1996). In that case, the district court certified a class under Rule 23(b)(3) of all nicotine-dependent persons in the United States who had purchased and smoked cigarettes manufactured by defendants (along with the estates, spouses, children, relatives, and "significant others" of these nicotine-dependent smokers). The claims dated back to 1943. The Fifth Circuit reversed, finding that individual issues of reliance and choice of law, among others, would predominate over common issues. The court echoed *Rhone-Poulenc*'s concerns regarding the pressures to settle class actions and the Seventh Amendment problems in bifurcated jury trials.

The Supreme Court, in the late 1990s, decided two important mass tort class action cases. Both cases involved settlement classes in connection with exposure to asbestos.

In the first decision, *Amchem Products, Inc. v. Windsor*, 521 U.S. 591 (1997), discussed in § 9.1, the Supreme Court rejected a Rule 23(b)(3) settlement class consisting of all persons who had been exposed occupationally to asbestos manufactured by one or more of the twenty defendants in the case and who had not yet filed an asbestos-related lawsuit against one of the defendants (along with the spouses, parents, children, and other relatives of those class members). The Supreme Court held that the proposed class did not satisfy the predominance requirement because it involved individuals who were exposed to different asbestos-containing products, for different amounts of time, in different ways, and over different periods. Furthermore, the class members had developed a variety of symptoms because of their exposures, with some having no symptoms at all. Moreover, choice-of-law problems counseled against predominance, as did conflicts between present and future (exposure-only) claimants.

Two years later, the Court decided *Ortiz v. Fibreboard Corp.*, 527 U.S. 815 (1999). *Ortiz*, which is discussed in detail in § 4.2, involved a mandatory "limited fund" settlement class that had been certified under Rule 23(b)(1)(B). The defendant, Fibreboard Corporation, having a net worth of approximately $235 million, was litigating with its insurance companies over disputed coverage for what promised to be billions of dollars of asbestos liability. Fibreboard agreed with its insurance carriers to establish a settlement fund of approximately $1.5 billion, which then became the "limited fund" against which a mandatory class of asbestos claimants claimed entitlement under various tort theories. Unlike the defendants in *Amchem*, the defendant in *Ortiz*, by virtue of the mandatory class action, stood to gain a definitive cap on its asbestos liability by forcing all claimants to recover from a fund consisting almost entirely of insurance proceeds, thereby permitting the corporation to continue with virtually all of its net worth intact. The Supreme Court held that the class did not qualify for certification under (b)(1)(B). Although the Court stopped short of holding that limited-fund settlement classes could never be certified under (b)(1)(B) in mass tort settlement cases, it stated that "the applicability of Rule 23(b)(1)(B) to a fund and plan purporting to liquidate actual and potential tort claims is subject to question." *Id.* at 864.

(4) Responses to Judicial Skepticism

It would be a mistake to view such decisions as *Rhone-Poulenc*, *Castano*, *Amchem*, and *Ortiz* as the end of aggregate mass tort lawsuits. Mass tort class actions—and lawsuits that function similarly to class actions—continue to be filed, and some of those cases have been successful.

First, federal courts have not shut the door altogether on mass tort class actions. One such example is a nationwide class action against a pharmaceutical company, which was certified and later settled. *In re Copley Pharm., Inc.*, 161 F.R.D. 456 (D. Wyo. 1995). Federal courts have also demonstrated a willingness to certify mass tort class actions in the settlement context. *See* § 9.1. Prominent recent examples include the *NFL Concussion* litigation and the *Deepwater Horizon* oil spill litigation. *See In re Nat'l Football League Players Concussion Injury Litig.*, 821 F.3d 410 (3d Cir.), *cert. denied sub nom. Gilchrist v. Nat'l Football League*, 137 S. Ct. 591, and *cert. denied sub nom. Armstrong v. Nat'l Football League*, 137 S. Ct. 607 (2016); *In re Oil Spill by the Oil Rig Deepwater Horizon in the Gulf of Mex., on Apr. 20, 2010*, 910 F. Supp. 2d 891 (E.D. La. 2012), *aff'd sub nom In re Deepwater Horizon*, 739 F.3d 790 (5th Cir. 2014) (economic and property damage); *In re Oil Spill by the Oil Rig Deepwater Horizon*, 295 F.R.D. 112 (E.D. La. 2013) (medical benefits).

Second, plaintiffs have generally found more receptive audiences in state courts than in federal courts. Of course, CAFA has made it more difficult for plaintiffs to keep substantial, multistate class actions in state court. *See* § 8.3.

Third, theories have been advanced in both state and federal court to address some of the manageability problems in mass tort cases. One example is the so-called medical monitoring claim, under which plaintiffs exposed to a toxic substance allege that they should receive periodic medical observation at the defendant's expense, even though they have exhibited no physical symptoms. Plaintiffs asserting medical monitoring claims have argued, albeit with only limited success, that such claims can be brought on a classwide basis. *See* § 4.1.

In addition, as discussed in Chapters 14, 15, and 16, parties are increasingly using non-class mechanisms—especially MDL—to litigate and settle mass tort cases.

B.   OTHER ISSUES IN MASS TORT CASES

The recent trend in mass tort class actions discussed above is only one of many important topics in the mass tort context. This section identifies several other important issues.

(1) Exposure-Only Claimants

One important issue in mass tort class actions is whether a "future claimant," *i.e.*, a person who has been exposed to a harmful substance but has shown no ill effects, can sue for damages. In the context of asbestos and other harmful substances, some courts have allowed such claims to go forward, reasoning that, even prior to the display of any symptoms, exposed individuals have suffered injury at the cellular level.

Other courts have refused to certify classes alleging only exposure but no physical injury, finding that the proposed classes did not meet the prerequisites of Rule 23. The reasoning of these courts has varied. Some courts have found that individualized questions, such as the degree and length of exposure and the potential for resultant injury, predominated over common questions. Other courts have pointed to the difficulty in giving notice to exposure-only plaintiffs, who may not know that they were even exposed and who may lack adequate information to determine whether to opt out of the class.

In *Ortiz v. Fibreboard*, 527 U.S. 815 (1999), the Supreme Court raised, but did not decide, whether "exposure-only" plaintiffs lacked "injury in fact," and thus did not have standing to sue. 527 U.S. at 831.

(2) "Mature" Versus "Immature" Mass Torts

An important question that some courts have asked in ruling on class certification is whether the case involves a "mature" tort or an "immature" tort. Courts in recent years have been reluctant to certify immature tort cases—those in which there have been few individual trials and verdicts. As the *Manual for Complex Litigation (4th)* explains, "[a] court should be cautious before aggregating claims or cases, particularly for trial, learning first about the nature of the litigation and whether the issues are appropriate even for pretrial aggregation or consolidation." § 22.2.

The concept of mature versus immature torts was important to the Fifth Circuit's decision in *Castano*, which involved a putative nationwide class of nicotine-dependent smokers. The court stated that, because these types of "addiction as injury" cases had never been tried before, there was no "prior track record of trials" from which the district court could assess Rule 23(b)(3)'s predominance and superiority requirements. 84 F.3d at 747. Other courts, however, have rejected "maturity" as a consideration in deciding whether to certify a class. *See, e.g., Klay v. Humana, Inc.*, 382 F.3d 1241, 1272 (11th Cir. 2004).

(3) Problems of Classwide Proof in Mass Tort Cases

A major issue in mass tort cases (and sometimes in other types of class actions) is whether plaintiffs can prove damages on a classwide basis through the use of aggregate statistical proof (or "extrapolation"). As discussed in detail in § 5.6, although the Supreme Court's treatment of what it deemed "Trial by Formula" in *Wal-Mart Stores, Inc. v. Dukes*, 564 U.S.

338 (2011), raised concern about the future availability of such methods of proof, the Court's subsequent decision in *Tyson Foods, Inc. v. Bouaphakeo*, 136 S. Ct. 1036 (2016), has alleviated some of those concerns. Nonetheless, the use of classwide statistical proof still raises potential issues, especially in mass tort cases.

(4) Novel Negotiation Class

In the *National Prescription Opiate Multidistrict Litigation*, the district judge certified a novel "negotiation class" that would allow a supermajority of the class to bind the entire class to a lump sum settlement (and to the allocation of that settlement). *In re National Prescription Opiate Litigation*, 332 F.R.D. 532 (N.D. Ohio 2019). The process was devised by one of the special masters in the case, the late Francis McGovern, along with Harvard Law Professor William Rubenstein, to assure the defendants that any settlement would result in global peace (or close to global peace), and not a resolution in which there would be large numbers of opt outs. *See* Francis McGovern & William Rubenstein, *The Negotiation Class: A Cooperative Approach to Class Actions Involving Large Stakeholders*, 99 Tex. L. Rev. ___ (forthcoming 2020).

The underlying cases are suits by cities and counties alleging that drug manufacturers exaggerated the benefits (and understated the risks) of opioid prescription medications and that drug distributors failed to monitor, investigate, or report suspicious prescription orders. Plaintiffs argued that

Rule 23 permitted such a negotiation class, and that such a class was especially suitable for the sophisticated governmental class members involved. The district court certified the class under both Rule 23(b)(3) and Rule 23(c)(4). On appeal, the Sixth Circuit reversed in a split decision that was rendered just as this text was going to press. *In re National Prescription Opiate Litigation*, ___ F.3d ___, 2020 WL 5701916 (6th Cir. 2020).

§ 11.2 EMPLOYMENT DISCRIMINATION CLASS ACTIONS

This section discusses several important issues that have arisen in employment discrimination class actions. Class actions are widely used in cases claiming that an act of discrimination is part of a larger pattern of similar conduct. For example, an African-American who claims that he was terminated during a reduction-in-force because of his race and that less qualified white employees were retained may also claim that other similarly situated African-Americans were the victims of discrimination. If the requirements of Rule 23 are satisfied, such claims may be pursued on a classwide basis.

Multi-party race, color, religion, sex, and national origin claims have been brought as class actions under Title VII of the Civil Rights Act of 1964, 42 U.S.C. §§ 2000e *et seq.*, and multi-party race claims have been brought under 42 U.S.C. § 1981. Likewise, multi-party disability discrimination claims have been brought as class actions under the Americans

With Disabilities Act (ADA), 42 U.S.C. §§ 12101 *et seq.* By contrast, cases alleging age discrimination under the Age Discrimination in Employment Act of 1967 (ADEA), 29 U.S.C. §§ 621–34, are not subject to Rule 23 but are subject instead to different procedures under a separate statutory scheme applicable to "collective" actions. This section examines both Rule 23 discrimination suits and ADEA collective actions.

This section—like prior parts of this text—refers repeatedly to the Supreme Court's decision in *Wal-Mart Stores, Inc. v. Dukes*, 564 U.S. 338 (2011). A student or practitioner cannot analyze class certification issues in the employment context (or virtually any other context) without taking into consideration that landmark case. Although *Dukes* poses new challenges for plaintiffs, employment discrimination class actions continue to be certified. *See* Robert H. Klonoff, *Class Actions Part II: A Respite from the Decline*, 92 N.Y.U. L. Rev. 971 (2017) (discussing cases).

A.   RULE 23 CASES

(1) Applicability of Rule 23 Requirements in Discrimination Cases

Prior to the Supreme Court's decision in *East Texas Motor Freight System, Inc. v. Rodriguez*, 431 U.S. 395 (1977), a number of lower courts took the view that the requirements for class certification should be liberally construed in Title VII cases, and that the requirements of Rule 23 did not need to be applied strictly. *Rodriguez*, however, made clear that, while "suits alleging racial or ethnic discrimination are often by their very nature class suits, involving classwide wrongs[,] . . . careful attention to the requirements of Fed. R. Civ. P. 23 remains nonetheless indispensable." *Id.* at 405.

The Court reiterated the point five years later in *General Telephone Co. of Southwest v. Falcon*, 457 U.S. 147 (1982), noting that "a Title VII class action, like any other class action, may only be certified if the trial court is satisfied, after a rigorous analysis, that the prerequisites of Rule 23(a) have been satisfied." *Id.* at 161. More recently, the Court reaffirmed the "rigorous analysis" approach in *Dukes*, 564 U.S. at 350–51. In light of *Rodriguez*, *Falcon*, and *Dukes*, courts must apply the Rule 23 requirements as stringently in Title VII cases as they do in other kinds of cases.

One context that has been greatly impacted by *Rodriguez* and *Falcon* is the "across-the-board" claim of discrimination. Such a claim involves all persons allegedly affected by a particular type of discrimination. For instance, in an "across-the-board" class action, a female plaintiff claiming discrimination in hiring might seek to represent female employees who claimed discrimination in promotion opportunities, other female employees who claimed that they were terminated based on their sex, and still other female employees who claimed discrimination in pay. Relying on Rule 23(a)'s typicality requirement, the Supreme Court in

Falcon raised serious doubts about the general viability of "across-the-board" class actions.

In *Falcon*, a plaintiff who alleged that he was not *promoted* by the defendant because he was Mexican-American attempted to represent a class that included Mexican-Americans who alleged that they were not *hired* because they were Mexican-American. Reversing the lower courts, the Supreme Court held that plaintiff could not represent such a class. The Court reasoned that "it was error for the District Court to presume that respondent's claim was typical of other claims against [the defendant] by Mexican-American employees." 457 U.S. at 158–59. According to the Court, "[i]f one allegation of specific discriminatory treatment were sufficient to support an across-the-board attack, every Title VII case would be a potential companywide class action." *Id.* at 159. The Court could "find nothing [in Title VII] to indicate that Congress intended to authorize such a wholesale expansion of class action litigation." *Id.* In an important footnote, however, the Court stated that "[s]ignificant proof that an employer operated under a general policy of discrimination conceivably could justify a class of both applicants and employees if the discrimination manifested itself in hiring and promotion practices in the same general fashion." *Id.* at 159 n.15. The Court gave as an example the use of "entirely subjective decision making processes" and the use of a "biased testing procedure to evaluate both applicants for employment and incumbent employees." *Id.*

Following *Falcon*, many courts have refused to certify across-the-board classes. This trend will no doubt continue given the Supreme Court's strict approach to commonality in *Dukes. See* § 3.8.

(2) Distinction Between Disparate Impact and Disparate Treatment Claims

An important distinction is made in employment law between "disparate treatment" claims and "disparate impact" claims. In the former, the plaintiff must prove a discriminatory motive or intent on the part of the employer; in the latter, the plaintiff need only show that an employment practice had a discriminatory impact on a protected group, regardless of motive. An example of the latter would be an aptitude test that, while not designed to discriminate against African-Americans, had the effect of disproportionately excluding them from the better jobs. Courts have generally held that disparate impact cases should be more liberally certified as class actions because they are usually based on objective standards that are applied evenly to the employees in question. By contrast, as the Fourth Circuit has noted, "the disparate treatment pattern or practice must be one based upon a specific intent to discriminate against an entire group, to treat it as a group less favorably simply because of [discriminatory animus]. The greater intrinsic difficulty of establishing the existence and common reach of such a subjectively based practice is obvious." *Stastny v. S. Bell Tel. & Tel. Co.*, 628 F.2d 267, 274 (4th Cir. 1980).

(3) Rule 23(b) Requirements

Most employment class actions have been certified, if at all, under either Rule 23(b)(2) or Rule 23(b)(3). As explained in § 4.3, Rule 23(b)(2) was adopted in large part for civil rights cases, and numerous civil rights suits seeking injunctive relief have been certified under (b)(2). Prior to *Dukes*, most courts had historically allowed certification even if damages were also sought, as long as equitable relief was the principal relief sought. As discussed in § 4.3, *Dukes* has cut back on the ability of plaintiffs to bring (b)(2) actions that include claims for monetary relief.

Rule 23(b)(3) has been used as a vehicle for employment class actions seeking primarily damages. Although some courts have been liberal in certifying (b)(3) employment cases, others have been more restrictive. Courts granting certification have often relied upon allegations of a pervasive discriminatory practice. Courts denying certification have frequently emphasized the existence of individualized issues, such as whether the employer in fact discriminated against each class member or instead treated individual class members unfavorably because of legitimate, non-discriminatory reasons, including poor performance, excessive absenteeism, or misconduct. *Dukes* reinforced the importance of such individualized defenses in the employment context.

(4) Pattern-and-Practice Cases

Some courts have been receptive to certifying cases alleging a "pattern and practice" of discrimination.

These courts frequently divide such cases into two phases—liability and remedy—and certify solely the question of whether defendant engaged in a pattern and practice of discrimination. A finding of a pattern and practice permits an award of injunctive relief and establishes a rebuttable presumption that individual class members were victims of discrimination. Courts adopting this approach reason that, at the first phase, the class members need not establish that they were individually discriminated against. As a result, disparities from employee to employee are irrelevant. Accordingly, these courts conclude that a pattern-and-practice trial achieves efficiencies by adjudicating common issues without becoming sidetracked by individual employee-specific issues. Other courts, however, refuse to certify discrimination cases even when a pattern and practice is alleged. For instance, some courts reason that since a pattern and practice finding establishes only a rebuttable presumption, individualized issues will still exist in the remedial phase in deciding whether a particular class member was a victim of the pattern and practice of discrimination. In light of *Dukes*, which itself involved an alleged pattern and practice, courts will no longer be able to ignore such individualized issues in determining whether a class action should be certified under Rule 23. *See* § 3.8.

(5) Whether a Finding of No Pattern or Practice Precludes Subsequent Individual Actions

In *Cooper v. Federal Reserve Bank of Richmond*, 467 U.S. 867 (1984), the Supreme Court addressed whether, in light of a class action determination that no pattern and practice of discrimination existed, members of the class could bring individual discrimination claims. In a unanimous opinion, the Court held that such suits *could* be brought. As the Court explained, "a class plaintiff's attempt to prove the existence of a company-wide policy, or even a consistent practice within a given department, may fail even though discrimination against one or two individuals has been proved." *Id.* at 878. As a result, "the rejection of a claim of classwide discrimination does not warrant the conclusion that no member of the class could have a valid individual claim." *Id.* Thus, under *Cooper*, even if a pattern and practice is not found, individual class members are entitled to bring separate discrimination claims.

(6) Seventh Amendment Issues

Under the Civil Rights Act of 1991, jury trials are now authorized in Title VII cases. Previously, such cases were limited to bench trials. As a result, potential Seventh Amendment issues are implicated in trying Title VII cases. In particular, certification of bifurcated employment discrimination class actions—in which, for example, common issues are decided by one jury in the first phase and individual issues are decided by a different jury in the second phase—may be more difficult, at least in some circuits, in light of recent case law construing the Seventh Amendment right to jury trial. *See* § 5.6.

B. COLLECTIVE ACTIONS

(1) Overview of Age Discrimination Suits

The ADEA prohibits discrimination in employment on the basis of age against individuals age 40 and over. The ADEA has been interpreted to require plaintiffs to prove intentional discrimination. *Gross v. FBL Fin. Servs., Inc.*, 557 U.S. 167 (2009). As noted at the outset of this chapter, age discrimination suits under the ADEA are *not* subject to Rule 23. Instead, those actions follow the procedures of a labor-specific statute, the Fair Labor Standards Act, 29 U.S.C. § 216(b). The differences between the Rule 23 approach and the ADEA approach are substantial.

First, under the ADEA, the sole inquiry for a collective action is whether the individuals alleging discrimination are "similarly situated" to one another. The "similarly situated" inquiry is a fact-specific one focusing on whether the individuals were subject to a single discriminatory decision, policy, or plan. Although some courts have held that the Rule 23 criteria apply in ADEA cases, other courts have held otherwise. Under the latter approach, no specific inquiry into numerosity, adequacy, typicality, and commonality is required, and the plaintiffs need not satisfy any of the Rule 23(b) criteria.

Second, suits under Rule 23 are either "opt-out" actions ((b)(3)) or mandatory class actions in which opt outs generally are not allowed ((b)(1), (b)(2)). By contrast, ADEA actions are "opt-in" actions: A plaintiff is *not* part of the collective action unless he or she affirmatively opts into the class by filing a written consent to join the action. Although all of these types of actions are commenced by representative plaintiffs, the size of an ADEA collective action depends on how many other individuals take affirmative steps to become part of the suit.

Third, plaintiffs who opt into an ADEA collective action have full party status, unlike unnamed class members in Rule 23 actions. Thus, each ADEA plaintiff is a named party to advance his or her own individual case. To be sure, the court has wide latitude in structuring the trial. It may, for example, try all of the opt-in plaintiffs at one time, rendering a judgment as to each, or it may have a liability phase, focusing solely on whether there is a pattern and practice of discrimination, and a subsequent remedial phase to determine the remedy for each opt-in plaintiff who proves that he or she was subjected to the pattern and practice. Because relatively few ADEA collective actions have gone to trial, there is little case law on trial structure for ADEA collective actions.

(2) Notice to Plaintiffs in ADEA Cases

Because the notice requirements of Rule 23 do not apply to ADEA cases, courts have faced legal issues regarding the propriety of notice in ADEA cases. The contexts of Rule 23 and ADEA are very different for purposes of notice. In a Rule 23 opt-out case, notices are sent to putative class members, who will be bound unless they opt out. In ADEA cases, by contrast, notices (when authorized) are sent to people who will not be part of the case unless they affirmatively opt in.

In *Hoffmann-La Roche Inc. v. Sperling*, 493 U.S. 165 (1989), the Supreme Court addressed whether the district court could authorize notice to potential members of the collective action on whose behalf an ADEA case has been brought. The Court held that a district court has discretion to send out notices to potential plaintiffs advising them of the suit and giving them a cutoff date for filing written requests to opt into the case. The Court recognized that "once an ADEA action is filed, the court has a managerial responsibility to oversee the joinder of additional parties to assure that the task is accomplished in an efficient and proper way." *Id.* at 170–71. The Court rejected the argument—based on the differences between Rule 23 and ADEA actions—that the district court should not be allowed to send notices to people who have not yet opted into the case.

(3) Certification of an ADEA Case as a Collective Action

As discussed in § 5.3, courts in Rule 23 cases have discretion in certain cases to grant or deny class certification without discovery. Some courts do so; others allow limited discovery; and still others allow close to full merits discovery. In other words, the Rule 23 cases tend to be very fact-specific.

The ADEA cases tend to follow a more predictable two-stage pattern. At the first stage, the court decides whether to give notice of the action to potential plaintiffs. Applying a lenient standard, courts generally grant conditional certification of an ADEA case as a collective action. Then, courts usually allow a period of discovery to address whether the claims of the plaintiffs who opt in are similarly situated to each other. At the conclusion of discovery, courts apply a much higher standard with respect to whether the certification decision should remain intact. District courts have frequently decertified the action at the second stage on the ground that the opt-in plaintiffs are not similarly situated. *See, e.g., Mooney v. Aramco Servs. Co.*, 54 F.3d 1207 (5th Cir. 1995) (discussing case law). The reasons for decertification at the second stage are, among others, that the opt-in plaintiffs differ in age, job status, and job locations, and suffered adverse employment actions by different supervisors at different times for different asserted reasons.

That is not to say that all cases are decertified at stage two. For example, in *Thiessen v. General Electric Capital Corp.*, 267 F.3d 1095 (10th Cir. 2001), the Tenth Circuit held that the district court had erred in decertifying a collective ADEA action at stage two. The court reasoned that, although individualized issues may exist at the second phase of trial, the first phase—the pattern-and-practice phase—involved common issues and common defenses. Because of the common pattern-and-practice issues, the opt-in plaintiffs were similarly situated for purposes of 29 U.S.C. § 216(b).

§ 11.3　SECURITIES FRAUD CLASS ACTIONS

A.　OVERVIEW

In its most basic form, a securities fraud class action arises when a group of people lose money in the stock market as a result of an allegedly fraudulent statement or omission by a corporation. For example, if a pharmaceutical company promotes a new drug as a risk-free cure for a particular ailment and fails to disclose that the drug has potentially fatal side effects, a subsequent announcement regarding those side effects may cause the company's stock price to plummet. Shareholders whose portfolios dropped in value when the true facts were disclosed may wish to sue for damages. Frequently, however, the losses suffered by individual shareholders are too small to warrant separate lawsuits. Moreover, litigating separately for each shareholder the identical question of whether the company committed fraud in failing to disclose the side effects would be extremely inefficient. Thus, courts and commentators have often cited securities fraud suits as being well-suited for class treatment. That is not to say, however, that all securities suits are suitable to be brought as class actions. The facts of a particular case may dictate that certification of a securities class action would be inefficient or unfair.

This section addresses some of the major procedural issues that have arisen in securities fraud class actions. The particular focus is on class actions under section 10(b) of the Securities Exchange Act of

1934, 15 U.S.C. § 78a ("section 10(b)"), and Securities and Exchange Commission Rule 10b–5, 17 CFR § 240.10b–5 ("Rule 10b–5").

B.   ELEMENTS OF A RULE 10b–5 CLAIM

Most securities fraud class actions seek damages based on section 10(b) and Rule 10b–5 and are brought under Federal Rule of Civil Procedure 23(b)(3). Rule 10b–5 makes it unlawful for any person to "make any untrue statement of a material fact or to omit to state a material fact necessary in order to make the statements made, in light of the circumstances under which they were made, not misleading." To make out a claim under section 10(b) and Rule 10b–5, a plaintiff must allege and prove that the defendant made a representation or omission of material fact, upon which the plaintiff justifiably relied, and that caused the plaintiff to suffer damages.

(1)   The Reliance Element

The securities law issue that has generated the most analysis for class action purposes is the element of reliance. As noted above, reliance is required in claims under section 10(b) and Rule 10b–5 (although certain other securities statutes do not require reliance). As discussed in § 4.4, the need to show individual reliance upon a misrepresentation or omission is frequently a reason why fraud claims are not certified as class actions. Because reliance is specific to each individual, courts often find that individual issues predominate over common issues, thereby rendering a class action unsuitable under Rule 23(b)(3). In the securities area, reliance is a required element in a section 10(b)/Rule 10b–5 claim. Reliance provides the crucial link between a defendant's misrepresentation or omission and a plaintiff's decision to buy or sell a stock.

Courts have developed at least three potential ways in which a plaintiff can avoid having to show individual reliance: (1) the "fraud-on-the-market" theory; (2) the *Affiliated Ute* presumption; and (3) the "fraud-created-the-market" theory. If a particular case falls within one of these categories, a major impediment to class certification disappears. If not, then a court is likely to find that the need to prove reliance separately for each class member renders the case unsuitable for class treatment.

(2) Fraud-on-the-Market Approach to Reliance

The fraud-on-the-market doctrine assumes that shareholders rely not so much on what a company says or omits but on the fact that the market price of the stock takes into account all publicly available information and thus reflects a fair value for the stock. The theory is that when the corporation does not disclose material information, the stock price is an artificial one. For instance, in the above pharmaceutical example, the stock price was artificially inflated during the period when the true facts about the drug's side effects were withheld. When the true facts were revealed, the stock price dropped to reflect the stock's true value.

The fraud-on-the-market approach was endorsed by the Supreme Court in *Basic Inc. v. Levinson*, 485 U.S. 224 (1988). *Basic* involved a class of shareholders who sued under Rule 10b–5, claiming that they sold their shares at artificially depressed prices because the company falsely denied that it was engaged in merger discussions. After the class members sold their stock, the company announced an offer by another company to buy all outstanding shares of its stock. In analyzing the claims, the Supreme Court noted that "[r]equiring proof of individualized reliance from each member of the proposed class effectively would have prevented [the class members] from proceeding with a class action, since the individual issues then would have overwhelmed the common ones." *Id.* at 242. The Court then addressed fraud on the market as a way of avoiding the need to adjudicate individual reliance. Under that doctrine, a person who trades in stock is presumed to have done so in reliance on the validity of the price set by the market, even where the price is artificially high or low because of the company's misstatements or omissions. This presumption only arises, however, if certain requirements are met.

Most importantly, the market must be an "efficient" one—*i.e.*, one in which the market price of a security accurately reflects all publicly disclosed information. A heavily traded stock on a major stock exchange, such as the New York Stock Exchange, almost certainly would qualify. A stock that sells only in low volumes and does not trade on a major stock exchange generally would not qualify. In *Basic*, the Court upheld the lower courts' determinations that the company's stock, which traded on the New York Exchange, traded in an efficient market.

Under *Basic*, however, the presumption of reliance resulting from an efficiently traded stock is rebuttable. As the Court noted, "[a]ny showing that severs the link between the alleged misrepresentation and either the price received (or paid) by the plaintiff, or his decision to trade at a fair market price, will be sufficient to rebut the presumption of reliance." *Id.* at 248. The Court gave the following examples of how the presumption could be rebutted: (1) if "market makers" (dealers who buy and sell the particular security on their own account) knew the truth about the company's merger plans; (2) if news of the merger discussions was in fact public at the time of the alleged fraud (a situation sometimes referred to as "truth-on-the-market"); and (3) if someone sold shares because of issues unrelated to the merger talks, despite knowing or believing that the company was presenting false information about the status of merger discussions. In each of these circumstances, the shareholder cannot be said to have relied on the false statements. *Id.* at 248–49.

Courts have looked at a variety of factors in evaluating whether a stock is traded in an efficient market. These include, among others: average weekly trading volume; number of analysts following the stock; market capitalization of the company; and evidence of a relationship between the announcement of major news and the effect on stock price. Courts have indicated that the assessment of whether a stock trades in an efficient market must be based not on mere allegations but on a careful analysis of the evidence, under a standard of proof similar to that required for obtaining a preliminary injunction or resolving jurisdictional disputes. *See, e.g., Unger v. Amedisys, Inc.*, 401 F.3d 316 (5th Cir. 2005).

One issue decided by the Supreme Court relating to *Basic* is whether a "scheme liability" theory—enabling investors to sue for fraud against third parties—is available under the 1934 Securities Exchange Act. In *Stoneridge Investment Partners LLC v. Scientific-Atlanta Inc.*, 552 U.S. 148 (2008), investors brought a class action under section 10(b) of the Securities Exchange Act of 1934 and SEC Rule 10b–5 against vendors and customers for allegedly helping a cable television operator inflate its earnings in financial statements that they knew investors would rely upon. The Supreme Court held that the vendors and customers did not have a duty to disclose. Moreover, because the defendants did not make their deceptive acts public, it was impossible for the investors to have relied upon the defendants' deception. Even in the absence of a public statement, the investors contended that the defendants' conduct was part of a scheme to mislead investors, thereby triggering the *Basic* presumption of reliance. The Court rejected that contention, noting that it was the cable company alone that filed the misleading financial statements.

In its 2014 decision in *Halliburton Co. v. Erica P. John Fund, Inc.*, 573 U.S. 258 (2014) (*Halliburton II*), the Supreme Court addressed the question of whether it should overrule *Basic*. The defendant advanced several arguments for doing so, including: (1) the evidence suggests that securities markets are not in fact "efficient markets"; (2) *Basic* wrongly assumes that investors rely on the integrity of the market price of a stock when deciding to invest; and (3) *Basic* cannot be reconciled with recent case law governing class certification, because it allows plaintiffs to simply plead—rather than prove—that the Rule 23 requirements for class certification are satisfied. In a split decision, the majority rejected those arguments and refused to overrule *Basic*, reasoning:

> In securities class action cases, the crucial requirement for class certification will usually be the predominance requirement of Rule 23(b)(3). The *Basic* presumption does not relieve plaintiffs of the burden of proving—before class certification—that this requirement is met. *Basic* instead establishes that a plaintiff satisfies that burden by proving the prerequisites for invoking the presumption—namely, publicity, materiality, market efficiency, and market timing. The burden of proving those prerequisites still rests with plaintiffs and (with the exception of materiality) must be satisfied before class certification. *Basic* does not, in other words, allow plaintiffs simply to plead that common questions of reliance predominate over individual ones, but rather sets forth what they must prove to demonstrate such predominance.

573 U.S. at 276.

Halliburton II was not a complete victory for plaintiffs, however. The Court held that defendants are entitled to an opportunity to rebut the *Basic* presumption *before* class certification "through evidence that an alleged misrepresentation did not actually affect the market price of the stock." Most courts, however, have been unpersuaded by defendants' efforts to take advantage of this evidentiary opportunity. *See* Robert H. Klonoff, *Class Actions in the Year 2026: A Prognosis*, 65 Emory L.J. 1569, 1588–89 (2016) (citing cases).

(3) The *Affiliated Ute* Presumption of Reliance

A second way in which plaintiffs can avoid individualized proof of reliance in securities cases is when defendants are alleged to have failed to disclose a material fact, as opposed to affirmatively misrepresenting a fact. When an *omission* is involved, individualized proof of reliance is not required. This principle was established by the Supreme Court in *Affiliated Ute Citizens v. United States*, 406 U.S. 128 (1972). In allowing an exception to the need for proving reliance on an individualized basis, the Court in *Affiliated Ute* recognized the practical difficulty in showing affirmative reliance on an omission, as opposed to showing reliance on a misrepresentation.

Although a case involving solely alleged omissions is clearly governed by *Affiliated Ute*, the courts are split on whether *Affiliated Ute* should apply when both omissions and misrepresentations are involved.

Some courts apply *Affiliated Ute* only if a 10b–5 case is based *solely* on omissions. Others apply the doctrine even when misrepresentations are involved as well, provided that the case is "primarily" one involving omissions.

(4) Fraud-Created-the-Market Theory

A third (very narrow) exception to the need for proving reliance on an individualized basis involves the situation in which defendants allegedly conspired to bring to the market securities that they knew were unmarketable. This doctrine, known as the "fraud-created-the-market" doctrine, applies only when the fraud is so extensive that the security should not be trading at all in an open and developed market. For example, the doctrine would apply to offering statements for stock issued by a startup company, when the company is part of a fraudulent scheme and has no value. A plaintiff relying on this exception must show that the underlying business is essentially worthless. Merely buying into what turns out to be a bad deal is not enough. Some courts, moreover, have rejected the fraud-created-the-market doctrine altogether. *See, e.g., Malack v. BDO Seidman, LLP*, 617 F.3d 743, 756 (3d Cir. 2010).

(5) Materiality of the Misrepresented or Omitted Fact

Basic also addressed the Rule 10b–5 element of materiality, offering a standard that can be assessed on a classwide basis. According to the Court, information that was misrepresented or withheld in a Rule 10b–5 case is material if there is "a substantial likelihood that the disclosure of the omitted fact would have been viewed by the reasonable investor as having significantly altered the 'total mix' of information made available." 485 U.S. at 231–32. This inquiry is an objective one and thus need not be made separately for each class member.

Courts have also developed several doctrines that enable them to determine, on a classwide basis, whether alleged misstatements or omissions are *immaterial* as a matter of law. One example, known as "puffing," involves positive, upbeat statements that are so vague that no reasonable investor would have relied on them. Another example is the "bespeaks caution" doctrine, which involves cautionary statements that accompany a written or oral communication. The cautionary statements are deemed to render the alleged omission or misrepresentation immaterial as a matter of law. For example, rosy forecasts of future growth may be deemed immaterial if accompanied by cautionary statements that the future is uncertain and that a significant period of lower earnings is possible.

Relying on *Basic*, the Supreme Court has rejected the use of a bright-line test for determining the materiality of adverse event reports. In *Matrixx Initiatives, Inc. v. Siracusano*, 563 U.S. 27 (2011), the issue was whether a plaintiff in a securities fraud class action could state a claim under section 10(b) and Rule 10b–5 based on a pharmaceutical company's failure to disclose reports of a possible link between its cold medicine and loss of smell, thereby misleading consumers. Defendant Matrixx countered that plaintiffs failed to allege a material misrepresentation because the reports did not disclose a statistically significant number of adverse events. The Court held that a lack of statistically significant data showing that a drug company's cold medicine caused adverse health effects did not necessarily preclude the data from being material to a class of investors. The issue turned on the precise factual context. According to the Court, "th[e] contextual inquiry may reveal in some cases that reasonable investors would have viewed reports of adverse events as material even though the reports did not provide statistically significant evidence of a causal link." *Id.* at 44.

Prior to 2013, courts had reached different conclusions as to whether plaintiffs were required to prove materiality before obtaining class certification on a fraud-on-the-market theory. In *Amgen Inc. v. Connecticut Retirement Plans & Trust Funds*, 568 U.S. 455 (2013) (discussed in § 5.2 with respect to the degree to which courts may evaluate the merits at the class certification stage), the Supreme Court held that proof of materiality is not a prerequisite to certification in such cases. The Court reasoned:

> While [the plaintiffs] certainly must prove materiality to prevail on the merits, we hold that such proof is not a prerequisite for class certification. Rule 23(b)(3) requires a showing that questions common to the class predominate, not that those questions will be answered, on the merits, in favor of the class.

> Because materiality is judged according to an objective standard, the materiality of [the defendant's] alleged misrepresentations and omissions is a question common to all members of the class.... [W]hether material or immaterial, [they] would be so equally for all investors composing the class.... As to materiality, therefore, the class is entirely cohesive: It will prevail or fail in unison.

568 U.S. at 459–560. *Amgen* has had an impact far beyond only securities fraud cases. *See* § 5.2.

(6) Zero Price Change

Some courts have found statements immaterial as a matter of law when disclosure of the alleged fraud did not result in a change in stock price. *See, e.g., Oran v. Stafford*, 226 F.3d 275 (3d Cir. 2000). Other courts, however, have refused to endorse that approach. *See, e.g., No. 84 Employer-Teamster Joint Council Pension Trust Fund v. Am. W. Holding Corp.*, 320 F.3d 920 (9th Cir. 2003).

(7) Loss Causation

The Supreme Court has held that an investor who alleges securities fraud must provide allegations that the purported fraud actually *caused* the loss at issue. *See Dura Pharm., Inc. v. Broudo*, 544 U.S. 336 (2005). It is generally not enough to allege simply that the price of the stock was inflated. As the Court explained:

[A]s a matter of pure logic, at the moment the transaction takes place, the plaintiff has suffered no loss; the inflated purchase payment is offset by ownership of a share that *at that instant possesses* equivalent value. Moreover, the logical link between the inflated share purchase price and any later economic loss is not invariably strong. Shares are normally purchased with an eye toward a later sale. But if, say, the purchaser sells the shares quickly before the relevant truth begins to leak out, the misrepresentation will not have led to any loss. If the purchaser sells later after the truth makes its way into the marketplace, an initially inflated purchase price *might* mean a later loss. But that is far from inevitably so. When the purchaser subsequently resells such shares, even at a lower price, that lower price may reflect, not the earlier misrepresentation, but changed economic circumstances, changed investor expectations, new industry-specific or firm-specific facts, conditions, or other events, which taken separately or together account for some or all of that lower price. . . . Other things being equal, the longer the time between purchase and sale, the more likely that this is so, *i.e.*, the more likely that other factors caused the loss.

Id. at 1631–32 (emphases in original).

A question related to loss causation is whether the plaintiff has to *prove* loss causation as a condition of class certification. The Supreme Court, reversing the

Fifth Circuit, unanimously held in 2011 that proof of loss causation was not required at the class certification stage. *Erica P. John Fund, Inc. v. Halliburton Co.*, 563 U.S. 804 (2011) (*Halliburton I*). The Court reasoned that, while proof of reliance was an element of class certification (one that, under *Basic*, could frequently be established through a rebuttable presumption of reliance), loss causation was not. According to the Court, "[t]he fact that a subsequent loss may have been caused by factors other than the revelation of a misrepresentation has nothing to do with whether an investor relied on the misrepresentation in the first place, either directly or presumptively through the fraud-on-the-market theory." *Id.* at 813.

C.   TRANSNATIONAL TRANSACTIONS

In *Morrison v. National Australia Bank Ltd.*, 561 U.S. 247 (2010), the Supreme Court addressed the extent to which the Securities Exchange Act of 1934 (the "Exchange Act") applies to transnational securities transactions. In that case, private foreign investors brought a putative class action against the National Australia Bank, alleging securities fraud related to foreign transactions. In the absence of clear congressional intent, the Second Circuit had formulated a "conduct-and-effects" test to determine the statute's extraterritorial reach for so-called "F-cubed" cases (*i.e.*, lawsuits filed in U.S. courts under U.S. securities laws by *foreign* plaintiffs against *foreign* issuers based on securities purchased on *foreign* exchanges). This test had been adopted and used by other circuit courts for almost four decades.

The Supreme Court, however, reversed, favoring a presumption against extraterritorial application of the Exchange Act. In a unanimous opinion, the Court held that the anti-fraud provision of the Exchange Act did not provide a private right of action to foreign plaintiffs suing a foreign defendant for misconduct connected to securities traded on foreign exchanges.

D. REFORM LEGISLATION

(1) The Private Securities Litigation Reform Act of 1995

Securities fraud class actions have been controversial. Critics contend that many of the lawsuits have been meritless, and that the threat of classwide verdicts has forced companies to settle even weak cases for significant sums of money, thereby injuring companies and their shareholders. Critics have also attacked the large fees that some plaintiff firms have received in such cases. On the other hand, defenders of these suits have argued that such suits have had a salutary effect on corporate conduct and have served to compensate shareholders injured by fraud.

The various criticisms convinced Congress to take a hard look at the situation. After extensive hearings, Congress enacted the Private Securities Litigation Reform Act of 1995 (the Reform Act or PSLRA). Pub. L. No. 104–67, 109 Stat. 737 (1995). The Reform Act contains a series of requirements governing federal securities fraud actions, including numerous requirements—in addition to those in Rule 23—that must be satisfied in securities class actions. Some of the major features of the Reform Act include the following:

(a)   Each named plaintiff who wishes to become a class representative must file a sworn certification stating that the plaintiff has read the complaint and authorized its filing, that the plaintiff did not purchase the security at issue at the direction of counsel or for purposes of participating in a securities fraud action, and that the plaintiff is willing to serve as a representative, including providing deposition and trial testimony. The sworn certification must also describe all transactions in the security made by the plaintiff during the class period; disclose any other federal securities fraud actions that the plaintiff has been involved in during the preceding three years; and confirm that the plaintiff will not accept any payment beyond his or her *pro rata* share of the recovery, except as authorized by the court (for such things as wage losses directly attributable to service as a class representative). 15 U.S.C. § 78u–4(a)(2); *see id.* § 78u–4(a)(4).

(b)   The Reform Act requires that, within twenty days of the filing of a securities fraud class action, the plaintiffs' attorneys must publish a notice in a "widely circulated" newspaper, advising potential class members of the suit, the claims involved, and the potential class period. The notice must also state that, within sixty days of the notice, any plaintiff may move the court to serve as lead plaintiff. The court is then required to "appoint as lead plaintiff the member or members of the purported plaintiff class that the court determines to be most capable of adequately representing the interests of class members." 15 U.S.C. § 78u–4(a)(3)(B)(i). In making this determination from among the persons who have submitted motions, the court is required to apply a rebuttable presumption that the person or group of persons having the "largest financial interest in the relief sought by the class" should be chosen "most adequate plaintiff," and should thus serve as class representative. 15 U.S.C. § 78u–4(a)(3)(B)(iii)(I). Some courts have permitted a group of unrelated investors to serve collectively as lead plaintiffs, but other courts have refused to endorse that approach. Additionally, the Eleventh Circuit has rejected the argument that a class representative's use of investment advisors to make investment decisions renders that representative atypical under Rule 23(a)(3). *Loc. 703, I.B. of T. Grocery Store & Food Emps. Welfare Fund v. Regions Fin. Corp.*, 762 F.3d 1248 (11th Cir. 2014).

Under the Reform Act, the individual selected as lead plaintiff has responsibility for selecting and retaining counsel, subject to court approval. 15 U.S.C. § 78u–4(a)(3)(B)(v).

(c) Courts may not award attorneys' fees that exceed a "reasonable percentage of the amount of any damages and prejudgment interest actually paid to the class." 15 U.S.C. § 78u–4(a)(6).

(d) Courts in securities fraud suits are required to make findings at the conclusion of the litigation as to whether any party or attorney violated Federal Rule of Civil Procedure 11(b) (a rule providing that attorneys who sign court papers thereby certify that the lawsuit is warranted under existing law or a good faith extension thereof). In making these findings, the court shall apply a presumption in favor of awarding attorneys' fees and costs if Rule 11 has been violated. 15 U.S.C. § 78u–4(c)(1).

(e)   To prevent the perceived use of burdensome and intrusive discovery to coerce an early settlement, the Reform Act provides for an automatic stay of discovery during the pendency of any motion to dismiss, except for discovery required to preserve evidence or prevent undue prejudice to a party. 15 U.S.C. § 78u–4(b)(3)(B).

(f)   The Reform Act requires that class action settlements generally cannot be placed under seal except for good cause shown, with good cause defined as "direct and substantial harm to any party." 15 U.S.C. § 78u–4(a)(5). Furthermore, any proposed settlement disseminated to a class must include, in addition to any other information required by the court, a statement of the amount of the settlement proposed to be distributed to the class (both in the aggregate and on a per share basis); a statement of the potential outcome of the case (if the parties agree on damages recoverable, then a statement of that amount; otherwise, a statement from each party concerning the issues on which there is disagreement); a statement of the attorneys' fees sought and an explanation in support of the request; the name and contact information of a representative of class counsel who is available to answer questions;

and a brief statement of the reasons for proposing a settlement. 15 U.S.C. § 78u–4(a)(7).

(g) The Reform Act imposes heightened pleading standards regarding the defendant's state of mind in securities fraud suits covered by the Act. 15 U.S.C. § 78u–4(b)(2). In *Tellabs, Inc. v. Makor Issues & Rights, Ltd.*, 551 U.S. 308 (2007), the Supreme Court made clear that, in analyzing whether facts pleaded give rise to a "strong" inference of scienter (15 U.S.C. § 78u–4(b)(2)), the court must find that the inference is "more than merely 'reasonable' or 'permissible'—it must be cogent and compelling, thus strong in light of other expectations." 551 U.S. at 310 (citations omitted). *See also Matrixx Initiatives, Inc. v. Siracusano*, 563 U.S. 27 (2011) (concluding that the plaintiffs properly pleaded scienter under the *Tellabs* standard).

Many proponents of the Reform Act believed that the legislation would dramatically reduce the number of securities fraud suits. That has not happened. While many types of class actions are in decline, federal securities class actions have continued to flourish. *See* Robert H. Klonoff, *Class Actions in the Year 2026: A Prognosis*, 65 Emory L.J. 1569, 1587–89 (2016).

In 2019, more than 400 securities class actions were filed in federal court. This marks the third consecutive year in which the number of filings has exceeded 400. *See* Jay B. Kasner, Scott D. Musoff & Susan L. Saltzstein, *In 2020, Securities Class Action Filings Likely to Continue Record Pace* (Skadden, Arps, Slate, Meagher & Flom LLP and Affiliates

2020), *available at* https://www.skadden.com/ insights/publications/2020/01/in-2020-securities-class-action-filings (last visited Sept. 14, 2020). In addition to the numerous cases filed in federal courts, the number of securities class actions filed in state courts increased in 2019. *See id.*

(2) Post-Reform Act Federal Removal Legislation

One response to the Reform Act is that plaintiffs' attorneys have looked more closely at state court options. In 1998, in response to this shift to state courts, Congress passed the Securities Litigation Uniform Standards Act of 1998, 15 U.S.C. § 77p (SLUSA). SLUSA provides for exclusive federal court jurisdiction in most securities fraud class actions and requires that federal law be applied. *See Merrill Lynch, Pierce, Fenner & Smith, Inc. v. Dabit*, 547 U.S. 71 (2006). As stated in the legislative history, SLUSA's purpose is "to prevent plaintiffs from seeking to evade the protections that Federal law provides against abusive litigation by filing suit in State, rather than in Federal, court." H.R. Rep. No. 105–803 (1998) (Conf. Rep.). The result is that the Reform Act and Rule 23 will govern the vast majority of securities fraud class actions.

Nonetheless, the state courts may play an increasingly important role going forward. As noted, the number of state court securities cases increased in 2019. And that trend may well continue in light of the Supreme Court's opinion in *Cyan, Inc. v. Beaver Co. Employees Retirement Fund*, 138 S. Ct. 1061

(2018). In *Cyan,* the Supreme Court resolved a split among the federal and state appellate courts about whether SLUSA gave federal courts exclusive jurisdiction over class actions alleging violations of the Securities Act of 1933 (1933 Act). The Court held that both federal and state courts had jurisdiction to adjudicate 1933 Act claims. *Id.* at 1069. The Court reasoned that the 1933 Act itself so provides, and that SLUSA did not change that result. Thus, such claims (if filed in state court) cannot be removed to federal court.

CHAPTER 12

DEFENDANT CLASS ACTIONS, DERIVATIVE SUITS, AND SUITS INVOLVING UNINCORPORATED ASSOCIATIONS

The traditional model of a class action is a suit by a class of plaintiffs against one or more individual defendants. This chapter discusses three types of aggregate actions that do not fit within that model: defendant class actions, shareholder derivative suits, and suits involving unincorporated associations. Defendant class actions are authorized by the text of Rule 23 itself; derivative suits are governed by Rule 23.1; and actions by or against the members of an unincorporated association are governed by Rule 23.2.

§ 12.1 DEFENDANT CLASS ACTIONS

A. OVERVIEW

Most class actions are brought *by* a class of plaintiffs. Rule 23, however, permits suits *against* a class a well. Rule 23(a) provides that "[o]ne or more members of a class may sue *or be sued* as representative parties" (emphasis added). In fact, the Supreme Court recognized the concept of a defendant class action over 150 years ago. *Smith v. Swormstedt*, 57 U.S. (16 How.) 288 (1853).

Relatively few class actions today are defendant class actions. As a result, the law is sparse, and a number of issues raised by commentators have not been settled—or even widely addressed—by the courts.

Some of the most frequent uses of defendant class actions are in securities litigation, patent infringement litigation, and civil rights litigation. In securities litigation, defendant classes often include claims brought by stock purchasers who allege fraud against a large number of brokerage houses involved in underwriting a stock offering. In patent infringement cases, defendant class actions often involve a party seeking to enforce a particular patent against a defendant class of infringers. In the civil rights area, plaintiffs often seek certification of defendant classes consisting of large numbers of state officials (for example, the sheriff in each county of a state), thus enabling plaintiffs to enjoin all of the relevant public officials from enforcing state laws that violate the plaintiffs' statutory or constitutional rights.

Rule 23 provides no meaningful guidance for applying class action principles to defendant classes. Indeed, many of the Rule 23 concepts were designed for plaintiff class actions and are not easily applied to defendant classes. The following sections address some of the most significant defendant class issues.

B.   RULE 23 CRITERIA AND DEFENDANT CLASSES

(1) Overview

As with plaintiff classes, a plaintiff suing a class of defendants must satisfy all of the threshold criteria (adequate class definition, a representative who is a member of the class, a claim that is not moot, and Article III standing). These requirements raise no major concerns in the context of defendant class actions. A defendant class must also satisfy the criteria of Rule 23(a)—numerosity, commonality, adequacy of representation, and typicality. Although numerosity and commonality generally have not been difficult issues in defendant classes, the typicality and adequacy requirements have raised some unique questions. Finally, a defendant class, like a plaintiff class, must also satisfy one of the subdivisions of Rule 23(b) (namely, (b)(1)(A), (b)(1)(B), (b)(2), or (b)(3)). Like the Rule 23(a) requirements, the Rule 23(b) criteria have posed some difficult issues for courts in defendant classes. The areas of difficulty are addressed below.

(2) Typicality

The Rule 23(a)(3) requirement—that "the claims or defenses of the representative parties [be] typical of the claims or defenses of the class," *see* § 3.9—generally raises no special issues in the context of defendant class actions. If a representative defendant has a unique issue or circumstance, that representative may be deemed atypical and thus not qualified to serve.

The more complicated typicality issues arise in the context of "bilateral" class actions—in which a class of plaintiffs sues a class of defendants. Courts have held that a named plaintiff who has no claim against a particular defendant cannot be typical of those class members who do have claims against that defendant. Under that approach, the only plaintiff class representative who could satisfy typicality would be one who has a claim against every defendant, and in some circumstances no such class member may exist. Thus, the fact that the suit is brought against a class of defendants complicates a named plaintiff's task in establishing typicality to represent a plaintiff class.

The exception to this rule of typicality is when the plaintiffs have alleged a conspiracy among the defendants or there is a "juridical link" among the defendants—namely, a legal relationship that unites defendants in a way that makes a single lawsuit more efficient than separate suits against the individual defendants. Examples of juridical links would be several underwriters who are each accused of having a role in a fraudulent prospectus, and state officials from various parts of the state who apply the same challenged regulation, even though only one official actually dealt with the particular plaintiff class representative.

(3) Adequacy of Representation

Rule 23(a)(4) requires, as a prerequisite to certification, the presence of adequate class representatives and class counsel. *See* § 3.10; *see also* Fed. R. Civ. P. 23(g) (addressing adequacy of counsel). The adequacy requirement poses several unique issues in the case context of defendant class actions.

First, because the plaintiff selects the class representative for the defendant class, the person named as the representative may not want to serve in that capacity and may, in fact, vigorously oppose the very notion of a defendant class. In a plaintiff class, a representative's opposition to class certification would obviously be disqualifying. In a defendant class, however, courts may view a representative's objection to class certification as confirming that the representative will vigorously assert the interests of the defendant class. An enthusiastic defendant, by contrast, might be acting in collusion with the plaintiff.

Second, because the defenses asserted by various defendants may differ, courts must scrutinize whether a defendant class representative has a conflict of interest in representing multiple defendants. The handful of courts that have addressed the issue have generally found defendant class representatives adequate, notwithstanding a potential conflict.

Third, a defendant class representative may be inadequate if his or her claim is small relative to the class as a whole. Courts may view the representative as having so little at stake that he or she would prefer to admit liability than to spend the time and resources defending a class action. By contrast, courts are less likely to reject plaintiff class representatives merely because their personal stake in the controversy is small.

(4)   Rule 23(b)(1)(A) Classes

Rule 23(b)(1)(A) encompasses defendant classes. It applies when "prosecuting separate actions by *or against* individual class members would create a risk of . . . inconsistent or varying adjudications with respect to individual class members that would establish incompatible standards of conduct for the party opposing the class" (emphasis added). Nonetheless, despite the wording of (b)(1)(A), defendant classes are not frequently certified under that subdivision. A major reason is the difficulty in showing the risk of "incompatible standards of conduct for the party opposing the class." In a defendant class, the focus is on whether the *plaintiff* (who is opposing the class) would be subject to incompatible standards. But a plaintiff who simply recovers against some, but not all, defendants is not thereby subjected to incompatible standards.

(5)   Rule 23(b)(1)(B) Classes

Rule 23(b)(1)(B) also contemplates suits against defendant classes. It allows for class certification when "prosecuting separate actions by *or against* individual class members . . . would create a risk of . . . adjudications with respect to individual class members that, as a practical matter, would be dispositive of the interests of the other members not parties to the individual adjudications or would substantially impair or impede their ability to protect their interests" (emphasis added). *See* § 4.2. Again, there is not a wide body of case law in the context of defendant class actions, but examples can certainly be found. For instance, some courts have certified defendant classes under (b)(1)(B) consisting of the partners of a general partnership with joint and several liability, reasoning that a finding of tort or contractual liability against one partner could substantially impair the other partners from mounting a defense.

(6)   Rule 23(b)(2) Classes

Unlike Rules 23(b)(1)(A) and (b)(1)(B), the language of Rule 23(b)(2) does not expressly refer to defendant class actions. Rule 23(b)(2) authorizes a class action when "the party opposing the class has acted or refused to act on grounds that apply generally to the class so that final injunctive relief or corresponding declaratory relief is appropriate respecting the class as a whole." *See* § 4.3. Courts are divided over whether defendant classes are allowed under Rule 23(b)(2). *See Henson v. East Lincoln Twp.*, 814 F.2d 410 (7th Cir. 1987) (discussing case law). Courts that have permitted such class actions generally have not attempted to justify that result based on the wording of Rule 23(b)(2). Nonetheless, some litigants seeking a (b)(2) defendant class have relied on the "sue or be sued" language of Rule 23(a) and argued that this wording supports defendant classes under all of Rule 23(b)'s subdivisions. Examples of (b)(2) defendant classes have included suits to enjoin classes of government officials from enforcing an unconstitutional statute.

Courts refusing to certify (b)(2) defendant classes point out that the defendant (the alleged wrongdoer), not the plaintiff, is always the one who will have "acted or refused to act on grounds generally that apply to the class." They also point out that the Advisory Committee Notes relating to (b)(2) refer solely to plaintiff classes.

(7) Rule 23(b)(3) Classes

Rule 23(b)(3) authorizes an opt-out class when common questions of law or fact "predominate" over individual questions and a class action is "superior" to other methods for resolving the disputes. *See* § 4.4. The opt-out feature of Rule 23(b)(3)—as opposed to the mandatory nature of classes under (b)(1) and (b)(2)—raises special issues in the context of defendant class actions. Obviously, defendants usually have a much stronger interest in opting out of a class than do plaintiffs. Individual class members in a plaintiff class action generally will opt out only if (1) they believe they can do better through separate lawsuits, or (2) for some personal reason they do not want to be involved, even as an unnamed class member. In most plaintiff class actions, the number of opt outs is small, since class members tend to like the convenience of taking a passive role but still being allowed to share in the recovery. In the context of a defendant class action, however, there may be strong incentives to opt out. Among other things, plaintiffs may not bother to sue those defendants who opt out. Courts are split on whether the possibility of massive opt outs prevents a defendant class action from being the superior device for adjudicating the claims. In some circumstances, courts have minimized opt-out concerns by noting that plaintiffs would simply join, as individual defendants, those defendants who choose to opt out.

C.   OTHER ISSUES

In addition to issues under Rule 23(a) and (b), defendant classes have occasionally raised issues involving statutes of limitations, notice, and personal jurisdiction.

(1) Statutes of Limitation

As discussed in § 8.1, the filing of a plaintiff class action generally tolls the statute of limitations with respect to all putative class members. The tolling doctrine raises complicated issues in defendant class actions. If applied to unnamed defendant class members, tolling could result in unfairness because those unnamed members may not be notified of a pending suit within the statute of limitations period and thus may not know, for example, that they need to preserve evidence to defend a claim. On the other hand, application of the tolling doctrine provides judicial economy. Without tolling, individual plaintiffs would be required to file a multiplicity of suits to protect themselves from a denial of class certification, resulting in a waste of judicial resources—the very problem that class actions are supposed to combat. Few courts have had the opportunity to consider tolling as it applies to a defendant class, and those that have done so are divided as to whether the filing of a defendant class action tolls the statute of limitations as to unnamed class members.

(2) Notice

Consistent with the law governing plaintiff classes, courts have required notice to members of defendant classes certified under Rule 23(b)(3). With respect to (b)(1) and (b)(2) classes, some courts have held that due process mandates notice to members of a defendant class, even if Rule 23 does not. Those courts (and various commentators) have noted the serious ramifications of an absent defendant class member being subjected to a judgment without notice.

(3) Personal Jurisdiction

In *Phillips Petroleum Co. v. Shutts*, 472 U.S. 797 (1985), discussed in § 7.1, the Supreme Court left open the issue of whether a court must have personal jurisdiction over the members of a defendant class in order for those members to be bound by the court's decision. Few lower courts have addressed this issue, and those that have are divided. Some focus on facilitating the use of the class action device for defendant classes (a goal that would be frustrated if personal jurisdiction requirements applied); others focus on the perceived unfairness of binding defendants over whom there are insufficient contacts.

§ 12.2   SHAREHOLDER DERIVATIVE SUITS

A.   OVERVIEW

Rule 23.1 authorizes shareholders to file suit on behalf of the corporation when the corporation itself has failed to take appropriate action against its directors, controlling shareholders, or third parties. The rule likewise entitles members to enforce the rights of an unincorporated association when the latter has failed to do so. A shareholder derivative action is similar to a class action. In both, the named plaintiff is asserting its own interests and those of others similarly situated. In addition, Rule 23.1 shares several procedural requirements with Rule 23: The named plaintiff must "fairly and adequately" represent the interests of other shareholders; a derivative action cannot be dismissed or settled without court approval; and "[n]otice of a proposed settlement, voluntary dismissal, or compromise must be given to shareholders . . . in the manner that the court orders."

Shareholder derivative suits, however, differ from class actions in certain respects, most importantly in the nature of the alleged injury. In a shareholder derivative suit, the allegedly aggrieved party is the corporation—not the individual shareholders—and any recovery is for the benefit of the corporation. Another difference is that, unlike Rule 23(b)(3), Rule 23.1 contains no provision for opting out of the action. *See, e.g.,* Angel R. Oquendo, *Six Degrees of Separation: From Derivative Suits to Shareholder Class Actions*, 48 Wake Forest L. Rev. 643 (2013) (discussing differences between derivative suits and suits under Rule 23).

Prior to 1966, provisions relating to shareholder derivative suits were part of Rule 23. In 1966, however, Rule 23.1 became a separate rule.

B.   REQUIREMENTS OF RULE 23.1

Rule 23.1 sets forth a number of requirements for maintaining a shareholder derivative suit. These include: (1) the claim asserted must belong to the corporation; (2) the plaintiff must have been a shareholder at the time of the alleged wrongdoing; (3) the plaintiff must demand that the corporation file suit on its own behalf or allege why such a demand would be futile; (4) the action must not be collusive, or designed to confer federal court jurisdiction; (5) the plaintiff must "fairly and adequately" represent the interests of other shareholders similarly situated; (6) court approval must be secured prior to settlement or dismissal; and (7) notice of a proposed settlement or dismissal must be given to the shareholders in "the manner that the court orders." These requirements are discussed below.

(1) Derivative Injury Requirement

Under Rule 23.1, the claim asserted must belong to the corporation and not any individual shareholder. In categorizing the claim, courts look to the type of injury suffered. If the injury is suffered by all shareholders jointly as a result of their status as such, then the claim belongs to the corporation. By contrast, if the injury suffered is unique to the plaintiff shareholder, then the suit may not be maintained as a derivative action. Examples of derivative claims include claims of mismanagement resulting in injury to the company; a claim that the corporation failed to pursue an antitrust action; and a claim of tortious interference with the corporation's contract. On the other hand, claims to prevent dilution of voting rights, claims of interference with a shareholder's right to vote, and claims for fraudulent sale of stock have been classified as distinct shareholder injuries that cannot support a derivative action. Courts are divided over whether insider trading claims are derivative (on the theory that a corporation is harmed by a drop in stock price and damage to its reputation) or direct (on the theory that individual shareholders are harmed when the value of their stock drops).

(2) Plaintiff Must Be a Shareholder at the Time of the Alleged Wrongdoing

The person bringing a derivative suit must have been a shareholder at the time of the alleged wrongful conduct. Some courts have adopted an exception when the alleged wrongdoing began prior to the plaintiff's stock ownership but continued after the stock was purchased. Other courts, however, have refused to embrace such an exception.

(3) Demand for Corporate Action

Before bringing a derivative suit, a plaintiff-shareholder must make a demand on the corporation to file the proposed lawsuit on the shareholder's behalf. A demand gives the board the opportunity to address the alleged wrongdoing, encourages intra-corporate problem solving, and allows the board to control any resulting litigation.

In general, a demand should provide several pieces of information, including the nature of the potential claim, injury suffered, and relief sought. Courts usually require that the board be given adequate time to respond, which in complicated cases could mean several months. After receiving a demand, the board may either commence a suit on the corporation's behalf or reject the demand.

A plaintiff need not make a demand on a corporation if such demand would be futile. To establish futility, plaintiff must demonstrate that the board was biased, acted in bad faith, or had a financial interest in the matter. Establishing futility is difficult because courts usually defer to the board's decisions.

Only after making a demand (that is denied) or establishing futility is the plaintiff free to bring a derivative suit.

(4) Derivative Actions May Not Be Collusive

A plaintiff must allege that the derivative action is "not a collusive one"—namely, that it is not designed to confer federal jurisdiction where none would otherwise exist. The purpose of this requirement is to prevent transfer of a small number of shares of stock to someone who is not the real party in interest but whose residence enables the suit to be based on federal diversity jurisdiction.

(5) Plaintiff Must Fairly and Adequately Represent the Interests of Other Similarly Situated Shareholders

As in Rule 23 class actions, a derivative plaintiff must "fairly and adequately" represent the interests of other shareholders similarly situated. Some courts hold that this requirement entails two inquiries: (1) the qualifications of the plaintiff's attorney, and (2) whether plaintiff has any interests antagonistic to those of the class. Other courts focus on the vigor with which the plaintiff will pursue the corporate claim, the commonality of interests between the plaintiff and the other shareholders, and the representative's familiarity with the case.

(6) Notice of a Proposed Settlement to Shareholders

Like Rule 23(e), Rule 23.1 requires that notice of a proposed settlement be given to all shareholders in a manner directed by the court. The notice should provide the shareholders with sufficient information to decide whether to contest the settlement. Although the rule does not set out what the notice should contain, courts recognize that it normally should describe the pending action (including the types of claims asserted), set forth the basic terms of the proposed settlement, inform shareholders of their right to object, and tell them where they may obtain additional information.

(7) Court Approval of Settlement or Dismissal

Like Rule 23(e), which governs class action settlements, Rule 23.1 provides that a derivative action may not be dismissed or compromised without court approval. In evaluating the fairness of a proposed settlement, courts look at, among other things, the likelihood of success if the case went forward to trial.

Even after the Supreme Court's *Devlin* decision (*see* § 9.1), lower courts are divided over whether a nonparty shareholder must intervene at the trial court level in order to contest the fairness of a settlement on appeal. The Supreme Court has not definitively resolved the issue.

§ 12.3 CLASS ACTIONS INVOLVING UNINCORPORATED ASSOCIATIONS

A. OVERVIEW

The Federal Rules of Civil Procedure contain a separate rule—Rule 23.2—addressing class actions by or against unincorporated associations. At common law, such entities (which include civil rights groups, religious organizations, and nonprofit public interest groups) were not legal entities and often could not be made parties to a lawsuit. The only way for an unincorporated association to sue or be sued, therefore, was to join all its members, a potentially insurmountable task. Even then, such a suit was not always economically viable, because the only damages recoverable were from the members' personal assets, not from the assets of the association.

Early on, some state legislatures enacted laws enabling unincorporated associations to sue and be sued as entities in their state courts. In 1922, the Supreme Court held in *United Mine Workers of America v. Coronado Coal Co.*, 259 U.S. 344 (1922), that an unincorporated association could be sued in federal court, even if state law said otherwise, if the purpose of the suit was to enforce a substantive federal right. In 1938, the holding of that case was codified by the passage of the original Federal Rule of Civil Procedure 17(b), which in relevant respects remains unchanged today. Rule 17(b) states, in pertinent part:

> [A] partnership or other unincorporated association with no ... capacity [to sue or be sued] under [the] law [of the state where the district court is held] may sue or be sued in its common name to enforce a substantive right existing under the United States Constitution or laws.

Rule 17(b) thus permits an unincorporated association to sue and be sued as an entity when the purpose of the suit is to enforce a substantive federal right.

Of course, not all cases in federal court are based on federal question jurisdiction. Many litigants rely on the diversity statute, 28 U.S.C. § 1332, to bring state-law claims in federal court. Rule 17(b) established that, with respect to diversity actions, the federal court should look to the law of the state in which it is sitting to determine the capacity of an unincorporated association to sue or be sued. But even after the enactment of Rule 17(b), many states adhered to the common law rule that denied unincorporated associations the capacity to sue or be sued. As a result, the ability to sue an unincorporated association in a diversity case still depended upon the laws of the individual states.

Moreover, Rule 17(b) did not address the problem that, even if state law permitted an unincorporated association to sue or be sued, such an association would often be unable to satisfy the requirements of diversity jurisdiction. The reason is that federal courts look to each member's citizenship to determine diversity, and unincorporated associations whose members reside in multiple states would frequently have one or more members with the same citizenship as the opposing party.

B.   ENACTMENT OF FEDERAL RULE 23.2

(1) Diversity Jurisdiction Issues

Rule 23.2, adopted in 1966, facilitates suits based on diversity by allowing representative actions by (or against) members of an unincorporated association. Rule 23.2 states:

> [A]n action brought by or against members of an unincorporated association as a class by naming certain members as representative parties . . . may be maintained only if it appears that those parties will fairly and adequately protect the

interests of the association and its members. In conducting the action the court may issue appropriate orders corresponding with those in Rule 23(d), and the procedure for settlement, voluntary dismissal, or compromise of the action shall correspond with that provided in Rule 23(e).

In explaining Rule 23.2, the Advisory Committee Notes state:

Although an action by or against representatives of the membership of an unincorporated association has often been viewed as a class action, the real or main purpose of this characterization has been to give "entity treatment" to the association when for formal reasons it cannot sue or be sued as a jural person under Rule 17(b).

As the Note explains, Rule 23.2 gives entity treatment to an association that *cannot* be sued as an entity under state law. This explanation raises the issue of whether Rule 23.2 may be used if state law *permits* an unincorporated association to sue and be sued as an entity. If Rule 23.2 cannot be invoked when state law allows the association to sue or be sued as an entity, then securing diversity jurisdiction will be difficult because the citizenship of each member of the association will be considered, as opposed to simply the citizenship of the representative parties. Courts have taken two views on this question.

Most courts have adopted a restrictive view of Rule 23.2, finding such an approach compelled by the plain language and logical implication of the above-quoted Advisory Committee Notes. These courts conclude that Rule 23.2 applies only when state law does not give an unincorporated association capacity to sue or be sued as an entity.

Some courts, however, hold that Rule 23.2 may be invoked even if state law permits an association to sue and be sued. These courts reason that neither the language of Rule 23.2 nor the Advisory Committee Notes compel a contrary result, and that the issue of diversity jurisdiction should not turn on state law treatment of unincorporated associations.

(2) Limitation on Qualifying Organizations

Courts have broadly construed the kinds of organizations that qualify as unincorporated associations under Rule 23.2. These include labor unions, fraternal organizations, athletic leagues, political parties, and student organizations. Rule 23.2 does not, however, apply to organizations that were formed only after the events at issue in the lawsuit, such as an organization formed specifically for the purpose of litigating a class action suit.

(3) Incorporation of Rule 23 Requirements into Rule 23.2

An important issue under Rule 23.2 is whether the requirements of Rule 23 apply. Because Rule 23.2 explicitly references Rule 23(d) (concerning court orders in the conduct of class actions) and Rule 23(e) (concerning court approval of dismissal or compromise), these parts of Rule 23 unquestionably apply. Furthermore, Rule 23.2, like Rule 23(a)(4), provides that "the representative parties will fairly and adequately protect the interests of the association and its members," and courts use the same basic criteria for determining adequacy under Rule 23.2 as under Rule 23(a)(4). But Rule 23.2 does not state whether the requirements of Rule 23(a)(1), Rule 23(a)(2), Rule 23(a)(3), Rule 23(b), or Rule 23(c) apply.

The majority view is that, other than those provisions or requirements explicitly referenced in Rule 23.2, the requirements of Rule 23 do not apply. Courts taking that view reason that, because Rule 23.2 refers expressly to subdivisions (d) and (e) of Rule 23, and also refers to adequacy of representation, the drafters knew how to incorporate the provisions and concepts of Rule 23 when they intended to do so.

By contrast, a minority of courts have held that *all* of the requirements of Rule 23 apply to class actions under Rule 23.2. These courts reason, among other things, that while Rule 23.2 does not include a numerosity or commonality requirement, certifying a Rule 23.2 class that is not numerous or that lacks significant common issues would make no sense.

CHAPTER 13

ETHICAL ISSUES IN CLASS ACTIONS

As noted in § 3.10, in recent years courts have focused more attention than ever on ethical misconduct by counsel. This is particularly true in the settlement context. *See* Robert H. Klonoff, *Class Actions in the Year 2026: A Prognosis*, 65 Emory L.J. 1569, 1623–35 (2016). It is important to recognize, however, that ethical issues can arise in all aspects of a class action. This chapter surveys some of the key ethical issues.

§ 13.1   KEY ETHICAL ISSUES

A.   OVERVIEW

Class actions raise a host of potential ethical issues for both plaintiffs' counsel and defense counsel. Although the number of court decisions finding class counsel to have engaged in ethical violations is relatively small (particularly when compared with the overall number of class action cases litigated), there is an extensive body of commentary discussing difficult ethical issues faced by class action attorneys. Moreover, several courts have addressed these issues in recent years. As a result, ethical issues are a significant topic in many courses on complex litigation, class actions, and mass torts.

Most state bar associations have enacted versions of either the ABA Model Rules of Professional Conduct (the Model Rules) or the ABA Model Code of Professional Responsibility. The Model Rules are used below to illustrate some of the ethical issues relating to class actions. A state's relevant ethical rules must, of course, be consulted for specific guidance on a case-by-case basis.

B. ATTORNEY COMMUNICATIONS WITH CLASS MEMBERS

Communications with class members are discussed in depth in Chapter 6. *See* § 6.2. This section supplements that material, highlighting key ethical concerns.

(1) Pre-Certification Communications

Prior to certification, it is unlikely that unnamed class members will have had any communication with counsel for the class representative, let alone anything approaching an attorney-client relationship. As a result, some courts addressing the issue have held that unnamed class members are not deemed to be represented by class counsel prior to certification. This conclusion has important ramifications.

First, from the perspective of the plaintiffs' lawyer, this means that the lawyer cannot view the unnamed class members as "clients" and must follow restrictions on lawyer solicitation and advertising, such as those contained in Model Rules 7.1, 7.2, and 7.3.

From the defense standpoint, if unnamed class members are not represented by counsel prior to certification, then the "represented person rule" does not apply. That rule provides that, "[i]n representing a client, a lawyer shall not communicate about the subject of the representation with a person the lawyer knows to be represented by another lawyer in the matter, unless the lawyer has the consent of the other lawyer or is authorized to do so." Model Rule 4.2. Nonetheless, some courts apply the represented person rule when a putative class action suit is *filed*, even before the court rules on class certification. These courts reason that, while unnamed class members are not yet clients, they are nonetheless players in litigation, and class counsel has a fiduciary duty to them even prior to certification. Adding to these points, some commentators have noted concerns about defense lawyers engaging in settlement discussions with, or taking formal statements from, unnamed class members at the pre-certification stage.

For additional discussion of communications with class members prior to certification, including the propriety of court orders restricting such communications, *see* § 6.2.

(2) Post-Certification Communications

After a class is certified, it is well accepted that the unnamed class members are treated as clients of class counsel unless and until they opt out of the class. This means that defense counsel are subject to the represented person rule, and they generally may not communicate directly with unnamed class members without the consent of class counsel.

Business communications not involving the suit are usually permitted, however.

For additional discussion of communications with class members after class certification, *see* § 6.2.

C.   CONFLICTS OF INTEREST

(1)   Collusion Between Plaintiffs' Counsel and Defense Counsel in Settlements

Courts and commentators have occasionally raised concerns that, in some cases, plaintiffs' counsel and defense counsel may have colluded to reach a settlement that is not in the class members' best interests. The concern is that, because defendants want to minimize their overall payment and plaintiffs' counsel want to maximize their fees, settlements end up offering little to the class members themselves.

This concern frequently arises in the context of so-called coupon settlements, *see* § 9.2, although the thrust of the attack is generally on the fairness of the settlement itself rather than upon the ethical conduct of the lawyers. In one important case, the Third Circuit invalidated a coupon settlement in a nationwide class action and remanded the case for further findings. *In re General Motors Corp. Pick-Up Truck Fuel Tank Prods. Liab. Litig.*, 55 F.3d 768 (3d Cir. 1995). Although the court did not find the lawyers' conduct unethical, it did note the need for courts to "effectively monitor for collusion . . . and other abuses." *Id.* at 787. Concerns about collusion and meager settlement recoveries for class members are further discussed in Chapter 9.

CAFA singles out coupon settlements for special judicial scrutiny. *See* § 9.2.

(2) Conflicts Among Class Members

Another potential ethical issue arises when the same lawyers represent both present and future claimants. In *Amchem Products, Inc. v. Windsor*, 521 U.S. 591 (1997), for example, a proposed settlement covered both present claimants alleging exposure to asbestos and future claimants who also alleged exposure but who had not developed any physical injuries. The Supreme Court discussed the concerns about having the same lawyers represent both present and future claimants:

> In significant respects, the interests of those within the single class are not aligned. Most saliently, for the currently injured, the critical goal is generous immediate payments. That goal tugs against the interest of exposure-only plaintiffs in ensuring an ample, inflation-protected fund for the future.

Id. at 595.

The Supreme Count reiterated these concerns in *Ortiz v. Fibreboard Corp.*, 527 U.S. 815 (1999). In *Ortiz,* the Supreme Court struck down the certification of a single nationwide class consisting of both present and future claimants and stated that, to address conflicts of interest, district courts should divide such massive classes into subclasses under

Rule 23(c)(5), with separate counsel for each subclass. On a separate conflicts issue, the Court in *Ortiz* expressed concern that some of the counsel for the class had a conflict arising from their separate representation of certain non-class claimants, whose settlements were in part contingent upon a successful settlement of the class suit. *See* § 4.2.

Other conflicts among clients may also make representation by a single lawyer inappropriate. For example, some class members may be more interested in recovering damages, while others may be more interested in securing injunctive relief. In a mass torts case, some class members may want to maximize the award to those with personal injuries, while others may seek to maximize the award for property damages. This problem may require the creation of subclasses represented by separate class representatives and counsel.

(3) Conflicts Between Class Counsel and the Class Representatives

Courts generally do not allow attorneys to serve as both class representatives and counsel to the class. The concern is that an attorney cannot be objective if he or she has a stake in both the attorneys' fees and the class members' recovery. Courts have raised similar concerns when the class representative is the spouse, law partner, employee, or close relative of the class attorney. *See, e.g.*, *Eubank v. Pella Corp.*, 753 F.3d 718 (7th Cir. 2014) (overturning class settlement on adequacy grounds in part because lead class counsel was the lead class representative's son-in-law). Conflicts may also arise if plaintiffs' counsel simultaneously represents the defendant in other, unrelated matters.

For additional discussion of conflicts involving class counsel, *see* § 3.10.

(4) Percentage-of-the-Fund Fee Awards

Class counsel are frequently compensated based on a percentage of the recovery. *See* § 9.4. Ethical issues sometimes arise because class counsel with a large financial stake in the litigation may have more incentive to settle than any individual class member, especially when the settlement includes a generous sum earmarked for attorneys' fees and insubstantial distributions to the individual class members. In addition, such attorneys may tend to focus solely on potential monetary recovery, and thus fail to pursue non-monetary relief that may be of more benefit to class members than a very small *pro rata* distribution of money. Although this type of conflict potentially exists in non-class litigation, the client in traditional litigation is generally in a better position to ensure that the lawyer follows the client's directions. In a class action with a large number of class members, the class lawyer cannot, as a practical matter, follow the instructions of every class member. Although courts have alluded to the ethical issues of percentage recoveries in class actions, the discussions generally occur in the context of a court's authority to review and approve settlements pursuant to Rule 23(e), not in the context of alleged ethical violations by counsel.

D. OTHER ETHICAL ISSUES

(1) Advancing Costs of Litigation

Jurisdictions are split over whether a plaintiff lawyer may ethically advance costs in a class action with no expectation that such costs will be recouped. The approach depends in part on the particular ethical canons adopted in the jurisdiction. Under ABA Model Rule 1.8, a lawyer may pay for costs, without recovery from the client, even if the suit is unsuccessful. By contrast, under Disciplinary Rule 5–103(b) of the ABA Code of Professional Responsibility, a lawyer may advance costs only if the client remains "ultimately liable." But even in states adopting the latter canon, some courts have carved out an exception for class actions, holding that requiring class members to be ultimately liable for costs would undermine Rule 23 and impose unfair hardships on the class representatives. Other courts have held that, while class representatives must reimburse counsel for costs, that obligation extends not to all costs incurred, but only to their *pro rata* share (which, in a class action involving numerous class members, would normally be relatively small).

For additional discussion of issues involving litigation costs, including third-party litigation funding, *see* § 9.5.

(2) Restrictions on Right to Practice

The canons of ethics universally prohibit agreements restricting a lawyer's right to practice law. Under those canons, it is unethical for a lawyer to agree, as part of a classwide or individual settlement, not to bring additional claims against the defendant. The concern is that such agreements deprive similarly situated people of the right to counsel of their choice. Although this concern is not unique to the class action context, it is especially likely to occur in such cases, given a defendant's strong interest in avoiding further class litigation.

(3) Failure to Communicate with Class Members

Model Rule 1.4 provides that attorneys have a duty to keep their clients reasonably informed about the status of their matters. This rule poses unique challenges in class actions with large numbers of class members. Several commentators have argued that class action lawyers have a duty to communicate with individual clients under this rule, even when there are hundreds or thousands of class members, and have suggested the use of the Internet, toll-free telephone numbers, and television hook-ups for "town meetings" as ways to enable class counsel to keep in touch with class members.

(4) Serial Objectors

As discussed in § 9.1, an increasingly prevalent ethical issue in the settlement context is the presence of "serial" or "professional" objectors—those raising meritless objections to settlements (often on appeal) in order to extort payment from class counsel. Such objections—typically lawyer-driven—can delay settlement until class counsel agrees to pay the objector to withdraw the objection or dismiss the appeal. This conduct has garnered significant attention from courts in recent years, and many courts have publicly admonished various attorneys for their conduct in representing objectors. The 2018 rule changes specifically address the problem of serial objectors. *See* § 9.1.

CHAPTER 14

MULTIDISTRICT LITIGATION

The multidistrict litigation (MDL) statute, 28 U.S.C. § 1407, was enacted in 1968. It provides, in relevant part, that "[w]hen civil actions involving one or more common question of fact are pending in different [federal] districts, such actions may be transferred to any district for coordinated or consolidated pretrial proceedings." Such transfers are made by a special panel, established under section 1407, known as the Judicial Panel on Multidistrict Litigation (the "MDL Panel"). The MDL Panel consists of seven federal circuit and district court judges designated by the Chief Justice of the United States. The purpose of section 1407 is to achieve judicial efficiency in *pretrial* proceedings. As discussed below, section 1407 requires that each case be sent back to its original district court for trial.

Since the statute's enactment, the MDL Panel has transferred more than half a million cases for coordinated proceedings. Such cases have included antitrust, securities, mass tort, employment, patent, and product liability suits. Virtually every recent, high-profile aggregate settlement has involved the MDL process—including the *BP Deepwater Horizon Oil Spill* litigation, the *Equifax Data Breach litigation,* the *National Football League Concussion* litigation, the *Volkswagen Clean Diesel* litigation, and the *National Prescription Opiate* litigation. Indeed, MDL cases constitute about 50 percent of the entire federal civil docket (excluding Social Security cases and various types of prisoner actions).

This chapter provides a brief overview of the MDL process. For a more detailed discussion of all aspects of MDL practice and procedure, *see* ROBERT KLONOFF, FEDERAL MULTIDISTRICT LITIGATION IN A NUTSHELL (West 2020).

§ 14.1 HOW MDL WORKS

A. INITIATION OF PROCEEDINGS UNDER SECTION 1407 AND THE ROLE OF THE MDL PANEL

Under section 1407, a transfer may be initiated *sua sponte* by the Panel or by motion of "a party in any action in which transfer . . . may be appropriate." 28 U.S.C. § 1407(c)(i), (ii). Upon the initiation of transfer proceedings, the MDL Panel is required to notify all parties in all cases in which transfers are sought, and to conduct a hearing to determine whether coordinated pretrial hearings are warranted.

The pendency of transfer proceedings before the Panel does not limit the jurisdiction of the court in which the action is pending. Nor are pretrial proceedings suspended pending the Panel's decision. All discovery in progress and orders by the transferor court remain in effect during and after transfer proceedings unless modified by the transferee court.

B. STANDARDS FOR TRANSFER

To order pretrial coordination or consolidation, the MDL Panel must determine that one or more common factual questions exist in the various separate cases and that transfer will promote "the convenience of the parties and witnesses and . . . the just and efficient conduct of [the] actions." 28 U.S.C. § 1407(a). The Panel need not find that common issues will predominate over individual issues, but only that common issues exist and that transfer will facilitate judicial efficiency.

As the *Manual for Complex Litigation (4th)* points out, transfer is appropriate when the common issues are numerous, complex, and not susceptible to informal coordination. Transfer is usually not suitable when relatively few cases are pending, when the issues are simple, or when informal coordination among courts would suffice (such as when the actions are all in close proximity to each other). The Panel can order transfer even if all of the parties object. The fact that cases may be at different stages of discovery is not necessarily fatal to MDL treatment, because the MDL judge can "group the pretrial proceedings on different discovery tracks according to the common factual issues," and can ensure that "no party [will have to] participate in pretrial proceedings unrelated to that party's interests." *In re Multi-Piece Rim Prods. Liab. Litig.*, 464 F. Supp. 969, 974 (J.P.M.L. 1979).

C.   SELECTION OF THE TRANSFEREE COURT

In selecting the transferee court, the MDL Panel considers a wide variety of factors. These include the location of the various cases; the locations of the parties, witnesses, and pertinent evidence; the experience of the various judges being considered;

the number of cases pending in the districts being considered; whether discovery is at a later stage in one of the districts; and the convenience of the parties. *See Manual for Complex Litigation (4th)* § 20.131, at 221 (describing factors considered). The Panel is not bound by the recommendations of the parties and need not limit its choice to a judge who currently has one or more of the cases at issue.

D. EFFECT OF A TRANSFER ORDER

When the MDL Panel enters a transfer order (and the order is filed with the transferee court), the transferor court loses jurisdiction over the case. Prior to that time, however, the transferor court remains free, notwithstanding a pending motion to transfer, to enter any order that the court deems appropriate, including an order remanding the case to state court for lack of jurisdiction. As noted, when a case is transferred, all orders entered by the transferor court remain in effect unless the transferee court modifies them.

Upon transfer, the transferee court has authority to administer all pretrial aspects of the case, including discovery and motions (such as summary judgment motions). The power to administer all pretrial aspects of the case is extremely important, since most MDL cases settle prior to trial and thus are never transferred back to the transferor court.

The transferee court has the power to rule on jurisdictional issues, such as motions to remand for lack of federal question or diversity jurisdiction. Importantly, in rulings involving state law, the transferee court is bound by the law that would have governed if the case were still in the transferor court. In rulings involving federal law, courts frequently hold that the law of the transferee court's circuit applies, but some courts (in some circumstances) apply the law of the transferor court's circuit.

E. SETTLEMENT OF MDL CASES

Predictably, in settling claims on an aggregate basis, defendants generally prefer to settle all claims at once to avoid a risk of future liability for the same conduct. Class action settlements under Rule 23 serve that purpose well. In MDL proceedings, however, a settlement will only be binding on those particular litigants who settle. Given that multidistrict litigation has supplanted class actions as the primary vehicle for resolving mass torts and certain other types of cases, scholars have expressed concern that this dynamic can lead to troublesome MDL settlement terms designed to ensure maximum participation by plaintiffs. *See, e.g.,* Howard M. Erichson & Benjamin C. Zipursky, *Consent Versus Closure,* 96 Cornell L. Rev. 265 (2011) (criticizing *Vioxx* settlement). Additionally, it is worth noting that settlements in MDL proceedings are not subject to the rigorous standards and protections of Rule 23(e). Thus, while some judges may treat MDL cases as "quasi class actions," such treatment occurs without the transparency of a binding rule governing settlement.

F.   REMAND AND TRIAL OF MDL CASES

In 1998, the Supreme Court ruled—contrary to the then-prevailing practice—that under section 1407, a transferee court is prohibited from assigning a case to itself for trial. *Lexecon Inc. v. Milberg Weiss Bershad Hynes & Lerach*, 523 U.S. 26 (1998). Rather, because section 1407 is for pretrial purposes only, a transferee court, at the conclusion of pretrial proceedings, must remand the case to the transferor court for trial.

Of course, upon remand, a party may ask the transferor court to transfer the case to the transferee court for trial under 28 U.S.C. § 1404(a) (discussed in § 16.1), which authorizes a district court to transfer a case in the interests of justice and for the parties' and witnesses' convenience. There is no assurance, however, that a transferor court will grant such a request. Other possible ways to secure trial by the transferee court notwithstanding *Lexecon* are described in the *Manual for Complex Litigation (4th)* § 20.132, at 224–25. In all events, almost all MDL cases are settled or otherwise resolved by the transferee court at the pretrial stage, and thus are never sent back to the transferor courts.

G.   REVIEW OF MDL PANEL RULINGS

No appeal or review is available for an MDL Panel decision denying a motion to transfer. Other orders of the MDL Panel are reviewable only by extraordinary writ pursuant to 28 U.S.C. § 1651. The MDL statute prescribes which federal court of appeals shall hear a particular type of extraordinary writ. For instance, petitions for extraordinary writ to review transfer orders or orders subsequent to transfer shall be filed in the federal circuit having jurisdiction over the transferee court. 28 U.S.C. § 1407(e). In practice, orders of the MDL Panel are almost never challenged.

H.   APPEALABILITY OF ORDERS DISMISSING INDIVIDUAL CASES

In *Gelboim v. Bank of America Corp.*, 574 U.S. 405 (2015), the Supreme Court held that the dismissal of a case that was part of a larger MDL was a final order under 28 U.S.C. § 1291 and thus was immediately appealable. The case, an antitrust suit, was dismissed because plaintiffs could not show antitrust injury. The Court ruled that "the order dismissing [plaintiffs'] case in its entirety removed [plaintiffs] from the consolidated proceeding, thereby triggering their right to appeal under § 1291." 574 U.S. at 412.

§ 14.2   BELLWETHER TRIALS IN MDL PROCEEDINGS

A "bellwether" trial refers to the trial of a limited number of plaintiffs' cases in a large MDL, with the results providing useful information but not being binding on cases not subject to trial. Bellwether trials allow the transferee judge and counsel for both sides to gather information on the litigation, test theories and defenses, and ultimately facilitate settlement.

In selecting cases for bellwether trials, the transferee court and counsel will generally create a pool of trial-ready cases that represent a cross-section of cases in the MDL. Once the pool has been selected, the parties conduct ordinary, case-specific discovery in each case. The transferee court and counsel will then select the cases that will actually be tried. The transferee court may prescribe various methods for making the final selections, such as random selection, selection by the court, or a certain number of selections afforded to counsel for each of the parties. *See generally* Eldon E. Fallon, Jeremy T. Graybill & Robert Pitard Wynne, *Bellwether Trials in Multidistrict Litigation*, 82 Tul. L. Rev. 2323, 2346–65 (2008).

One of the primary advantages of bellwether trials is efficiency. By gathering key information in the context of early trials, the parties may be able to agree to an acceptable settlement structure relatively early in the litigation. Of course, bellwether trials can be expensive. And because the cases are all being tried in the transferee court's district, the outcomes and jury pools may not be representative of possible outcomes elsewhere in the country.

§ 14.3 POLICY AND REFORM ISSUES

Given its prominence for resolving massive litigation, the MDL process has been the subject of extensive commentary and debate. Some scholars and attorneys have raised concerns that MDL proceedings lack the extensive procedural safeguards of Rule 23, including Rule 23(e)'s settlement review criteria (designed to deter collusive settlements) and Rule 23(h)'s judicial review of attorneys' fee awards. Critics also complain that MDL judges make a host of crucial rulings without the availability of interlocutory review. In addition, concern has been expressed that the plaintiffs' attorneys selected for leadership roles tend to be repeat players, thus increasing the possibility of collusion and exorbitant fees.

Of course, existing MDL practices have their staunch defenders—including prominent members of the bench, bar, and academy—who argue that MDL judges provide careful oversight, and that the repeat player phenomenon merely reflects the fact that some attorneys have proven themselves to be skilled and reliable to handle these complicated, high-profile cases.

In 2014, the Duke Law Center for Judicial Studies, in conjunction with 22 experienced MDL attorneys for both plaintiffs and defendants, drafted a list of "Standards and Best Practices for Large and Mass-Tort MDLs." *See* https://law.duke.edu/sites/default/files/centers/judicialstudies/MDL_Standards_and_Best_Practices_2014-REVISED.pdf (last visited July 30, 2020). That document provides concrete suggestions on how MDL courts can improve fairness and efficiency.

Since 2017, the Federal Advisory Committee on Civil Rules has been looking into possible rule changes impacting MDL practice. It is not clear whether that review will lead to actual proposed rule changes.

§ 14.4 COORDINATION OF FEDERAL
AND STATE CLAIMS

Section 1407 only applies to cases within the federal court system, as does transfer under 28 U.S.C. § 1404(a) (discussed in § 16.1). Consolidation under Rule 42 (discussed in § 15.6) is even more restrictive: It is limited to cases pending before the *same* federal court. In short, apart from bankruptcy (*see* § 16.4), there is no existing legal mechanism for consolidating related federal and state cases.

This is a serious gap: Many of the leading multiparty cases over the last several decades have involved separate lawsuits pending in both federal and state courts. There are several reasons why this has been the case. First, many plaintiffs' lawyers will deliberately select state court over federal court whenever possible. *See* § 7.2. Second, depending on the residence of the parties, the nature of the pleadings, and the particular federal court's attitude regarding removal, some state cases will be successfully removed to federal court, while others will be remanded to state court (or not removed in the first place). Finally, some plaintiff attorneys may choose to file suit in federal court (for instance, because they have chosen to assert federal law claims as well as state-law claims), while others may focus solely on state-law claims in an effort to remain in state court.

Despite the lack of a formal coordination device, federal and state judges with related cases sometimes coordinate their cases on an informal basis, particularly when the judges are within the same state. Matters for coordination may include discovery, motions practice, coordinated appointment of lead counsel, and scheduling of trials and other proceedings. *See Manual for Complex Litigation (4th)* §§ 20.31–20.313 (discussing types of informal coordination). Indeed, to achieve such coordination, the MDL Panel sometimes transfers related federal cases to a federal court that is located where similar state cases are pending. As the *Manual* points out, coordination is least difficult when common counsel are involved and when the cases are centered in one state (or relatively few states). Coordination is much harder when the cases are geographically dispersed throughout the country and myriad lawyers are involved.

Proposals have been put forth to address the issue of coordinating federal and state claims. Perhaps the most elaborate and widely publicized of these proposals was made by the ALI's *Complex Litigation Project* in 1994. That proposal would allow removal from state court to federal court of a case not qualifying for diversity jurisdiction when (1) the case arose from the same transaction or occurrence (or series of transactions or occurrences) as a case in federal court, and (2) the cases share a common factual or legal question. A proposed "Complex Litigation Panel" (modeled after the Judicial Panel on Multidistrict Litigation) would decide whether to allow removal, and also whether the removed case should be consolidated with the case or cases already pending in federal court. Under a proposed choice-of-law provision, the court presiding over the cases would in many instances be allowed to apply a single, uniform law to the cases, even if the cases arose from multiple states.

Under the ALI proposal, removal could be initiated upon the motion of any party to a state proceeding or upon certification by a state judge before whom one of the actions was pending. The Complex Litigation Panel would then decide whether removal was appropriate. In addition, the proposal would in some circumstances allow cases in federal court to be transferred to state court for coordination with similar cases.

The ALI proposal generated substantial controversy—including federalism concerns—and did not make any headway in Congress. Nonetheless, the proposal is intriguing and is worthy of discussion and debate. Scholars have offered their own proposals as well. *See, e.g.,* William W. Schwarzer, Alan Hirsch & Edward Sussman, *A Proposal to Amend the Multidistrict Litigation Statute to Permit Discovery Coordination of Large-Scale Litigation Pending in State and Federal Court*, 73 Tex. L. Rev. 1529 (1995) (proposing amendment to section 1407 with features similar to the ALI proposal).

CHAPTER 15

NON-CLASS AGGREGATION DEVICES UNDER THE FEDERAL RULES OF CIVIL PROCEDURE

In many instances, a class action is not necessary to achieve the efficiencies of party aggregation. Indeed, as noted in § 4.4, a court evaluating the superiority of a class action under Rule 23(b)(3) is required to address other aggregation devices. Moreover, some aggregate cases are not suitable for class action treatment, and thus counsel looking for efficiencies must consider other aggregate options (as well as separate lawsuits for each claimant). Thus, it is important to understand the requirements not only of class actions and multidistrict litigation, but also of other devices for litigating claims on a multi-party basis.

This chapter addresses the various multi-party devices under the Federal Rules of Civil Procedure. These include permissive joinder (Rule 20), compulsory joinder (Rule 19), impleader (Rule 14), interpleader (Rule 22), intervention (Rule 24), and consolidation (Rule 42). Chapter 16 addresses several other multi-party devices.

§ 15.1 PERMISSIVE JOINDER OF PARTIES

A. OVERVIEW

The Federal Rules of Civil Procedure distinguish between circumstances in which joinder is permissible and those in which it is required when feasible. This section addresses permissive joinder.

Rule 20 governs permissive joinder of plaintiffs as well as defendants. In other words, Rule 20 governs the circumstances in which multiple plaintiffs can join together against a particular defendant (or defendants), and the circumstances in which a plaintiff (or plaintiffs) may sue multiple defendants.

The rule constitutes an expansion of the common law, which allowed joinder only when plaintiffs claimed a joint right or sued multiple defendants based on a theory of joint liability. Rule 20 contains no similar limitations.

Permissive joinder is designed to promote efficiency and avoid multiple, duplicative, and sometimes inconsistent suits involving similar issues. As a result, Rule 20 is construed liberally. *See United Mine Workers of Am. v. Gibbs*, 383 U.S. 715 (1966). Despite its salutary purposes, however, joinder under Rule 20 is not mandatory. Compulsory joinder is governed by Rule 19 and discussed in § 15.2. A plaintiff is free to sue multiple defendants separately or to decline to join with other plaintiffs having similar claims.

Rule 20 is a procedural rule and thus governs joinder in all federal court actions, even those based on diversity. On the other hand, because joinder is simply procedural, it does not create or alter substantive rights under either federal or state law. Thus, the mere fact that Rule 20 authorizes joinder in a particular circumstance says nothing about whether the particular claims have merit.

Rule 20 joinder should not be confused with impleader. The latter, which is governed by Rule 14 (discussed in § 15.4), addresses the situations in which an existing defendant can bring *additional* parties into the case. Similarly, joinder should be distinguished from intervention under Rule 24 (discussed in § 15.5), which allows *nonparties* to intervene in certain circumstances and become parties.

B.   JOINDER OF PLAINTIFFS

Federal Rule 20(a) allows for joinder of plaintiffs as parties if (1) "they assert any right to relief jointly, severally, or in the alternative with respect to or arising out of the same transaction, occurrence, or series of transactions or occurrences"; and (2) there is "any question of law or fact common to all plaintiffs." Both requirements must be satisfied, based on the allegations in the complaint, before Rule 20 joinder will be allowed.

When joinder is authorized, each plaintiff becomes a party to the case. In contrast to a class action, no one plaintiff speaks for the group as a whole, and each plaintiff may be represented by separate counsel (although in most cases a small number of attorneys end up representing the entire group).

(1) Same Transaction or Occurrence

Courts have generally adopted a flexible, case-by-case approach in evaluating whether the plaintiffs allege the same transaction or occurrence or a series of similar transactions and occurrences. Some courts look to case law under Federal Rule of Civil Procedure 13 for guidance, because that rule contains a "transaction or occurrence" requirement in connection with cross-claims and compulsory counterclaims. Courts typically examine whether there is a logical relationship between the plaintiffs' claims. This is a fact-based inquiry. For instance, the transaction or occurrence requirement is frequently satisfied if the plaintiffs are complaining about the same behavior of the same defendant in the same time frame, such as a stock broker's misrepresentations about a particular stock to several clients during a specific time period.

Other courts focus on whether, based on the factual similarities, joinder would be fair to the defendant. For example, courts have allowed joinder of plaintiffs who complain of similar harassment or beatings by the same police officers, even if the individual plaintiffs were victimized at different times over a period of months.

On the other hand, courts may refuse to allow joinder of multiple plaintiffs who complain about different kinds of conduct by the same defendant, such as when one plaintiff alleges sexual harassment by a supervisor and another alleges that the supervisor committed race discrimination in making promotion decisions. Likewise, courts have held that the "transaction or occurrence" test is not satisfied if plaintiffs all complain about an allegedly defective product, such as an automobile, but the plaintiffs used the product in different ways, at different times, and in different locations. In general, while prior court decisions are instructive, they are of only limited value in determining whether a specific set of facts involves the same transaction or occurrence.

(2) Common Question of Law or Fact

In addition to the transaction or occurrence element, Rule 20(a) requires the existence of a common question of law or fact. This "common question" requirement appears in many places in the Federal Rules, including class actions (Rule 23(a)(2)), permissive intervention (Rule 24(b)), and consolidation (Rule 42(a)). In all of these situations, only one common legal or factual question must exist. Under Rule 20(a), in contrast to Rule 23(b)(3), there is no requirement that common questions predominate over individual questions.

Traditionally, the common question requirement has been easily satisfied in the joinder context. Indeed, if the "transaction or occurrence" requirement is satisfied, it is almost always possible to identify at least one common factual or legal question. Examples of potentially common issues include whether a product used by multiple plaintiffs is inherently defective; whether a pollutant to which multiple plaintiffs were exposed is toxic; and whether an airline crash involving numerous injured plaintiffs was caused by pilot negligence.

Nonetheless, courts have occasionally denied joinder for lack of a common legal or factual question—for example, when multiple plaintiffs sue the same defendant for discrimination but the employment decisions were made by different supervisors in different corporate divisions.

As explained in § 3.8, the Supreme Court in *Wal-Mart Stores, Inc. v. Dukes*, 564 U.S. 338 (2011), made it harder for plaintiffs in putative class actions to satisfy commonality. Thus far, it does not appear that *Dukes* has impacted the treatment of commonality in the non-class setting.

Because the transaction or occurrence requirement is separate from the common question requirement, it is possible that the latter requirement, but not the former one, will be satisfied. For instance, assume that an agency denies permits to different people at different times for the same reason. The question whether the reason is lawful is common, even though different transactions or occurrences are involved. In this situation, even though Rule 20 joinder is not appropriate, a court may allow the parties' claims to be consolidated for trial or pretrial proceedings under Rule 42 (discussed in § 15.6).

Even if the two requirements for permissive party joinder are satisfied, a court is not required to authorize joinder. Rather, the decision whether to permit joinder is within the discretion of the trial court. Although joinder is generally encouraged when the requirements are met, a court may refuse to allow it when, under the particular facts, joinder would cause undue jury confusion that would not be remedied by a limiting instruction.

(3) Interest in Obtaining All Relief Granted

Rule 20(a)(3) makes clear that joinder is appropriate even if the plaintiff is not "interested in obtaining . . . all the relief demanded." Thus, joinder is not defeated simply because a particular plaintiff is not seeking all of the damages sought by other plaintiffs, or is litigating only certain of the causes of action set forth in the complaint.

C. JOINDER OF DEFENDANTS

As noted above, Rule 20 allows for joinder of defendants as well as joinder of plaintiffs. The requirements for joining defendants under Rule 20(a) are essentially the mirror-image of those governing plaintiffs: (1) a claim asserted against multiple defendants jointly, severally, or in the alternative involving the same transaction or occurrence, or series of similar transactions or occurrences; and (2) one or more common legal or factual questions. The major difference is that, when Rule 20 is invoked by plaintiffs, the plaintiffs usually have *chosen* to sue collectively, whereas when defendants are joined under Rule 20, they generally are placed in that position involuntarily by the plaintiff.

Defendants have been joined in a variety of situations. Examples include: cases alleging negligence by the servant and invoking *respondeat superior* against the master; defendants who are alleged to be jointly and severally liable for tortuous conduct; parties who are allegedly all guilty of patent infringement; and parties who share a common interest in the property involved in the case.

On the other hand, courts have sometimes refused to permit joinder of defendants who are alleged to have engaged in similar wrongful conduct (such as similar anti-competitive business practices) but who are not linked by a conspiracy, concerted action, or some other theory.

Under Rule 20(a)(3), defendants may be joined even if they are not "interested in ... defending against all the relief demanded." For example, a defendant who is sued on multiple claims can be joined with another defendant who is sued on only some of the claims.

D.   ORDERS TO AVOID PREJUDICE

Rule 20(b) allows a court in which parties are joined to issue orders necessary to prevent embarrassment, prejudice, or delay. The one specific type of order mentioned in Rule 20(b) is that the court may order separate trials. For example, separate trials may be ordered for some or all of the joint plaintiffs out of concern that a jury would confuse the claims of the various plaintiffs or find defendants liable as to all plaintiffs simply because of the sheer number of plaintiffs raising the same claim. The court also has authority to order joint trials on common issues, followed by separate trials on individual issues. Regardless of whether the trials are separate or joint, the court has the authority to allow for joint discovery.

E. MISJOINDER OF PARTIES

Rule 21 of the Federal Rules of Civil Procedure provides that "[m]isjoinder of parties is not ground for dismissing of an action." Rather, the court has broad discretion to add or drop parties—either at a party's request or *sua sponte*—"at any time," including on appeal. Moreover, "the Court may also sever any claim against a party." Rule 21's statement that dismissal is not appropriate for misjoinder does not apply, however, when an indispensable party is absent from the case and cannot be joined. *See* § 15.2.

F. JURISDICTIONAL ISSUES

Joinder under Rule 20 must satisfy not only the requirements of the rule itself but also the requirements of subject matter jurisdiction. Under the supplemental jurisdiction statute, enacted in 1990, 28 U.S.C. § 1367(a), when a case is based on federal question jurisdiction, a court has discretion to exercise supplemental jurisdiction over all properly joined plaintiffs or defendants, including all related pendent state-law claims. On the other hand, when jurisdiction is based solely on diversity jurisdiction, 28 U.S.C. § 1367(b) governs. Section 1367(b) states:

> In any civil action of which the district courts have original jurisdiction founded solely on section 1332 of this title [diversity of citizenship], the district courts shall not have supplemental jurisdiction under subsection (a) over claims by plaintiffs against persons made parties under Rule 14, 19, 20 or 24 of the Federal Rules of Civil Procedure, or over claims by

persons proposed to be joined as plaintiffs under
Rule 19 of such rules, or seeking to intervene as
plaintiffs under Rule 24 of such rules, when
exercising supplemental jurisdiction over such
claims would be inconsistent with the
jurisdictional requirements of section 1332.

In prohibiting supplemental jurisdiction over "claims
by persons proposed to be joined as plaintiffs," section
1367(b) cites Rule 19 but not Rule 20. As a result,
prior to *Exxon Mobil Corp. v. Allapattah Services,
Inc.,* 545 U.S. 546 (2005) (*see* § 8.2), considerable
confusion existed among the courts regarding when,
if at all, supplemental jurisdiction could be invoked
in a case in which multiple plaintiffs (joined under
Rule 20) filed a suit against a single defendant, but
only some plaintiffs satisfied the amount-in-
controversy requirement. In *Allapattah,* the Court
applied supplemental jurisdiction in this context
(involving a child whose personal injury claim
against a single defendant met the jurisdictional
amount but whose family members' emotional
distress and economic damages claims did not).

§ 15.2 COMPULSORY JOINDER
OF PARTIES

A.   OVERVIEW

Generally, the choice of which defendants to sue
belongs to the plaintiff. In some circumstances,
however, joinder of either additional plaintiffs or
additional defendants (or both) is required to ensure
fairness to the defendant, to nonparties who might be

affected by the case, and to the judicial system. Rule 19 of the Federal Rules of Civil Procedure governs compulsory joinder.

To determine whether to order compulsory joinder, courts apply a three-step inquiry. First, a court must determine whether a party should be joined if feasible under Rule 19(a). This inquiry is often phrased by the courts as whether the joinder of the party is "necessary," although Rule 19 does not use that term. Second, if the party is necessary, a court must then decide whether joinder is feasible. For example, joinder is not feasible when there is no personal jurisdiction over the absent party. Third, if a court finds that joinder of the absentee is not feasible, the court must then decide whether the party is indispensable under Rule 19(b). If the absentee is found to be indispensable, then the case cannot go forward and must be dismissed. Unlike Rule 20, which is liberally construed, courts are frequently reluctant to mandate joinder under Rule 19 or to dismiss the action because joinder is not feasible.

The absence of necessary and indispensable parties is usually raised by an existing party in the case, but the issue may also be raised by the court *sua sponte*. The purpose of Rule 19 is to protect absent individuals—as well as those before the court—from inconsistent judicial determinations or impairment of their interests. Compulsory joinder also saves judicial resources by preventing multiple trials of similar issues.

The issue of whether a party should or must be joined is a procedural one, and thus is governed by Federal Rule 19 even in diversity cases.

B.   DETERMINATION OF WHETHER THE ABSENT PARTY IS NECESSARY

The threshold Rule 19 issue is whether an absent party is necessary and thus should be joined if feasible. If the party is not necessary, then the court does not even reach the question whether the case must be dismissed if the party cannot be joined. As discussed below, Rule 19(a) provides several circumstances in which a nonparty is necessary.

(1)   Rule 19(a)(1) ("Complete Relief" Clause)

Rule 19(a)(1) requires joinder (if feasible) when "in [the] person's absence, the court cannot accord complete relief among existing parties." The focus under the "complete relief" clause of Rule 19(a)(1) is on prejudice to parties, not to the nonparty whose joinder is at issue. As the Advisory Committee Notes point out, "[c]lause (1) stresses the desirability of joining those persons in whose absence the court would be obliged to grant partial or 'hollow' rather than complete relief to the parties before the court."

Under Rule 19(a)(1), only meaningful relief must be available, not necessarily every kind of relief that is theoretically possible. The issue arises, for example, when only two of several obligors under a contract are joined as defendants. If all of the obligors are jointly and severally liable under applicable law, then the absent obligor is not essential to provide complete relief to the plaintiff. Similarly, as the Supreme Court held in *Temple v. Synthes Corp.*, 498 U.S. 5 (1990), joint tortfeasors are not necessary parties, and thus an absent joint tortfeasor need not be joined under Rule 19.

(2) Rule 19(a)(1)(B)(i) ("Impair or Impede" Clause)

Rule 19(a)(1)(B)(i) requires joinder if feasible when the absent person "claims an interest relating to the subject of the action," and resolution of the case in the person's absence may "impair or impede the person's ability to protect the interest."

The "impair or impede" clause of Rule 19(a)(1)(B)(i) focuses on whether the rights of the *absent* person would be harmed without joinder, in contrast to Rule 19(a)(1)(A)'s focus on prejudice to parties. The phrase "claims an interest" is somewhat confusing, because the absent party normally will not have claimed anything. The phrase is usually interpreted to mean "has an interest" in the subject matter of the case. The interest must be sufficiently significant so that the absentee needs the protection of party status.

Whether a nonparty's interests would be impeded absent joinder generally involves a case-specific inquiry. Most courts nonetheless agree on some basic parameters. On the one hand, a mere *stare decisis* effect of an action on an absent person is not enough to trigger Rule 19(a)(1)(B)(i). On the other hand, if issue preclusion or collateral estoppel could be used against the absent person based on rulings in the case, then the absent person's interests would clearly be impaired or impeded by an adverse ruling. Between these two extremes, it is difficult to articulate precise principles.

The "impair or impede" clause serves the same purpose as intervention under Rule 24 (*see* § 15.5), namely, to avoid impairment of the absentee's interests. Intervention, however, is a mechanism used by the absentee to enter the case, whereas compulsory joinder will usually be invoked by the defendant (or the court). The right to intervene is meaningless, of course, if the absentee has no knowledge of the litigation.

(3) Rule 19(a)(1)(B)(ii) ("Multiple Liability" Clause)

Rule 19(a)(1)(B)(ii) requires joinder when the absent person has an interest in the subject matter and resolution of the case in the person's absence would "leave an existing party subject to a substantial risk of incurring double, multiple, or otherwise inconsistent obligations because of the interest." The inquiry under Rule 19(a)(1)(B)(ii) is whether adjudication without the absent person would expose *existing* parties—almost always the defendant—to the risk of multiple or inconsistent obligations. For example, a defendant might incur double obligations when a receiver claiming the proceeds to a life insurance policy sues in state court and an alternate beneficiary makes a claim in federal court.

C.   FEASIBILITY OF JOINDER

If a party is deemed necessary under any of the three clauses discussed above, the court must then determine whether joinder is feasible. Under Rule 19(a), joinder is feasible only when the requirements of personal jurisdiction, subject matter jurisdiction, and venue can be satisfied. In addition, joinder is not feasible if the nonparty would be entitled to assert immunity from suit. Whether lack of independent subject matter jurisdiction prevents joinder depends upon whether supplemental jurisdiction can be utilized. As noted in connection with Rule 20 (*see* § 15.1), the supplemental jurisdiction statute (28 U.S.C. § 1367) can be invoked in cases involving federal question jurisdiction. In diversity suits, however, joinder of parties under Rule 19 must satisfy the requirements of diversity. The confusion among the courts that had existed under Rule 20 prior to *Exxon Mobil Corp. v. Allapattah Services, Inc.,* 545 U.S. 546 (2005) (*see* § 15.1) does not exist for Rule 19, which specifically precludes supplemental jurisdiction over "claims by persons proposed to be joined as plaintiffs *under Rule 19*" (emphasis added). Nonetheless, several courts have criticized section 1367(b)'s distinction between Rule 20 permissive joinder and Rule 19 compulsory joinder.

D.   RESOLUTION WHEN PERSON SHOULD BE JOINED BUT JOINDER IS NOT FEASIBLE

Under Rule 19(b), if a person who should be joined to the suit cannot be joined, then a court must decide "whether, in equity and good conscience, the action should proceed among the parties or should be dismissed." Rule 19(b) identifies four factors that a court should consider in making this determination.

First, a court should examine "the extent to which a judgment rendered in the person's absence might prejudice that person or existing parties." As the Advisory Committee Notes explain:

> The first factor brings in a consideration of what a judgment would mean to the absentee. Would the absentee be adversely affected in a practical sense, and if so, would the prejudice be immediate and serious, or remote and minor? The possible collateral consequences of the judgment upon the parties already joined are also to be appraised. Would any party be exposed to a fresh action by the absentee, and if so, how serious is the threat?

For example, an absent party would clearly be prejudiced if the action had collateral estoppel or *res judicata* implications for that party. Likewise, a defendant in a case in which other potential defendants cannot be joined could, in certain circumstances, satisfy this standard by arguing that it would have to bear the entire cost of liability in the case.

Second, Rule 19(b)(2) instructs courts to consider "the extent to which any prejudice could be lessened or avoided ... by (A) protective provisions in the judgment; (B) shaping the relief; or (C) other measures." Examples of such protective provisions and measures include a defensive interpleader action by the purportedly prejudiced defendant (*see* § 15.4); intervention by the purportedly prejudiced nonparty (§ 15.5); and allowing a plaintiff to pursue only monetary damages when declaratory relief would prejudice a nonparty who cannot be joined.

Third, Rule 19(b)(3) instructs courts to examine "whether a judgment rendered in the person's absence would be adequate." The inquiry here is simply whether *meaningful* relief to the existing parties would be available, even if some forms of relief are not available. This factor overlaps to some extent with the second factor.

In many instances, if the relief claimed could be recovered from the existing defendant, the fact that other defendants could be held liable as well does not undermine the adequacy of a judgment solely against the existing defendant. For example, if a corporate employer is sued for the tortious conduct of plaintiff's supervisor and is capable of providing the remedies sought by the plaintiff, the inability to join the plaintiff's supervisor ordinarily would not require dismissal.

Fourth, Rule 19(b)(4) instructs courts to weigh "whether the plaintiff would have an adequate remedy if the action were dismissed for nonjoinder." As the Advisory Committee Notes put it, "the court should consider whether there is any assurance that the plaintiff, if dismissed, could sue effectively in another forum where better joinder would be possible." For example, if a case is dismissed from federal court (because the necessary party would defeat diversity jurisdiction) but the plaintiff could sue all of the essential parties in state court, that fact would weigh in favor of dismissing the case.

The issue of whether to dismiss the action or go forward is ultimately committed to the trial court's discretion. The four factors cited in Rule 19(b) are not exhaustive or ranked in importance. The issue involves a fact-specific weighing of the fairness to all affected persons of dismissal versus continuing with the case. *See, e.g., Republic of the Philippines v. Pimentel*, 553 U.S. 851, 862–63 (2008) (discussing factors bearing on "whether to proceed without a required person"). Courts are usually reluctant to dismiss a case under Rule 19(b) unless the prejudice from going forward would be considerable. *Cf. id.* at 864 (dismissal required under Rule 19(b) because of absence of the Republic of the Philippines).

E.   PROCEDURAL ISSUES

The issue of failure to join a necessary or indispensable party may be asserted in a responsive pleading, by motion for judgment on the pleadings, or at trial. According to Rule 12(h)(2), the responsive defense of "failure to join a person required by Rule 19(b)" may be raised at any time, including trial. Indeed, failure to join an indispensable party is deemed so critical to fundamental fairness that it can be raised even after trial or on appeal, and may be raised by the appellate court *sua sponte*. Of course, when the defense is raised late in the proceedings, a court will examine whether the plaintiff would be unfairly prejudiced and whether the delay was in good faith or instead was the result of strategic considerations.

§ 15.3 IMPLEADER

A. OVERVIEW

Rule 14 of the Federal Rules of Civil Procedure allows a "defending party" (a defendant or a plaintiff who is subject to a counterclaim) to file a complaint at any time after commencement of suit against "a nonparty who is or may be liable to it for all or part of the claim against it." Prior to 1946, Rule 14 allowed this sort of third-party practice—commonly known as impleader—if the third-party defendant was potentially liable directly to plaintiff. Under the 1946 amendment, however, impleader is allowed only if the third-party defendant is liable to the third-party plaintiff (in the event of the third-party plaintiff's liability to the plaintiff). The rationale for the change is that a defendant should not be able to force a plaintiff to sue an additional party that the plaintiff has chosen not to sue, simply because that additional party may also be liable to the plaintiff.

Impleader promotes judicial efficiency by allowing third-party claims to be tried together with the main claims, and it prevents inconsistent adjudications that could arise if such claims were adjudicated separately. To illustrate, were it not for impleader, then B—in a suit brought by A—would have to defend the suit without the presence of C, even though C would be legally liable to B if B were held liable to A. B would then have to bring a separate suit against C. Not only would the two suits be inefficient, but there would be a risk of inconsistent adjudications (for example, in the suit by B against C, C might prevail by showing that A's claim is meritless, even though A already succeeded in its case against B).

Although impleader in federal court is governed by Rule 14, a court in a diversity case may need to examine state substantive law to ascertain whether the nonparty could in fact be liable to defendant in whole or in part if defendant were found liable to the plaintiff.

B.   CIRCUMSTANCES IN WHICH IMPLEADER IS ALLOWED

Impleader is allowed only when the claim at issue is contingent upon or derivative of the main claim. In other words, impleader is allowed only if the third-party defendant would be liable to the defendant (the third-party plaintiff) in whole or in part if the defendant were found liable to the plaintiff. Unlike permissive joinder under Rule 20, it is not sufficient that the claim is part of the "same transaction or occurrence" and involves a common legal or factual question.

Contingent or derivative liability can arise in several situations. One common situation is indemnification, which applies when one party agrees (or is held by law) to hold someone else harmless for certain liabilities. For instance, if a builder agrees to indemnify the manufacturer of equipment for any injuries caused by the use of the equipment by the builder's employees, and a worker injured by such equipment sues the manufacturer, the manufacturer can implead the builder, assuming that the impleader is timely and no other procedural impediments exist. Likewise, an insured who is sued for tortious conduct may seek indemnification from an insurance company that has agreed to insure against such claims in whole or in part.

A second type of contingent liability is contribution. Most states have statutes providing a right of contribution among persons who are jointly or severally liable in tort for the same personal injury or property damage. Thus, a defendant sued for a tort can implead other persons subject to joint or several liability.

A third common type of contingent or derivative liability is subrogation, in which one person stands in the shoes of another for purposes of pursuing a claim. For instance, if an insured party sues his or her insurance company to recover for injuries suffered in an auto accident, the insurance company can implead the driver whose alleged negligence caused the accident.

Courts generally hold that, as long as the claim is contingent or dependent upon the main claim, the liability of the third-party defendant to the third-party plaintiff need not be based on the same theory as the liability of the defendant to the plaintiff. Thus, the defendant may be liable to the plaintiff in tort, but may have a contractual claim against the third-party defendant.

Impleader is entirely permissive. Even if a nonparty may be liable to a defendant for all or part of a plaintiff's claim, the defendant is not required to implead the nonparty. A defendant may decide, for example, that it would rather sue the nonparty in another forum in a separate case, rather than bring that entity into the existing suit.

C.   WHEN LEAVE OF COURT IS REQUIRED FOR IMPLEADER

Under Rule 14, leave of court to serve a third-party defendant is not required if such complaint is filed within 14 days after the defendant serves its original answer. Thereafter, leave of court is necessary. In ruling on requests to allow impleader, courts consider, among other things, the efficiencies achieved by the third-party claim, the reasons for delay in filing the third-party claim, and the likely prejudice to existing parties and to the potential third party. In general, courts are willing to allow third-party claims that satisfy the elements of Rule 14 unless such claims are raised so late (such as on the eve of trial) that the existing or potential parties would suffer severe prejudice.

D.   ASSERTION OF DEFENSES

A third-party defendant can assert all defenses that it has against the original defendant, such as lack of personal jurisdiction, estoppel, and waiver. Likewise, the third-party defendant can generally assert defenses that the original defendant has against the plaintiff. For instance, if the plaintiff's claim has been released or is barred by the statute of limitations, the third-party defendant may assert those defenses, even if the third-party plaintiff decides not to do so. The third-party defendant cannot, however, assert defenses that are personal to the original defendant, such as arguing that the court lacks personal jurisdiction over the original defendant, that the original defendant was improperly served, or that the case was filed in an improper venue.

E.   PLEADING REQUIREMENTS

Subject to the requirement for seeking leave in certain circumstances, a third-party action is brought essentially like an original complaint, with the same requirements for service of process. The third-party defendant must answer the complaint in accordance with the Federal Rules of Civil Procedure.

F.   OTHER THIRD-PARTY PRACTICES

Rule 14 authorizes or requires additional claims or defenses once a third-party claim is filed. Thus, a third-party defendant is required under Rule 14 to assert any defenses to the third-party claim that exist under Rule 12. The third-party defendant is also required, as provided in Rule 13, to assert any compulsory counterclaims that it has against the third-party plaintiff and any cross-claims against other third-party defendants. Rule 14(a)(2)(D) also allows—but does not require—the third-party defendant to "assert against the plaintiff any claim arising out of the transaction or occurrence that is the subject matter of the plaintiff's claim against the third-party plaintiff." In addition, under Rule 14(a)(3), the plaintiff is allowed to "assert against the third-party defendant any claim arising out of the transaction or occurrence that is the subject matter of the plaintiff's claim against the third-party plaintiff," and the third-party defendant must then assert any defenses available under Rule 12.

Rule 14(a) also allows third-party defendants to implead additional parties (*i.e.*, fourth-party defendants) if the requirements of Rule 14 are satisfied.

Finally, Rule 14(b) allows a plaintiff to implead a new party when a counterclaim is asserted against it, provided that the rule "would allow a defendant to do so."

G.   MOVING TO STRIKE THIRD-PARTY CLAIMS

Under Rule 14(a), any party may move to strike a third-party claim or to have it severed or tried separately. Courts have considerable discretion in deciding whether to allow severance or separate trials. Courts will usually deny separate trials where the matters share common legal or factual issues unless a joint trial would result in jury confusion, substantial delay, or other demonstrable prejudice.

H.   JURISDICTIONAL REQUIREMENTS

If the main claim is properly based on federal jurisdiction, the filing of a third-party complaint will not defeat jurisdiction with respect to the main claim. Thus, where there is complete diversity in the main case, diversity is not defeated because a third party is a resident of the same state as the plaintiff or defendant. Nonetheless, while third-party claims cannot destroy jurisdiction over the main claim, a jurisdictional basis must exist to assert the third-party claim.

In cases in which the main claim is based on federal question jurisdiction, jurisdiction over the third-party claim may be based on supplemental jurisdiction (28 U.S.C. § 1367(a)). The issue is more complicated, however, in diversity cases. Under 28 U.S.C. § 1367(b), a court may not exercise supplemental jurisdiction "over claims *by plaintiffs* against persons made parties under Rule 14" (emphasis added). *See* § 15.1. Under this language, if a defendant impleads a third party in a diversity case, section 1367(b) would appear to allow supplemental jurisdiction over such a claim. By contrast, a plaintiff who attempts to assert a claim against the impleaded party cannot rely on supplemental jurisdiction. Similarly, if a defendant asserts a counterclaim against a plaintiff, and plaintiff attempts to implead a third party under Rule 14, section 1367(b) would appear to prohibit the invocation of supplemental jurisdiction.

It should be noted, however, that the last clause of Section 1367(b) limits the reach of the exceptions to supplemental jurisdiction, stating that those exceptions apply "when exercising supplemental jurisdiction over such claims would be inconsistent with the jurisdictional requirements of section 1332." One court has noted that, "without its last phrase, subsection (b) would ... except from supplemental jurisdiction a claim asserted by the plaintiff against the third-party defendant when that claim is a compulsory counterclaim to a claim by the third-party defendant against the plaintiff." *Gibson v. Chrysler Corp.*, 261 F.3d 927, 938 (9th Cir. 2001). As the court noted, "it would be both unfair and inefficient to forbid the plaintiff's compulsory counterclaim to that claim." *Id.*

§ 15.4 INTERPLEADER

A. OVERVIEW

Interpleader is an equitable device that allows an individual who confronts multiple—and potentially conflicting—claims regarding a particular fund or piece of property to resolve those claims in a single proceeding. This proceeding enables the "stakeholder" to avoid multiple liability, inconsistent judgments, and multiple lawsuits in different courts. In many ways, an interpleader is similar to a limited fund class action.

There are two types of interpleader in federal practice: "rule interpleader" (Fed. R. Civ. P. 22) and "statutory interpleader" (28 U.S.C. § 1335). Although the two forms of interpleader are similar, they differ in multiple respects, including their procedural and jurisdictional requirements. Both types of interpleader are entirely voluntary; the stakeholder is not required to invoke the device but may instead choose to litigate the claims separately. Because of its remedial nature, interpleader (both rule and statutory) is liberally allowed by courts.

B.   RULE INTERPLEADER

Rule interpleader may be invoked by a plaintiff as well as by a defendant. Rule 22(a) provides, in pertinent part, that "[p]ersons with claims that may expose a plaintiff to double or multiple liability may be joined as defendants and required to interplead. . . . A defendant exposed to similar liability may seek interpleader through a cross claim or counterclaim."

There are two broad requirements for rule interpleader: (1) the stakeholder's *bona fide* concern about multiple claims against a fund or piece of property; and (2) at least two adverse claimants.

(1) Stakeholder's   Concern   over   Multiple Claims

To invoke interpleader, the stakeholder must have a genuine concern that multiple claims will be asserted against a fund or piece of property. Numerous cases have made clear, however, that while the fear must be genuine and reasonable, the risk of multiple liability need not be imminent or certain to occur. A threat of having multiple claims asserted will suffice. *See State Farm Fire & Cas. Co. v. Tashire*, 386 U.S. 523 (1967).

Moreover, the stakeholder is not required to demonstrate the relative merits of competing claims or show that any individual's claim is meritorious. The stakeholder need only have a good faith concern regarding duplicative liability and multiple court proceedings. Indeed, the stakeholder is permitted to contend that *no* claim against the fund or property is warranted.

(2) At Least Two Adverse Claimants

This requirement simply means that at least two claimants must be competing for the limited fund or piece of property, and that the fund or property cannot be awarded simultaneously to multiple potential claimants. The potential claimants need not be hostile to each other, and need not even know of each other's existence.

(3) Jurisdiction, Venue, and Other Procedural Requirements for Rule Interpleader

Under Rule 22, there must be either complete diversity or federal question jurisdiction. For diversity, the stakeholder must be diverse from all claimants, and the amount in controversy must exceed $75,000. Venue is proper where all claimants reside, where the particular claims arise, or where a substantial part of the property at issue is situated. 28 U.S.C. § 1391. Rule interpleader is subject to the service of process requirements and territorial limitations of Rule 4. Rule 22 does not require the stakeholder to deposit the fund at issue with the court or to post a bond.

(4) Two Stages of an Interpleader

An interpleader is a two-stage process. In stage one, the court determines whether the interpleader device is properly invoked. If it is, the court may simply discharge the stakeholder, assuming the stakeholder concedes that one of the claimants is entitled to the fund or piece of property. Of course, if the stakeholder claims that *no* claimant is entitled to the fund or property, the stakeholder must remain in the case to litigate that contention. In the second stage, the court or jury adjudicates the merits and decides which, if any, of the claimants is entitled to the fund or piece of property.

C. STATUTORY INTERPLEADER

(1) Overview

The federal interpleader statute, 28 U.S.C. § 1335, was enacted in 1917. Like rule interpleader, statutory interpleader requires the stakeholder to have legitimate concerns over multiple claims with respect to money or property and requires that there be at least two adverse claimants. Thus, 28 U.S.C. § 1335 applies when "[t]wo or more adverse claimants . . . are claiming or may claim to be entitled to . . . money or property" in the custody or possession of the stakeholder.

(2) Jurisdictional and Other Procedural Requirements for Statutory Interpleader

The jurisdictional requirements for statutory interpleader are much easier to satisfy than those for rule interpleader, and many stakeholders thus find statutory interpleader more attractive. There are special diversity requirements in 28 U.S.C. § 1335: Diversity must only exist between two or more of the adverse claimants, not between the stakeholder and *all* claimants as required by Rule 22 and 28 U.S.C. § 1332; and the amount in controversy need only be $500, as opposed to the $75,000 requirement of Rule 22 and 28 U.S.C. § 1332. Unlike rule interpleader, which is subject to Rule 4's service of process requirements, 28 U.S.C. § 2361 allows nationwide service of process for statutory interpleader.

Under 28 U.S.C. § 1397, venue lies in the district where any claimant resides. Although this venue requirement is generally more liberal than that for rule interpleader, a stakeholder may occasionally prefer rule interpleader. For instance, if rule interpleader allows the stakeholder to sue where he or she resides, because the claim arose there or the property at issue is situated there, but statutory interpleader does not allow suit in that venue, because no claimant resides there.

Unlike rule interpleader, 28 U.S.C. § 1335 requires the stakeholder to deposit the money or property with the court or post a bond in an amount that the court deems proper. For this reason, some stakeholders may prefer rule interpleader.

One device available to a court in a statutory interpleader case is the power under 28 U.S.C. § 2361 to enjoin other court proceedings involving the same property. In other contexts, injunctions restraining other courts from proceeding are not normally allowed, so this is a significant device. There is, for example, no specific class action counterpart to 28 U.S.C. § 2361 that allows a court presiding over a class action to enjoin other judicial proceedings.

§ 15.5 INTERVENTION

A. OVERVIEW

Unlike the various other aggregation devices discussed above, which are controlled by parties to the suit, Federal Rule of Civil Procedure 24 allows a *nonparty* in certain circumstances to intervene in an action to protect its interests. By intervening, the nonparty becomes a party to the case. There are two kinds of intervention under Rule 24: intervention as of right and permissive intervention. There are strict requirements for intervention as of right. By contrast, the standards for permissive intervention are more flexible, although the court may limit permissive intervention to certain issues or phases in the case.

B. GENERAL REQUIREMENTS FOR INTERVENTION AS OF RIGHT

Under Rule 24(a), a party who files a timely application for intervention is entitled to intervene as of right when a federal statute confers "an unconditional right to intervene." Examples of statutes that allow certain private parties to intervene are the Fair Housing Act, 42 U.S.C. § 3612(*o*)(2), and the Securities Exchange Act of 1934, 15 U.S.C. § 78p(b). Other federal statutes permit intervention as of right by the United States or a state in certain circumstances, such as when the constitutionality of a federal or state statute is at issue.

In the absence of a statute, Rule 24 also authorizes a party to intervene as of right if four requirements are met: (1) the motion to intervene is "timely"; (2) the applicant "claims an interest relating to the property or transaction that is the subject of the action"; (3) the applicant "is so situated that disposing of the action may as a practical matter impair or impede the [applicant's] ability to protect its interest"; and (4) the applicant's interest is not "adequately represent[ed]" by "existing parties." Failure to satisfy any of these criteria is fatal. A fifth requirement arises where an intervenor seeks relief different from that sought by the original parties. In that circumstance, the intervenor must independently satisfy the criteria for standing under Article III of the U.S. Constitution. *See* § 3.5.

When the requirements for intervention as of right are satisfied, the court must allow intervention. It is not clear under the case law whether a court has authority to impose conditions or limitations on intervention as of right, such as allowing participation with respect to only certain issues or proceedings, and courts are usually reluctant to impose any such conditions.

(1)   Timeliness of a Motion to Intervene

Rule 24 imposes no specific time limit for intervening in a case. In rare circumstances, intervention may be appropriate even during (or after) trial or on appeal. In assessing whether an application for intervention is timely, courts consider numerous factors. These include the length of time that the party waited before intervening after becoming aware of the matter; the prejudice that the proposed intervenor would suffer if intervention were denied; the prejudice that existing parties would suffer if intervention were granted; and other case-specific circumstances bearing on the timeliness of intervention.

(2) The Applicant's Interest in the Subject Matter

This requirement is more flexible than that contained prior to the 1966 amendment to Rule 24. The prior version required that the proposed intervenor be legally "bound" by the result in the case. Read literally, that requirement arguably restricted intervention to situations in which the proposed intervenor would be bound by *res judicata*. As the Advisory Committee Notes indicate, the revised rule makes clear "that an applicant is entitled to intervene in an action when his position is comparable to that of a person under Rule [19(a)(1)(B)(i)] [governing compulsory joinder, *see* § 15.2]. . . , unless his interest is already adequately represented in the action by existing parties." According to the Advisory Committee Notes, "[t]he Rule [19(a)(1)(B)(i)] criterion imports practical considerations, and the deletion of the 'bound' language similarly frees the rule from undue preoccupation with strict considerations of *res judicata*." Nonetheless, even under the current rule, the applicant must have a direct, substantial, and legally protectable interest in the case. A mere abstract interest in the outcome of the case is not enough.

Some examples of this highly fact-specific inquiry are instructive. Courts have allowed a labor union to intervene as of right in an antitrust suit to oppose a consent decree that would shut down the plant where union employees worked. In addition, courts have also allowed property owners to intervene when their land would be affected by a proposed project at issue. They have also allowed employees to intervene in a Labor Department suit against their employer for violation of the Fair Labor Standards Act. Likewise, courts have allowed intervention by the real party in interest in a case, such as an insurer.

On the other hand, some (but not all) courts have refused to allow a person to intervene in litigation merely because the proposed intervenor would be impacted by the *stare decisis* effect of the suit. Similarly, persons who alleged that a complaint contained false allegations regarding them were not allowed to intervene as of right to seek sanctions against the plaintiffs' attorney. And courts have denied intervention as of right to a nonparty claiming that the production of records by a party could be incriminating to the proposed intervenor.

(3) Practical Impairment

The inquiry here is whether, absent intervention, the suit will foreclose the ability of the proposed intervenor to protect its interests. Courts look at, among other things, whether there are other proceedings and forums in which the proposed intervenor can protect its interests, and whether the proposed intervenor can make its position heard simply by filing an *amicus* brief.

(4) Inadequacy of Existing Representation

This element is generally not difficult to satisfy. The applicant meets its burden by showing that the existing representation *may* be inadequate. If the proposed intervenor would offer arguments and theories that the existing parties would not, then this standard is typically satisfied. On the other hand, this criterion is not satisfied if it is clear that an existing party has the same interests as the proposed intervenor and would likely make the same legal arguments that the proposed intervenor would make.

Showing inadequacy of representation is more difficult when the existing representative is a governmental entity charged with representing the interests of absentees. In that circumstance, courts usually presume that the existing representation is adequate. Nonetheless, when the applicant asserts a personal interest, as opposed to one common to the public, a court may find that even a governmental representative is inadequate.

(5) Standing

Prior to 2017, courts were split over whether a party seeking to intervene must establish Article III standing independently, or whether the presence of a case or controversy between the original parties is sufficient. The Supreme Court resolved this conflict in *Town of Chester, New York v. Laroe Estates, Inc.*, 137 S. Ct. 1645 (2017). In that case, developer Steven Sherman filed a suit against the Town of Chester (Town), asserting a regulatory takings claim under the Fifth and Fourteenth Amendments and alleging that the Town had obstructed his plans to build a subdivision on land that he owned. Real estate development company Laroe Estates, Inc., sought to intervene, filing a motion to intervene as of right. Laroe claimed to have an ownership interest in Sherman's land. Laroe asserted a regulatory takings claim and sought compensation for the taking of Laroe's interest in the property at issue.

In a unanimous opinion, the Court held that an intervenor as of right must establish standing independently if he or she seeks "relief that is different from that which is sought by a party with standing." *Id.* at 1651. This standing requirement, the Court noted, "includes cases in which both the plaintiff and the intervenor seek separate money judgments in their own names." *Id.* If, however, the intervenor seeks the same relief as is sought by a party with standing, then the intervenor does not need to establish its own standing. The Court could not determine if Laroe sought the same relief as Sherman or instead sought additional relief, such as a money judgment in Laroe's name, and thus remanded the case for further proceedings.

C. PERMISSIVE INTERVENTION

Under Rule 24(b), a nonparty may timely intervene in two circumstances. The first is when a federal statute confers "a conditional right to intervene." Rule 24(b)(1)(A). Statutes conferring a conditional right to intervene include the Fair Labor Standards Act, 29 U.S.C. § 216(b), and the Equal Education Opportunities Act, 20 U.S.C. § 1717. But even if a statute is applicable, it is up to the discretion of the court to determine if permissive intervention is justified.

The second circumstance in which permissive intervention may be allowed is when an applicant's "claim or defense . . . shares with the main action a common question of law or fact." Rule 24(b)(1)(B). This circumstance, unlike intervention as of right, does not require the intervenor to have a direct personal interest in the transaction or property at issue. In ruling on applications for permissive intervention, Rule 24(b)(3) requires the court to "consider whether the intervention will unduly delay or prejudice the adjudication of the original parties' rights." In addition, the court must determine whether the application to intervene is timely.

Because the requirements for permissive intervention are generally more liberal than those for intervention as of right, many courts that refuse to grant intervention as of right ultimately grant permissive intervention.

The "common question of law or fact" standard is the same as that applied to permissive joinder under

Rule 20 (*see* § 15.1) and the wording is similar to that applied to class actions under Rule 23(a)(2) (*see* § 3.8). This standard—which requires only a single common legal or factual issue—has not been difficult to satisfy, and courts have not adopted the stringent *Dukes* standard here. *See* § 3.8.

The timeliness inquiry is similar to that for intervention as of right, although some courts have been more stringent on the issue of timeliness when an applicant seeks only permissive intervention.

Rule 24(b) does not explicitly refer to adequacy of representation as a criterion for permissive intervention, but courts generally scrutinize this factor, just as they do for intervention as of right under Rule 24(a). Permissive intervention is unlikely to be granted when the applicant's interests are already adequately represented by the existing parties, especially when the existing party is the government. In those situations, intervention would unnecessarily complicate the litigation. Similarly, courts will consider whether the applicant has any unique input that may be significant and useful to the development of the issues, or whether such input would be counterproductive.

The question whether permissive intervention would unduly delay the rights of the original parties is one for the court's discretion. Prejudice could exist, for example, if the proposed intervenor would inject additional issues or witnesses into the case.

Unlike Rule 24(a), in which intervention is required if the criteria of the rule are satisfied, Rule

24(b) gives to the trial court the ultimate discretion to decide whether to allow permissive intervention, even if the criteria of Rule 24(b) are satisfied. As with intervention as of right, the cases involving permissive intervention are heavily fact-specific.

Courts will often impose conditions on permissive intervention, such as allowing intervention only for particular purposes or phases of the case. A person who is allowed to intervene only permissibly may also be denied the right to participate fully in discovery or trial proceedings.

It should be noted that the Article III standing analysis in *Town of Chester* arose in the context of intervention as of right. It remains an open question whether the analysis of *Town of Chester* applies in the context of permissive intervention.

D.   PROCEDURES FOR INTERVENTION

To seek intervention, a proposed intervenor must file a motion to intervene "accompanied by a pleading that sets out the claim or defense for which intervention is sought." Rule 24(c). The motion to intervene and the pleading must be served on all parties by the method required by Rule 5. The applicant becomes a party only if leave to intervene is granted.

E.   JURISDICTIONAL ISSUES

Intervenors must show an independent basis of subject matter jurisdiction to enter a federal case. Thus, an intervenor must plead a federal question, assert diversity of citizenship, or rely on supplemental jurisdiction. The requirements of supplemental jurisdiction are set out in 28 U.S.C. § 1367, quoted in § 15.1, which was enacted in 1990. (Prior to 1990, an independent basis for jurisdiction was required for permissive intervention but not for intervention as of right.)

Although the exercise of supplemental jurisdiction over the intervenor is permissible when federal question jurisdiction is involved, supplemental jurisdiction in diversity cases under section 1367(b) is more restrictive. Section 1367(b) does not permit supplemental jurisdiction over claims by non-diverse persons seeking to intervene as plaintiffs or over claims by plaintiffs against non-diverse intervenors.

F.   *AMICUS* PARTICIPATION

A person who is not allowed to intervene, either as of right or permissively, may in many cases obtain permission to participate as an *amicus curiae*, or "friend of the court." The role of an *amicus*, however, is usually limited to submitting briefs (and occasionally participating in oral argument). An *amicus*, unlike an intervenor, does not have the status of a party in the case.

§ 15.6 CONSOLIDATION

A.   OVERVIEW

Consolidation dates back to eighteenth-century England, when it was used to avoid multiple suits involving the same subject matter. In the United

States, the concept was authorized by federal statute in 1813, and was first embodied in Rule 42 in 1938. It filled an important gap caused by the early limitations on permissive joinder. *See* § 15.1.

Rule 42(a) provides that, when actions within a particular judicial district involve "a common question of law or fact," a court may "join for hearing or trial any or all matters at issue in the actions"; it may "consolidate the actions"; or it may "issue any orders to avoid unnecessary costs or delay." Rule 42(b), in turn, allows a court to order separate trials of any claim or issue "[f]or convenience, to avoid prejudice, or to expedite and economize."

B. NATURE AND PURPOSES OF CONSOLIDATION

A consolidation does not merge separate lawsuits; consolidated suits remain separate, and the parties in one case do not become parties in the other. The entry of separate judgments is required. This is true even when cases are consolidated for trial.

The purpose of consolidation is to further the convenience of the court and the parties, particularly when the cases involve the same witnesses and the same operative facts. Consolidation also serves to avoid inconsistent adjudications. Although Rule 42 speaks of consolidation for a joint hearing or trial, and although Rule 42 is located in the section of the Federal Rules on "trials," as opposed to the section on "parties" (where the other aggregation devices in this chapter are located), it is well settled that cases can be consolidated under Rule 42 for pretrial purposes (such as discovery) as well.

Consolidation is allowed only for cases "before the court." Thus, Rule 42 does not authorize a court to order transfer of a case from another court. By contrast, the Judicial Panel on Multidistrict Litigation may, in certain circumstances, order transfer to one district, for pretrial purposes, of cases pending in numerous federal courts. *See* § 14.1. A federal court may also, in certain circumstances, order transfer of a case to another federal court under 28 U.S.C. § 1404. *See* § 16.1.

C.   CONSIDERATIONS IN EVALUATING WHETHER TO CONSOLIDATE

In deciding whether to consolidate cases, courts look primarily at whether there is an identity of issues. Rule 42(a)—like Rule 20(a), Rule 23(a)(2), and Rule 24(b)—requires only a single common question of law or fact. Courts, however, are more likely to exercise their discretion to consolidate if there is substantial overlap of issues. Satisfaction of the common question requirement has traditionally not been difficult, and courts have not adopted the stringent *Dukes* standard here. *See* § 3.8.

Courts also look to whether there is an identity of parties. While the parties do not have to be identical, if there are too many differences between the parties to the cases, courts are less likely to order consolidation.

Unlike certain other aggregation rules, such as permissive joinder, there is no requirement that the cases being consolidated involve the same transaction or occurrence. Thus, the standards for obtaining consolidation are easier to satisfy than those for joinder.

A major issue with respect to consolidation is whether that procedure will result in jury confusion. For example, the Second Circuit has held that consolidation of numerous individual tort cases was inappropriate because of a strong risk that the jurors could not keep straight the facts and circumstances of each case. *Malcolm v. Nat'l Gypsum Co.*, 995 F.2d 346 (2d Cir. 1993). In some instances, however, concerns about jury confusion can be dealt with through special interrogatories and phased trials. And, if the number of consolidated cases is small, there is much less risk of jury confusion.

The decision whether to consolidate under Rule 42 is left to the sound discretion of the court. That discretion is not unfettered, however, and a trial court will be reversed if it creates a procedure that denies parties fundamental fairness.

D.   SEPARATE TRIALS

Rule 42(b) grants courts broad discretion to order separate trials on individual claims or issues and to bifurcate trials into liability and damages phases. The Advisory Committee Notes point out that "separation of issues for trial is not to be routinely ordered" but should "be encouraged where experience has demonstrated its worth." Bifurcation under Rule

42(b) has been deemed appropriate, for example, "where the evidence offered on two different issues will be wholly distinct, or where litigation of one issue may obviate the need to try another issue." *Athridge v. Aetna Cas. & Sur. Co.*, 604 F.3d 625, 635 (D.C. Cir. 2010). Bifurcation of defendants has also been used to prevent potential prejudice. For example, in *Shannon v. Koehler*, 616 F.3d 855, 858 (8th Cir. 2010), a civil rights case alleging excessive force by a police officer, the co-defendants—the city and police chief—were granted (under Rule 42(b)) a trial separate from that of the individual officer. As Rule 42(b) itself makes clear, however, separate trials and bifurcated proceedings must comport with the "federal right to a jury trial." *See* § 5.6.

CHAPTER 16

OTHER AGGREGATION AND COORDINATION DEVICES IN FEDERAL PRACTICE

This Chapter discusses federal court aggregation and coordination devices that are not contained in the Federal Rules of Civil Procedure. These are; (1) transfer under 28 U.S.C. § 1404; (2) the Multiparty, Multiforum Trial Jurisdiction Act of 2002; (3) coordination among federal courts; and (4) bankruptcy as an aggregation device. *See also* Chapter 14 (multidistrict litigation). Like the devices discussed in earlier chapters, all of these devices are designed to increase judicial efficiency in resolving complex claims.

In addition to the above-mentioned devices, this chapter addresses aggregate settlement of non-class cases.

§ 16.1 TRANSFERS UNDER 28 U.S.C. § 1404

A. OVERVIEW

Section 1404(a) provides for transfers from one federal court to another "[f]or the convenience of parties and witnesses, and in the interest of justice." Section 1404 may be invoked by the parties or by the court *sua sponte,* although courts rarely transfer cases under section 1404 on their own motion. Unlike multidistrict litigation under 28 U.S.C. § 1407 (*see* Chapter 14), section 1404 does not necessarily implicate multi-party situations: Section 1404(a) can be used to transfer a single case from one district to another. Nonetheless, because it can also be used to aggregate similar cases before a single court, section 1404(a) merits discussion.

B.   REQUIREMENTS FOR TRANSFER

Section 1404(a) contains a few basic requirements. Prior to recent legislation, one important requirement was that a case could only be transferred to a district or division "where it might have been brought." This requirement was applied strictly. In *Hoffman v. Blaski*, 363 U.S. 335 (1960), the Supreme Court held that a court cannot transfer a case, on the motion of a defendant, to a district in which the plaintiff did not have a right to sue. This was true in *Hoffman* even though the defendant, in seeking the transfer, was willing to waive lack of personal jurisdiction and venue over it in the transferee forum. As the Court noted, "the power of a District Court under § 1404(a) to transfer an action to another district is made to depend not upon the wish or waiver of the defendant but, rather, upon whether the transferee district was one in which the action 'might have been brought' by the plaintiff." *Id.* at 343–44. This strict limitation no longer applies, however. Under the Federal Courts Jurisdiction and Venue Clarification Act of 2011, upon consent of all parties, a district court may transfer a case to another district even if the transferee court is not one where the case could have been brought originally.

C.   FOR THE CONVENIENCE OF THE PARTIES AND WITNESSES

Transfer under section 1404(a) will not be allowed unless it promotes the convenience of the parties and witnesses. This inquiry looks at such factors as the location of the parties, witnesses, attorneys for the parties, and critical evidence, such as pertinent documents.

D.   INTEREST OF JUSTICE

The "interests of justice" factor "include[s] such concerns as ensuring speedy trials, trying related litigation together, and having a judge who is familiar with the applicable law try the case." *Heller Fin., Inc. v. Midwhey Powder Co.*, 883 F.2d 1286, 1293 (7th Cir. 1989). The goals underlying this factor are fairness and efficiency.

E.   USE OF SECTION 1404(a) AS AN AGGREGATION DEVICE

A transfer under section 1404(a) is effective for all purposes, including trial. This contrasts with section 1407, discussed in § 14.1, which is for pretrial purposes only.

Nonetheless, aggregation of multiple cases in multiple courts requires that each judge having such a case agree to a transfer. This is in sharp contrast with section 1407, in which the decision for all applicable federal cases is made by the Judicial Panel on Multidistrict Litigation.

Like section 1407, section 1404(a) may be used only for transfers between federal courts. It may not be used to transfer cases between state courts or between state and federal courts.

Despite its limitations, section 1404(a) has occasionally been used as a device to aggregate similar cases, such as the transfer of factually and legally similar asbestos cases to a single district where each of the cases could have been brought. *See, e.g., In re Joint E. & S. Dists. Asbestos Litig.*, 769 F. Supp. 85 (E. & S.D.N.Y. 1991).

§ 16.2 MULTIPARTY, MULTIFORUM TRIAL JURISDICTION ACT OF 2002

The Multiparty, Multiforum Trial Jurisdiction Act (MMTJA), enacted in 2003, provides for federal jurisdiction in a narrow category of mass accident cases, such as airplane and train crash cases, in which traditional diversity rules would have required the cases to be heard in state court. The Act grants federal district courts "original jurisdiction of any civil action involving minimal diversity between adverse parties that arises from a single accident, where at least 75 natural persons have died in the accident at a discrete location." 28 U.S.C. § 1369(a). The MMTJA also permits removal in cases that could have been brought in federal court pursuant to § 1369(a) under original jurisdiction. 28 U.S.C. § 1441(e)(1)(A). The technical requirements of the MMTJA are beyond the scope of this text, but it should be noted that there has been considerable litigation in the context of Hurricane Katrina over what constitutes a single accident for purposes of the MMTJA—as opposed to a natural disaster or series of accidents. In general, a catastrophic incident, such as a plane crash, building collapse, or fire will qualify as a single accident, whereas a natural disaster or a series of product liability suits will not.

§ 16.3 COORDINATION AMONG FEDERAL COURTS

As the *Manual for Complex Litigation (4th)* notes, even in the absence of transfer under the MDL statute or 1404(a), federal courts can achieve efficiencies through coordination. Coordination devices include (1) assigning all of the cases to a specially designated judge pursuant to 28 U.S.C. §§ 292–294 (relating to assignment of judges to other courts); (2) establishing an agreement among the judges assigned to the various cases that one case will be the lead case (with the other cases possibly being stayed); (3) conducting joint court hearings; (4) coordinating the appointment of experts, special masters, and lead counsel; and (5) coordinating discovery.

Coordination between federal and state courts is discussed in § 14.4.

§ 16.4 BANKRUPTCY AS AN AGGREGATION DEVICE

A detailed discussion of bankruptcy as an aggregation device would involve complicated issues under the bankruptcy code and is beyond the scope of this text. It should be noted, however, that a party in

bankruptcy may, in some circumstances, provide a
vehicle for aggregating multi-party cases. For
instance, if a company that declares bankruptcy is
one of several defendants in various mass tort cases,
that company's litigation will generally end up being
consolidated before a federal bankruptcy court, even
if the company's cases were originally in a number of
federal or state courts. And, as discussed below, in
rare situations other defendants may be able to have
their cases transferred to the bankruptcy court as
well.

Under 11 U.S.C. §§ 105 and 362, the filing of a
bankruptcy petition automatically stays all lawsuits
against the bankrupt or debtor, both in federal and
state court, and permits the debtor seeking
bankruptcy protection to obtain an injunction
against any state or federal proceedings that could
impact the debtor's estate. The cessation of lawsuits
is one of the major immediate benefits of seeking
bankruptcy protection. Through the stay and
injunction provisions of the Bankruptcy Code, the
status quo of an insolvent debtor can be preserved
temporarily to protect the debtor's assets.

After the entry of the stay, another aim of a
bankruptcy proceeding is the consolidation of all
claims against a debtor into one forum in order to
ensure an orderly and fair distribution to creditors.
Generally, parties who are litigating against the
debtor are creditors. There are statutory devices
available to help consolidate pending lawsuits in a
single federal court. As the *Manual for Complex
Litigation (4th)* notes in discussing mass tort cases,

"[t]he automatic stay, combined with the bankruptcy court's exclusive control of the debtor's assets, effectively centralizes that defendant's state and federal mass tort cases into a single federal court." § 22.5. Bankruptcy is thus a powerful aggregation device in this situation, particularly because it permits aggregation of both federal and state cases.

Although consolidating all of the legal claims against a bankruptcy debtor into one forum is not usually controversial, there has been significant controversy—particularly in the mass torts area—with respect to one aspect of bankruptcy court jurisdiction. Under 28 U.S.C. § 1334(b), "the district courts shall have original but not exclusive jurisdiction of all civil proceedings arising under title 11 [the Bankruptcy Code] or arising in or *related to* cases under title 11" (emphasis added). "Related to" jurisdiction does *not* require that the related matter be against the debtor claiming bankruptcy. All that is required is a sufficient link between the case and the bankruptcy proceeding. The purpose of section 1334(b) is "to grant comprehensive jurisdiction to the bankruptcy courts so that they might deal efficiently and expeditiously with all matters connected with the bankruptcy estate." *Celotex Corp. v. Edwards*, 514 U.S. 300, 308 (1995).

The Supreme Court has not definitively ruled on what constitutes "related to" jurisdiction, and the federal circuit courts are divided in their approaches. In some circuits, "related to" jurisdiction is quite expansive—permitting parties to use a bankruptcy proceeding as an aggregation device for lawsuits that are only indirectly related to a bankruptcy. "Related to" jurisdiction was utilized in two controversial mass tort cases to consolidate claims against nondebtor corporations: *In re Dow Corning Corp.*, 86 F.3d 482 (6th Cir. 1996), and *A.H. Robins Co. v. Piccinin*, 788 F.2d 994 (4th Cir. 1986).

In *A.H. Robins*, the debtor, A.H. Robins, sought bankruptcy protection in the Eastern District of Virginia as a result of massive litigation caused by defects in its Dalkon Shield intrauterine device. By seeking bankruptcy protection, A.H. Robins was protected by the automatic stay, but many plaintiffs sought to pursue the remaining codefendants. Asserting an interest in a common insurance policy, A.H. Robins sought to consolidate the claims in the Eastern District of Virginia. The district court agreed, and the Fourth Circuit upheld that decision, interpreting "related to" jurisdiction in an expansive way.

A similarly expansive approach was adopted in the *Dow Corning* case. That case involved Dow Corning, the debtor, and the other major silicone breast implant manufacturers. These manufacturers were defendants in thousands of federal district court lawsuits filed throughout the country that were consolidated and transferred to the Northern District of Alabama by the MDL Panel. The district court in Alabama thereafter certified a non-mandatory class for settlement purposes that established a $4.25 billion settlement fund. Although 440,000 women chose to remain in the settlement class, many thousands of women opted out to pursue individual claims. Because of the expected litigation costs of these many opt outs, Dow Corning filed a Chapter 11 petition in the Eastern District of Michigan.

With its Chapter 11 petition, Dow Corning obtained an automatic stay of all pending litigation against it. Subsequently, it sought a transfer of the pending opt-out claims to the federal district in which its bankruptcy proceeding was pending. This transfer included opt-out suits that had been initiated in state court but removed to federal court pursuant to 28 U.S.C. § 1452(a). Dow Corning indicated that it would seek, as part of a bankruptcy reorganization plan, a consolidated jury trial on the issue of whether silicone breast implants caused the diseases claimed by the plaintiffs. Such a transfer and consolidation of litigation pending all over the country would obviously bring substantial savings in litigation costs to Dow Corning. Dow Corning's codefendants also sought to transfer, to the Eastern District of Michigan, all of the cases in which they were named as codefendants so that they could participate in the consolidated trial requested by Dow Corning.

The district court granted Dow Corning's request but denied the requests of the other codefendants, ruling that there was no subject-matter jurisdiction over the claims of the codefendants because they were not "related to" Dow Corning's bankruptcy proceeding. The Sixth Circuit reversed, ruling that there was "related to" jurisdiction over the claims against the non-debtor defendants. The court reasoned that the threat of suits for contribution and indemnification (as well as the existence of joint insurance policies) was enough to establish a conceivable impact on the debtor's estate sufficient to invoke "related to" jurisdiction. The court remanded the case to the district court, however, to ascertain whether the district court should abstain from hearing the cases of the nondebtor defendants under various abstention provisions of the Bankruptcy Code.

Some courts, however, have applied a narrow approach to "related to" jurisdiction. For instance, in *Arnold v. Garlock, Inc.*, 278 F.3d 426 (5th Cir. 2001), the court distinguished *Dow Corning* from the asbestos claims before it on the ground that in *Dow Corning*, "each of the co-defendants was closely involved in using the same material, originating with the debtor, to make the same, singular product, sold to the same market and incurring substantially similar injuries." *Id.* at 440. By contrast, the asbestos defendants in *Arnold* "use[d] asbestos for brake friction products, insulation, gaskets, and other uses." *Id.* The court likewise distinguished *A.H. Robins* as involving a "unique" product. *Id.*

Another bankruptcy aggregation device that has emerged in the asbestos context is the "pre-packaged" bankruptcy, or "pre-pack." In a pre-packaged bankruptcy under 11 U.S.C. § 524(g)(1), the debtor may obtain bankruptcy protection for its asbestos liability by securing support for its reorganization plan by at least 75 percent of the debtor's voting asbestos claimants. This enables the debtor to obtain a "channeling injunction," which acts as an aggregation device by prohibiting any claim that is not brought in ("channeled" through) the bankruptcy court. A major criticism of pre-packs is that they often do not treat similarly situated claimants equitably. Pre-packs can be especially unfair to future claimants (a problem reminiscent of the one addressed in *Amchem* and *Ortiz*). *See* § 13.1; *see generally* Marl D. Plevin, Robert T. Ebert & Leslie E. Epley, *Pre-Packaged Asbestos Bankruptcies: A Flawed Solution*, 44 S. Tex. L. Rev. 883 (2003) (surveying the topic); *In re Combustion Engineering*, 391 F.3d 190 (3d Cir. 2004) (rejecting pre-pack because of inequitable distribution among claimants).

In short, bankruptcy courts can sometimes play a crucial role in major civil litigation. Perhaps the most prominent recent example is the prescription opioids litigation brought by cities and counties against drug manufacturers and distributors. Although the federal multidistrict litigation is proceeding in federal district court in Cleveland, Ohio, the claims against Purdue Pharma—a private company (owned by the Sackler family) that filed for bankruptcy in September 2019—are proceeding in U.S. bankruptcy court in White Plains, New York. Purdue Pharma has thereby benefited from an automatic stay of litigation brought by thousands of plaintiffs in federal and state courts. Moreover, the bankruptcy court extended the automatic stay protection of the bankruptcy laws to individual members of the Sackler family, who have also been sued for their roles in the opioid crisis, even though those family members have not filed for personal bankruptcy. Needless to say, the bankruptcy court's treatment of the Sackler family has been controversial and has been condemned by various state attorneys general and legal commentators.

§ 16.5 AGGREGATE SETTLEMENT OF NON-CLASS CASES

As discussed in § 9.1, the Supreme Court's *Amchem* opinion has sometimes posed difficulties for parties who wish to pursue a classwide settlement. In other circumstances, even if a classwide settlement is possible, parties may prefer a non-class mechanism in order to avoid the various requirements applicable to class actions.

One prominent recent example of a non-class aggregate settlement is the $4.85 billion agreement between multiple individuals who alleged that the drug Vioxx, manufactured by Merck, caused heart attacks and strokes. The settlement was complicated: it required that the lawyers for the claimants recommend the settlement to all claimants. If a claimant chose not to participate, the lawyer had to withdraw from representing that claimant. Virtually all claimants chose to participate. *Vioxx* and other recent non-class aggregate settlements have raised issues about the criteria that should be applied to such settlements. Because such claims are not brought under Rule 23, the Federal Rules do not mandate a fairness review, as required by Rule 23(e) for class actions. Courts that have reviewed such settlements have done so by analogizing them to class actions ("quasi" class actions).

One longstanding rule that governs such settlements is an ethical rule, adopted in all states, known as the aggregate settlement rule. Under that rule, when a lawyer or lawyers represent two or more claimants on a non-class basis and seek to settle the claims, each client must be given the opportunity, before agreeing to the settlement, to review the settlement terms of all other claimants subject to the settlement.

In its *Aggregate Litigation* project, published in 2010, the ALI examined the aggregate settlement rule and considered alternative mechanisms. A major concern that led to this examination was the ability of a claimant (or small number of claimants) to attempt to extract premiums in exchange for approval. This risk was thought to be particularly strong in circumstances where defendants were only willing to settle if all claimants agreed to participate.

The result of the ALI's work was a proposal that allows claimants and counsel to enter into an agreement, in advance of any settlement, that the claimants will be bound by the vote of a substantial majority of all claimants approving a settlement proposal. *Principles of the Law of Aggregate Litigation* § 3.17. Such an agreement requires that the claimants give informed consent after fully understanding what they are giving up. *Id.* Also, claimants can challenge a later settlement on the ground that they had not given informed consent or that their settlement allocation is unfair or inadequate. § 3.18. Thus far, while the ALI approach to aggregate settlement has been discussed by many commentators, it has not been widely adopted by courts. It was, however, the inspiration for the novel "negotiation class" adopted by the MDL judge in the *National Prescription Opiate* MDL. *See* § 11.1.

INDEX

References are to Pages
